I0819643

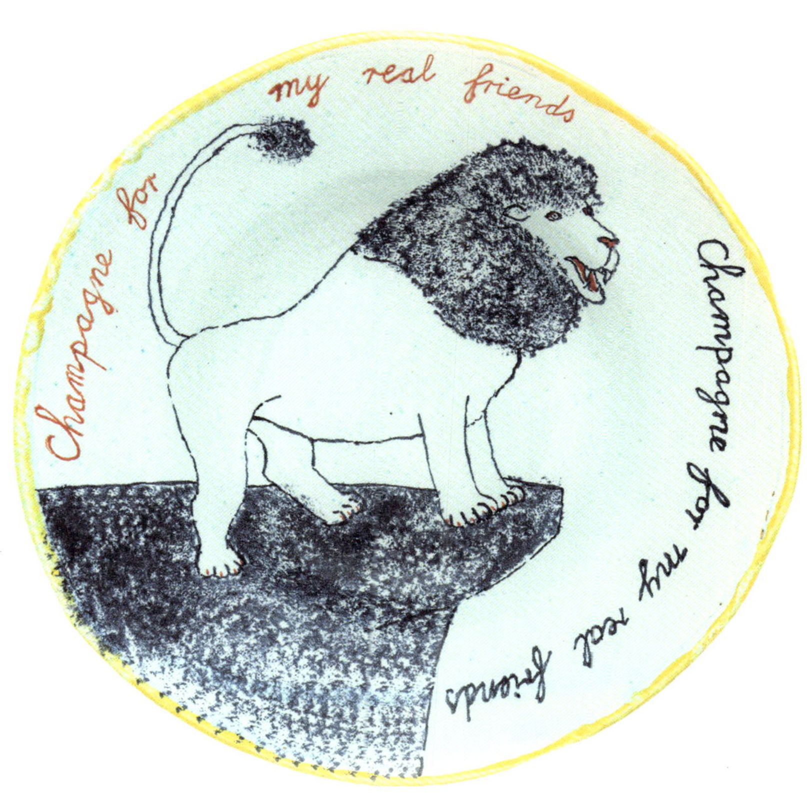
Champagne for my real friends
Champagne for my real friends

Things Made Over Time

Hylton Nel

STEVENSON HURTWOOD

Foreword

Kim Jones

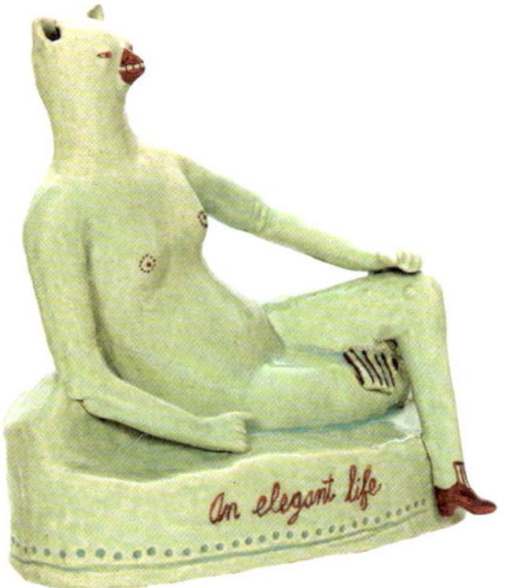

25 November 2019

I first met Hylton indirectly, through my friends the photographer Pieter Hugo and the gallerist Marc Barben – one of the directors of Stevenson, Hylton Nel's gallery in Cape Town, and the editor of this book. I met the work before the man. But it was through his ceramics that I had a very good idea of who the man was – they are full of life, with his life so very present in them. I was intrigued and knew that I had to meet him in person.

I've collected ceramics for many years, mainly Bloomsbury's Omega Workshop, and I have always liked a way of life shaping them – this happens quite literally in what Hylton does. His soft tones, his colour palette and what is portrayed – animals, nature, people – are all a reflection of his way of being in South Africa, both joyful and melancholy. I recognised so much in the work, both geographically and personally. The first thing I bought was a plate with a dog on it – it looked exactly like my dog, Dexter.

I then set off on a road trip with Pieter Hugo to meet Hylton.

It is a six-hour journey from Cape Town to the Karoo, into the desert to Calitzdorp, a small farming community where Hylton has lived for many years. I fell in love with Hylton and his home straight away – I immediately saw how he was fully living his work. In his house, at his studio, everywhere you look there is something, and always something to be inspired by. Like Hylton, I am a magpie, an inveterate collector. His house and his studio are one, there is no separation – what he does and how he lives are really who he is.

What struck me was his knowledge, a world of knowledge from eighteenth-century Staffordshire to Chinese Tang Dynasty pottery and a whole load of ceramics in between. Influences on his techniques are many and varied. And I

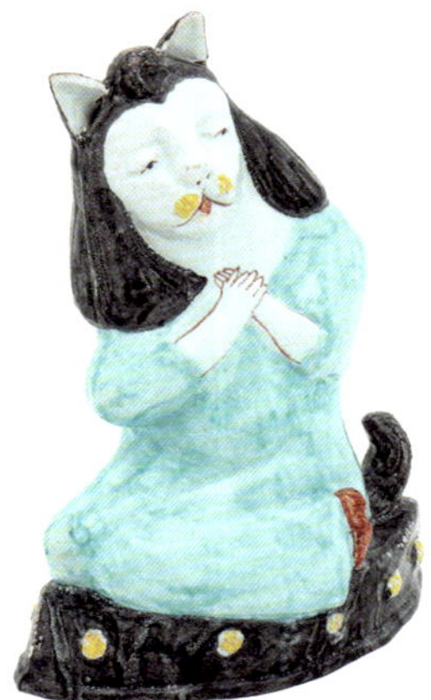

22 November 2010

was immediately attached to the work – it spoke to me of my love of Africa, my love of the medium and my fascination with Hylton himself.

Which led to the Dior Homme Summer 2025 collection, presented at Paris Fashion Week in June 2024, where I wanted to do something quite personal.

Hylton has visited my home. I live in a concrete box with glass and stainless steel, something very different from Hylton's style of house – but I also have Virginia Woolf's teapot. I think that's what he really came to visit. Hylton arrived when he had a show at Charleston, the Bloomsbury group museum and former country home in Sussex. The contrast between his retrospective show there and my house in London, full of objects, things and interiors, and moods that say so much about our lives, has informed the collection. It's about a way of living, the texture, the feel of it. it's an amalgam of all of that, of inspirational things.

Including the cats. Hylton Nel's giant cats on the catwalk are based on ones from my collection and Hylton's. These are the cats that spoke to me the most – they meowed to me.

Politics and poetics of cats

Tamar Garb

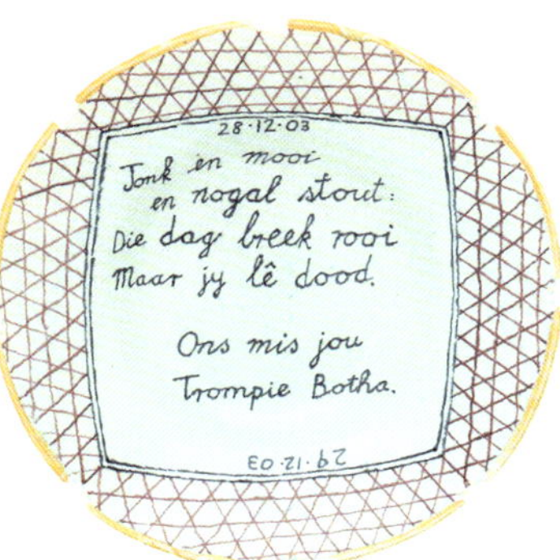

29 December 2003

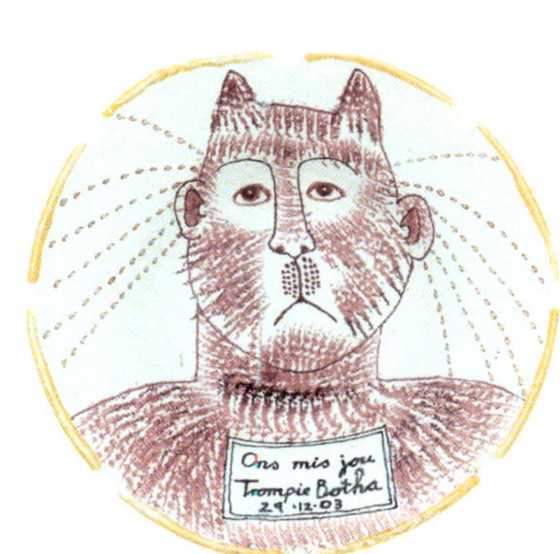

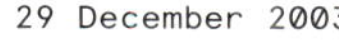
29 December 2003

A curious pair of plates, made to commemorate the death of a young man, Trompie Botha, in 2003, brings together the quirky juxtaposition of cats and crockery, text and image, domesticity and mortality that haunts much of Hylton Nel's practice as a potter. One of the plates bears a poem, written in Afrikaans, lamenting the loss of 'Trompie', a 'rent boy' described affectionately as 'young and beautiful' if 'naughty', but who now lies dead despite the dawn of day. 'Ons mis jou Trompie Botha', intones Nel beneath the painted verse, a sentence that he repeats as a memorial plaque pasted onto the furry chest of a knowing cat who stares out from an accompanying dish. Here the four-eared, whiskered creature fills the tondo-like surface with the gravitas of an ancient portrait bust, looking imperiously out, his features part-feline, part-human, his gaze measured and strong.

Cats, as witnesses and proxies, populate Nel's panoply of ceramic creatures. Photographs of his Calitzdorp studio (where he worked from 2002 to 2022, before moving across town) reveal a chorus of cats presiding over suspended and stacked plates, each inscribed with icons and idioms, sayings and quotes that embed language (verbal, visual, cryptic or straight) at the heart of his process of making. 'This plate is what I have to say,' suggests Nel, as if 'I' and 'it' are simple affairs. But the cat figure registers the ambivalence and internal dialogue this entails, suggesting the multiple identities and subjectivities that find themselves embedded on the pinched and painted clay surfaces that he makes. Neither gender nor creature secure, their androgynous and anthropomorphised fluidity makes them perfect sites for imaginative projection and play.

The cats can appear stately and grand or cuddly and cute. They are

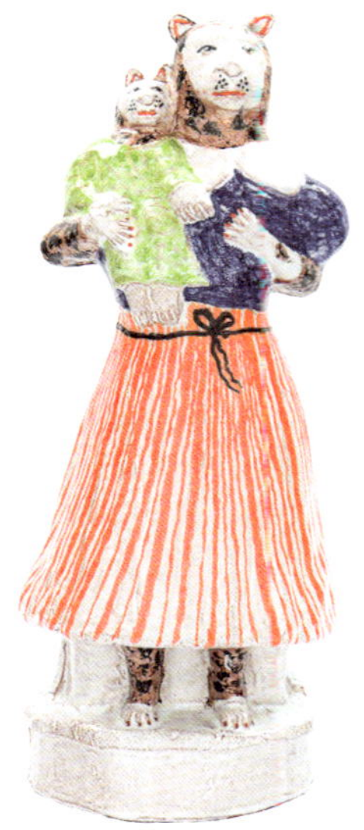

18 May 2021

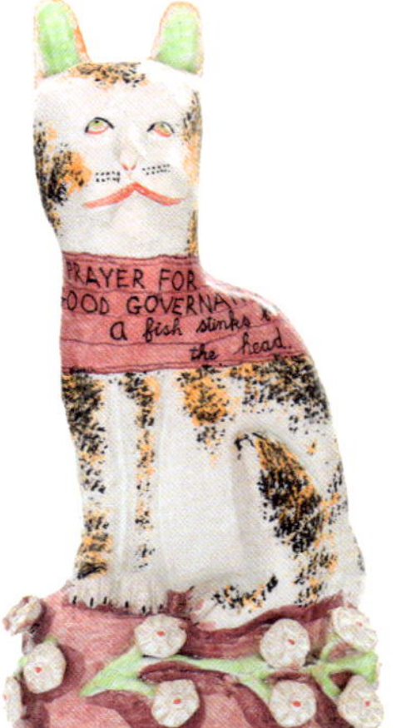

3 April 2013

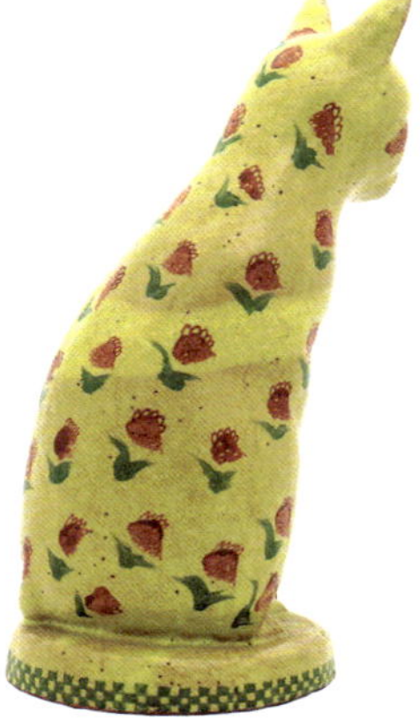

16 December 2007

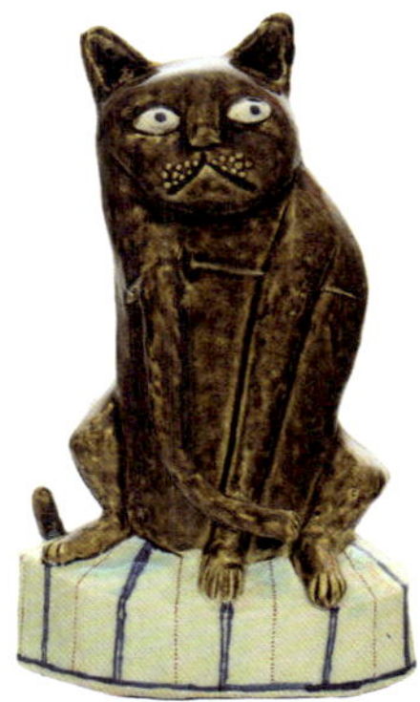

22 November 2019

alternately serious and silly. Some seem grumpy and rude, others benevolent and kind. With their mottled surfaces, brightly painted and glazed to indicate if not mimic the variegated patterns of fur, the cats defy all expectations of verisimilitude. Instead, they seem like story-book animals: pointy-eared, round-eyed, whiskered and weird, they bring an array of precedents to mind. Sometimes these relate to beloved objects in the artist's possession, like the miniature Staffordshire 'mother and child' pair, now multiplied and enlarged into striped-skirted, moustachioed matriarchs with their wriggly kittens in arms. At other times they invoke the grandeur of civilisations past, like the cat deities of ancient Egypt, where the animals were so revered that they were often mummified and preserved, regularly appearing as cat heads placed on human bodies to represent female gods. For Nel, the reverence for Dynastic Egypt goes back to his early reading of historical fiction, like the popular novels of Joan Grant, published in the 1930s and 40s, with their romantic tales set among pharaohs and priests. In these books, assorted felines from lionesses to African wildcats populate the narrative, testing and taunting the human characters in knowing and often manipulative ways. But there is nothing solemn or sententious about Nel's cats. If they are wise, it's in the manner of TS Eliot's cats with their ability to both embody and reflect upon human affectation and pride. Practical and resourceful, the cats in Eliot's panoply seem invariably aloof and savvy, looking on at human foibles with a degree of both scorn and indulgence.

For Nel, like Eliot, cats are both surrogates and soothsayers. He has spoken of their role as human substitutes, 'as both portraits and

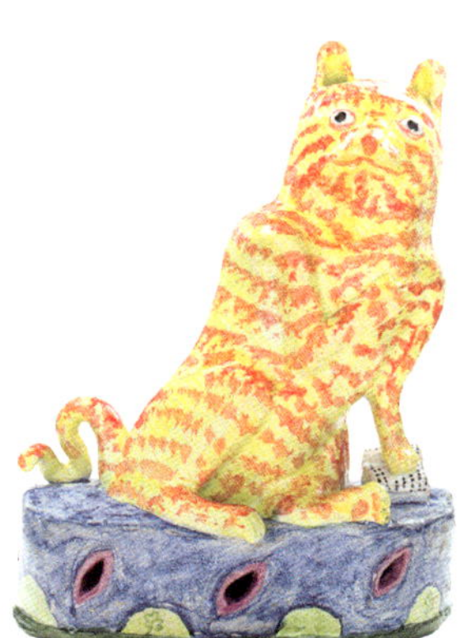

17 March 2021

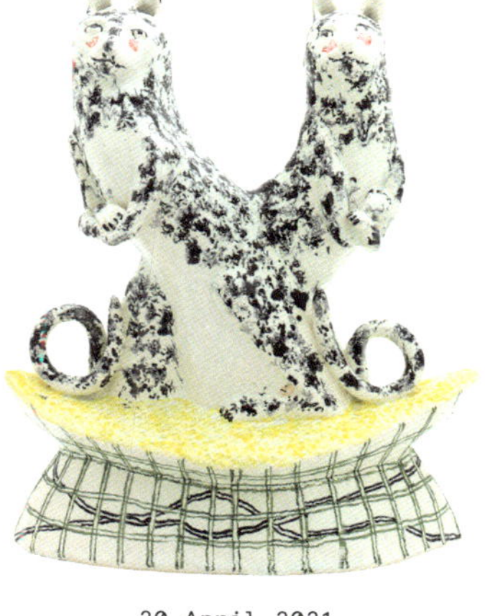

20 April 2021

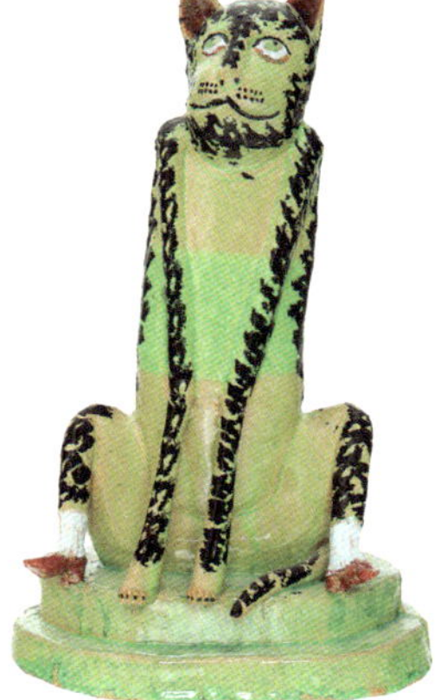

19 February 2013

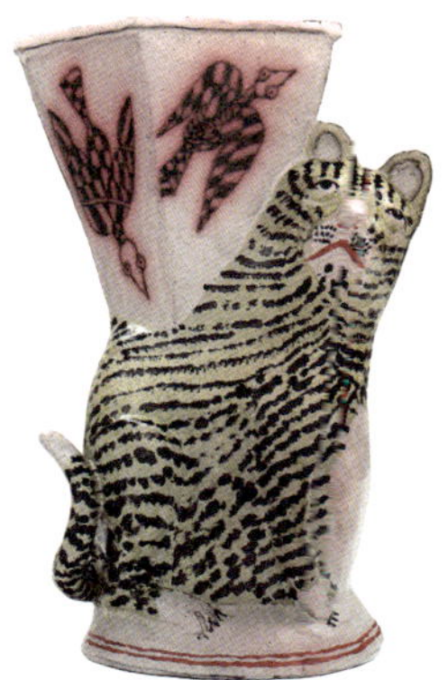

30 June 2021

self-portraits', which allows him to avoid 'being blatant' or literal in his suggestion or satirisation of people.[1] Instead the cats provide a form (moulded, glazed and decorated) through which multiple personalities are performed. They sit, paws propped on miniature books or decorated platforms, so that they cannot be safely identified or named. And yet collectively they appear to watch over an imperfect world, with a knowing and curious stance, much like the artist-potter himself.

The cat functions as both a curiosity and an ornament. Long used as a subject for decorative sculpture and ceramic figurines, cats serve, for Nel, as 'regular things', objects that enable him to squeeze his queer sensibility into a tradition that has a recognisable genealogy and lineage.[2] At the same time they allow for a certain pointed and irreverent humour. This is not only to be found in the expressions and quirky demeanour of the cats. Sometimes it is worn as a slogan or text that cuts against the cuteness and kitsch (Nel revels in the dangerous flirtation with the sentimentality and sweetness that the cat *bibelot* inevitably invokes) and provides the space for a political or polemical assertion.

Consider, for example, 'Prayer Cat' (3 April 2013), an elegant pink creature, seated on a floral encrusted plinth, emblazoned with an unlikely refrain. Written across its neck and chest are the words 'Prayer for Good Governance', followed by the epigram 'A fish stinks from the head'. The first is a cry from the heart that Nel has used repeatedly since the mid-1990s when, in the heady days of the transition from apartheid to democracy, he inscribed it on the bases of a number of multi-hued male figures.[3] The second is a piece of folk wisdom that seems to speak directly to the rot of contemporary

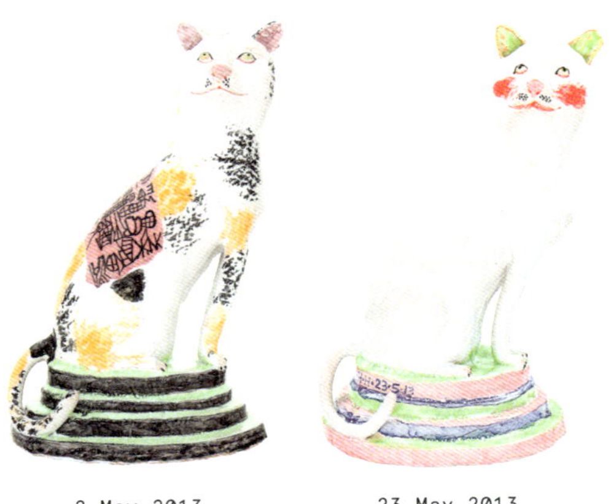

2 May 2013

23 May 2013

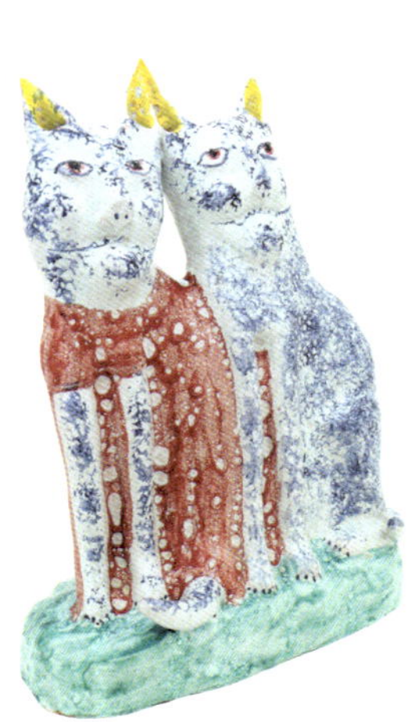

16 February 2012

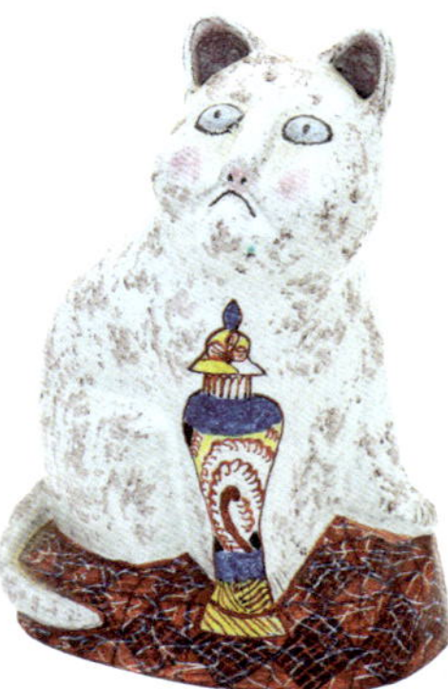

1 December 1995

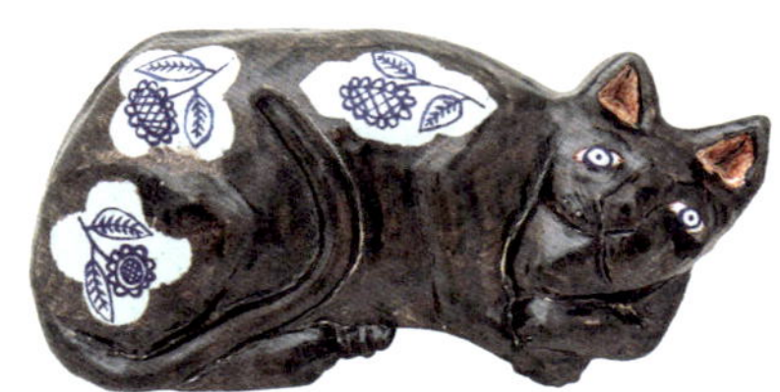

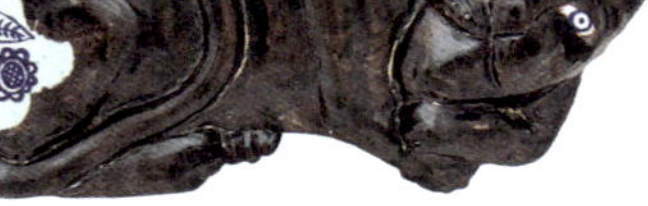

4 February 2003

corruption and the failure of political leadership, whether at home or abroad. Now the prayer seems like an innocent, somewhat futile hope given what the cat seems to know: that a great stink has been emitted and it stems from the very top. Inscribed on the stoneware tabby, with its comic-book features and compact body, the words, scrawled in Nel's familiar hand, appear to balance faith with failure, but never to resort to despair.

For one thing, making is an act of defiance and life. Nel has been making things in clay since the 1960s, and with an increasing sharpness of wit and satirical slant so that his figures and pots have become vehicles for observation and critical commentary. In their very form and shape they testify to a hand-made attachment to histories and traditions of making. The cats, for example, are pressed in slabs into concave, hand-made moulds, joined together to make their characteristic shapes, and then adapted with individuated appendages as well as add-on bits and bobs. Once fired, they are painted and glazed so that each has its unique if contiguous character. The plates and bowls use convex moulds which provide a basic shape that is then inscribed, pinched, pulled and textured, so as to form the base for images and texts. The processes are tactile and labour-intensive. And it is in the act of building and baking, painting and glazing that a connection to the world (and its multiple pasts/technologies) is felt. The relationship is palpable and real. As Nel says, making things with a recognisable lineage is a way of 'fitting in' and being a participant in the shared cultures and histories of the world.

And yet these pots and plates, fit for a king or a cat, provide platforms for more than their ornamental antecedents might suggest. They are

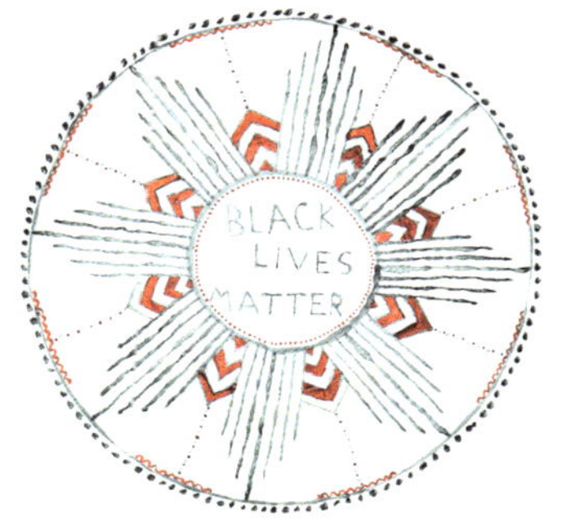

24 July 2020

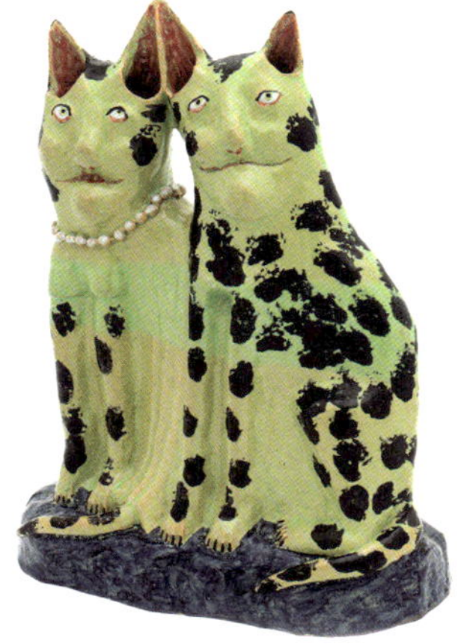

8 March 2013

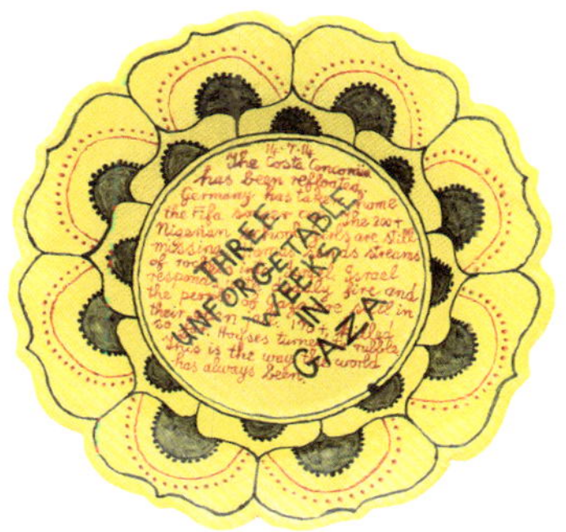

14 July 2014

22 April 2020

both functional and decorative (like much pottery), offering hospitality to food and suggesting the rituals of conviviality and company. They love to be used, held and shared. Often sexualised in reference and shape, they speak to human appetites and pleasures: a penis is propped on a throne, an arsehole is proffered on a plate, a profile asks to be touched.

But each bowl and plate, once shaped and set, like the 'Prayer Cat', acts too as a surface for poetic or polemical inscription. Sometimes it's a matter of birds or insects, flowers or motifs, usually extracted from a traceable source: a newspaper, a painting, a print, a pattern. At other times, it's a matter of words, whether in the form of private salutations and epistles or quotations drawn from literature and popular culture. Headlines, aphorisms, slogans and sayings are carefully chosen and applied, regularly referencing contemporary events and political controversies. Nel is attracted to powerful phrases and punchy lines. It's often the poetry of placards and posters that appears: 'Three Unforgettable Weeks in Gaza', 'Don the Con is Gone', 'Black Lives Matter'. At other times the personal rubs up against the public: 'Waiting for Covid 19', 'Off to China', 'Ons mis jou Trompie Botha'. It's the phrases as much as their popular resonances that appeal. No ordinary commemorative plates, these vessels nod to the reverence and deference accorded such historical objects with their official insignia and memorial messages. But now the plate is no official piece of memorabilia or propaganda. Instead, it becomes a personalised platform for protest and exposé, memory and experience, drawing from the language of the street or the private pathos of loss. Veering from the high-minded to the vulgar, from the

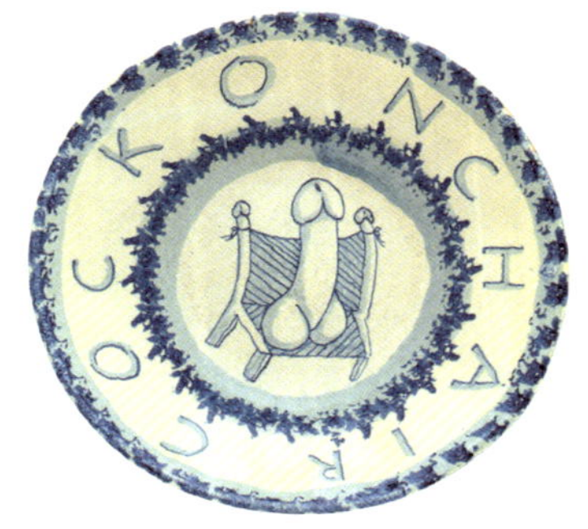

15 November 1996

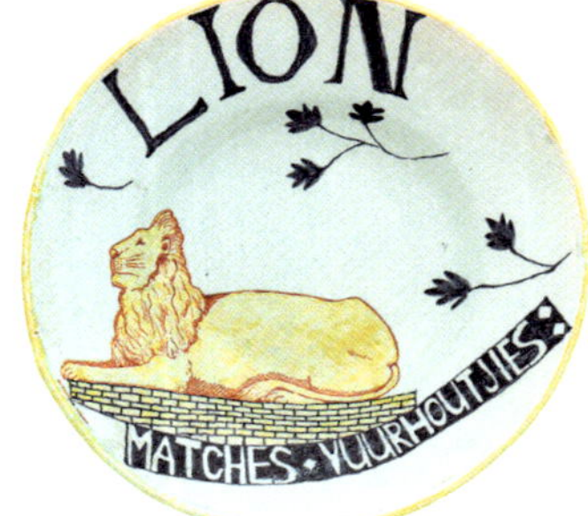

4 February 2004

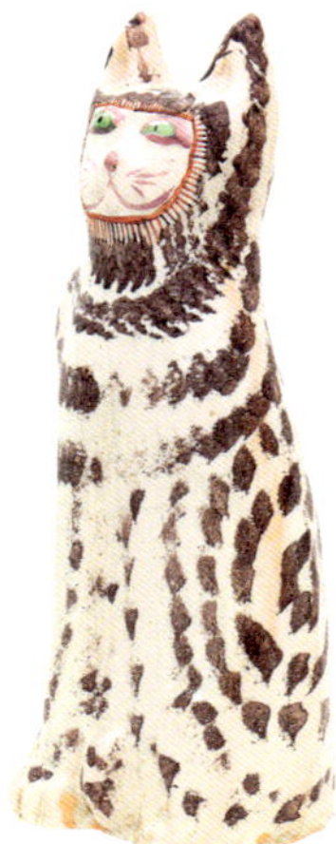

c.1991

celestial to the everyday, Nel populates his world in a radically democratic and unhierarchical way. All manner of things might make an appearance on a plate or a vase. Figural referents range from Renaissance prototypes to lewd graffiti. Both seem equally rich and true. The ignominious cohabit with the grand, the epic finds its echo in the miniscule. And the cats, curious, knowing and aloof, appear to look on, ciphers of wisdom and witness, themselves culled from history and clay. Not quite deities or fetishes – they are too funny and iconoclastic for that – they nevertheless appear quite separate from the world they survey. At once ornaments and oracles, pieces of high culture and kitsch, they scramble and destabilise our categories. And there's both a politics and a poetics in that.

1 See Michael Stevenson, 'Introduction', in *Hylton Nel: For Use and Display* (London: The Fine Art Society, 2017), np.
2 Nel makes this point to Stevenson: 'They are also a kind of shape that has been used as an ornament for a long time. From another perspective, being gay is a sort of minority position and at some levels one is not quite what one should be, and so another reason why I make cats is to try and fit into the world because such ornaments seem like regular things.' In *Hylton Nel: For Use and Display*.
3 *Prayer for Good Governance* was the name given to his show at the Fine Art Society in 1996.

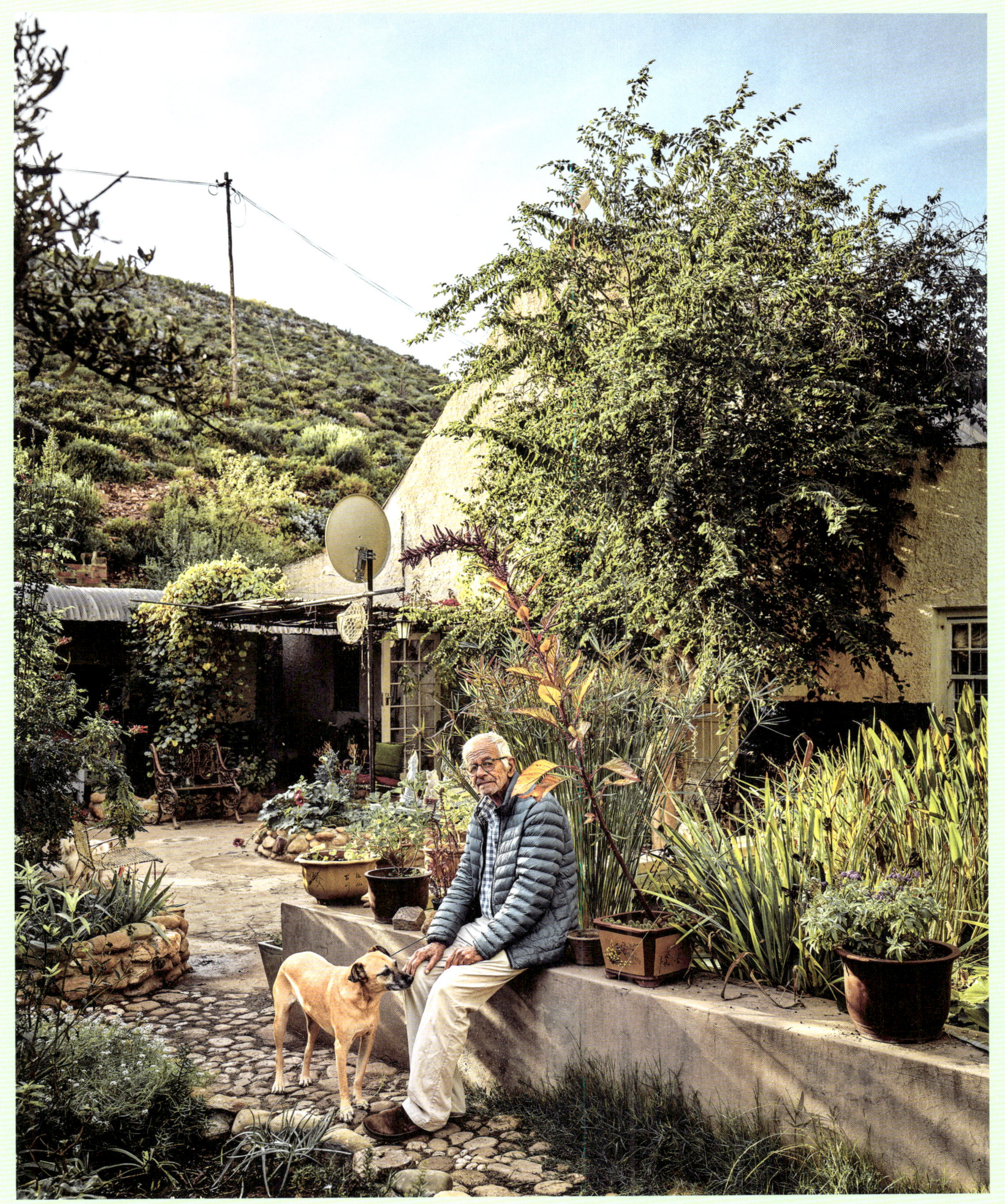

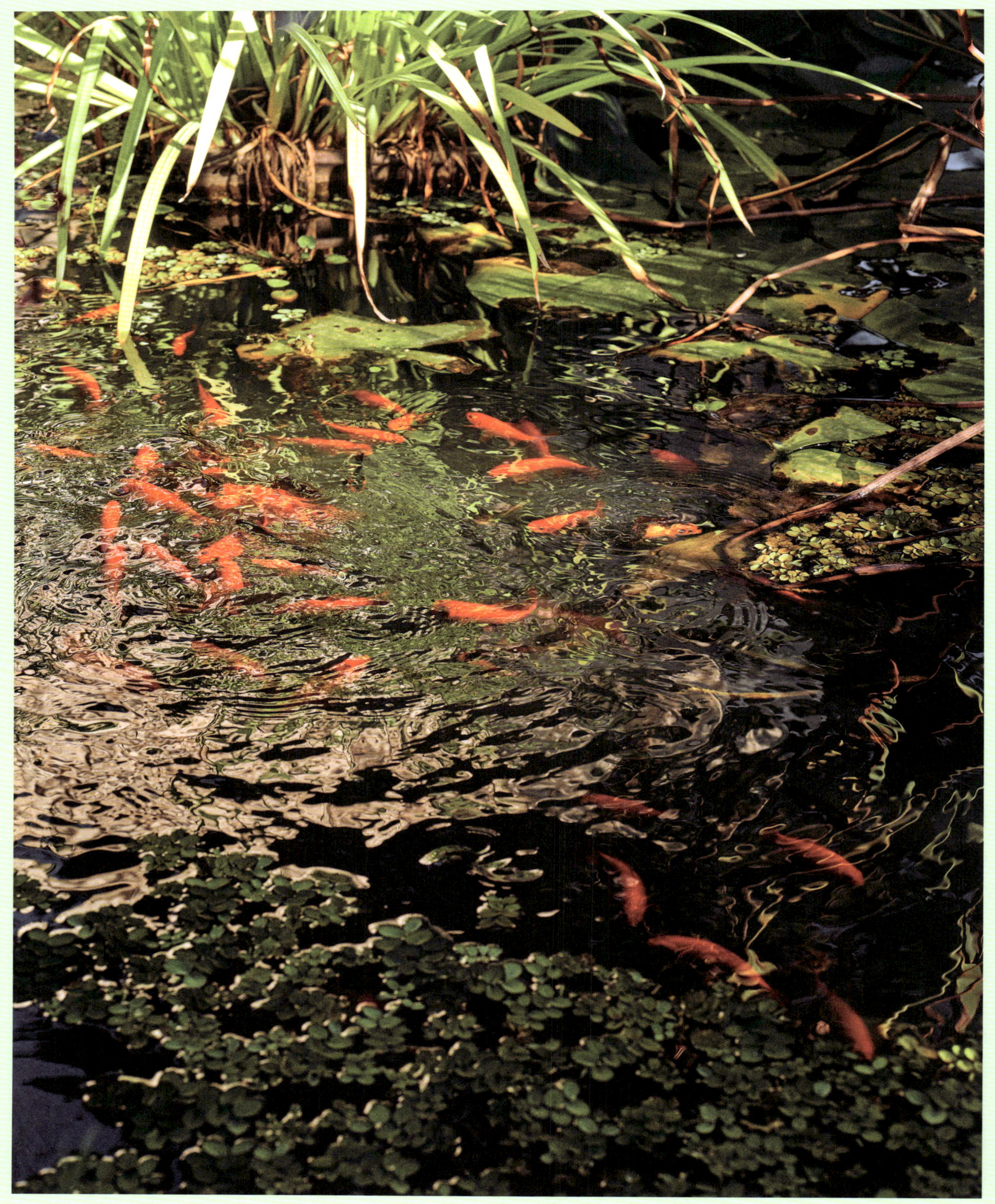

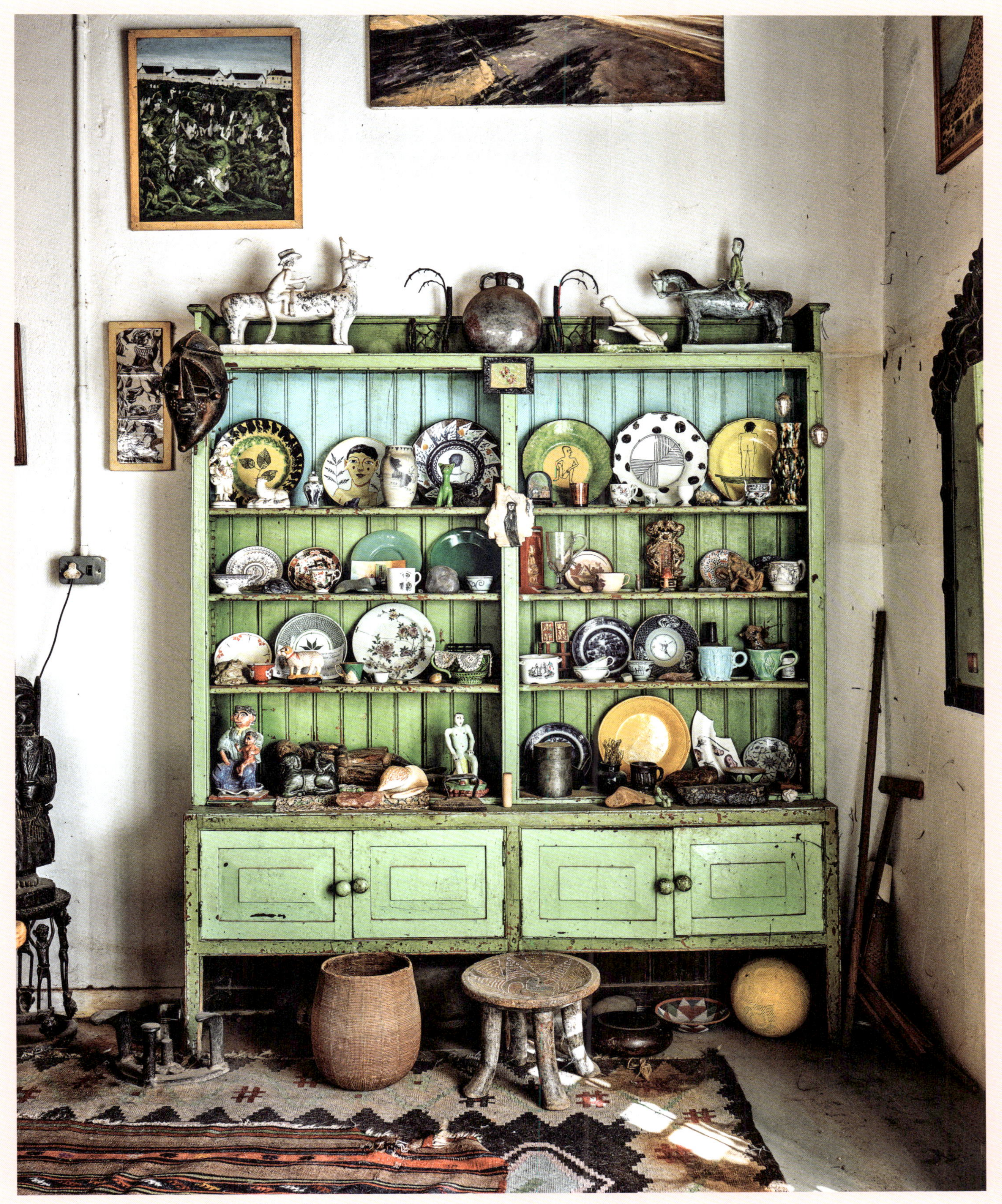

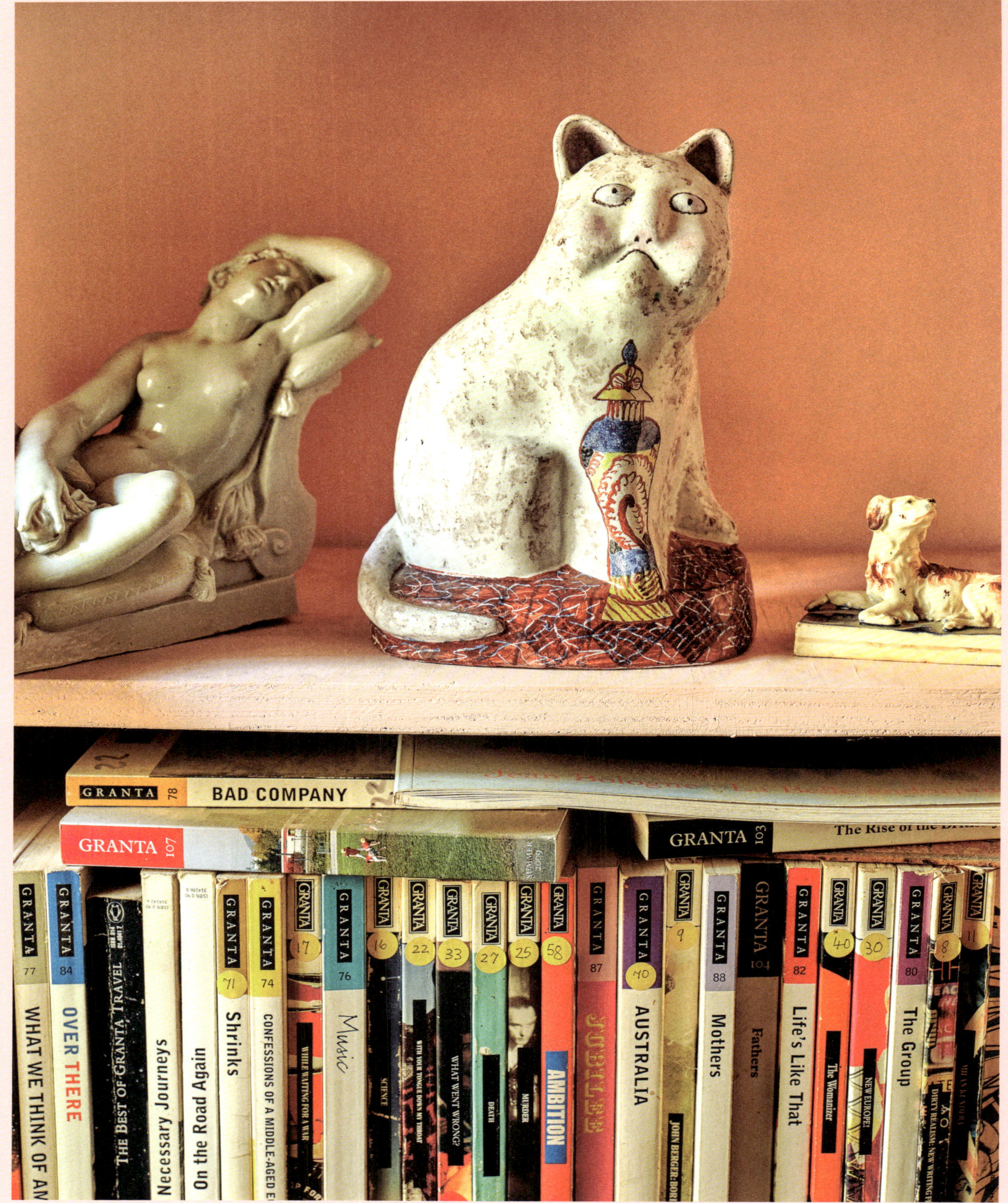

GRANTA 78 BAD COMPANY
GRANTA 107
GRANTA 103
GRANTA 84 OVER THERE
THE BEST OF GRANTA TRAVEL
Necessary Journeys
On the Road Again
GRANTA 71 Shrinks
GRANTA 76 Music
WHAT WENT WRONG?
AMBITION
GRANTA 87 JUBILEE
AUSTRALIA
GRANTA 88 Mothers
GRANTA 104 Fathers
GRANTA 82 Life's Like That
The Womanizer
NEW EUROPE!
GRANTA 80 The Group

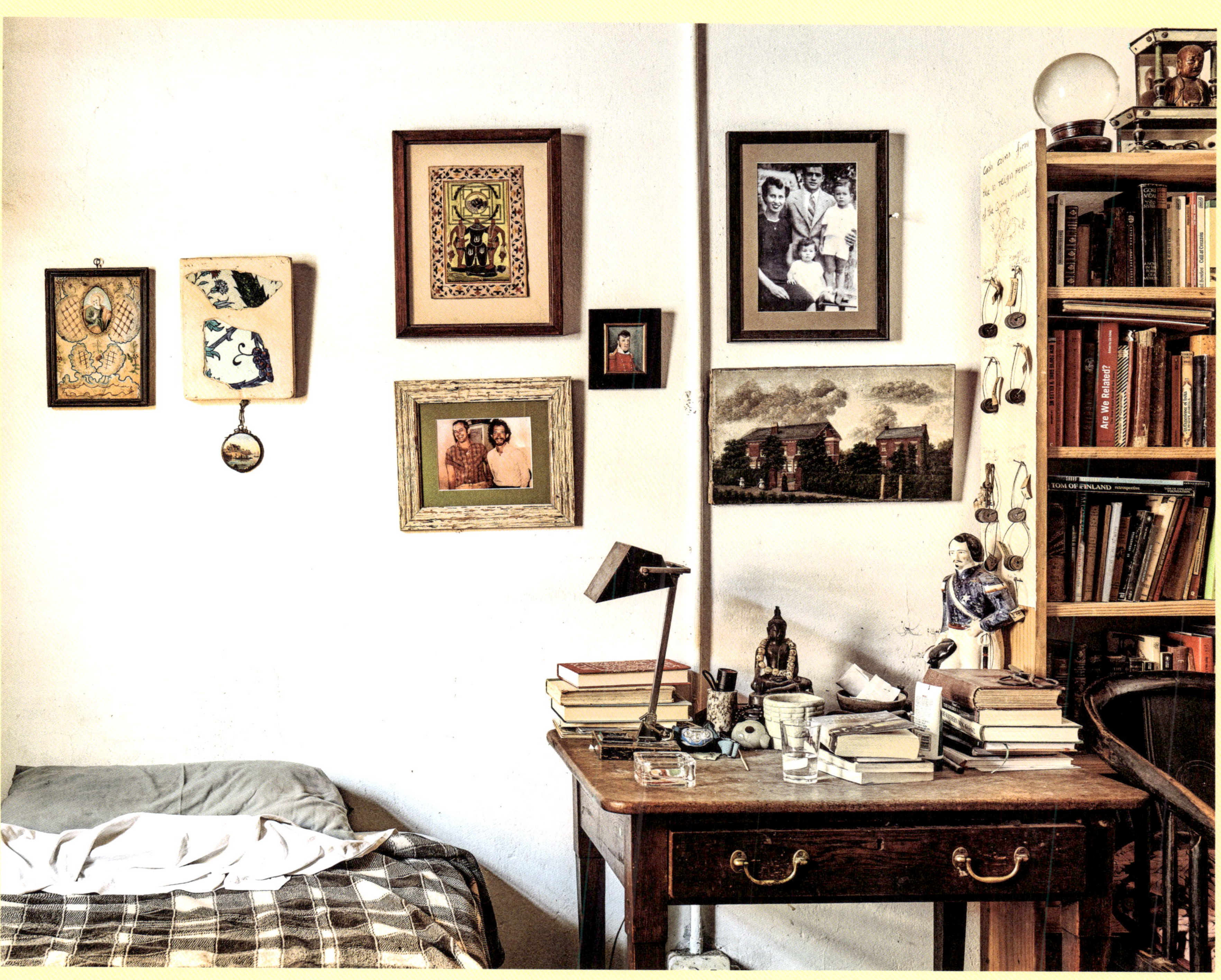
Are We Related?
TOM OF FINLAND

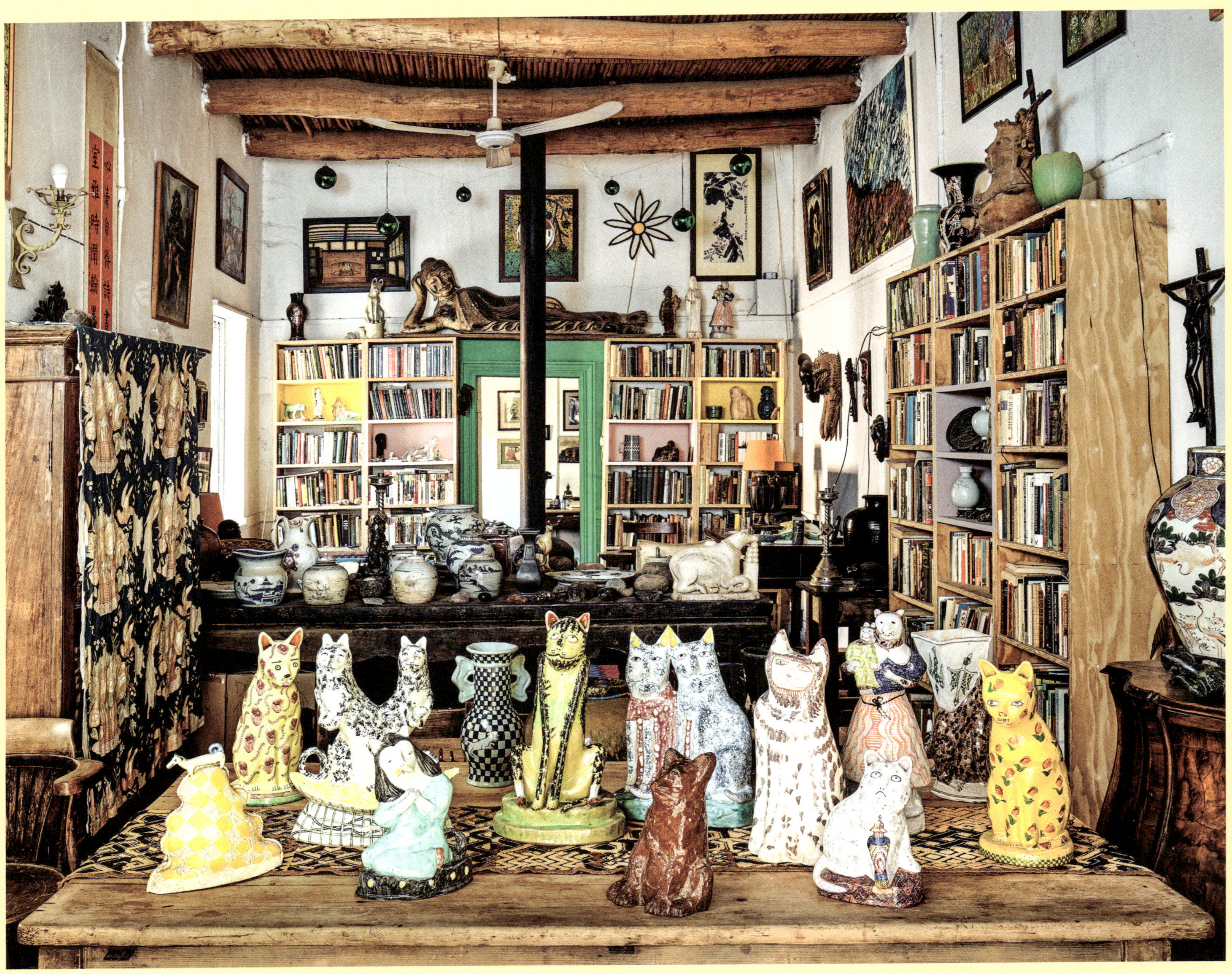

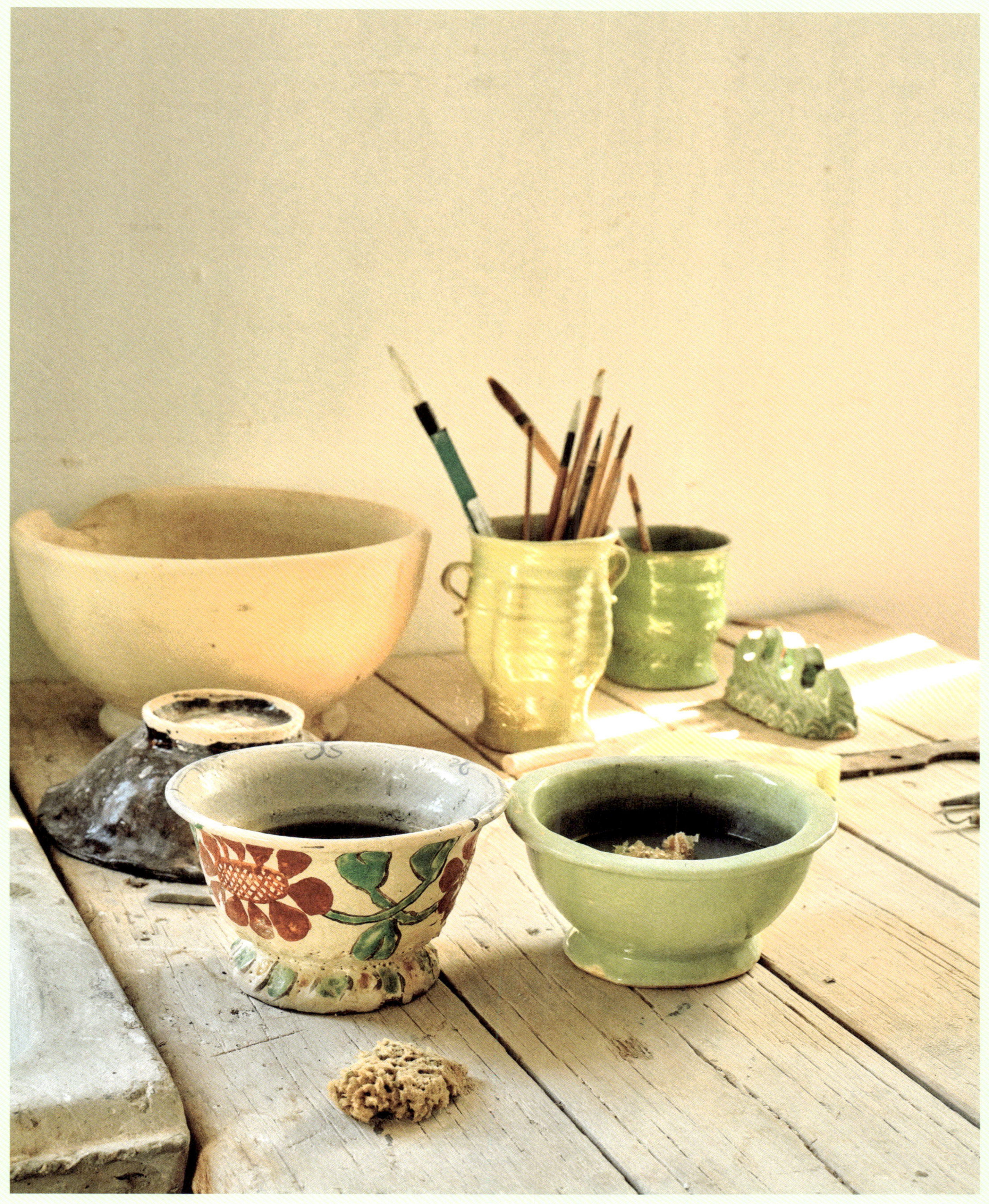

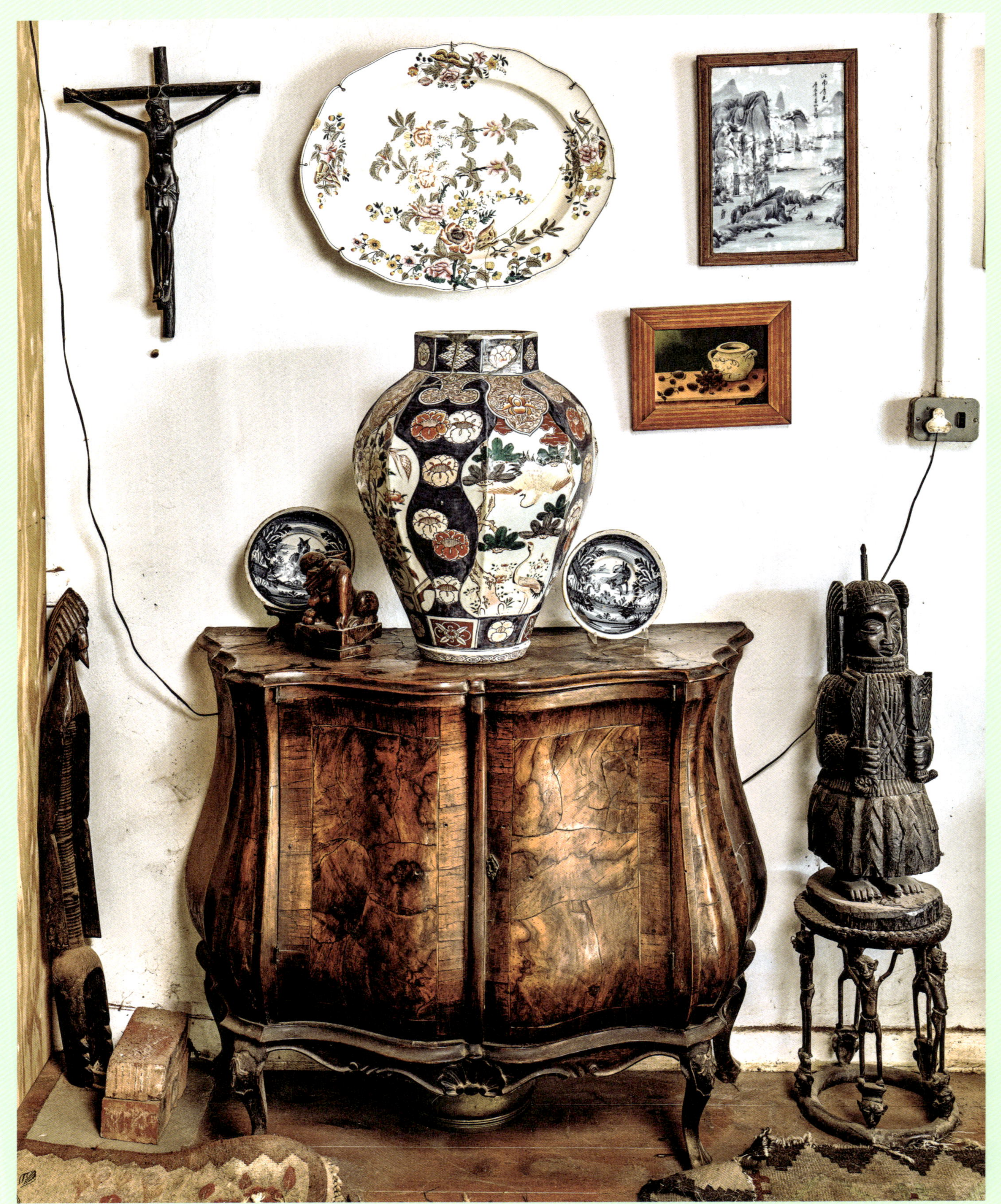

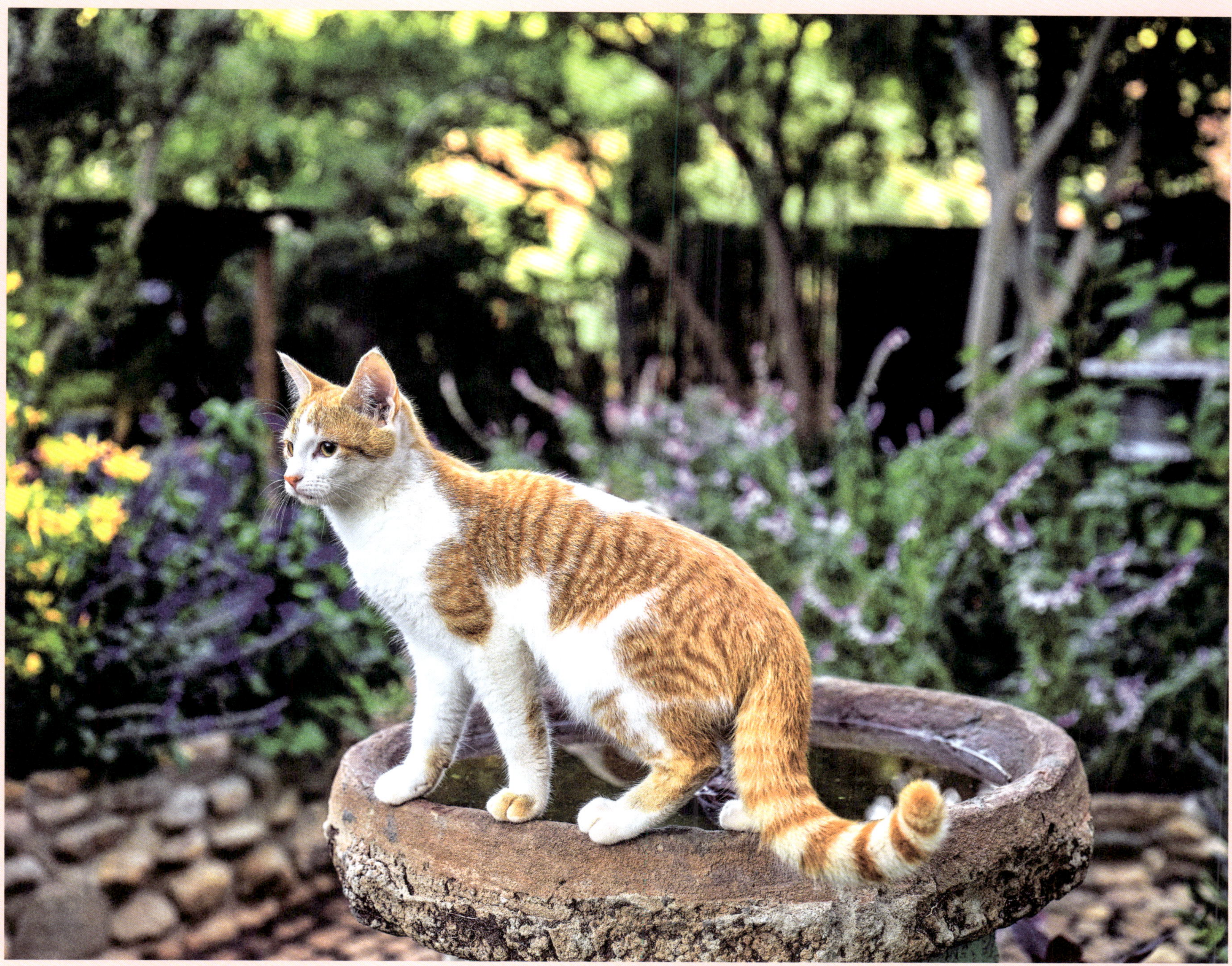

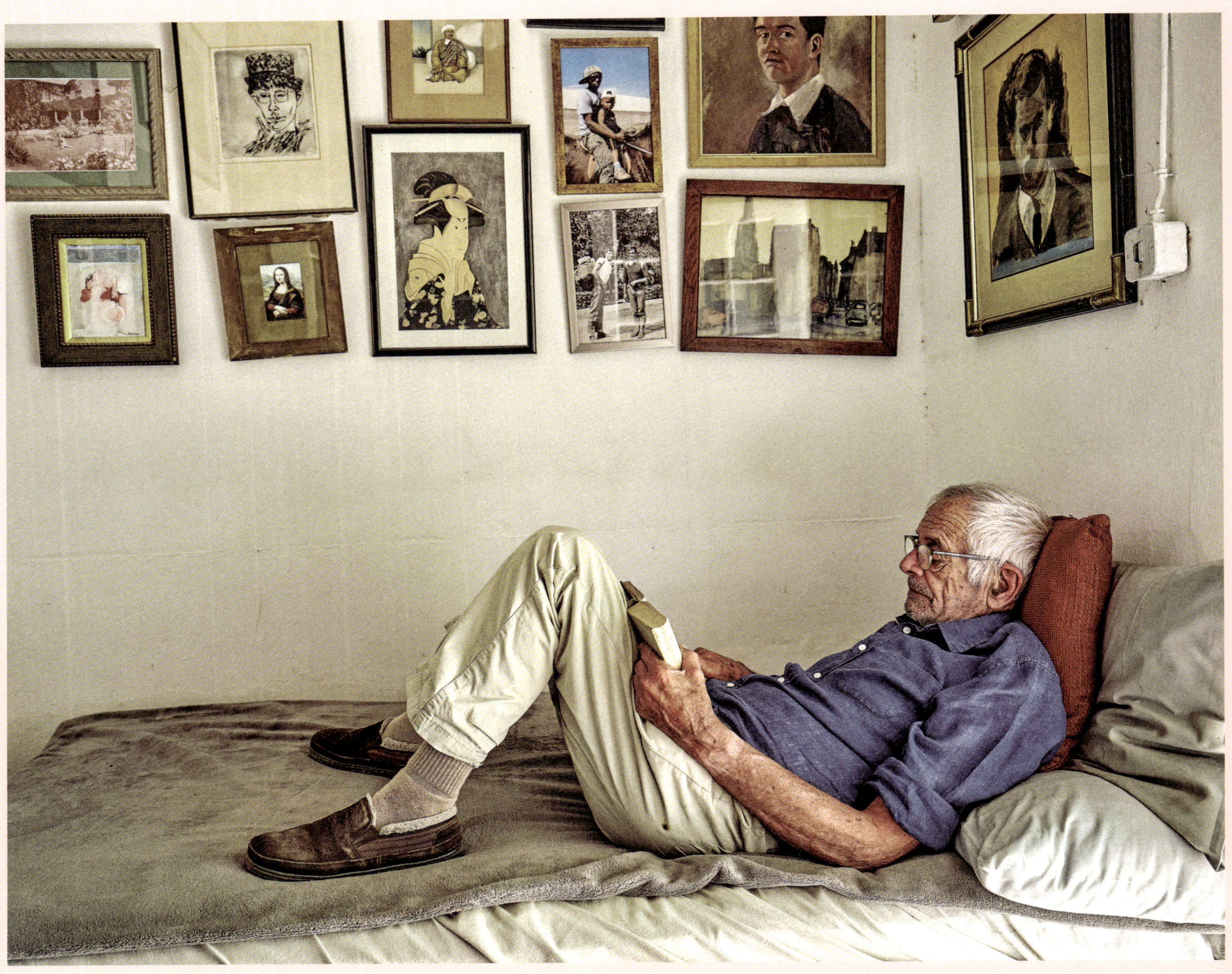

When you look at the variety of things I've made over time, sometimes they are made around the same time but look very different from one another; other things are separated by time but look very similar. As far as I am concerned they are the same, but in fact there are variations and changes. Things are 'of a time', there are flows, and sometimes they shift abruptly. I only see them clearly after a while, because at the time of making you're sort of in the middle of it. Time gives it distance. After a long time I can look at my things and think, 'That's nice,' but in the moment of making it, one is too close. You need time to see them.

HYLTON NEL
IN HIS OWN WORDS

In 1380 or thereabouts, the first book was published in Chinese on what's good stuff, what's better than other stuff, and all that. In the West the only known version of this book, *The Ko Ku Yao Lun*, was a fragment in the Bibliothèque Nationale in Paris, and that was the only access people had to it. The renowned collector Percival David was visiting the house of a high-born family in China and in their library he realised that he could be looking at the only surviving copy of the book. It soon passed into his possession, and he made it his life's work to translate it into English, although sadly he died before it was actually published. I was aware of his book, *Chinese Connoisseurship: The Ko Ku Yao Lun*, but couldn't afford it on the salary I was earning as a technician. Then it was remaindered, and I bought it for R20, a very low price. It's not everyone's cup of tea.

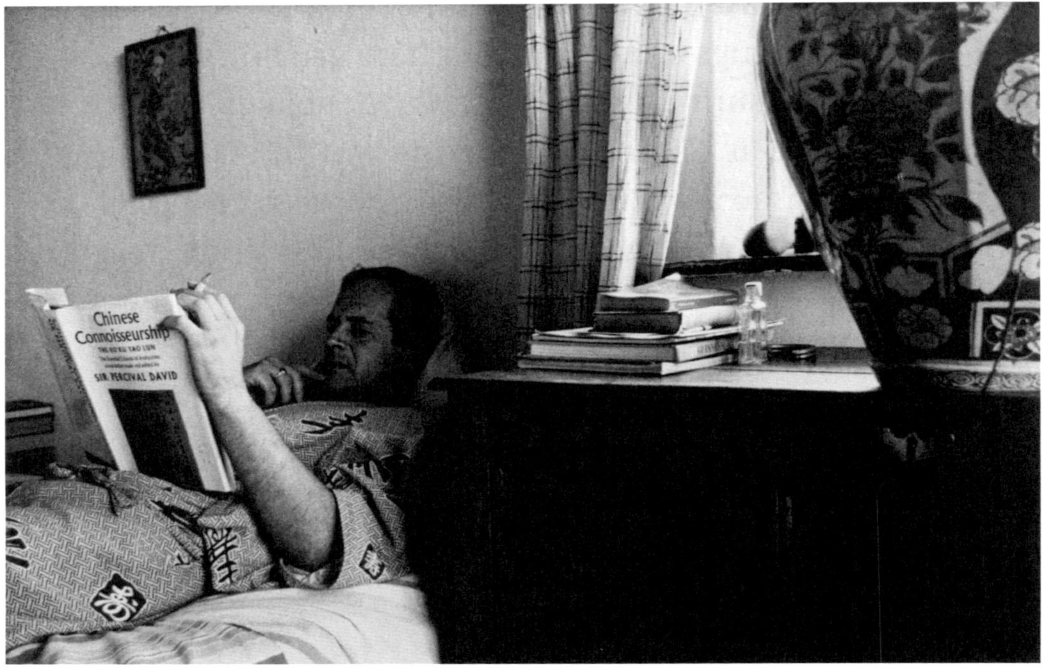

Photo by Bernard Wilke, Port Elizabeth, c.1982

The tiger is all that I have left from that time in Antwerp. It was from a postcard of a painting by George Stubbs. I slaved over the thing, and only after it was made I realised that a cat has a snout that sticks out and I had his face completely flat. The earliest cat.

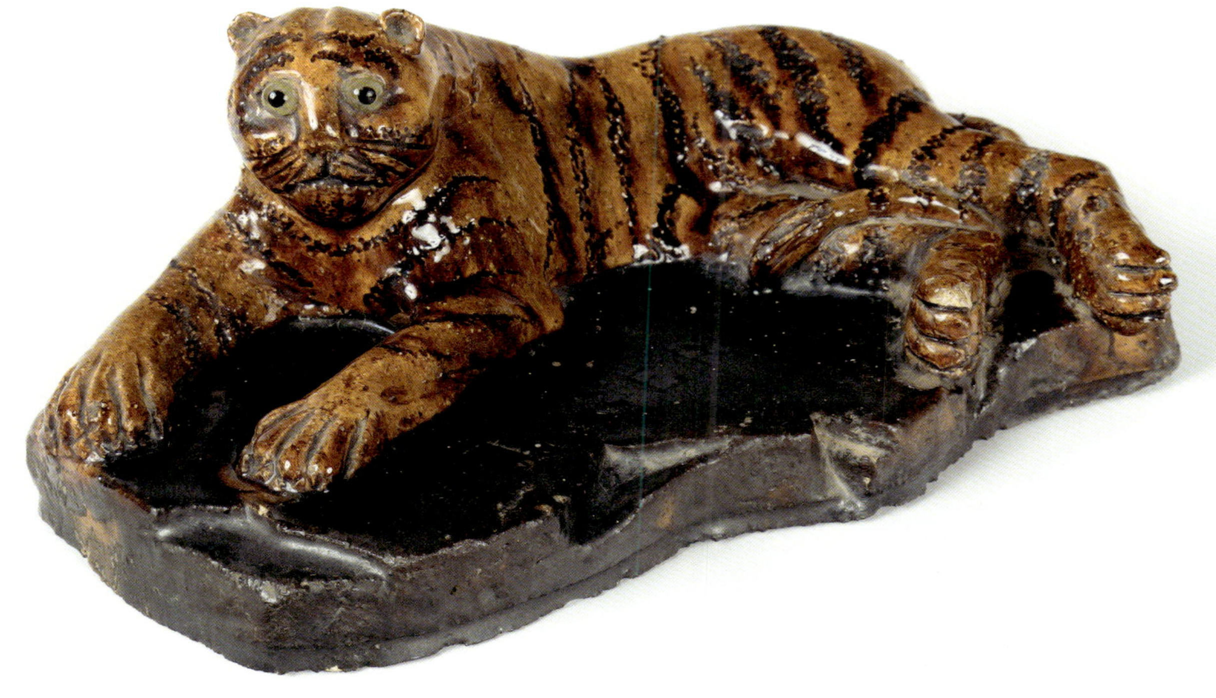

1967

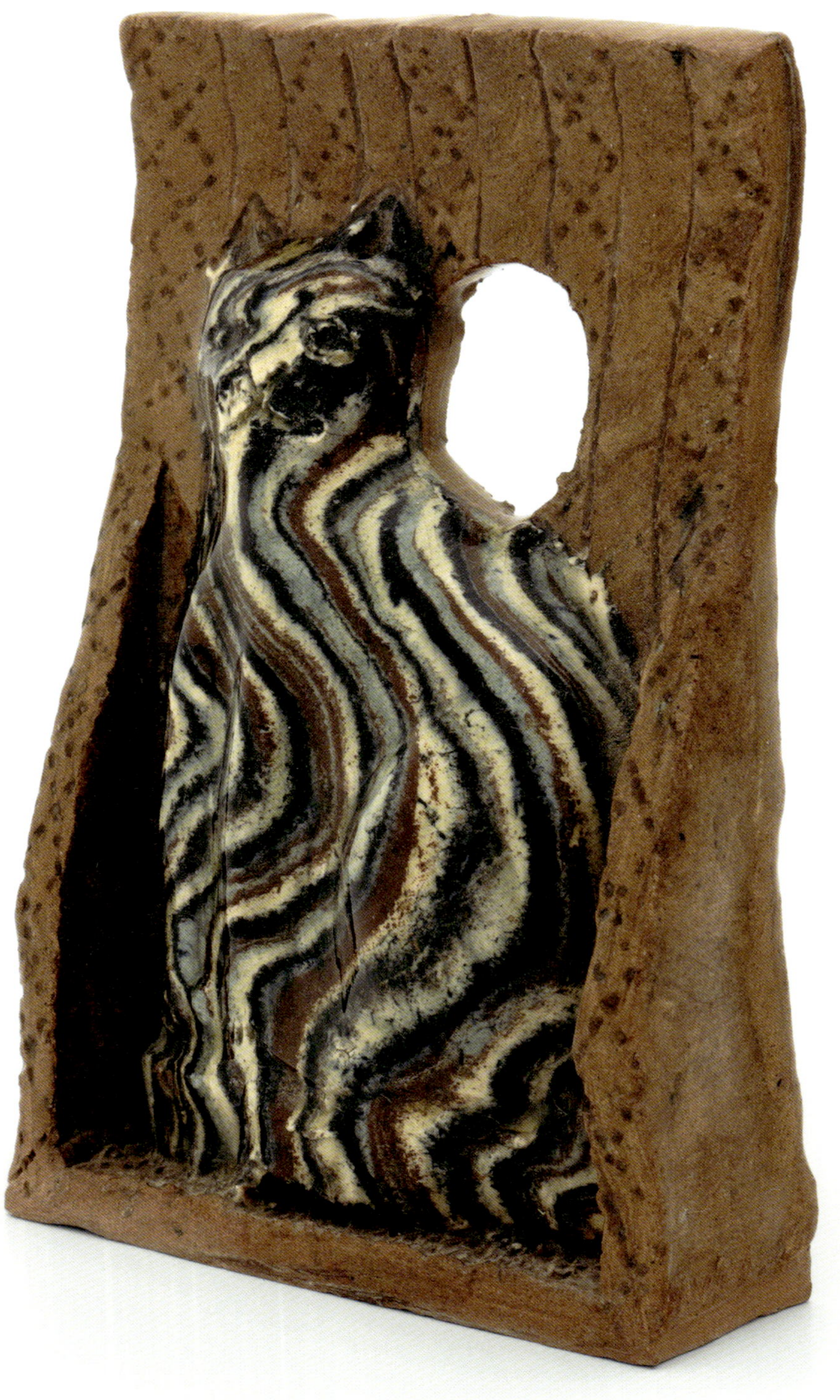

c.1974

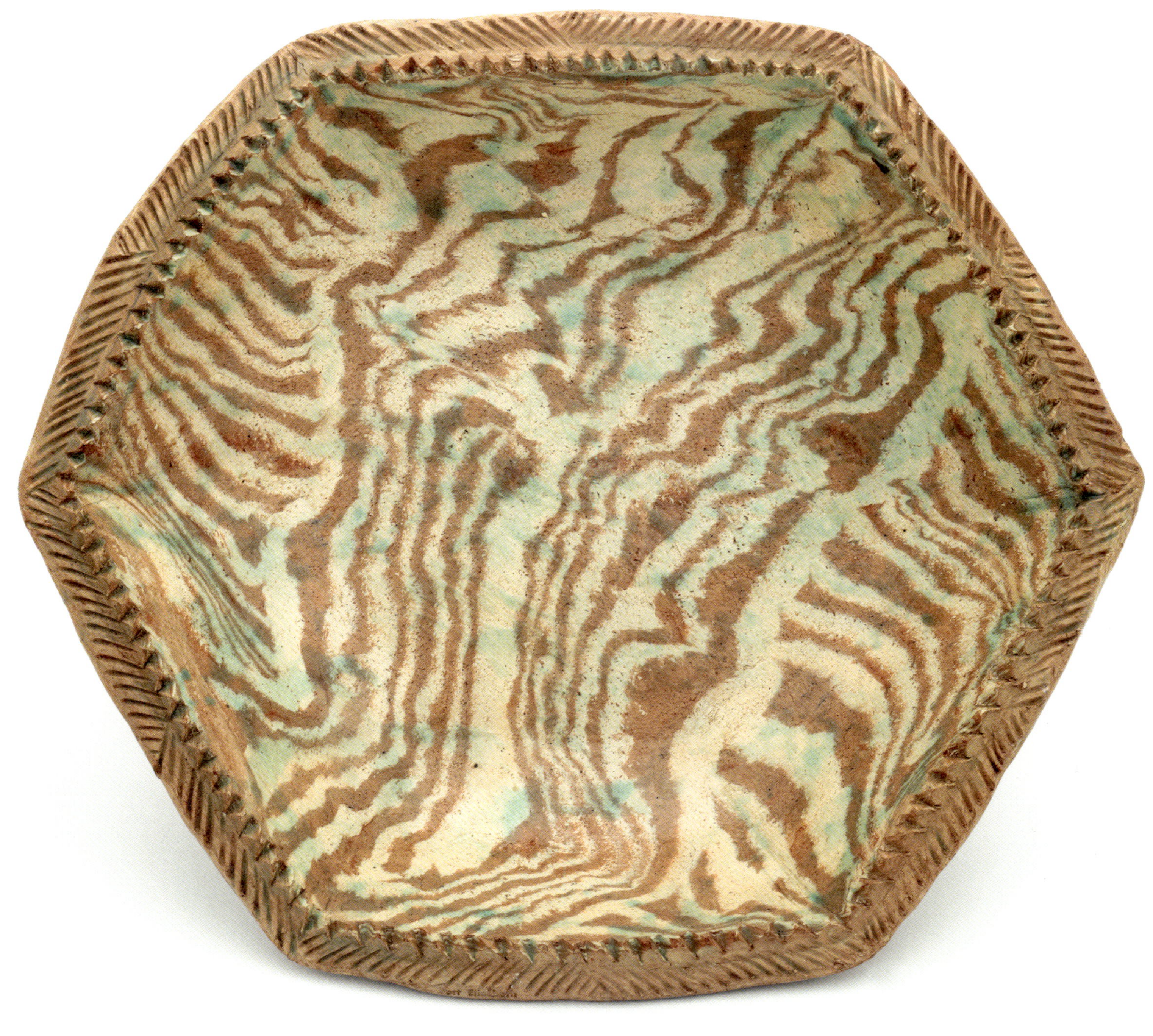

c.1975

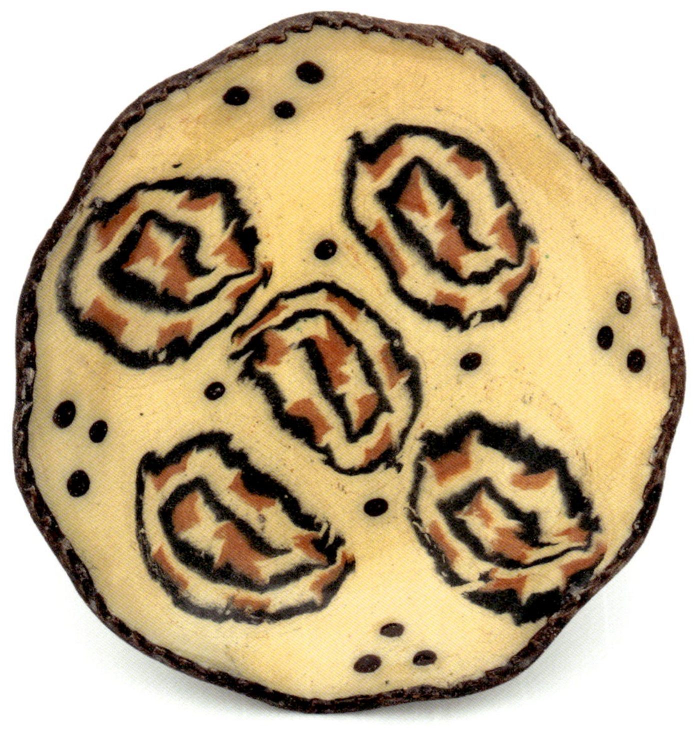

c.1975

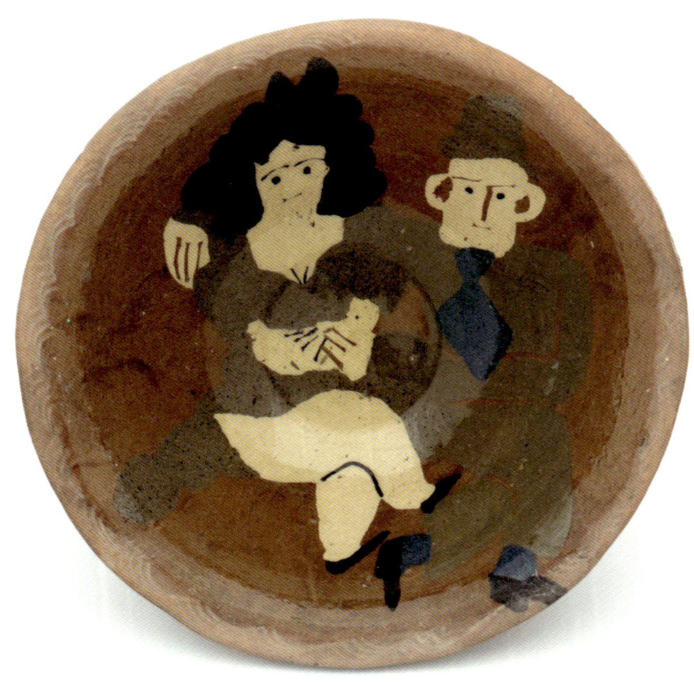

c.1972

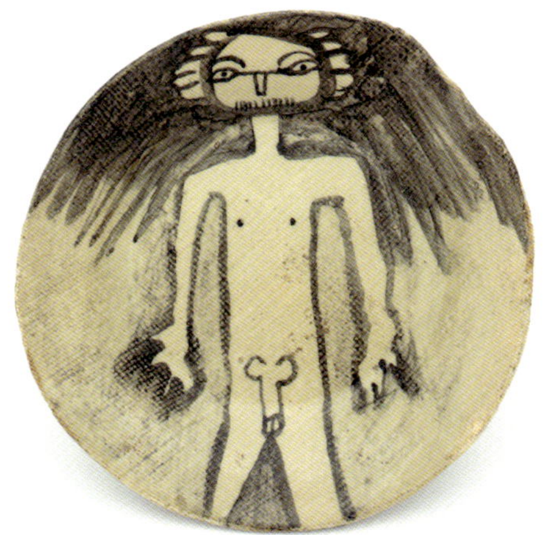

c.1976

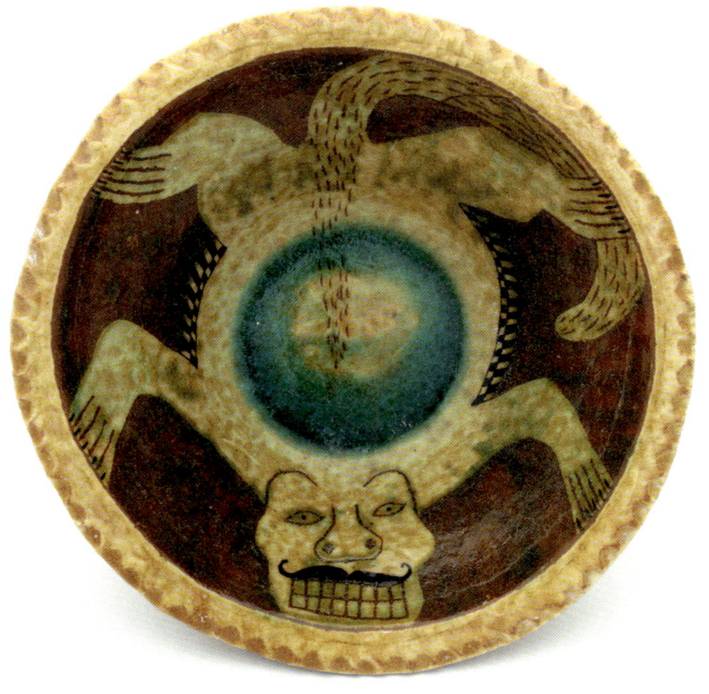

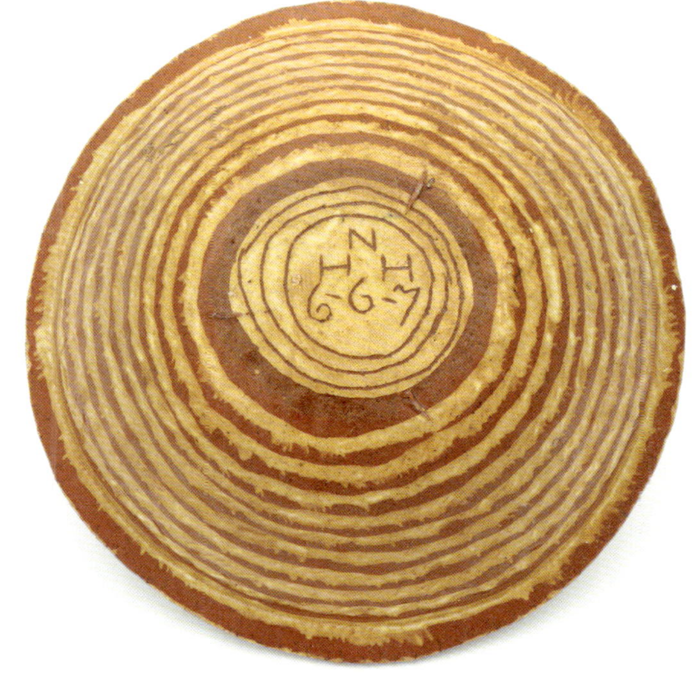

6 June 2007

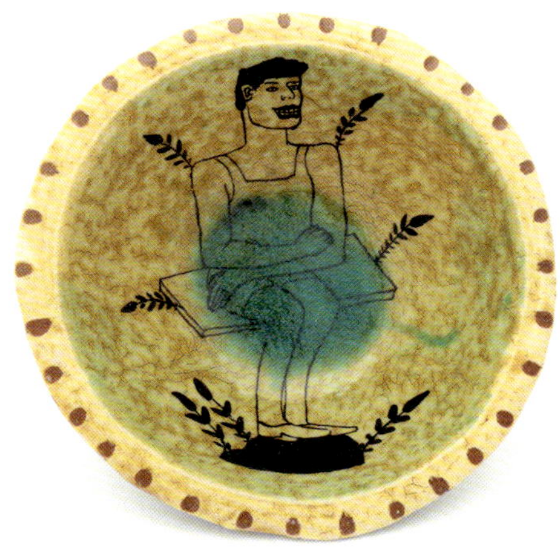

8 May 2007

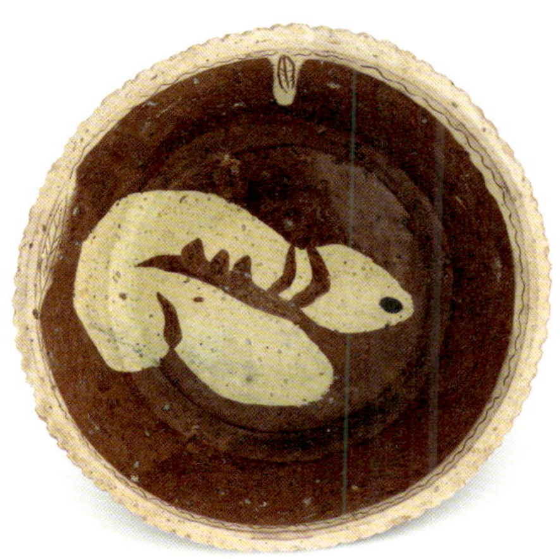

c.1972

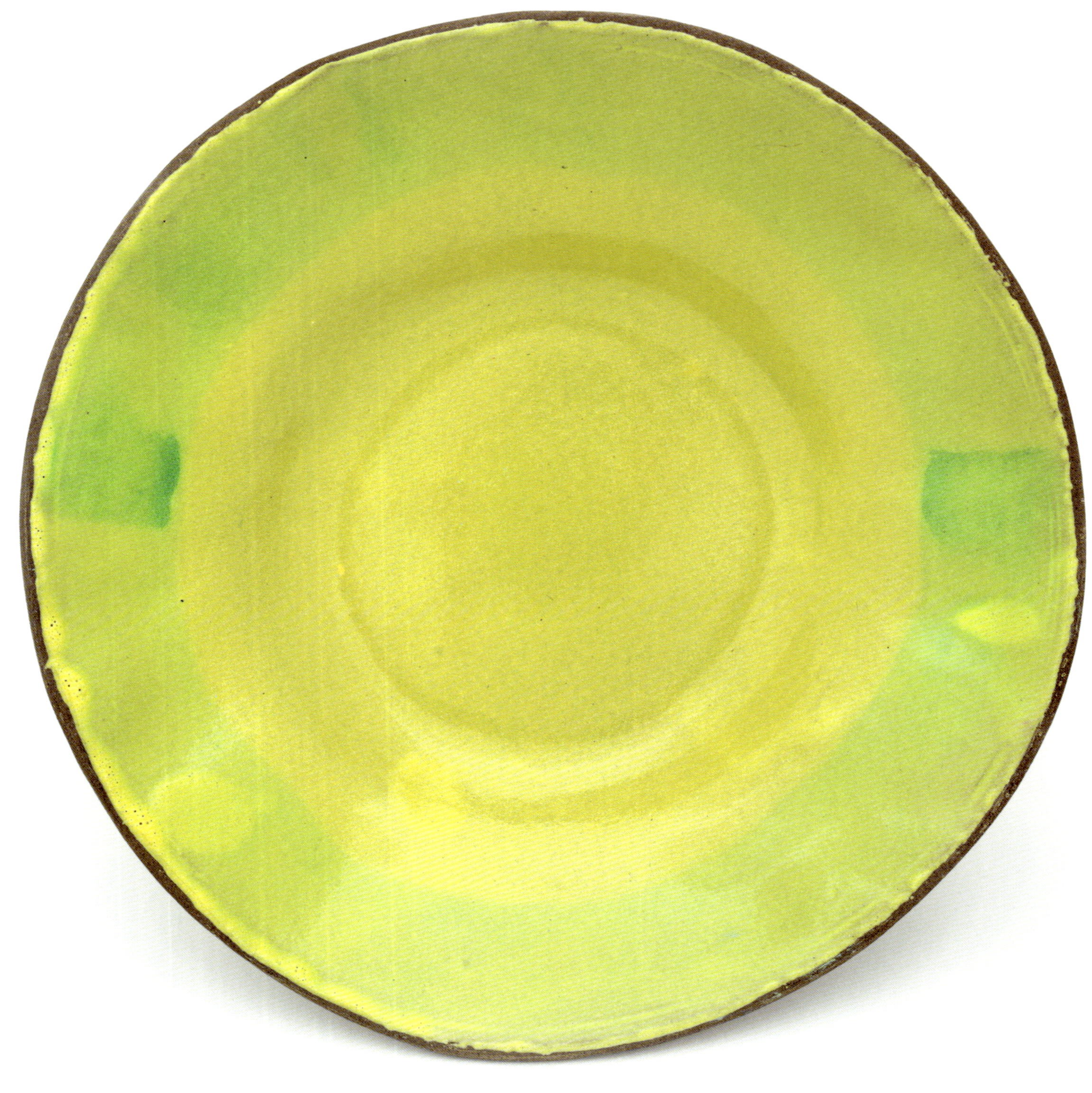

27 May 1995

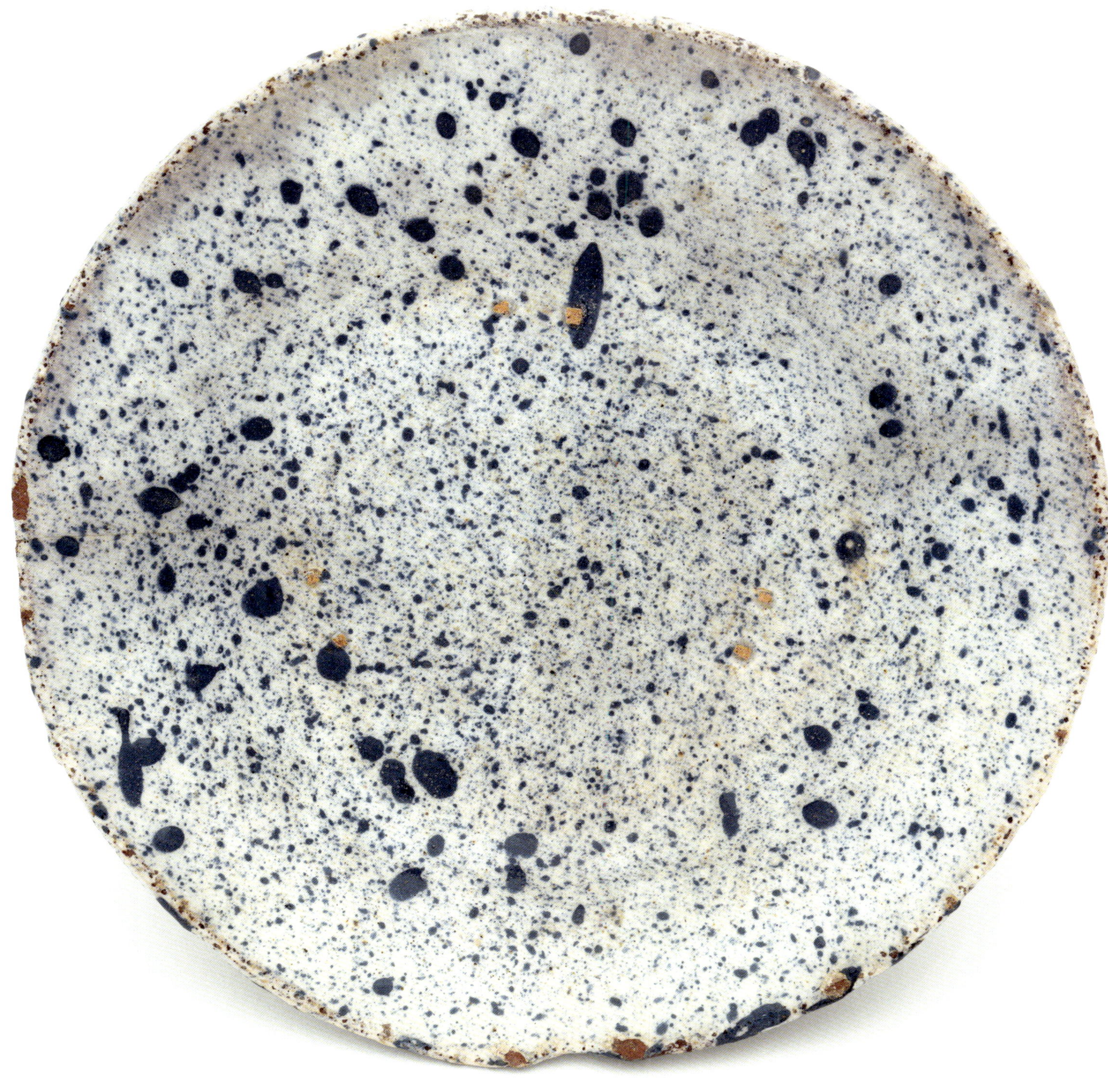

c.1976

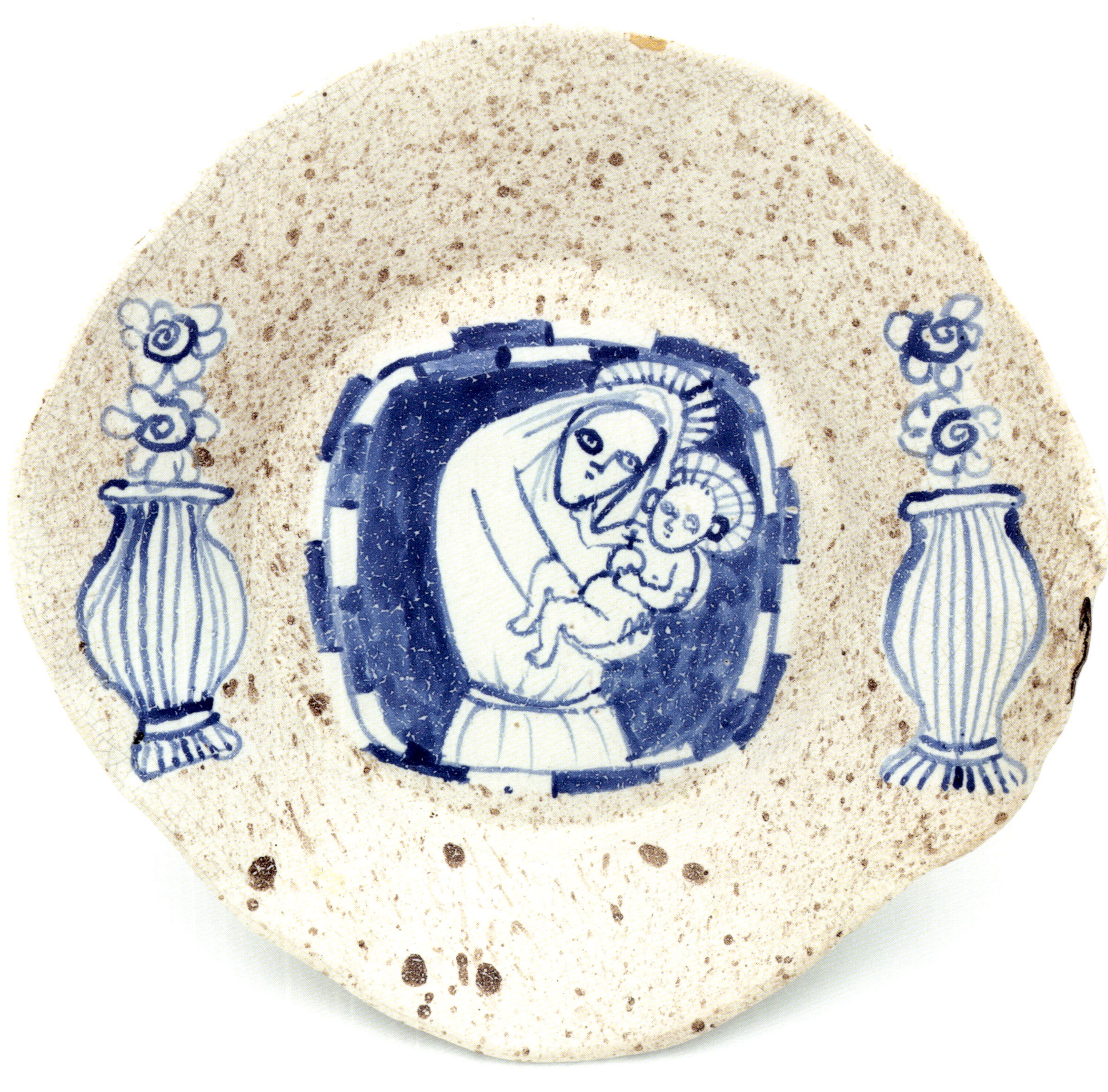

1987

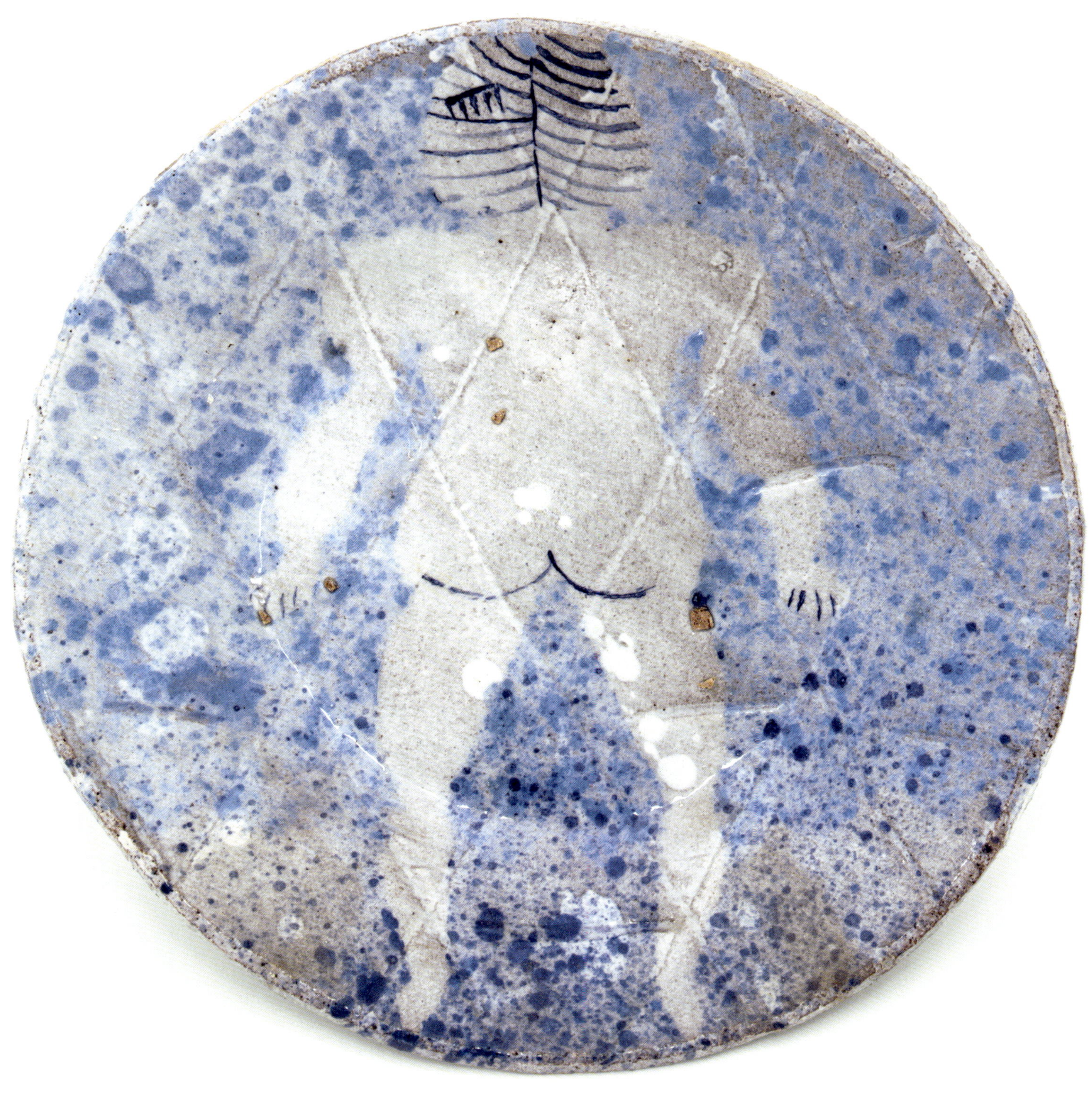

c.1982

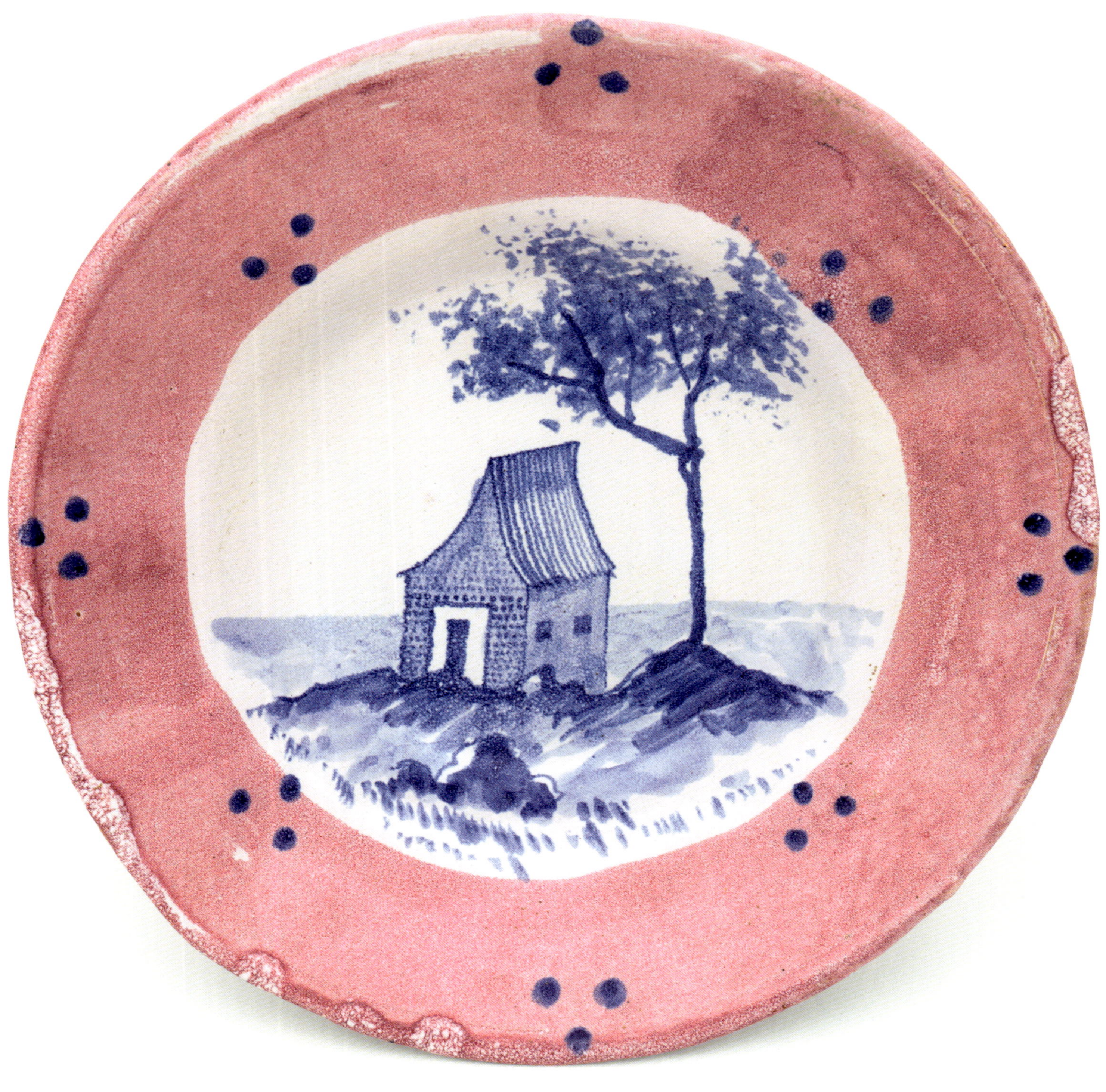

29 September 1995

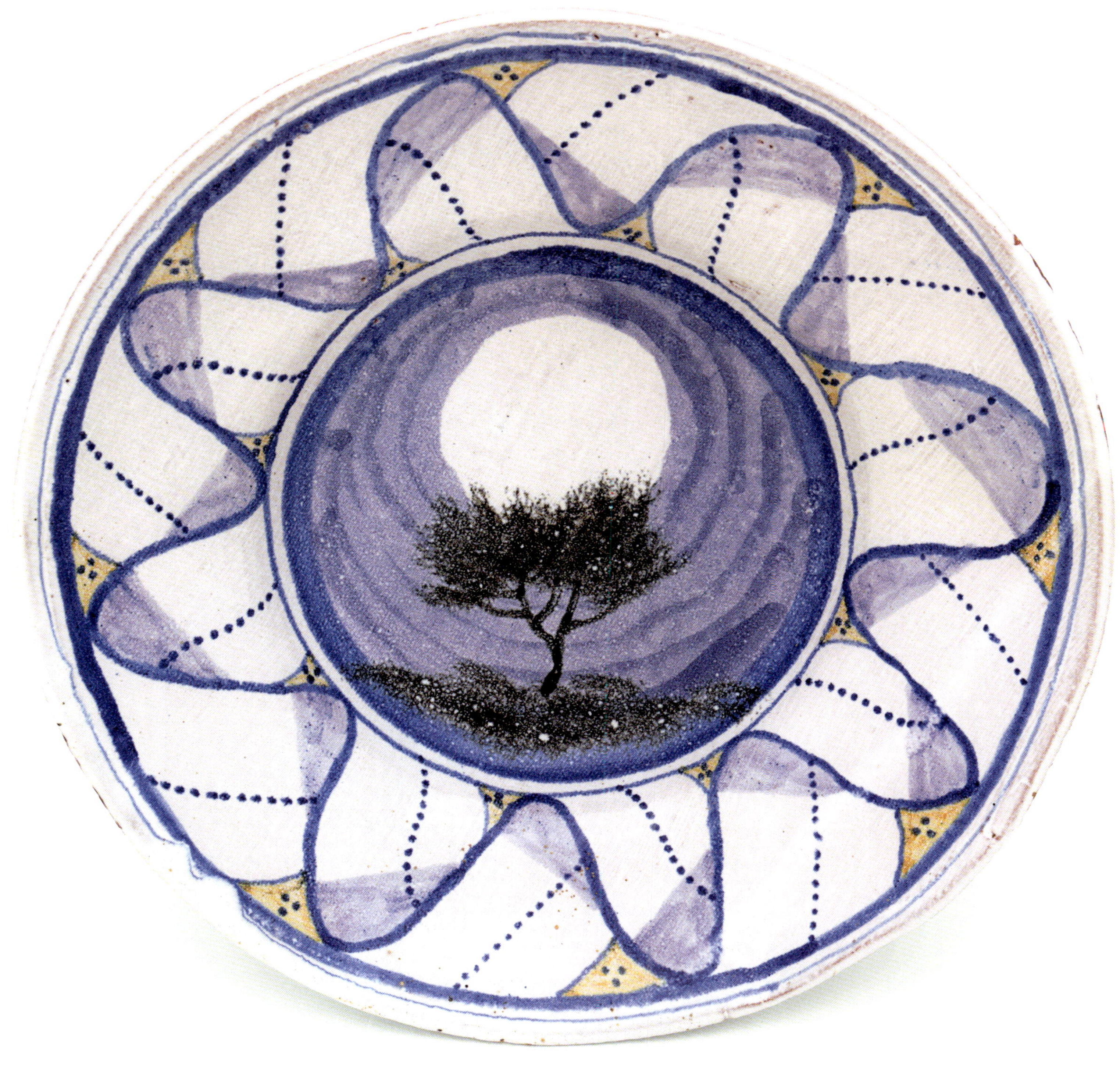

26 January 1999

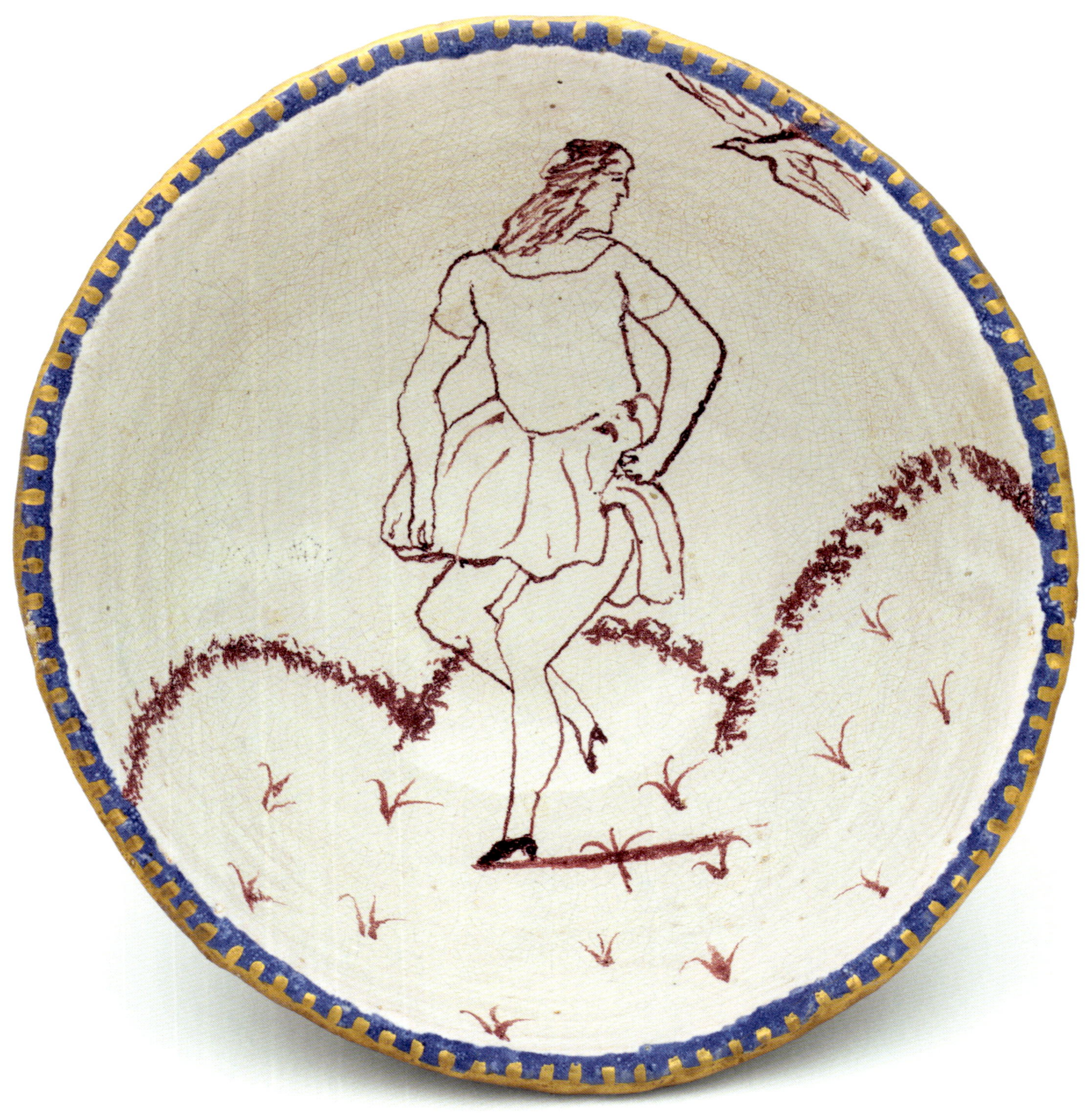

1990s

The bowl is a shape that makes sense. Historically, the form has emerged and evolved universally, so there is an infinite array of references – from cultures in China to Europe to Africa to the Middle East – to bring into one's own bowls. I like to make things that are just simple, ordinary, easy to use. Bowls themselves are versatile; they can be held with one hand, their contents scooped up with the other. The bowl's foot is there to prevent hot liquid burning your hands, so you can hold it, but the foot can also be used for a little wire to wrap around, to hang it up, for use and display.

I sort of live in this round shape. That's where I am working, always in this round shape, and usually it has a border to emphasise that, but sometimes I don't want to do a border, I want to simply flow out.

A lot of what I make is for utility, which I take across the road from the studio to the home. I use these things that I make from fire and earth. For me that is an enormous satisfaction. One of the reasons I make things is because I like things and want things. That's why I keep stuff back.

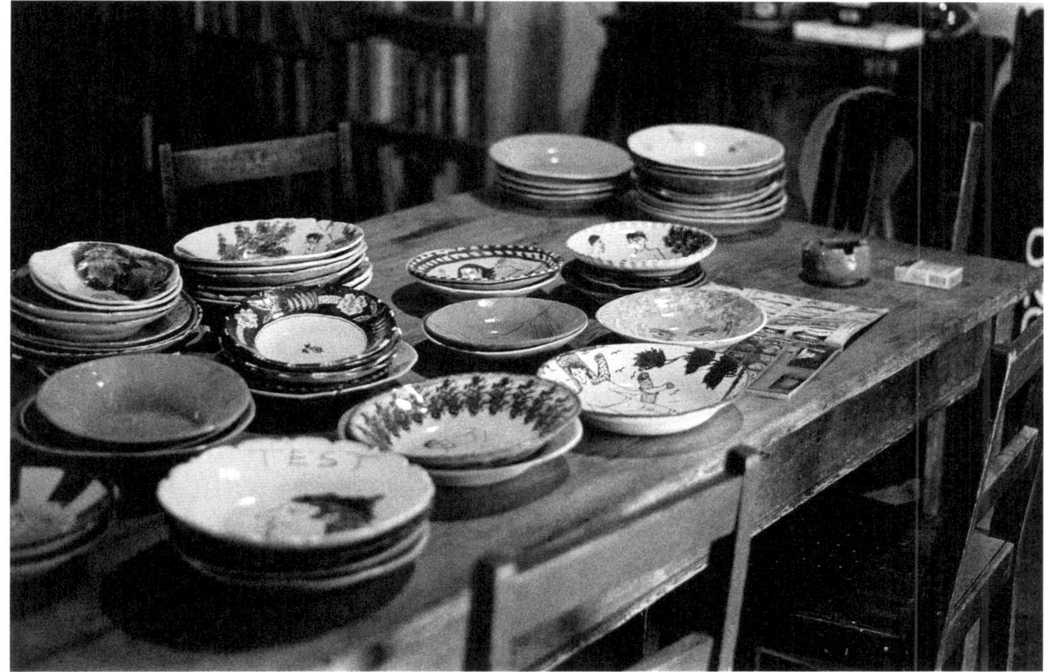

I am trying to get my ceramics to be part of life, a gesture, like sitting down on a chair, or setting a table, or frying an egg. What seems natural is what I am trying for. The idea of things that are born, not made, is something I think about quite often. That is what I see in a lot of the ceramics I admire – they seem just to be. So I try to make things that are just there. The fact that I use the things that I make every day helps me to anchor them in reality. It is not in our culture in this country to go and buy regional ceramics made by a local potter because machines and factories have taken over. For me it is important to make things that are real and that continue to be real.

I need a starting idea that fascinates me in some way; I want to see what it would look like if I did that and that and that. It has to interest me enough to want to pursue it. At the same time one tries to be practical. It's a lot of things and it's the whole thing.

What kind of shape am I using? A bowl shape, a basic shape. It can be useful, a basic usable shape. And the colour? What do I do with the edge, so that it feels easy? The weight of it, the shape of it. And then the outside of the bowl, which if it's hung on a wall wouldn't be visible, but somehow for the bowl to be complete it needs something on the outside, but what?

The glaze inspires me.

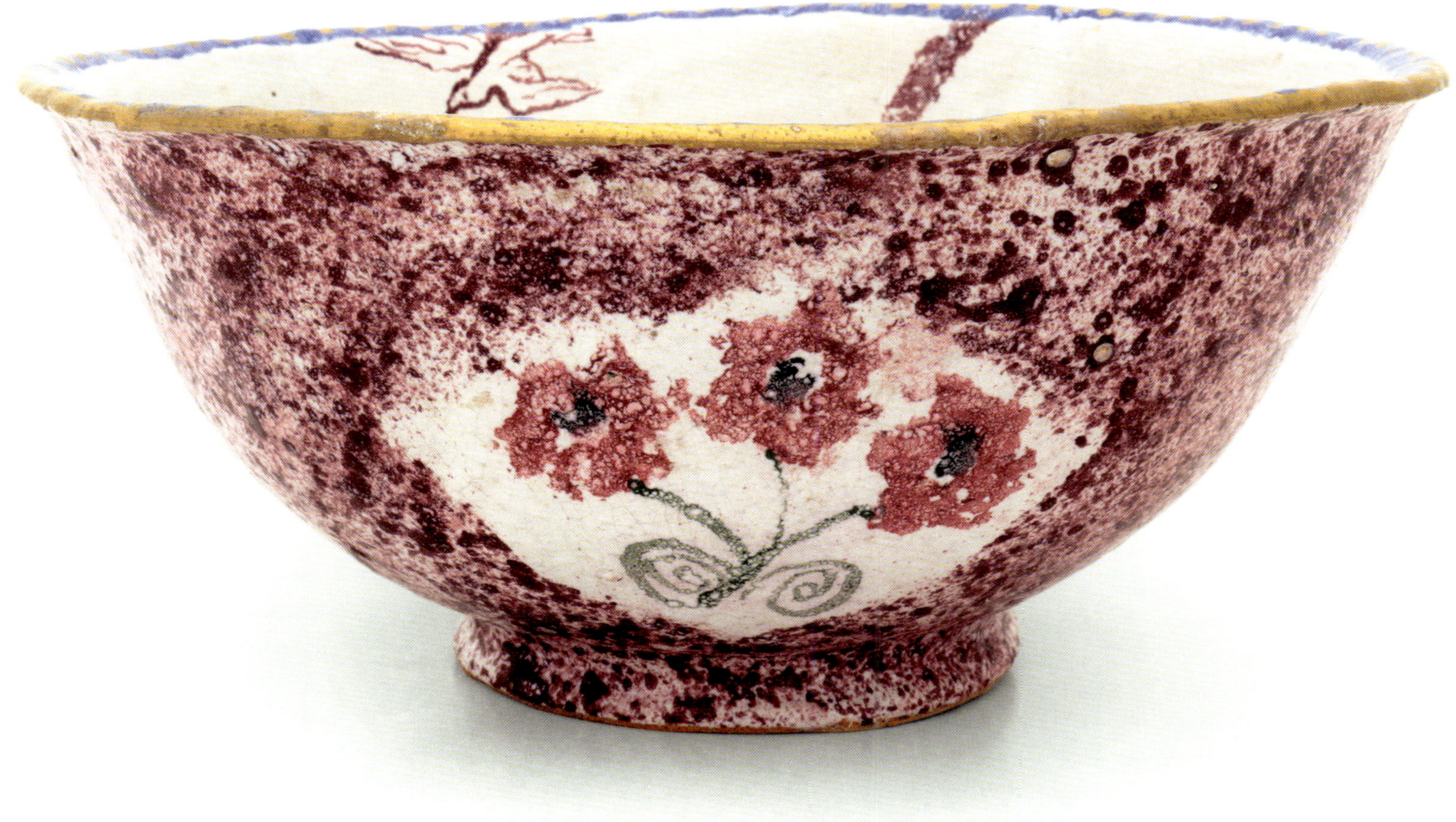

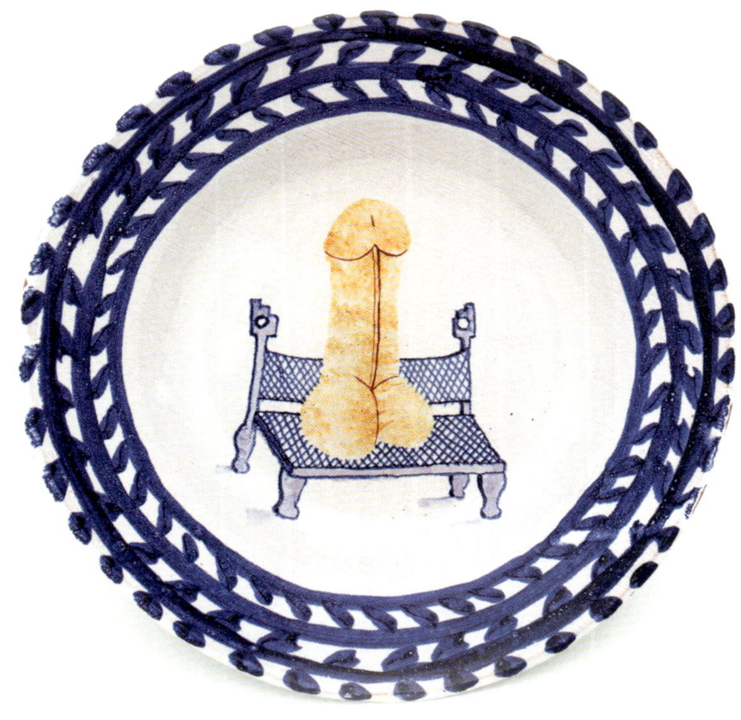

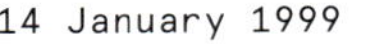

14 January 1999

20 November 2002

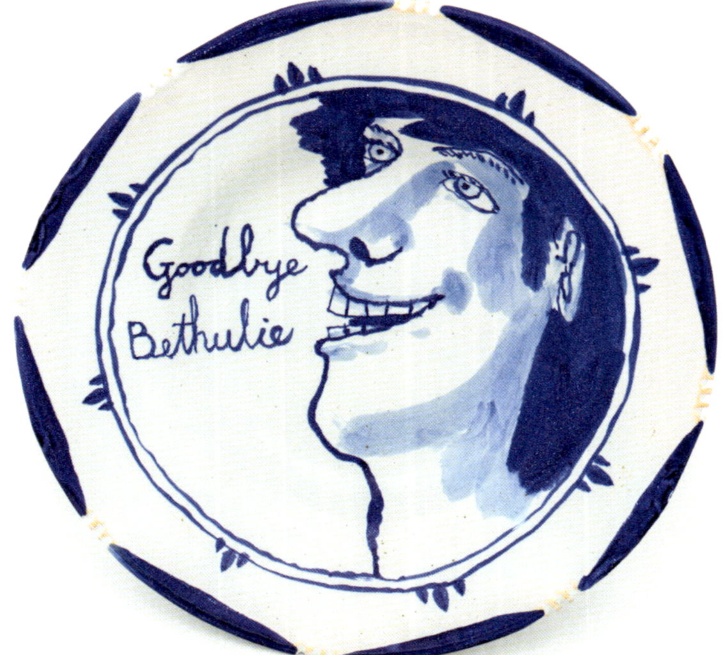

18 March 2002

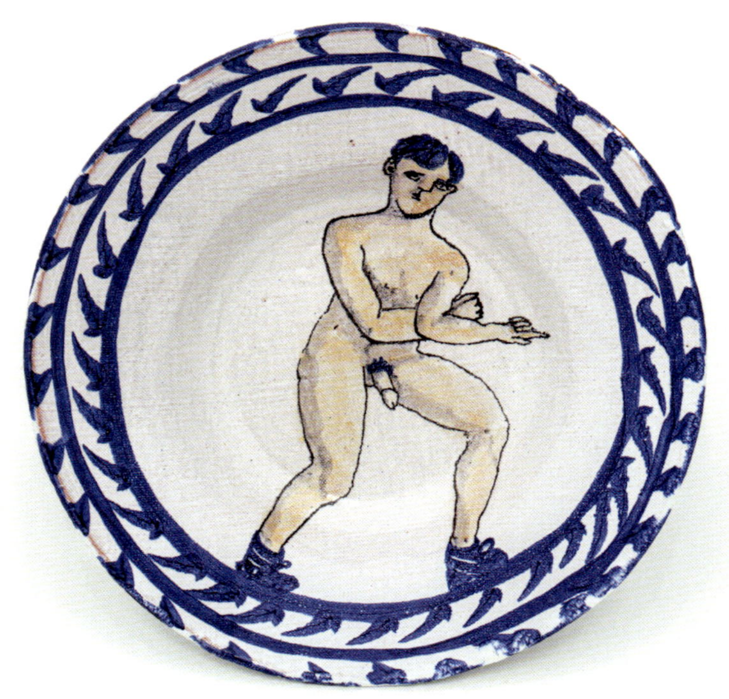

18 January 1999

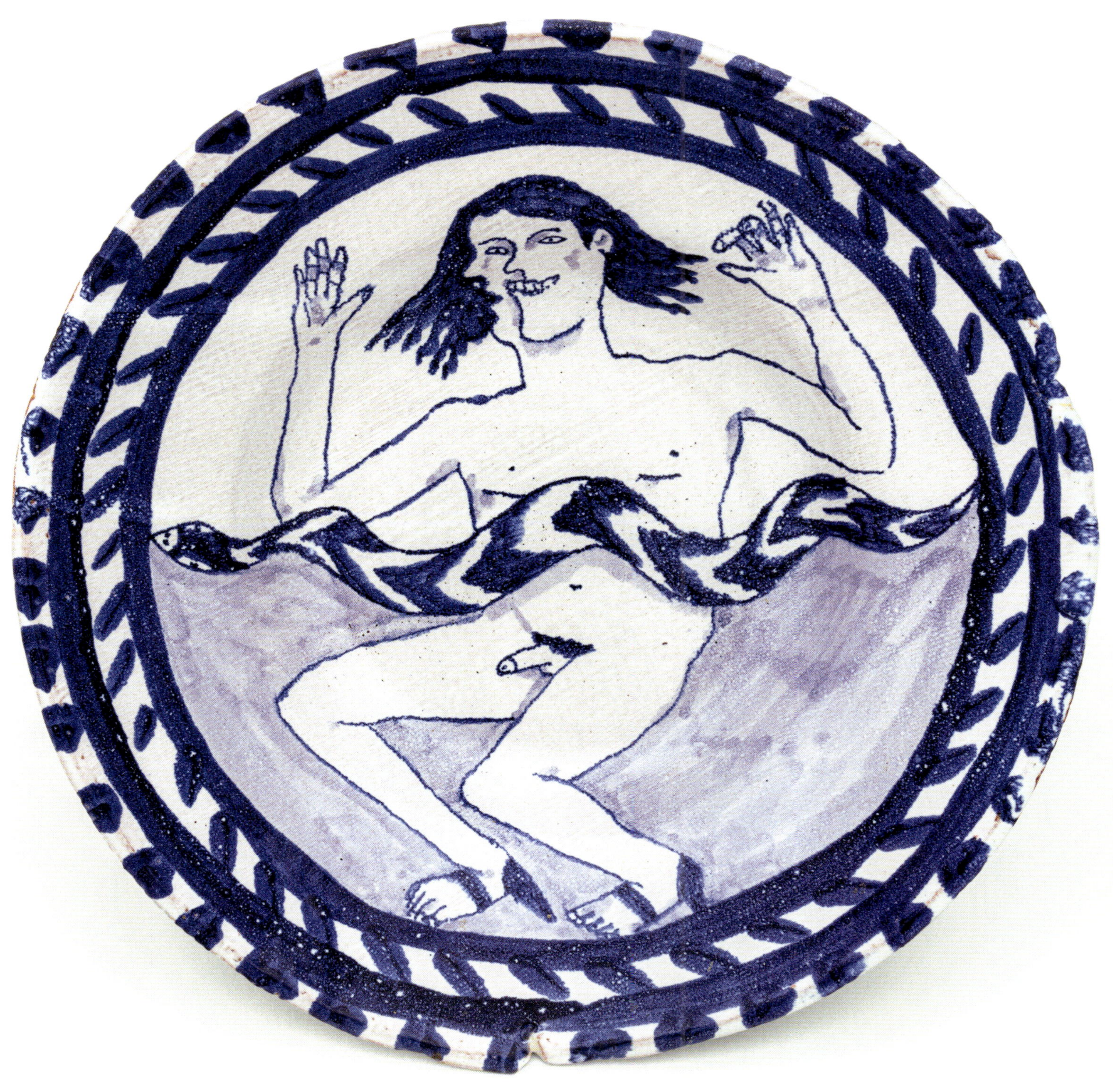

12 January 1999

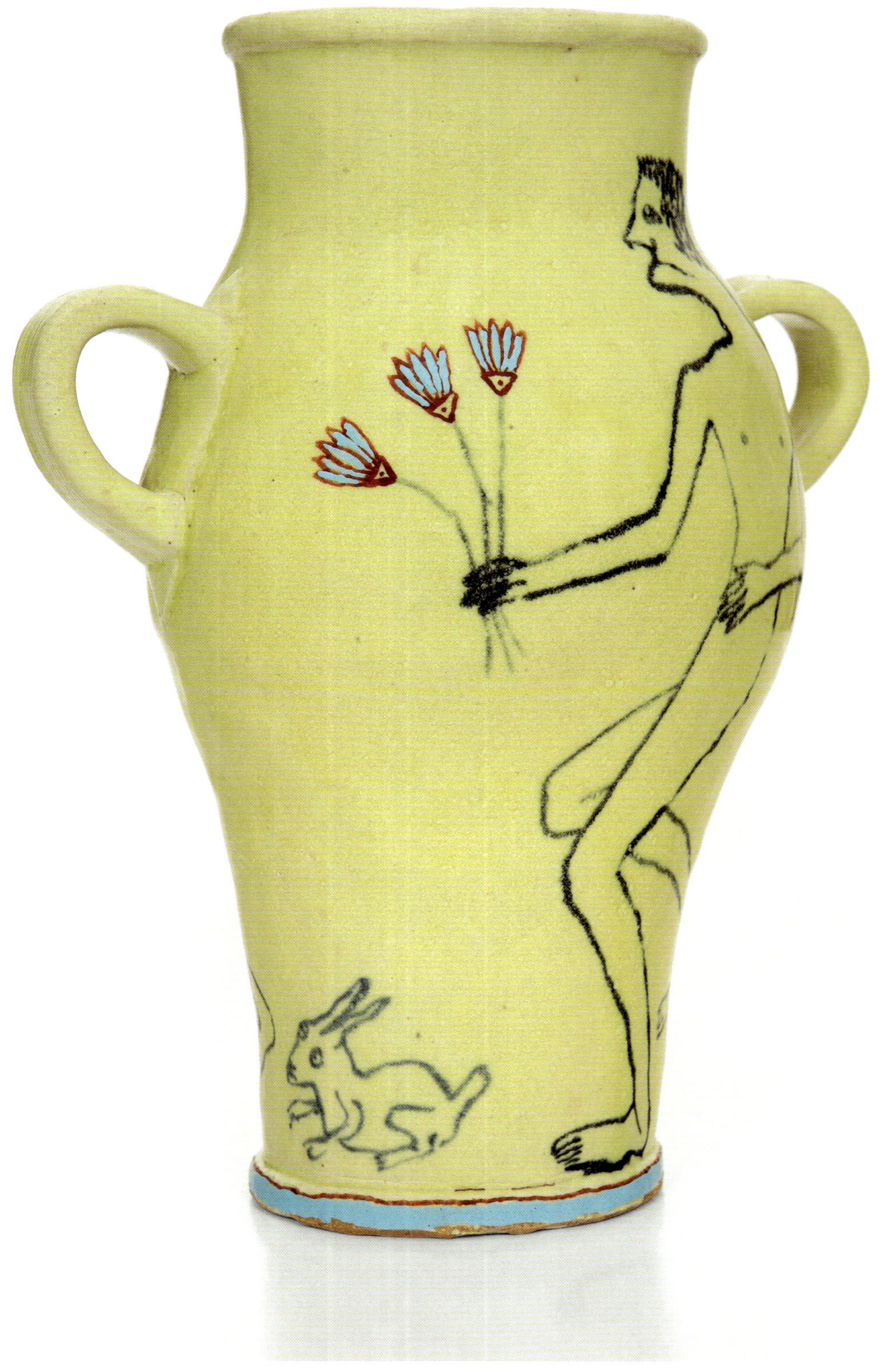

22 December 2016

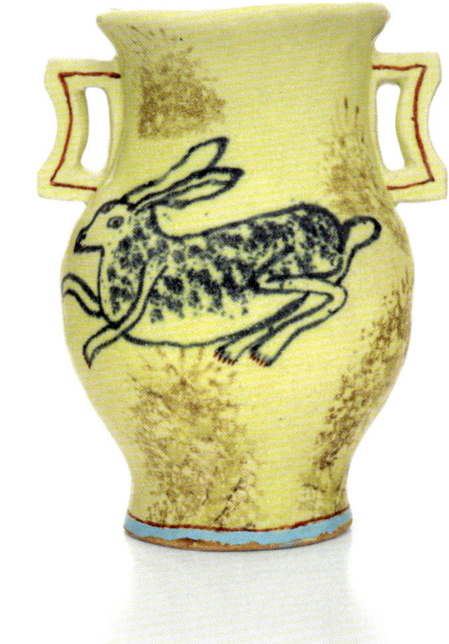

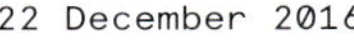

22 December 2016

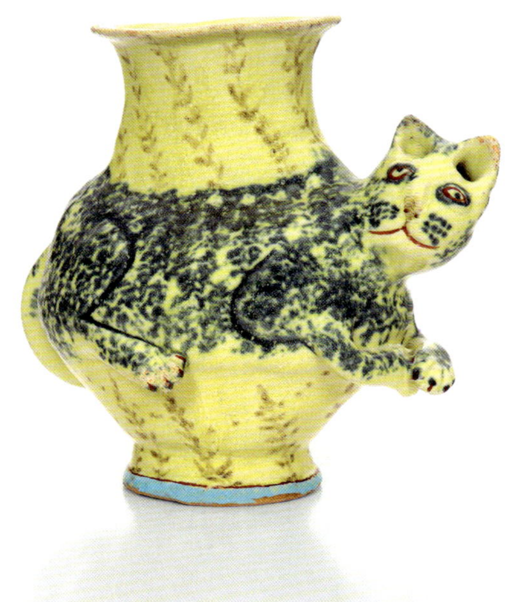

22 December 2016

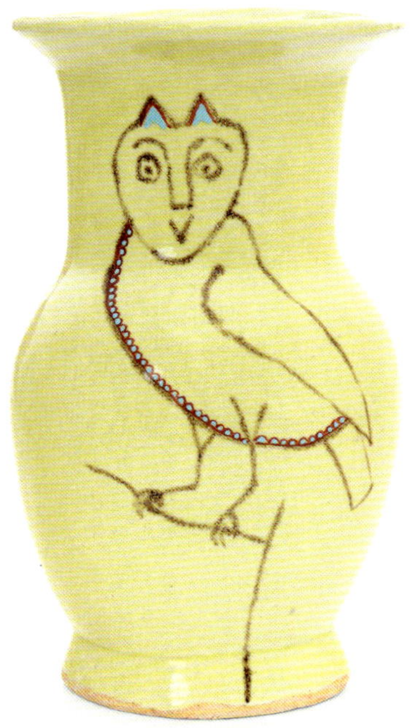

12 December 2017

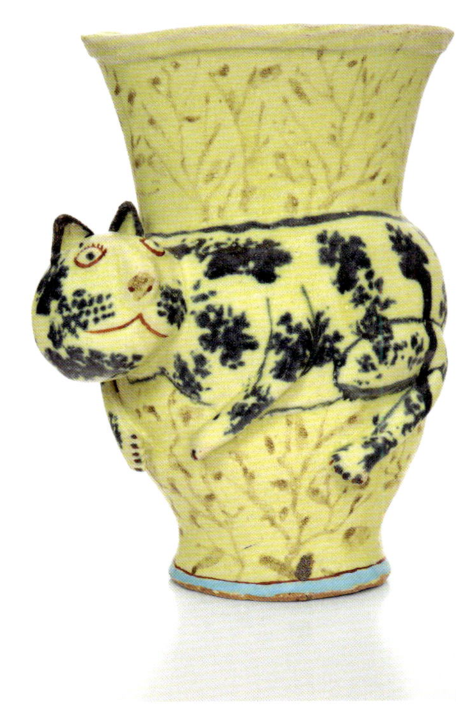

22 December 2016

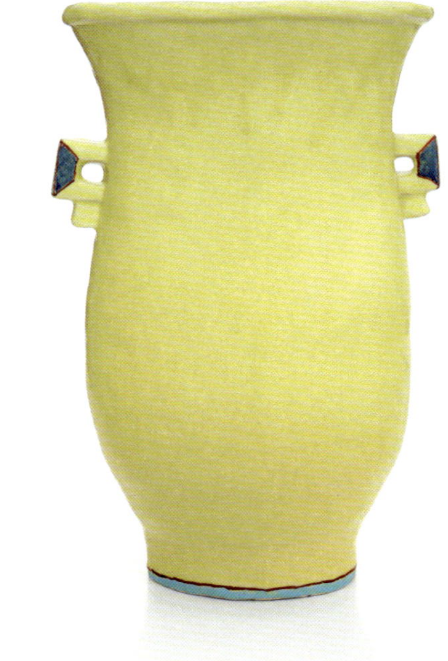

23 February 2017

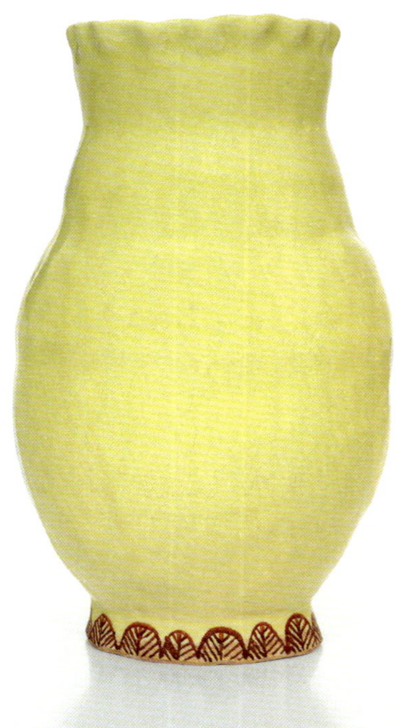

27 January 2017

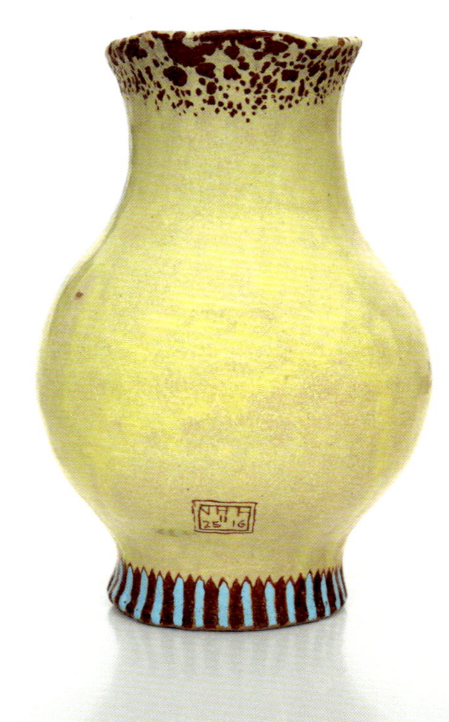

25 November 2016

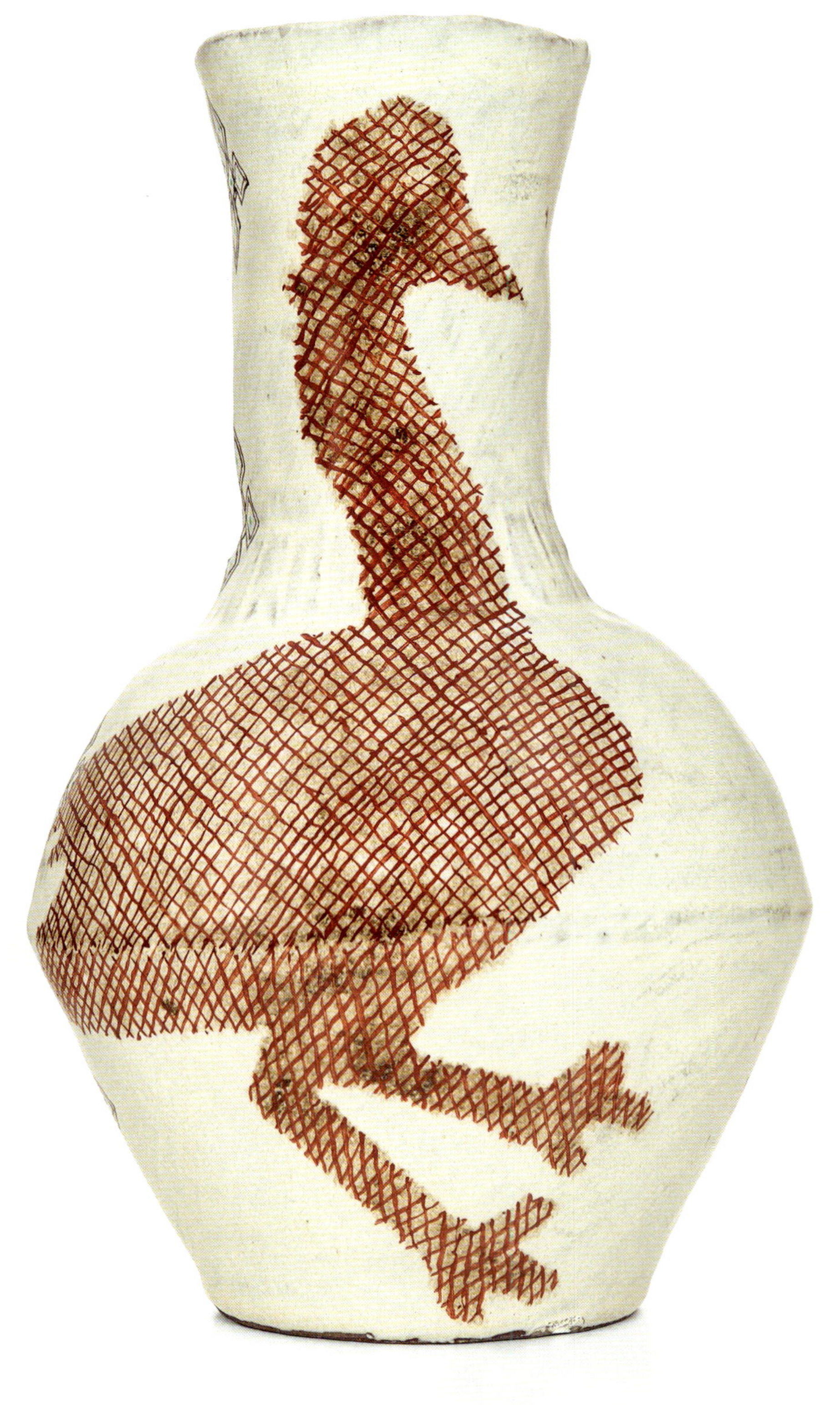

8 December 2014

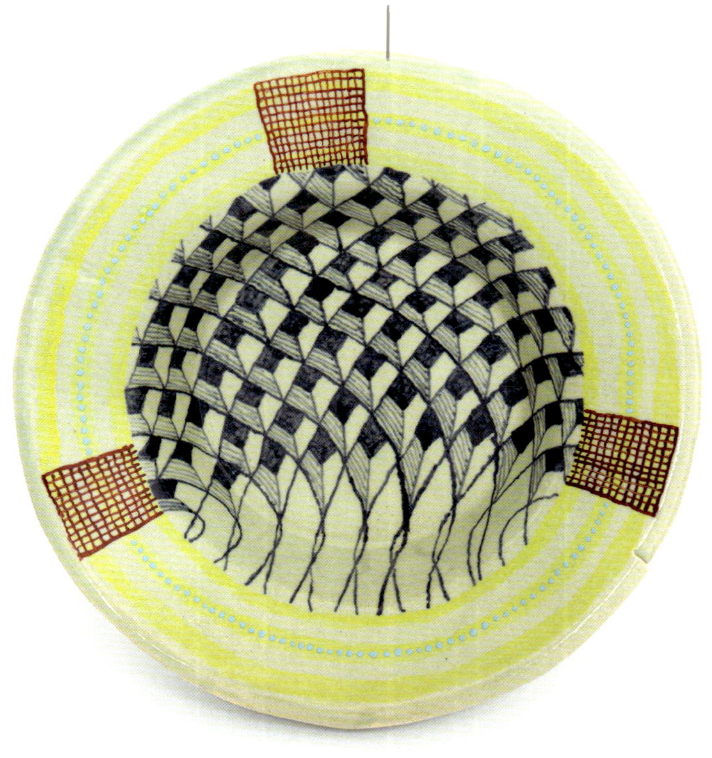

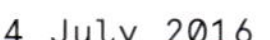

4 July 2016

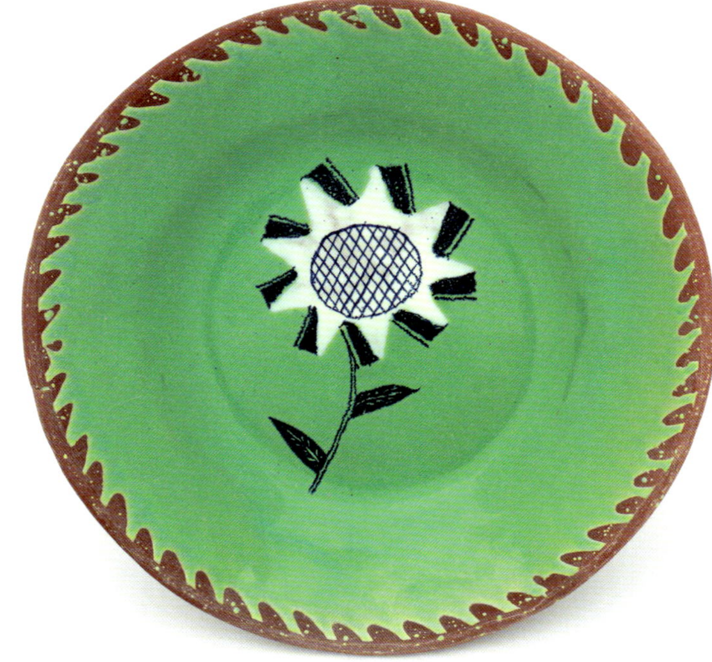

19 November 1997

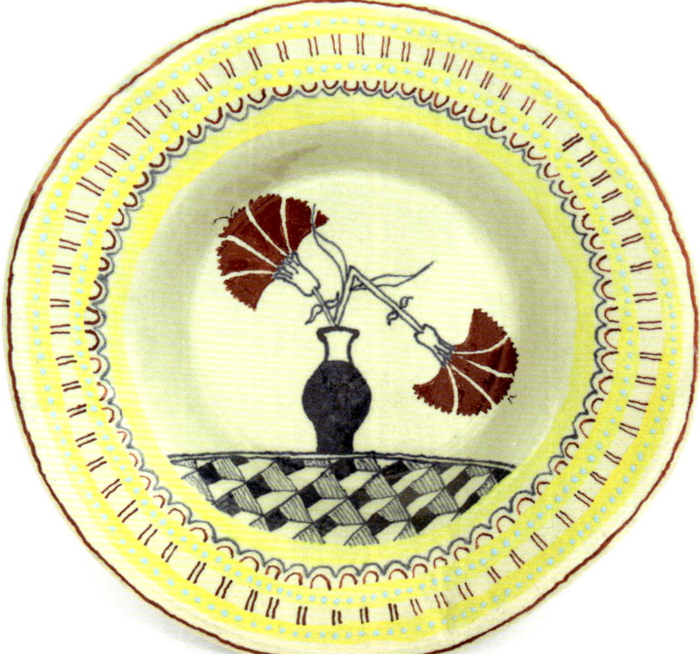

5 August 2016

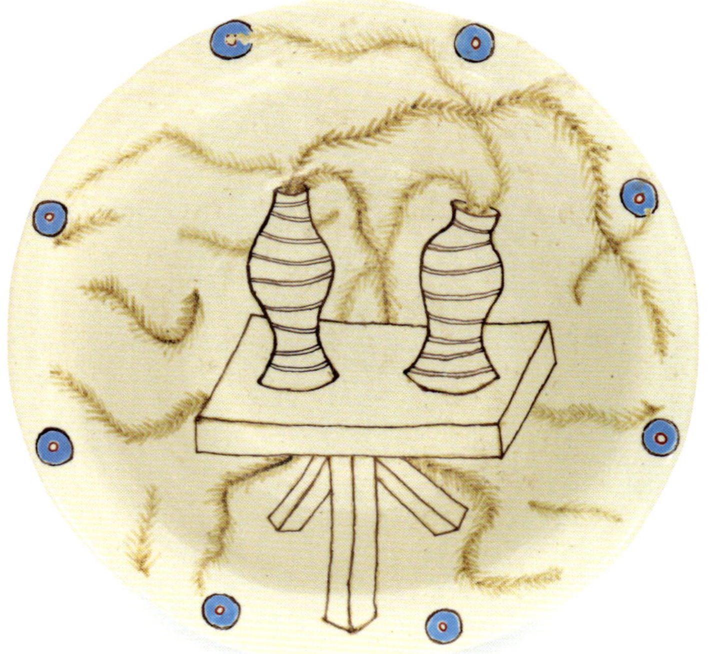

30 August 2017

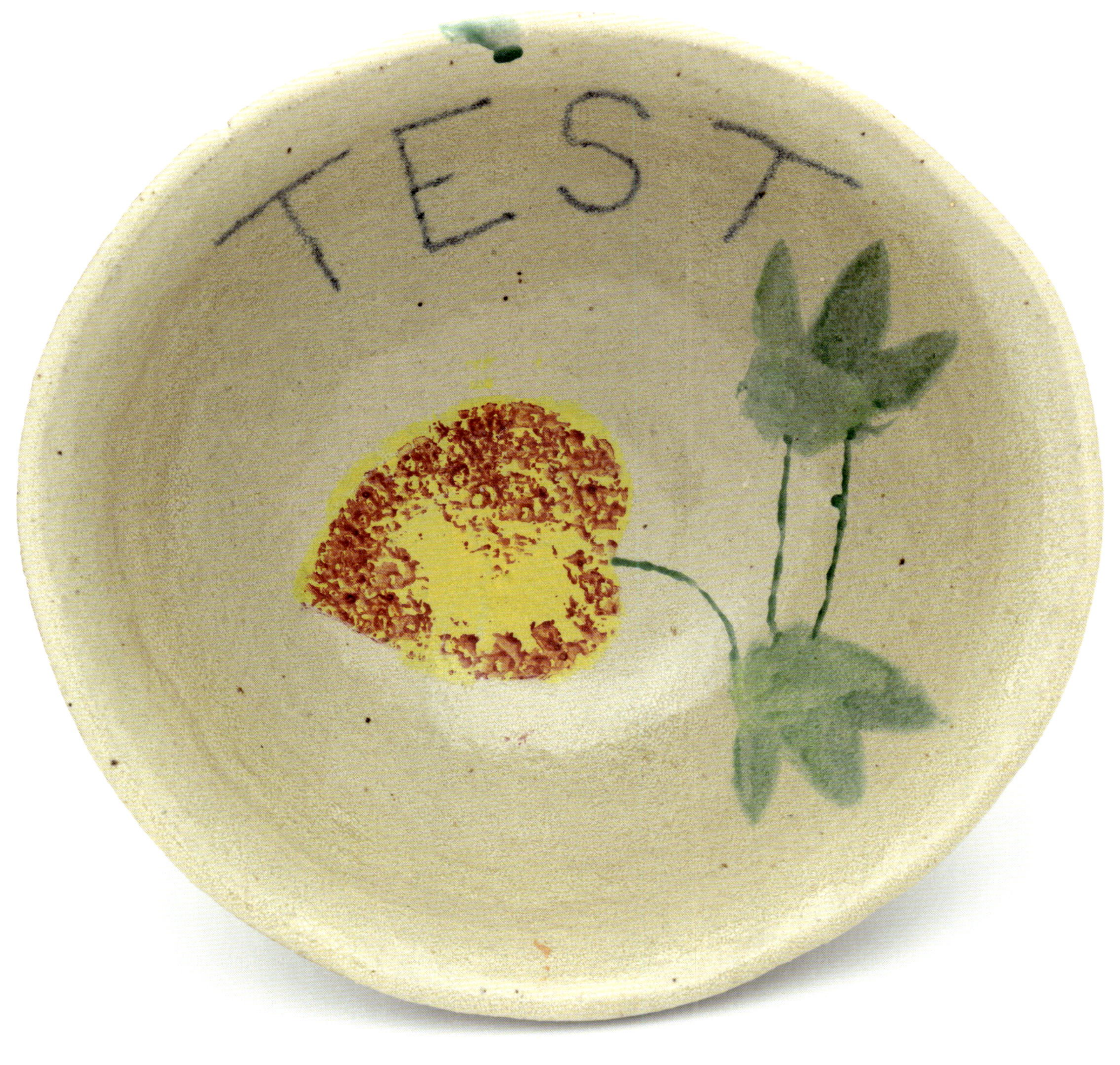

8 March 2016

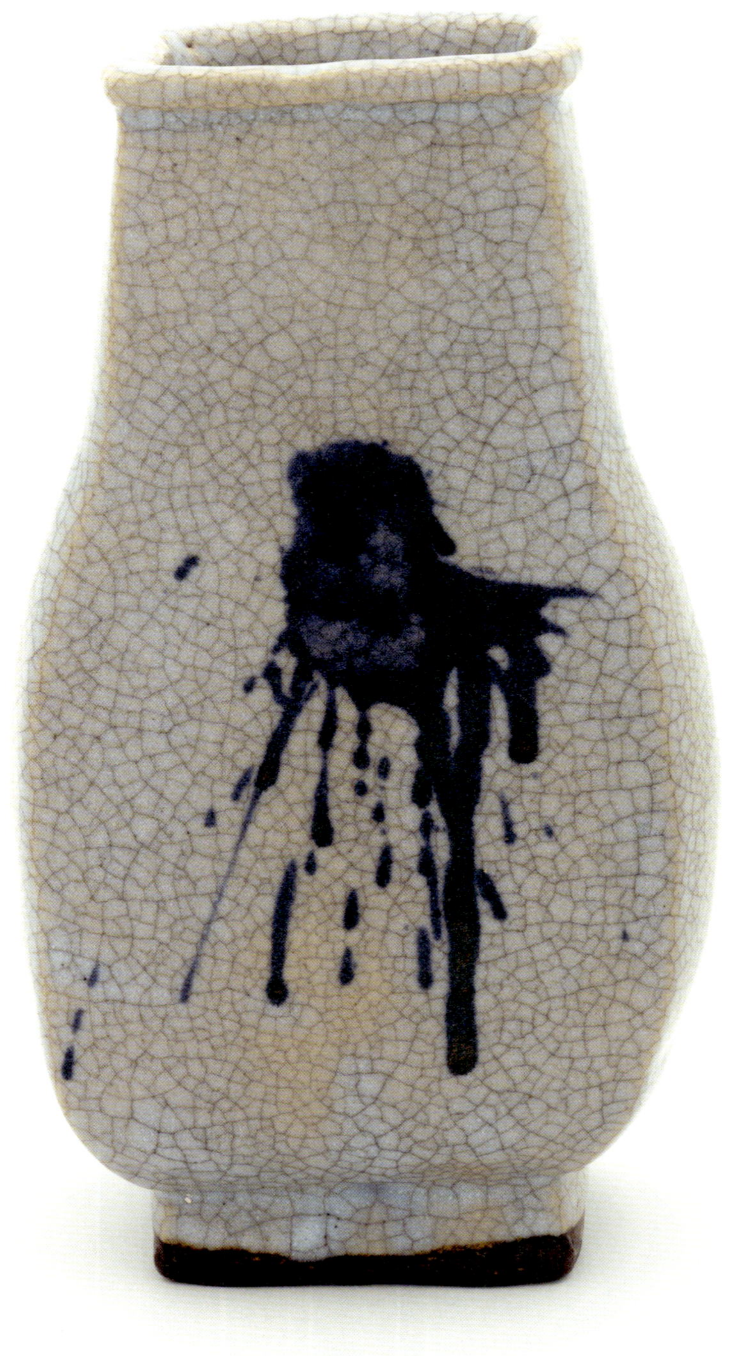

3 October 2011

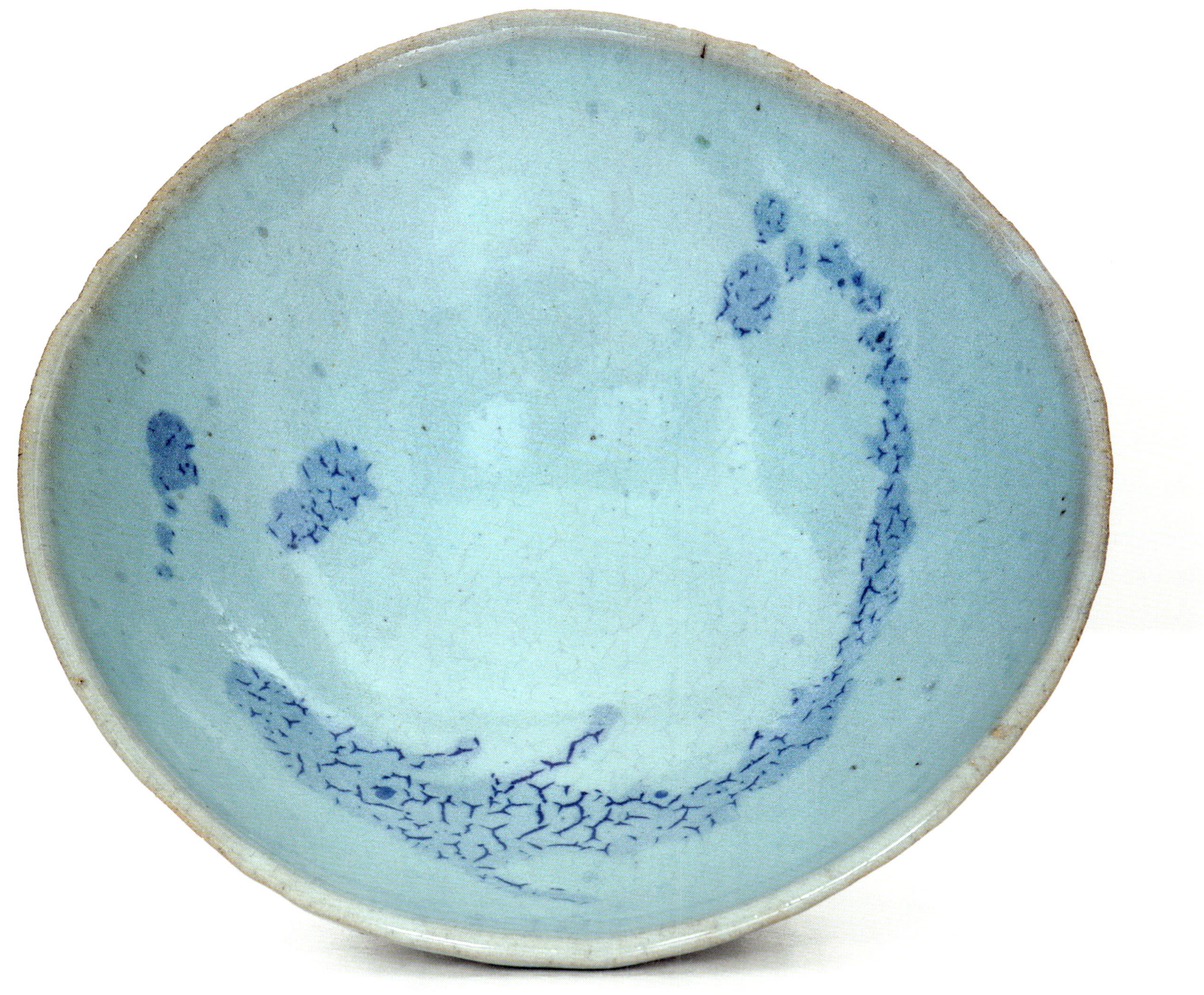

1 April 2015

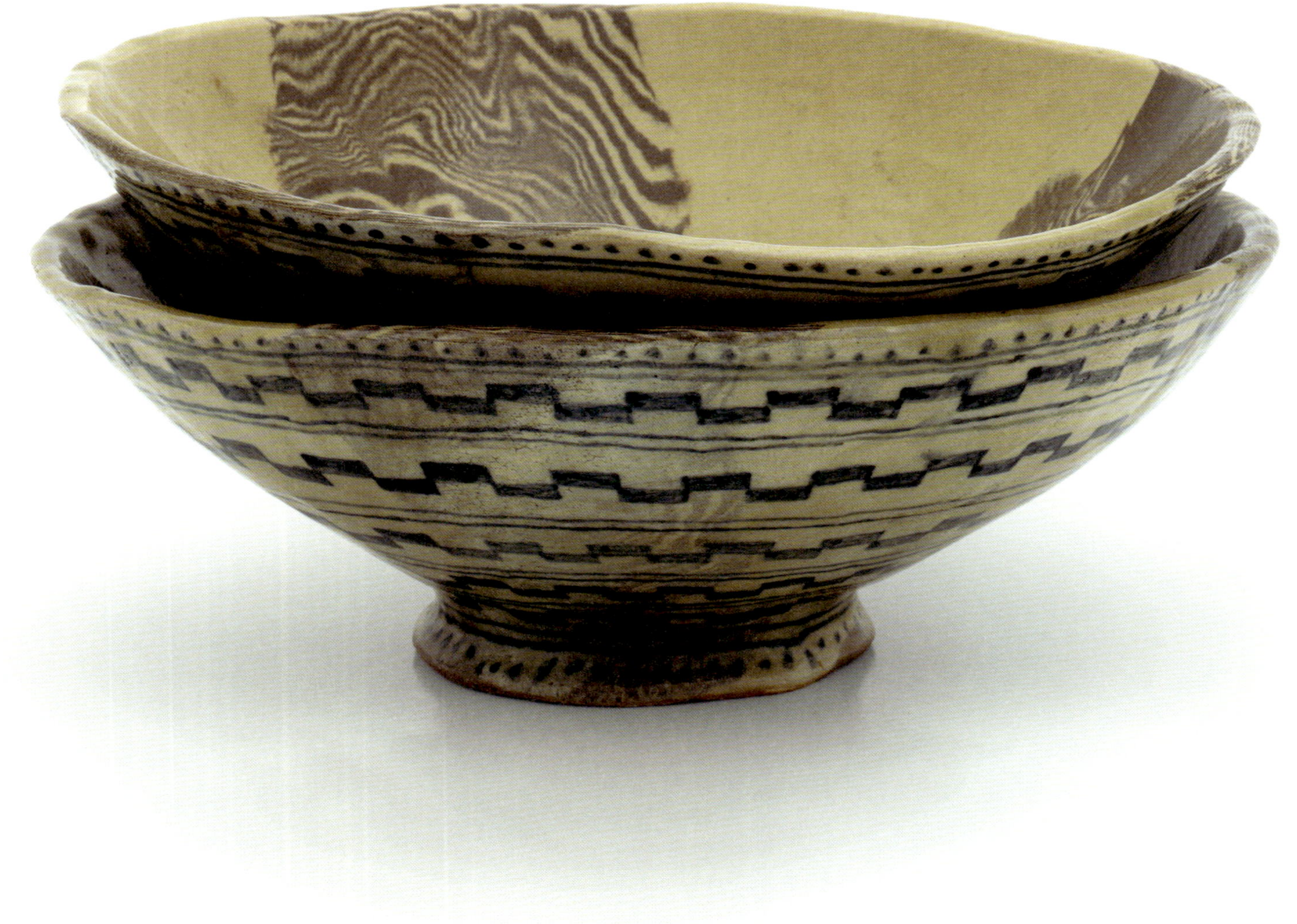

24 March 2014

I made the last bowls shallower than they used to be. They used to be very deep, and when I put the clay in it would want to come adrift, so I made them shallower. And then I make the foot spread a bit, so you can take a bit of wire and hang it on a wall.

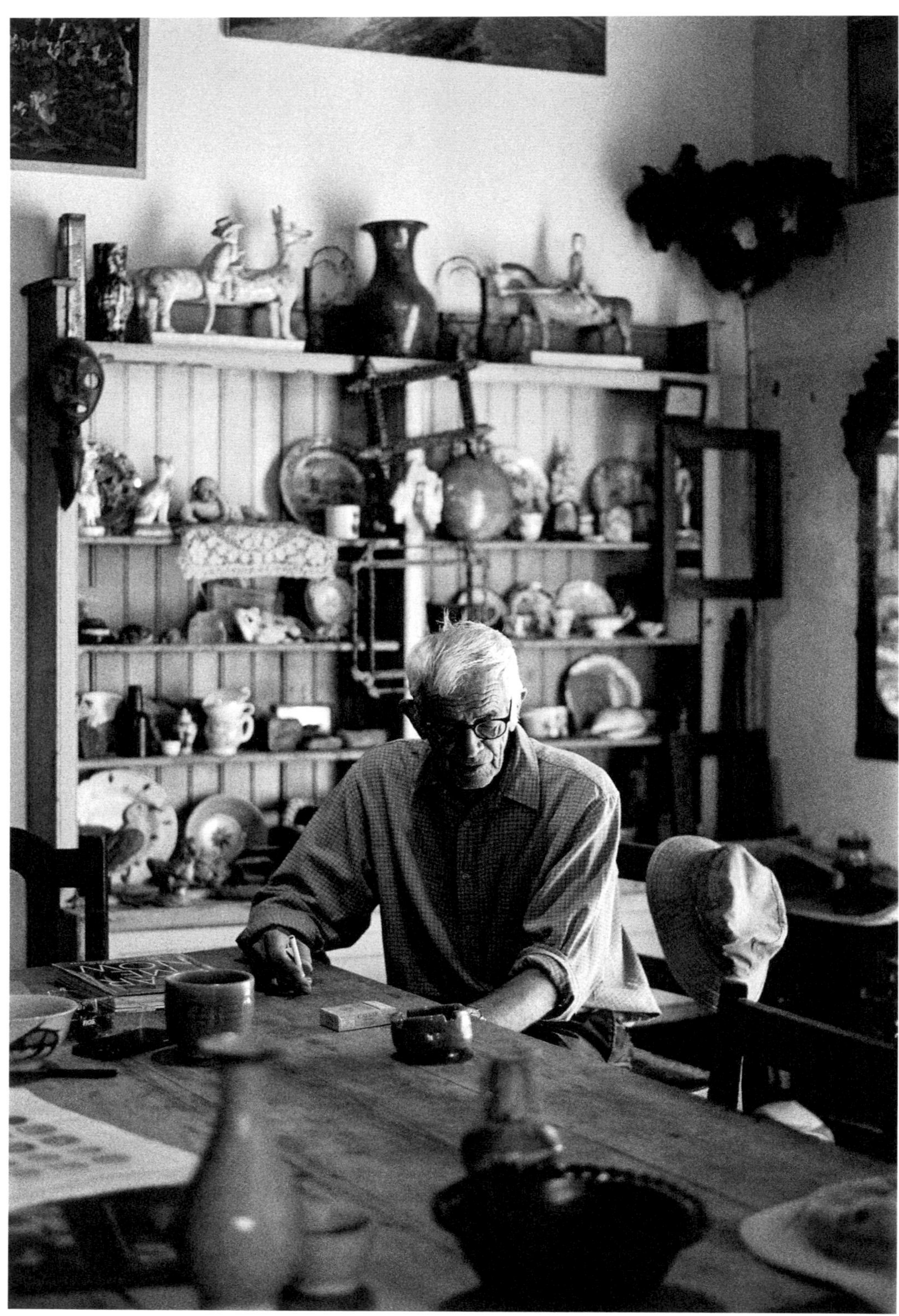

About work, what can I say? I take both East and West as my cultural heritage. I work as best I can with the past for inspiration. I dreamed the other night of the edge of a bowl. I saw a welt of turquoise-coloured glaze with a crackle. It had sort of folded over onto the inside of the bowl's edge.

Because fictile wares break, they must constantly be replaced. How infinitely poorer one's life would be without glazed pottery. I keep shelves filled with glazed pottery of many colours. These are all old things. Between them and me there is a dialogue. I can learn from them more readily than from the work of modern potters.

I always had an old Chinese pot around, but also a colourful piece of Staffordshire pottery.

I admire so many kinds of ceramic ware. Also many modern potters. Yet selfishly, to protect my vision I live in the country and don't see much modern work.

The Chinese have a way of describing beauty that evokes the high and the wide. Which is quite a nice way of putting it.

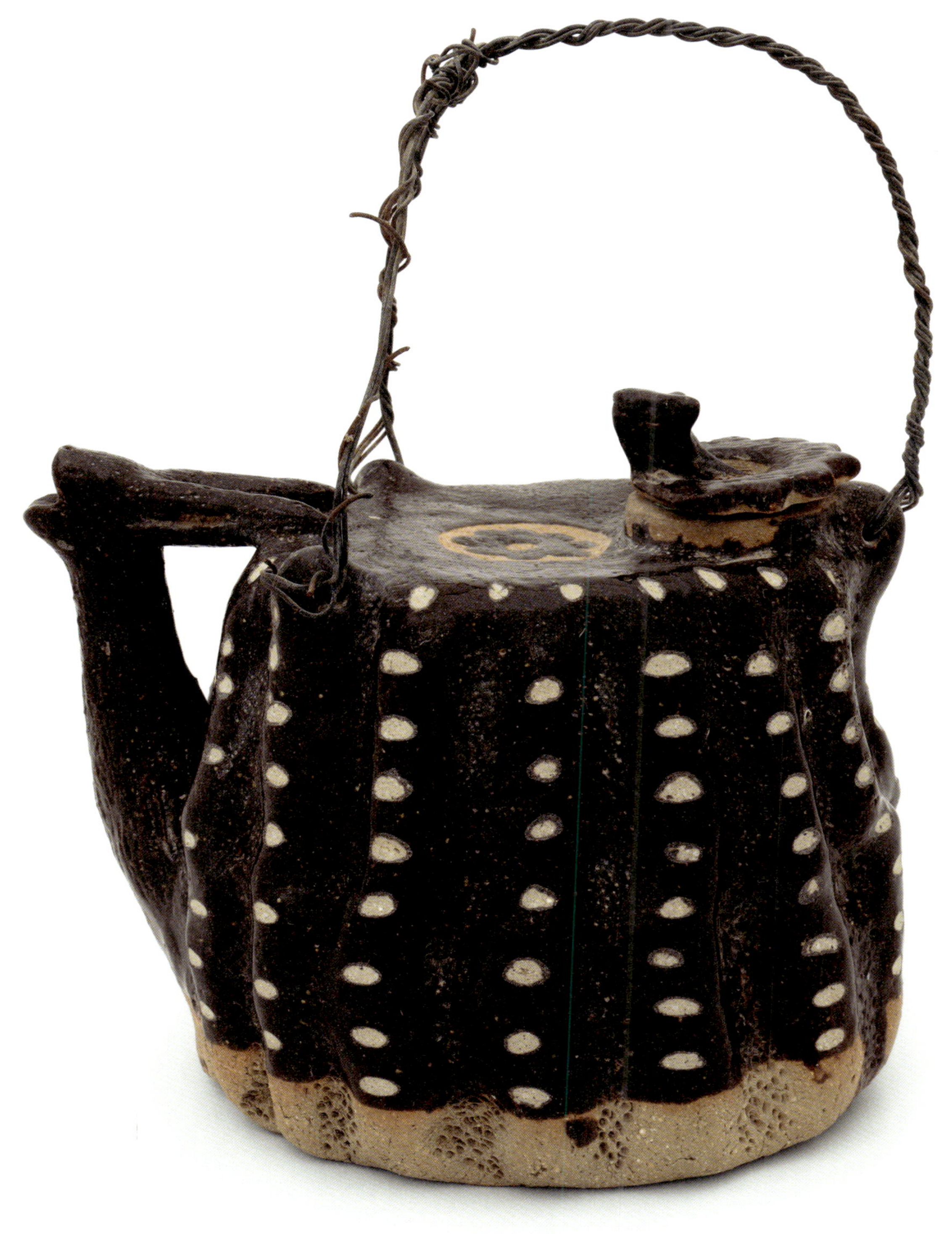

Late 1970s

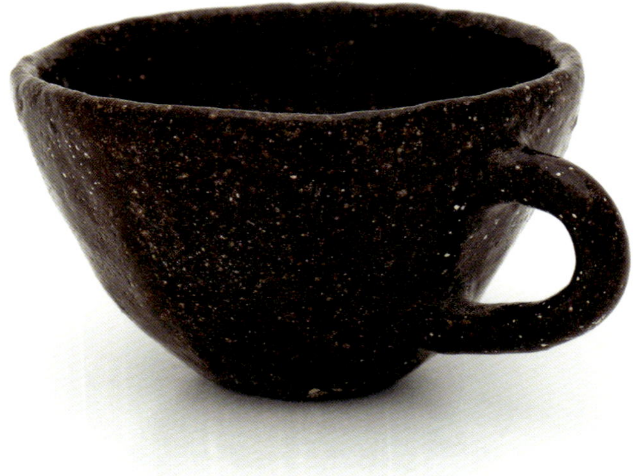

1980s

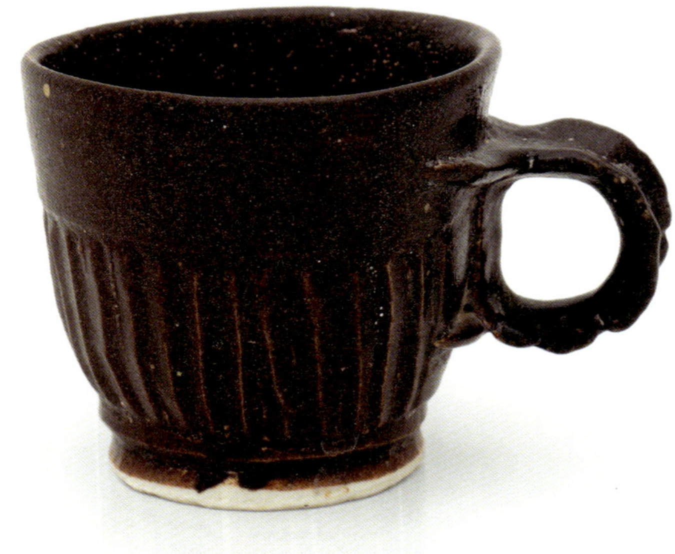

1980s

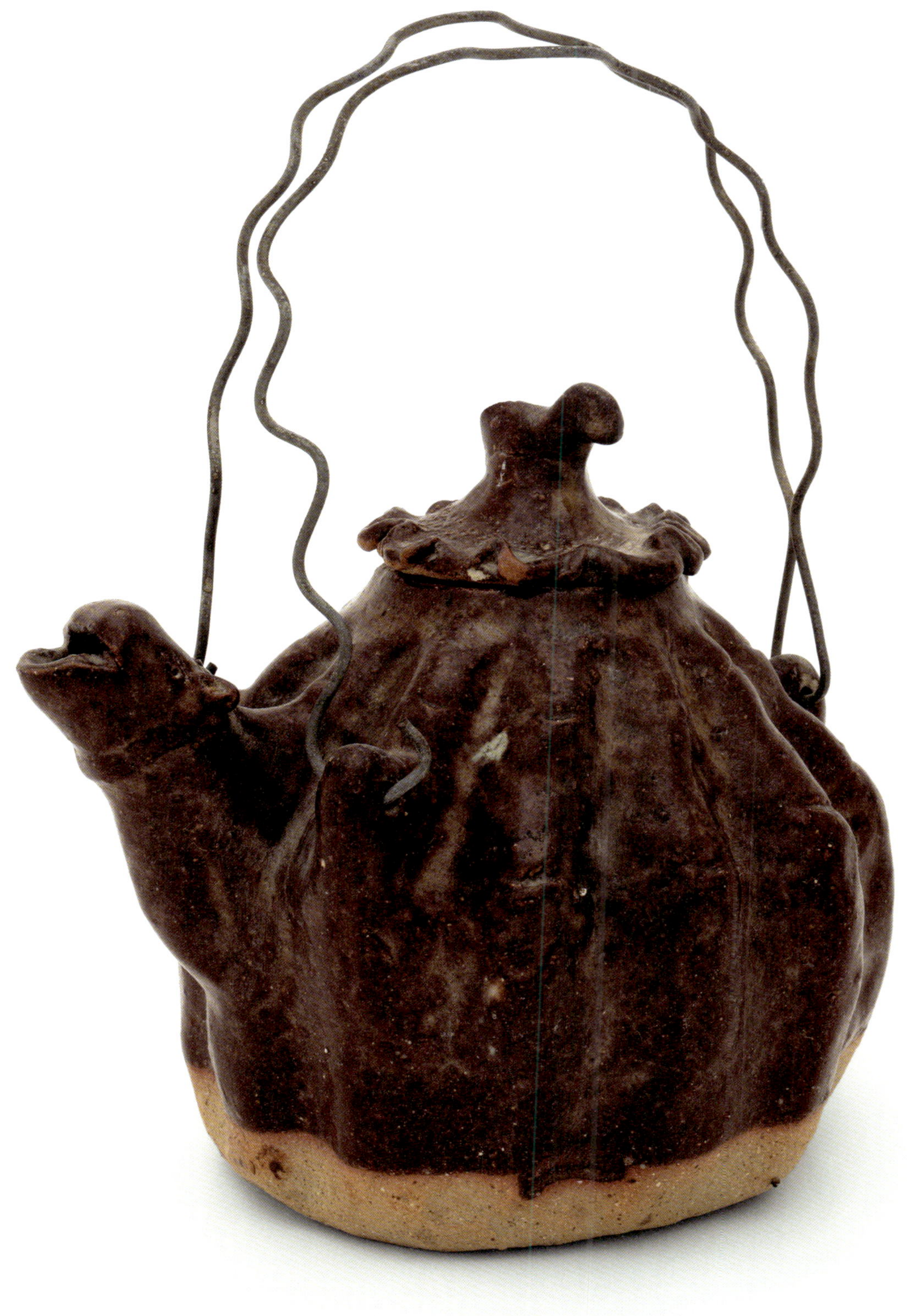

Late 1970s

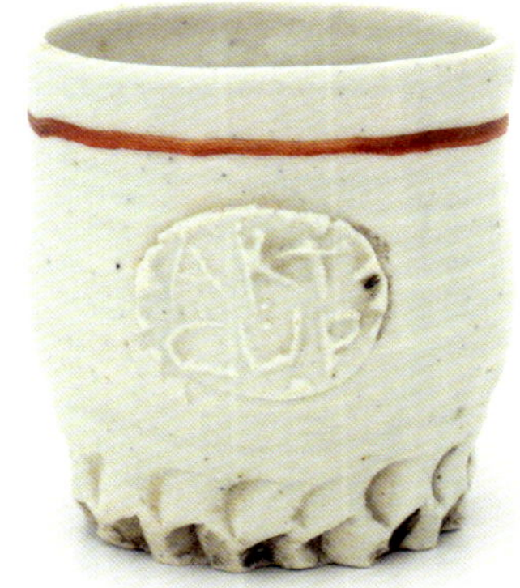

1980s

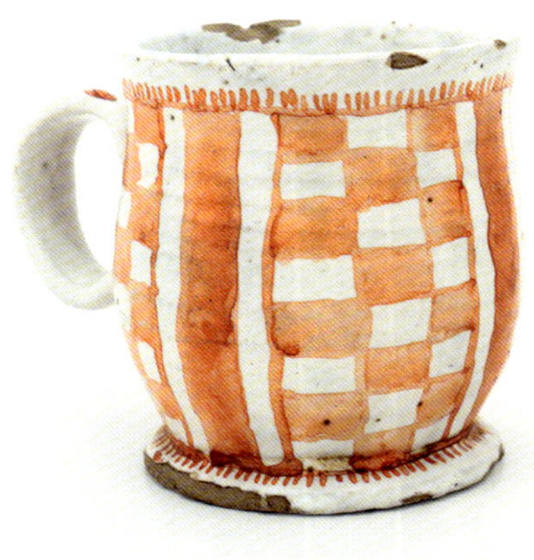

1980s

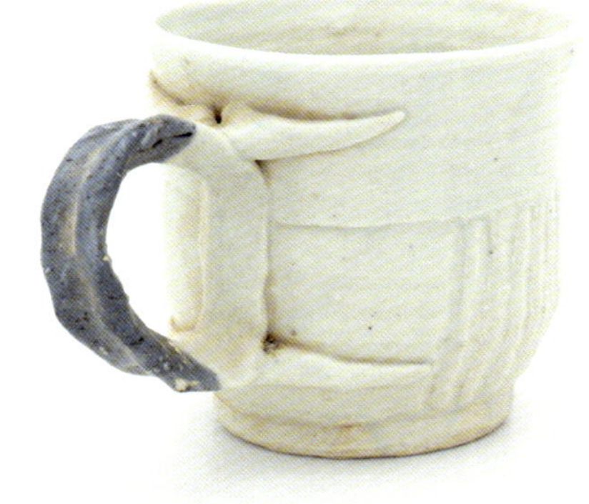

1980s

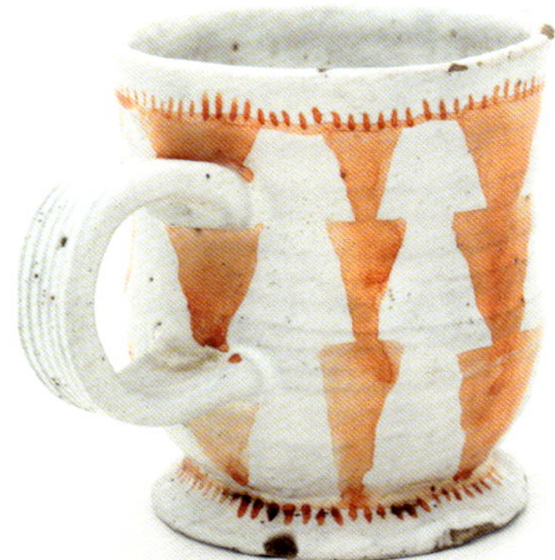

1980s

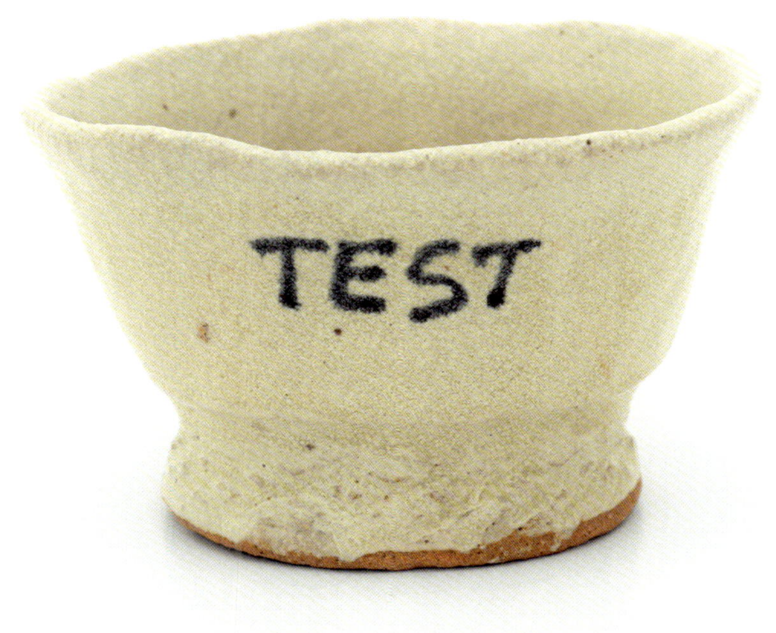

Undated

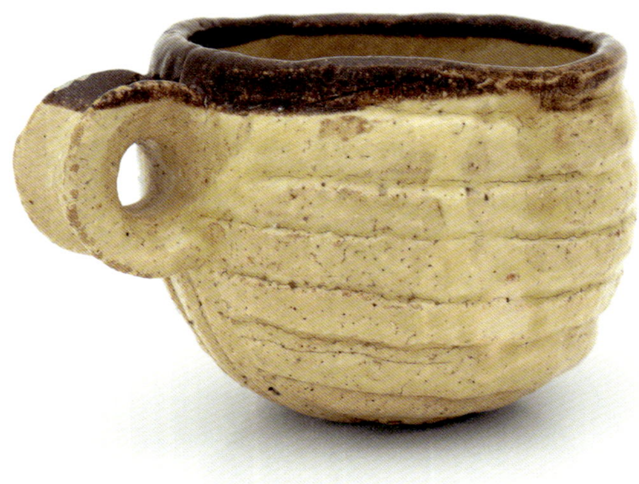

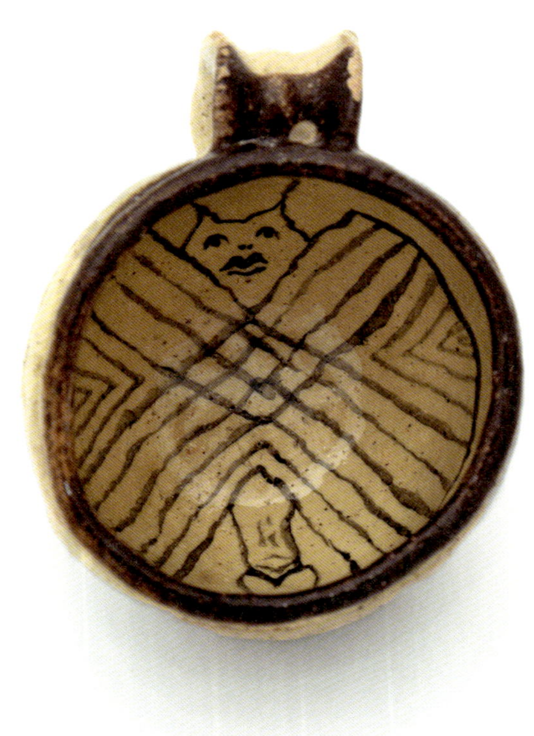

c.1982

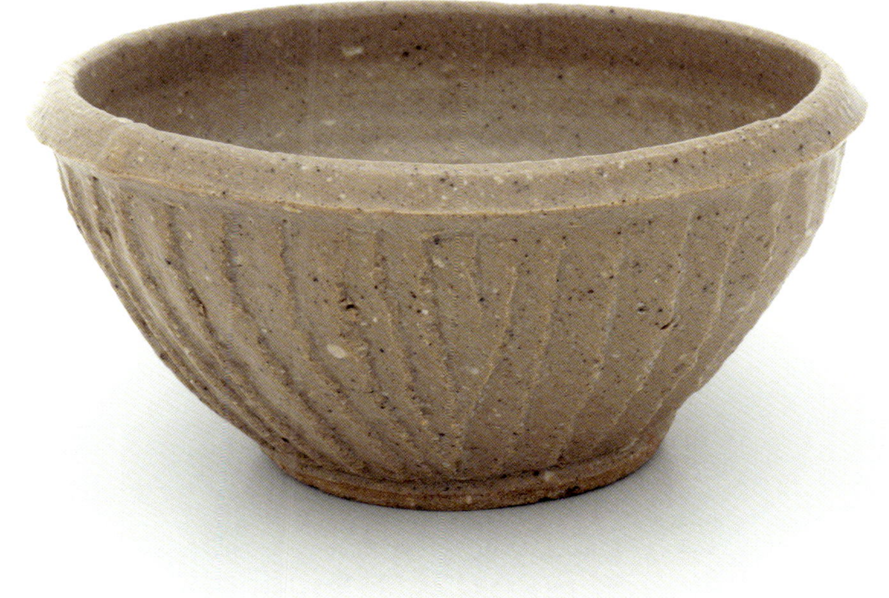

c.1971

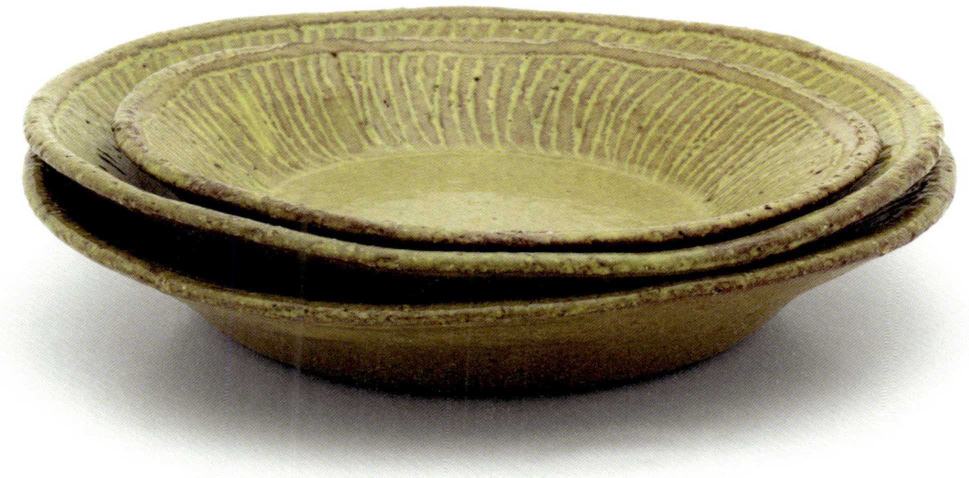

c.1982

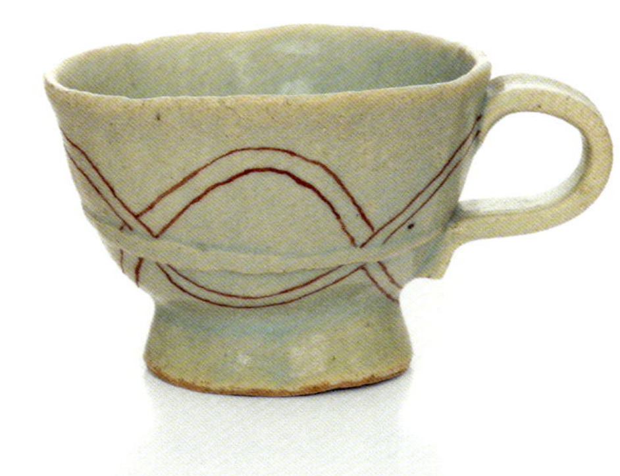

24 November 2016

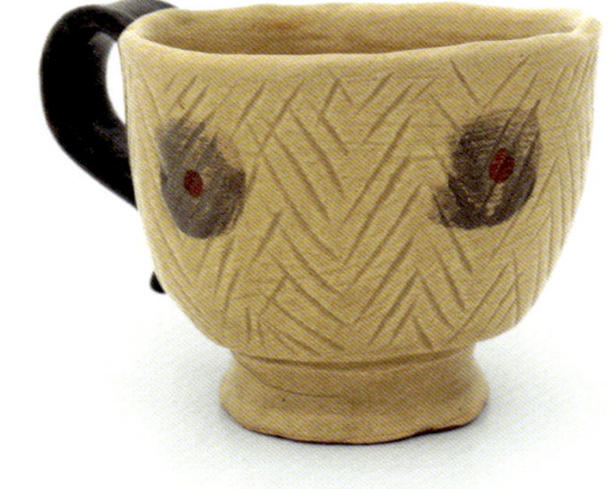

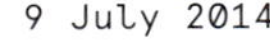

9 July 2014

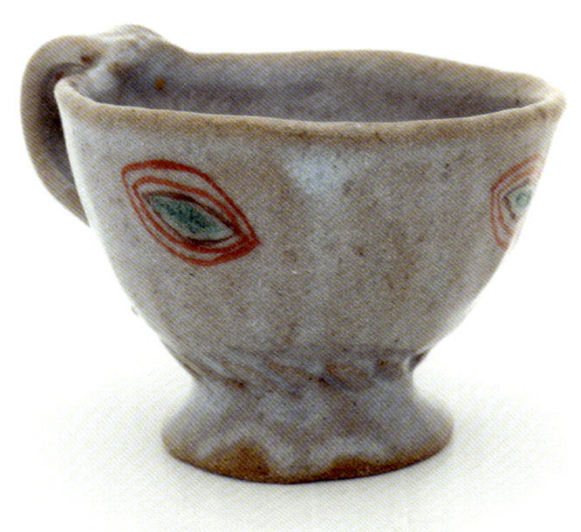

12 December 2011

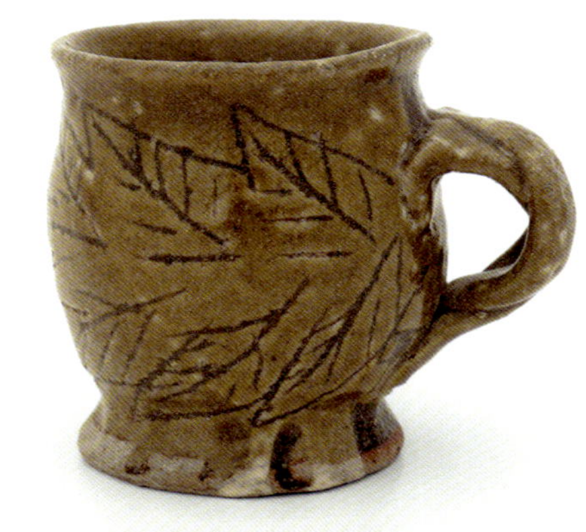

14 September 2021

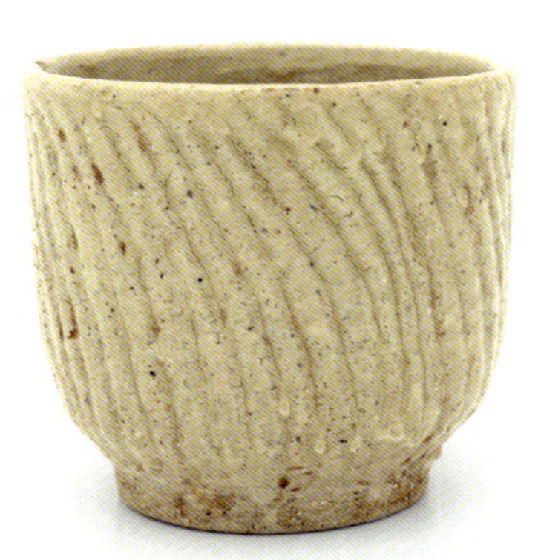

6 June 2007

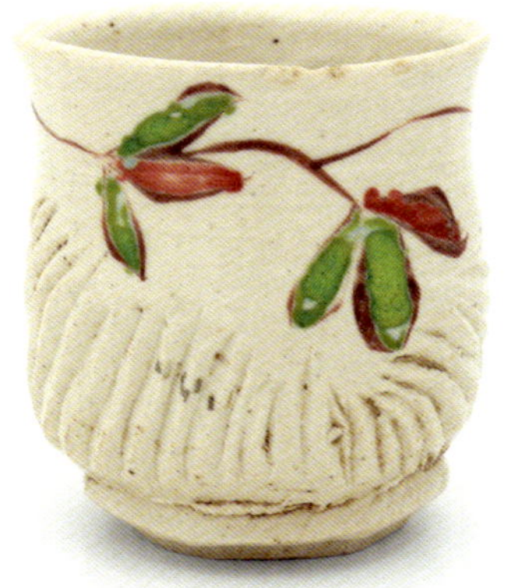

8 May 2007

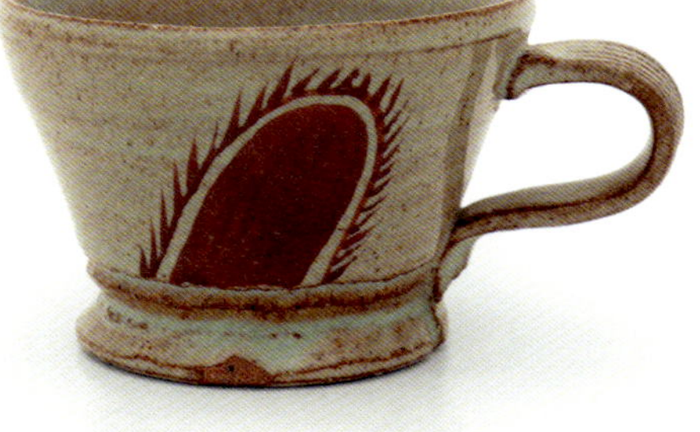

24 June 2013

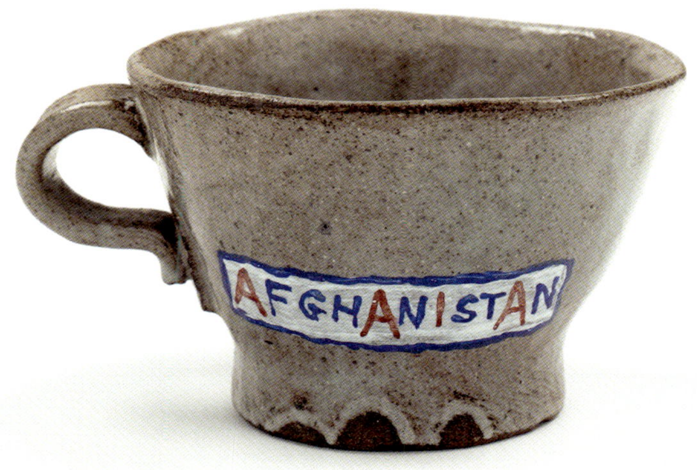

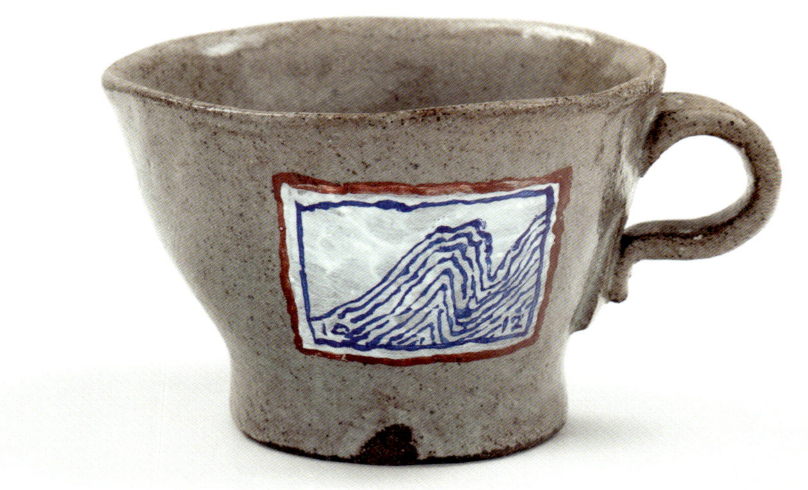

14 September 2021

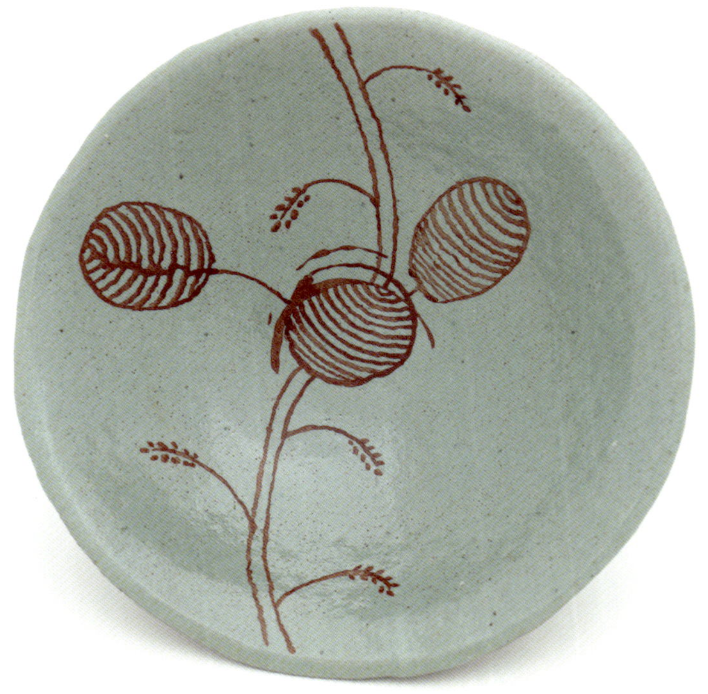

19 October 2021

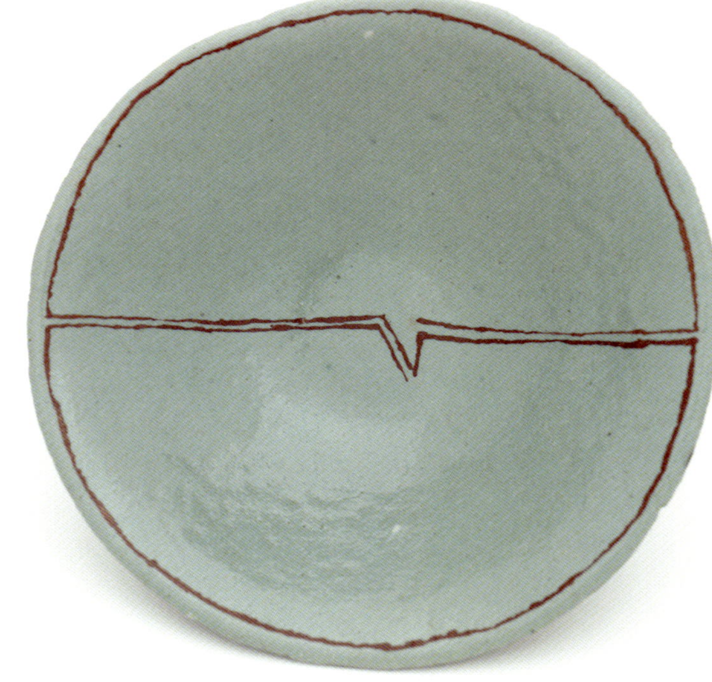

19 October 2021

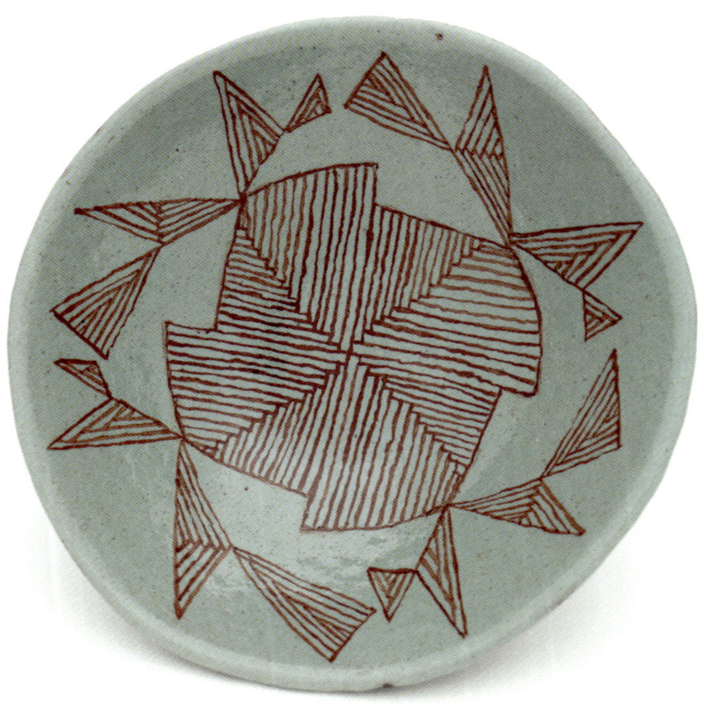

18 October 2021

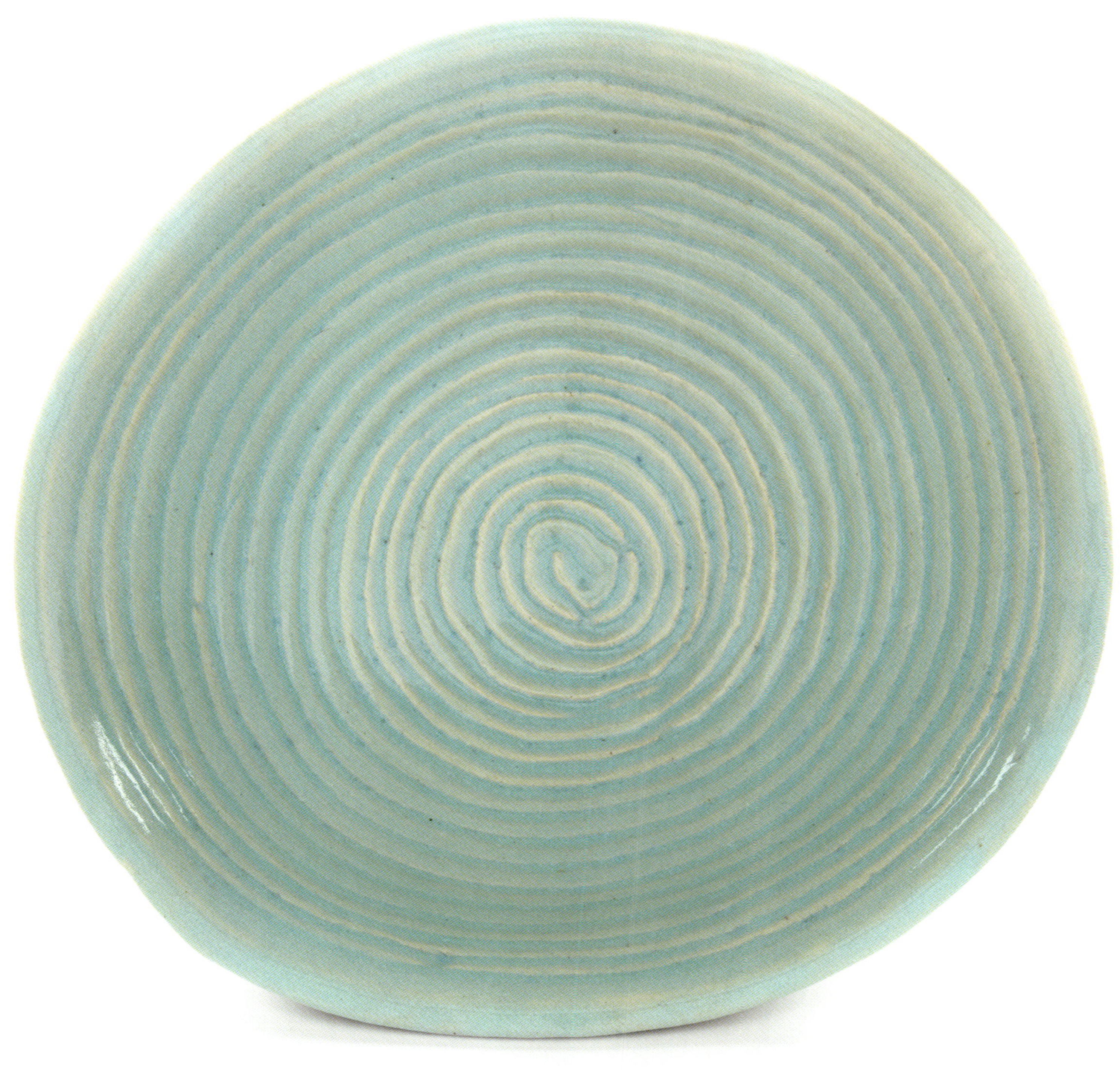

4 February 2020

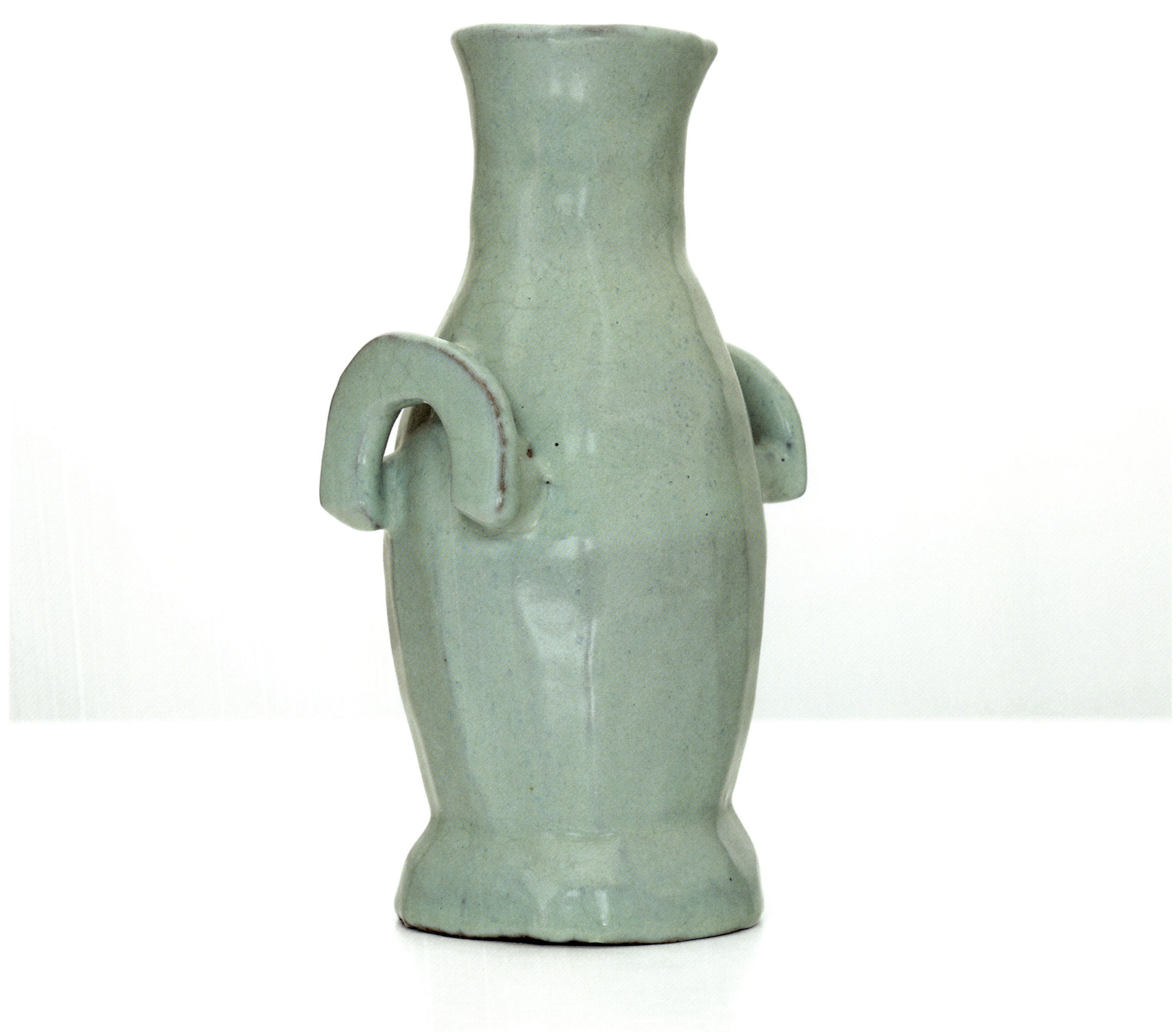

23 December 2014

There's precedent for my version of a celadon almost all over the Middle East, where people admired those Chinese celadons of a certain time. In this Muslim world they would import them in great quantity, but the local potters made their versions of it too, using copper like I do and firing it at a lower temperature. Mine are quite convincing as celadon-type things.

The slightly greenish glaze is very beautiful – a colour that comes naturally when you're using solid fuel to fire your kiln. It burns up the oxygen, and you make use of that. There's a very small amount of iron in the glaze, and if you reduce the oxygen at the right moment when the glaze is melting, it can change from a yellowish colour to that greenish colour. I have an electric kiln, but I still like the colour so instead of iron I use a little bit of copper to get that greenish colour.

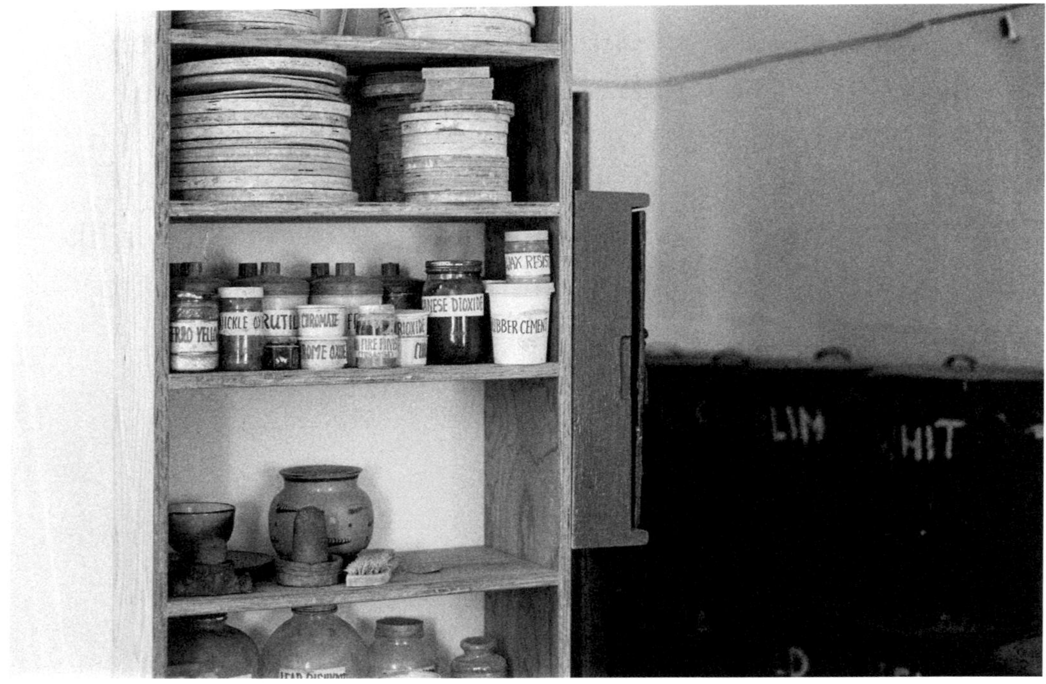

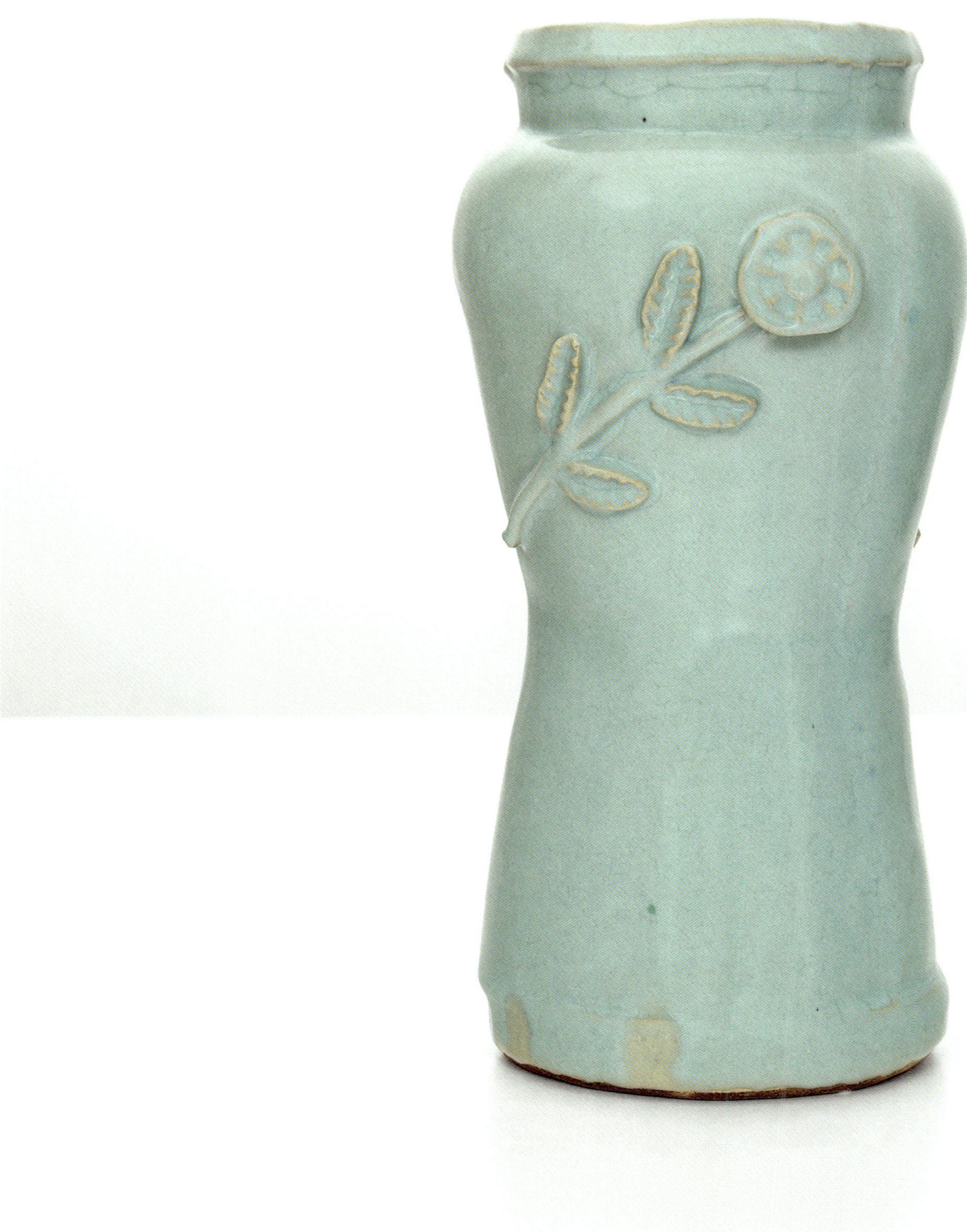

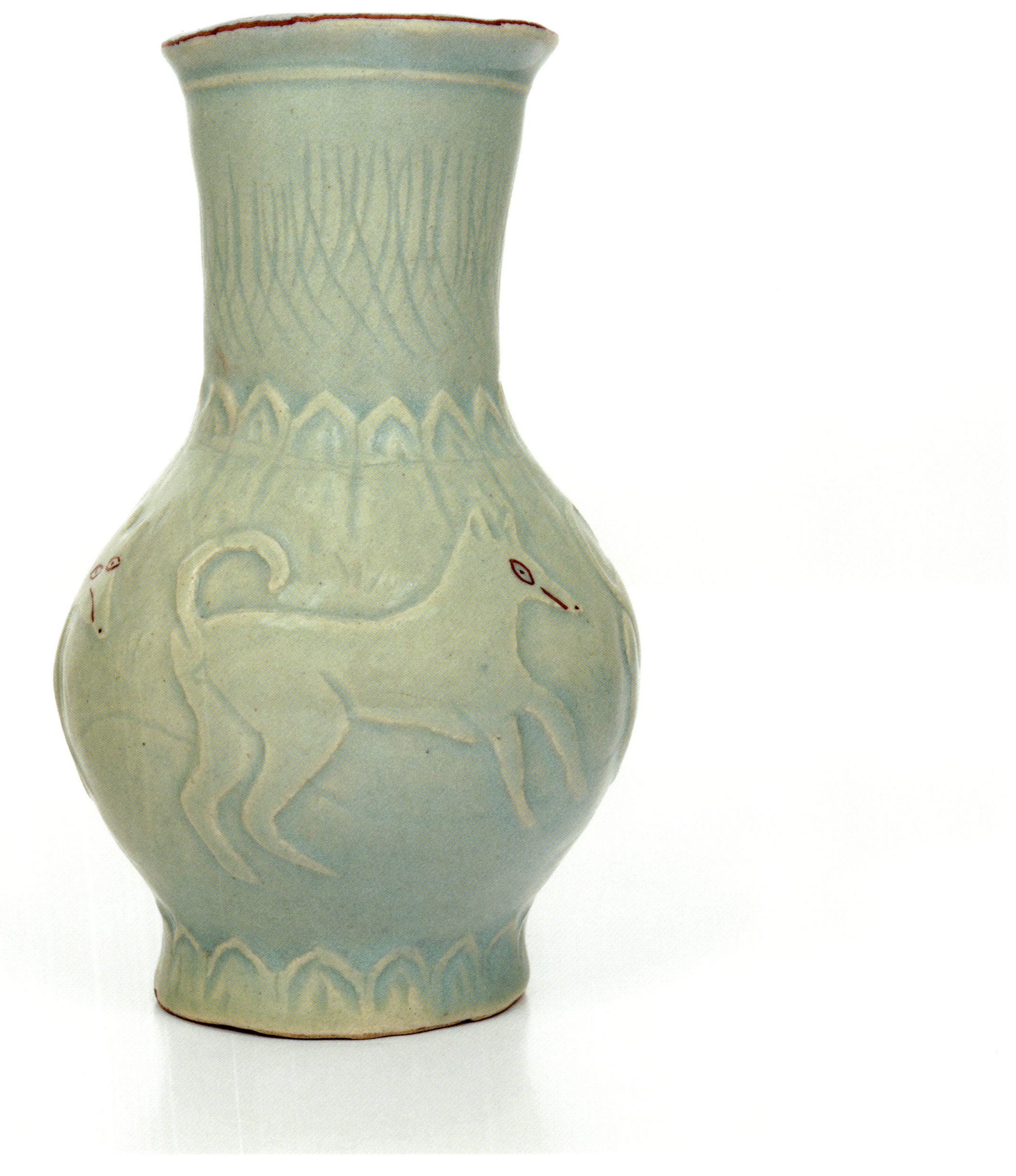

14 October 2016

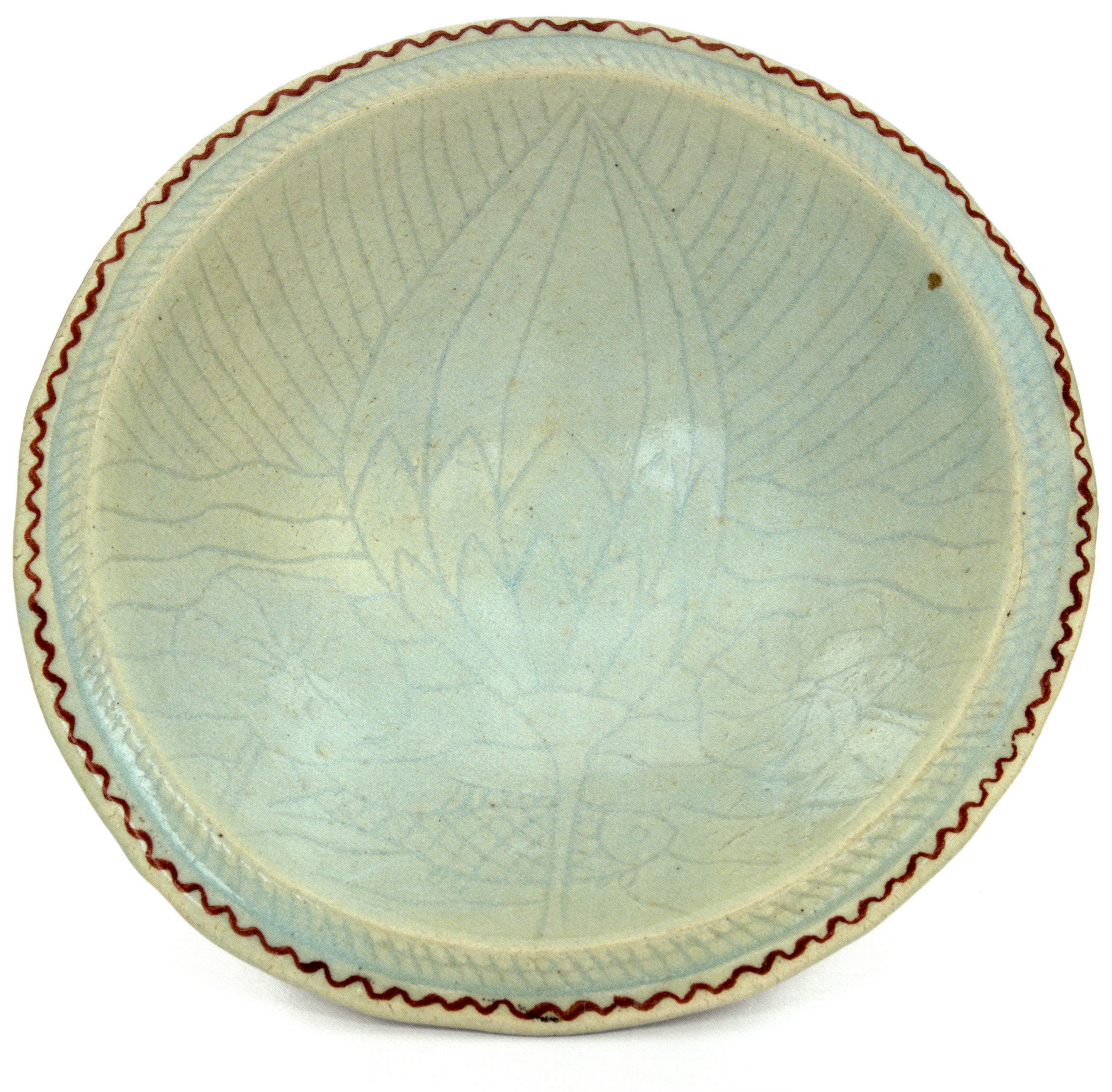

22 December 2016

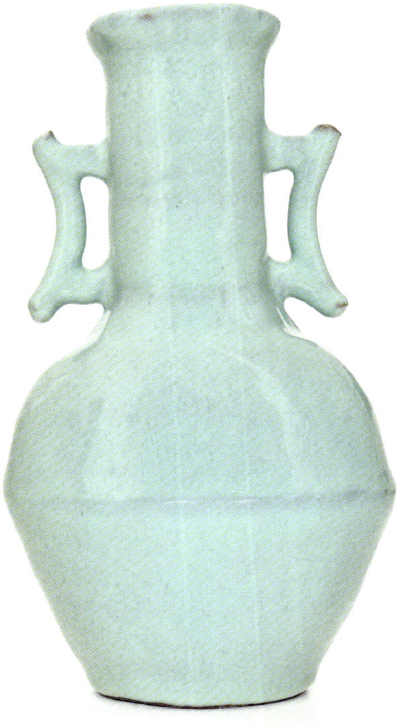

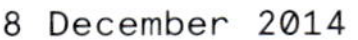

8 December 2014

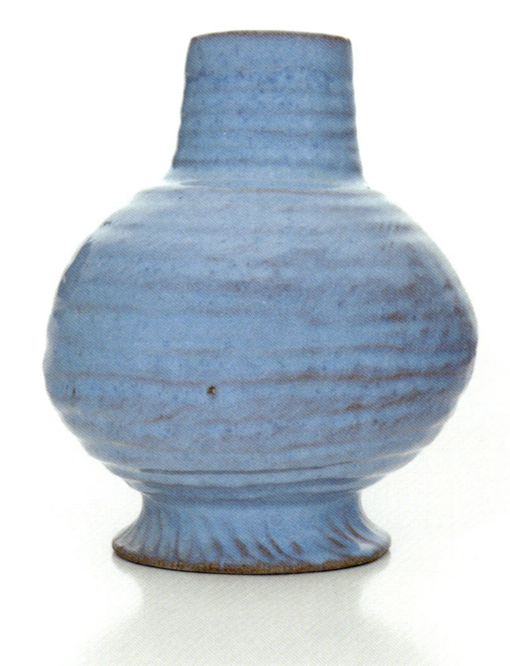

18 September 2004

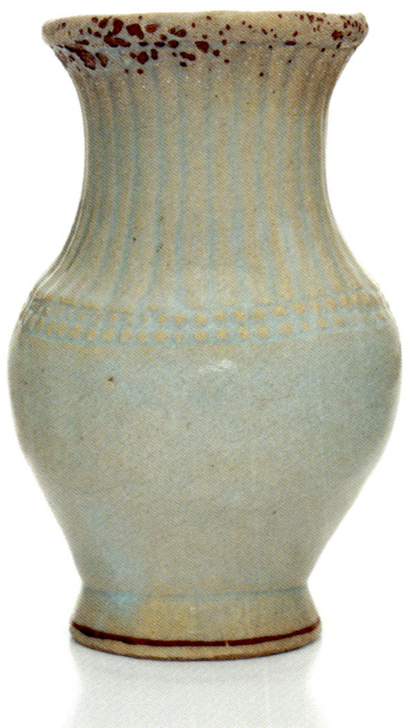

29 November 2016

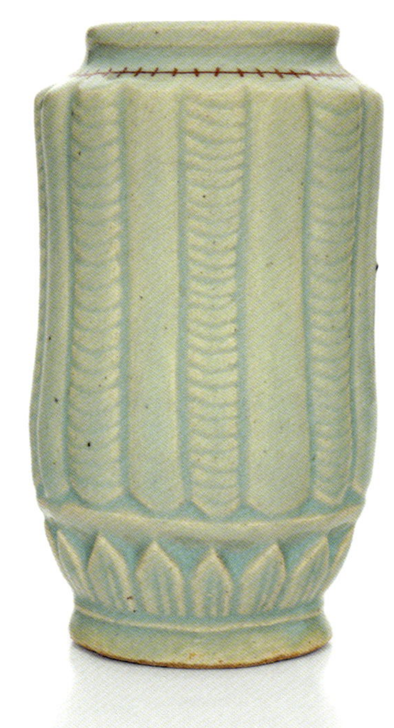

28 November 2016

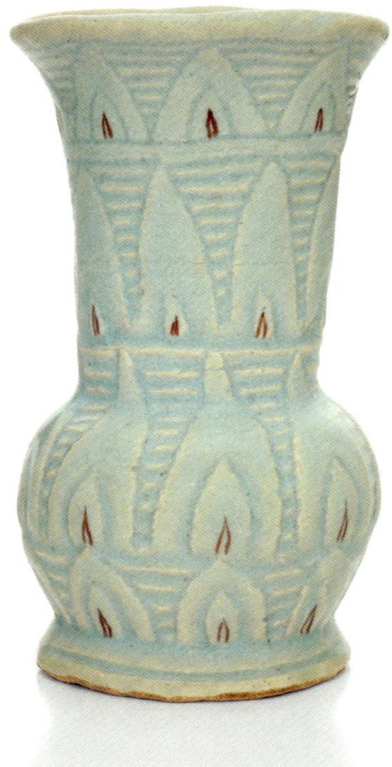

28 November 2016

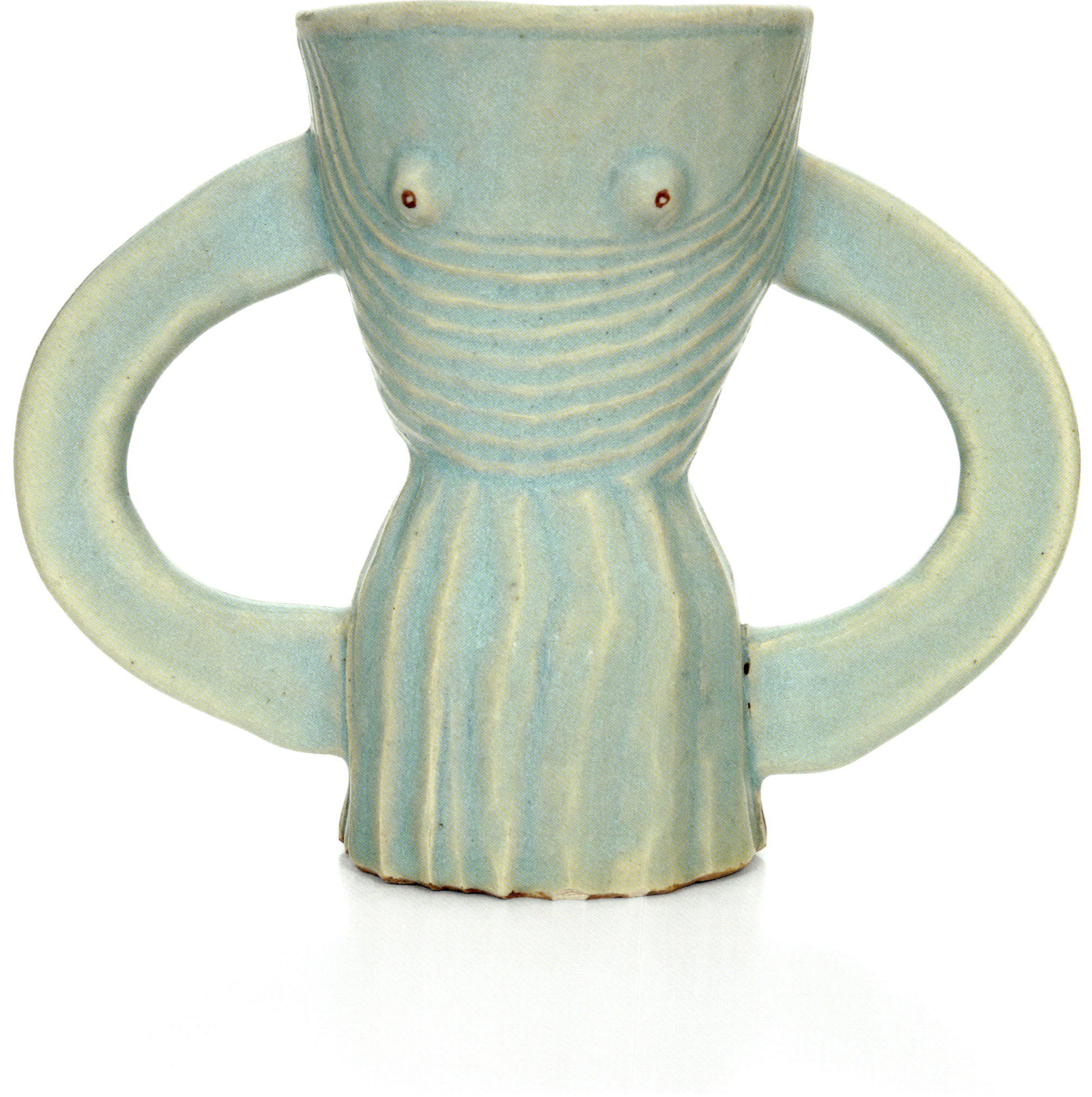

28 January 2016

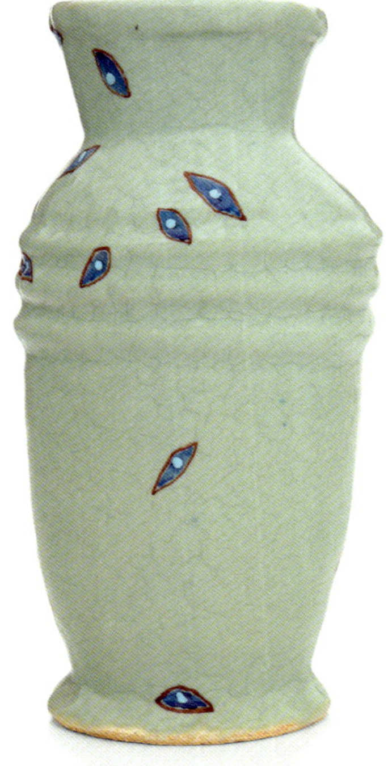

23 February 2017

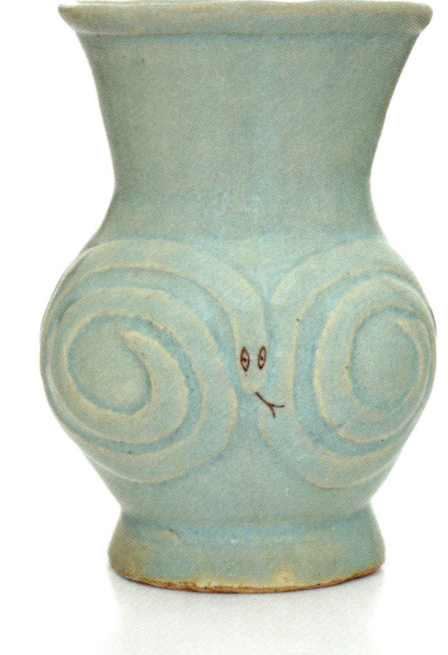

28 November 2016

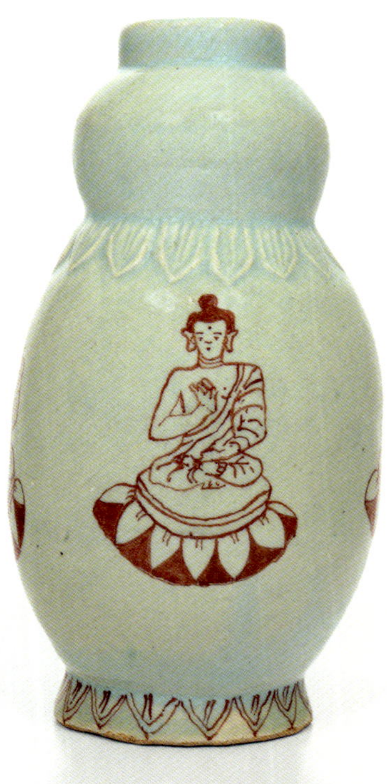

14 October 2016

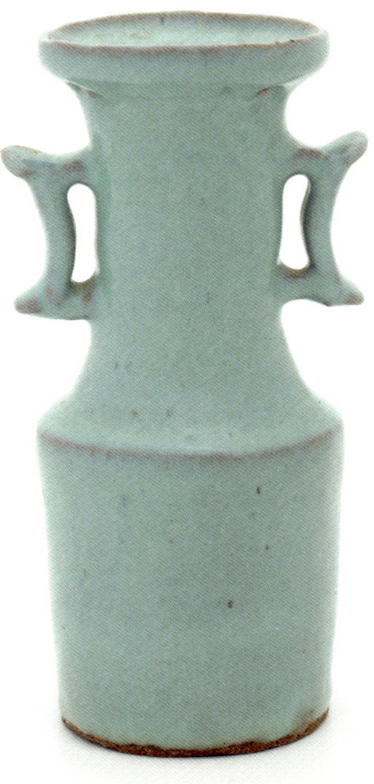

5 December 2016

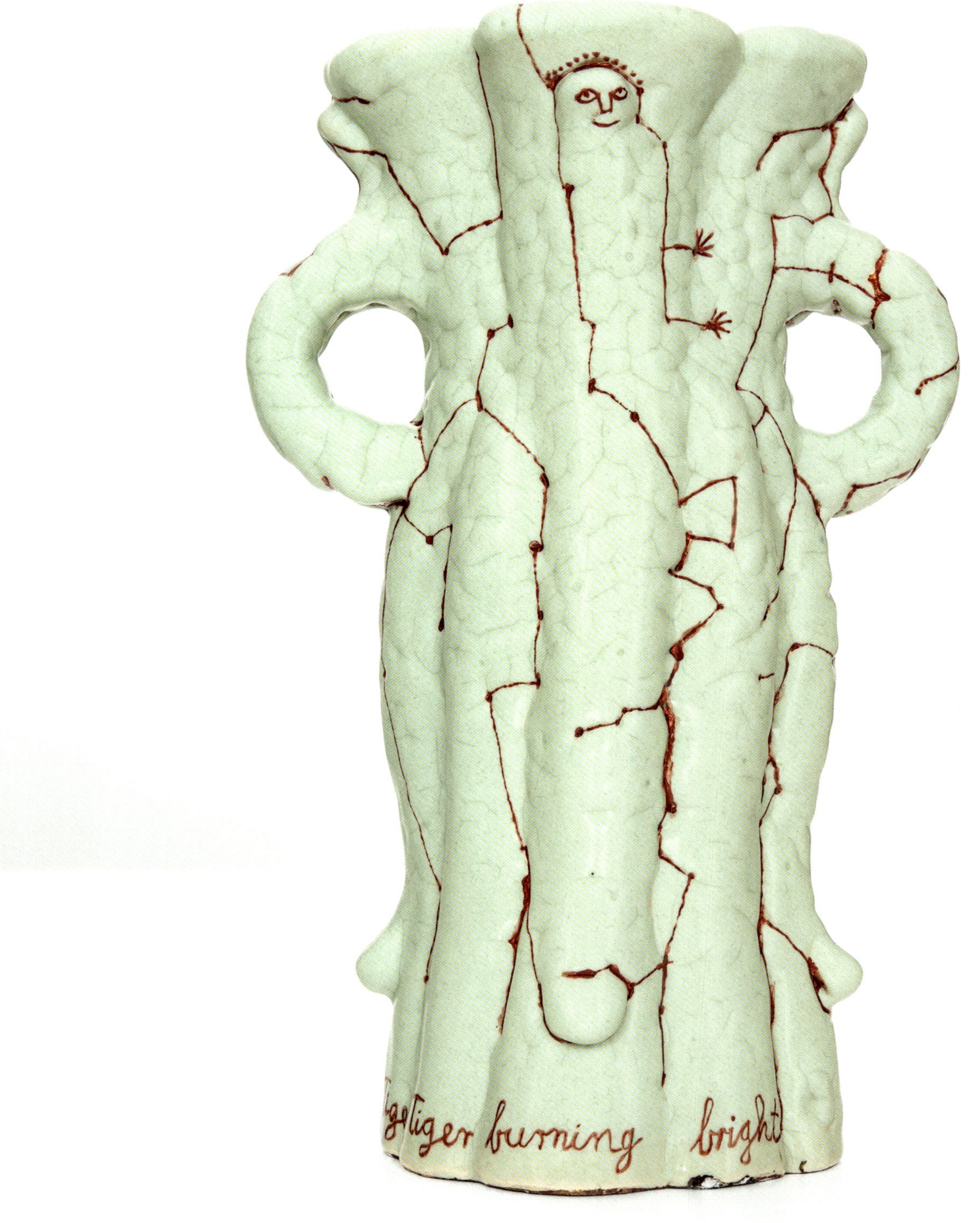

27 November 2014

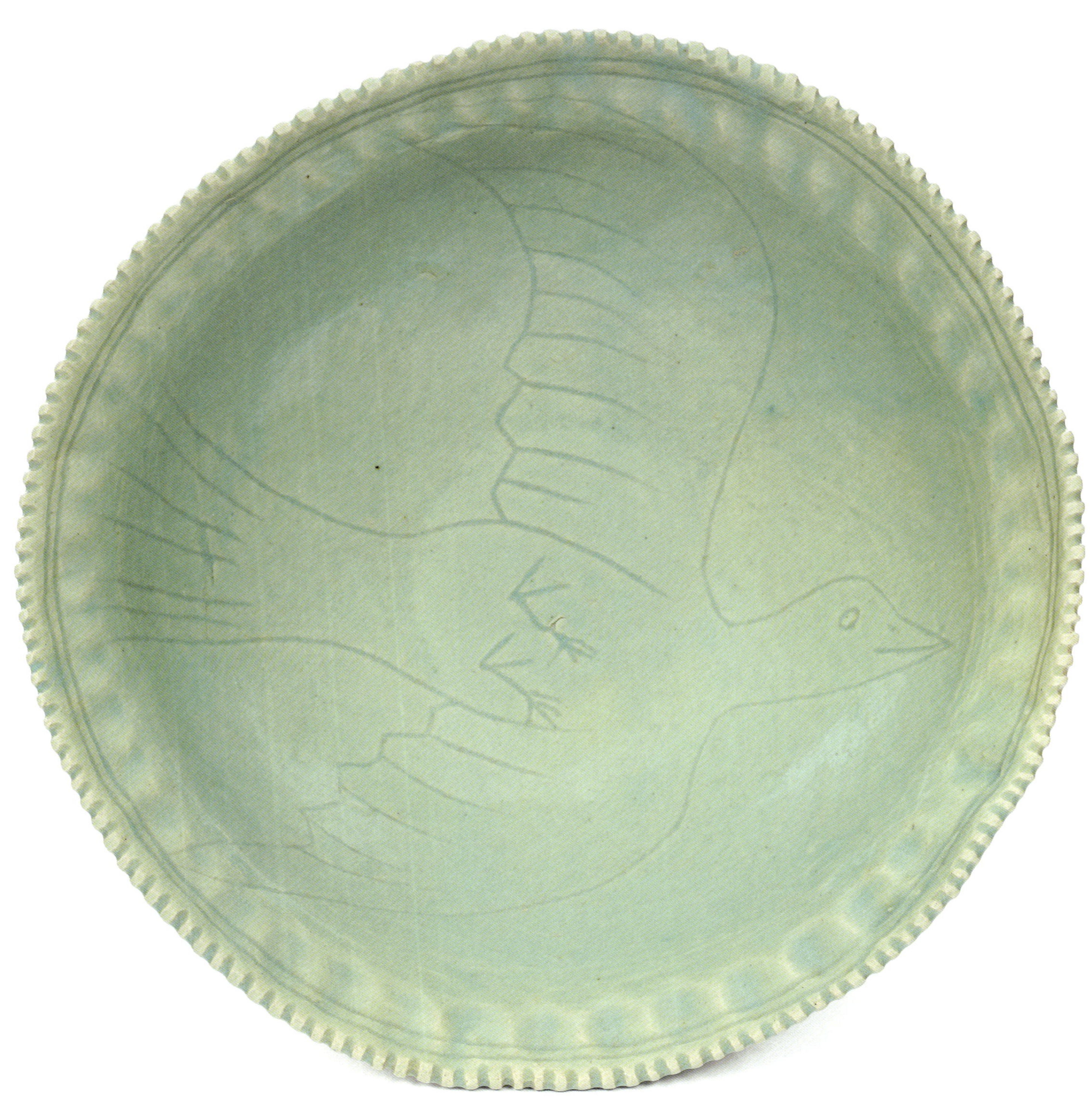

22 April 2019

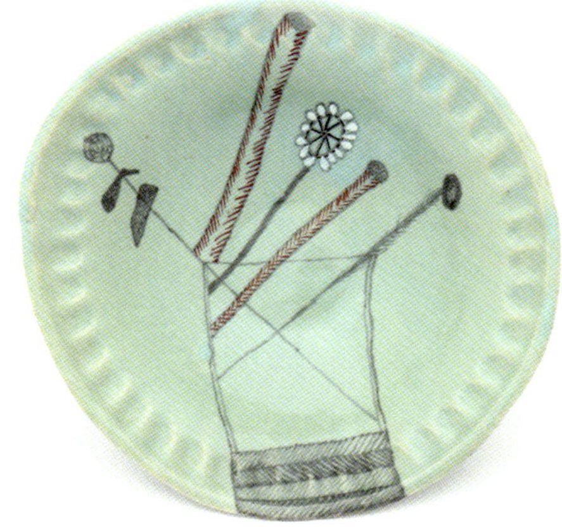

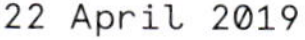

22 April 2019

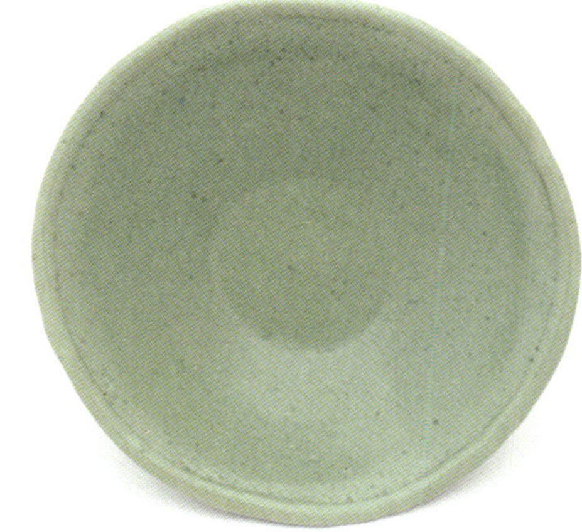

28 November 2014

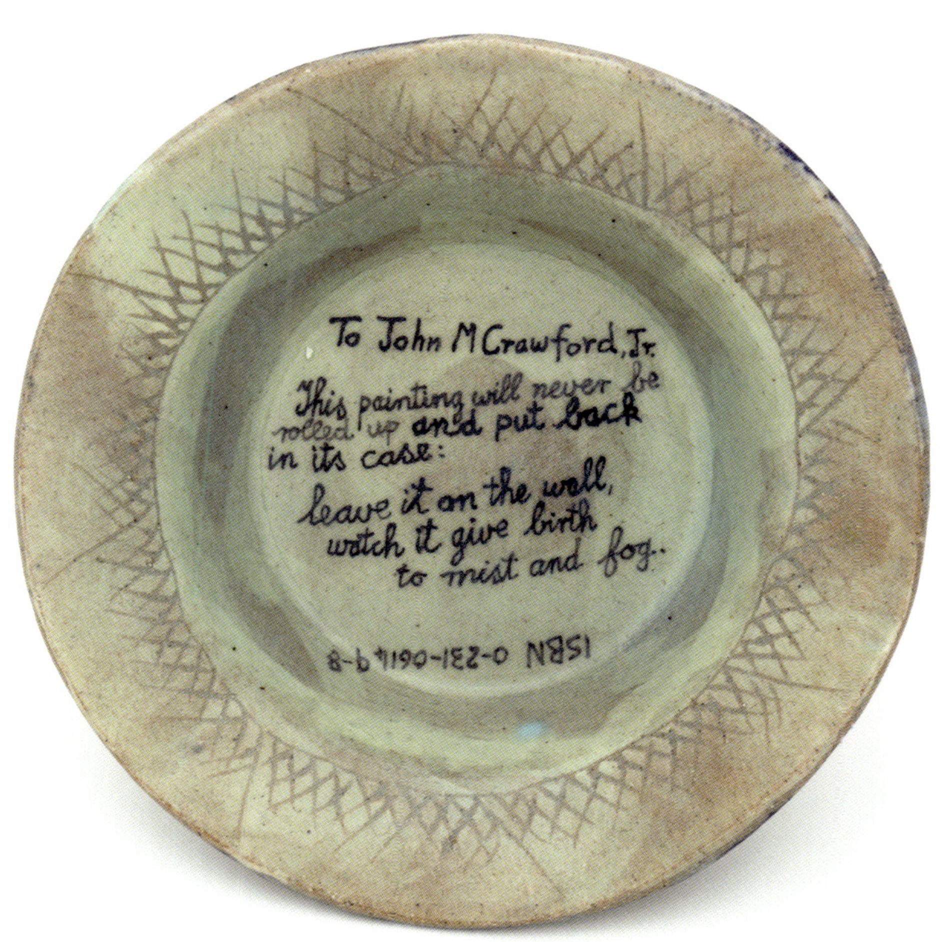

7 July 2015

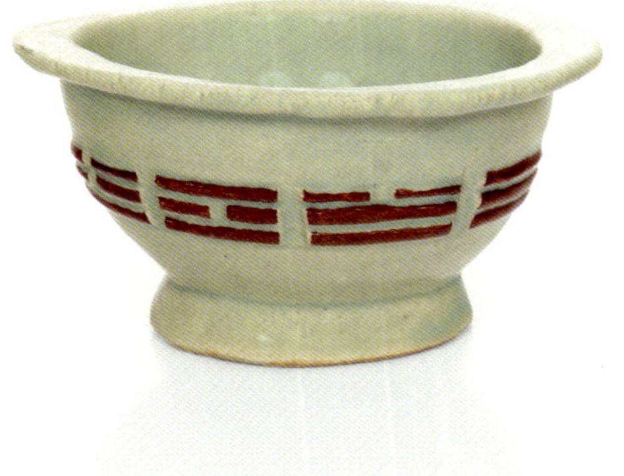

24 November 2016

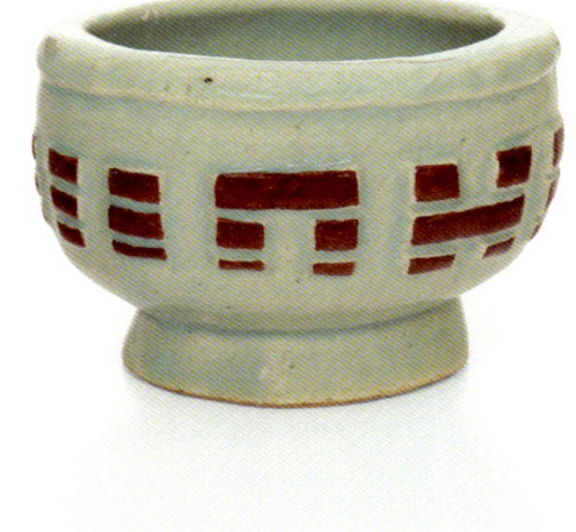

24 November 2016

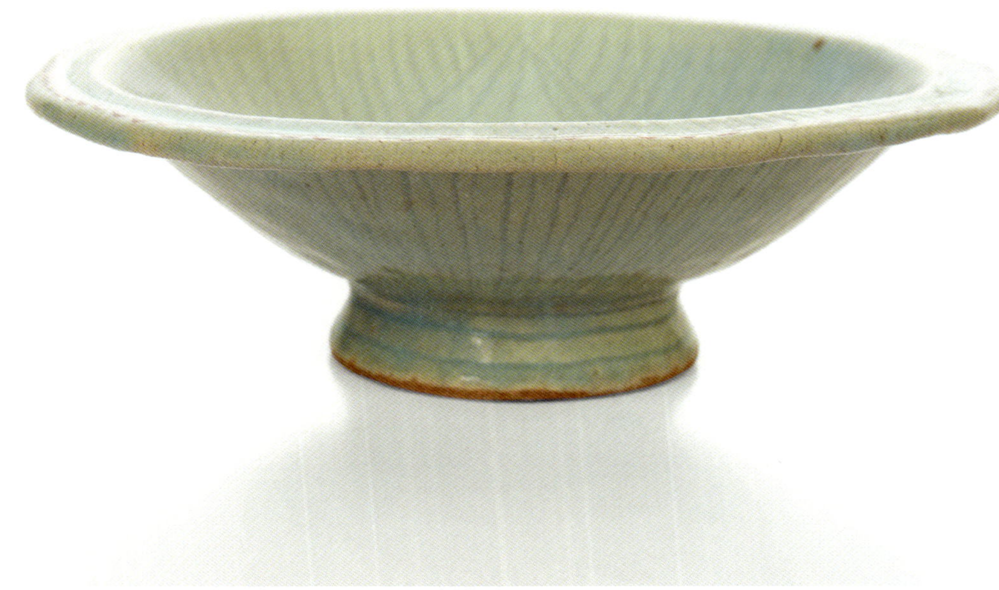

22 December 2016

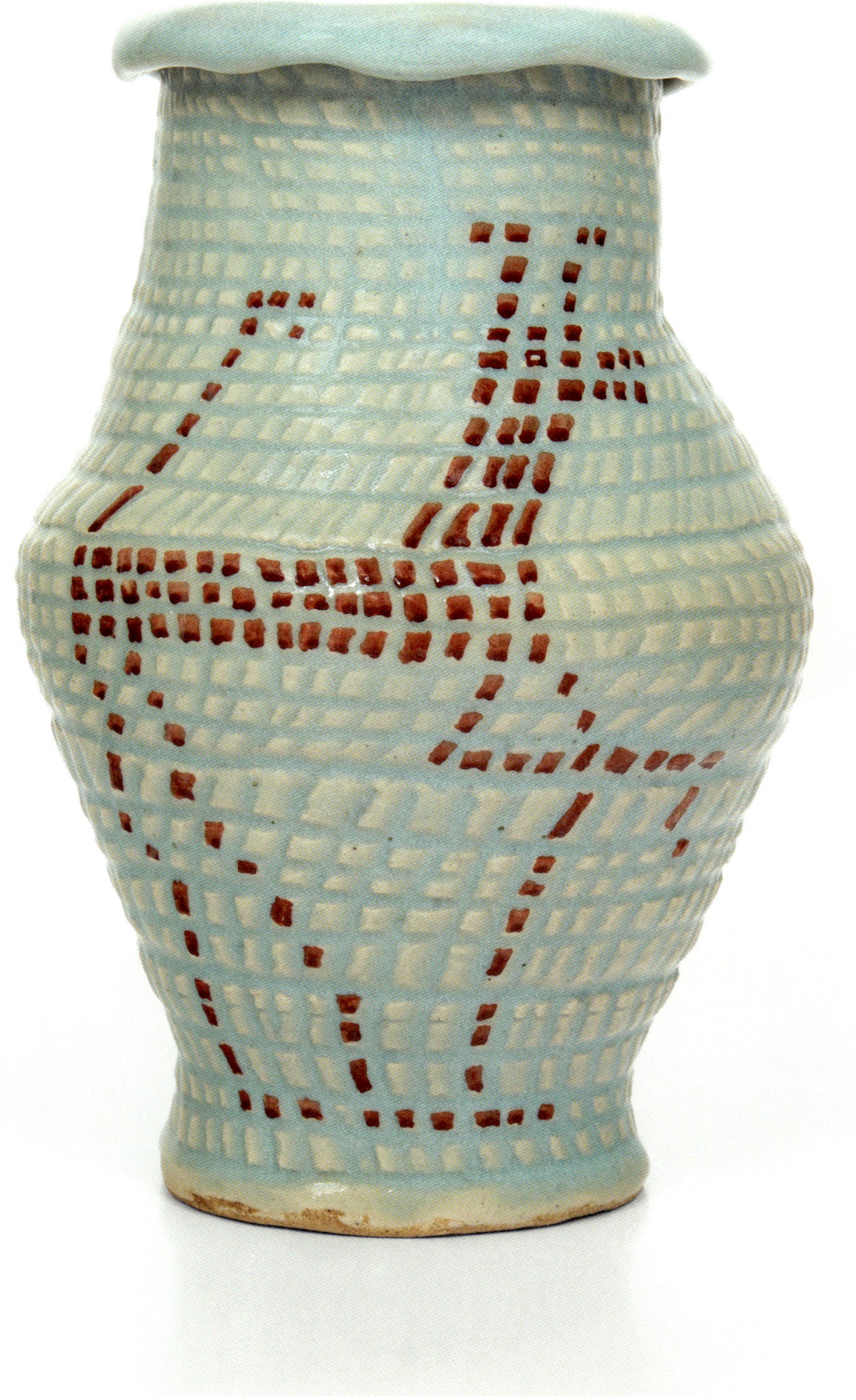

14 October 2016

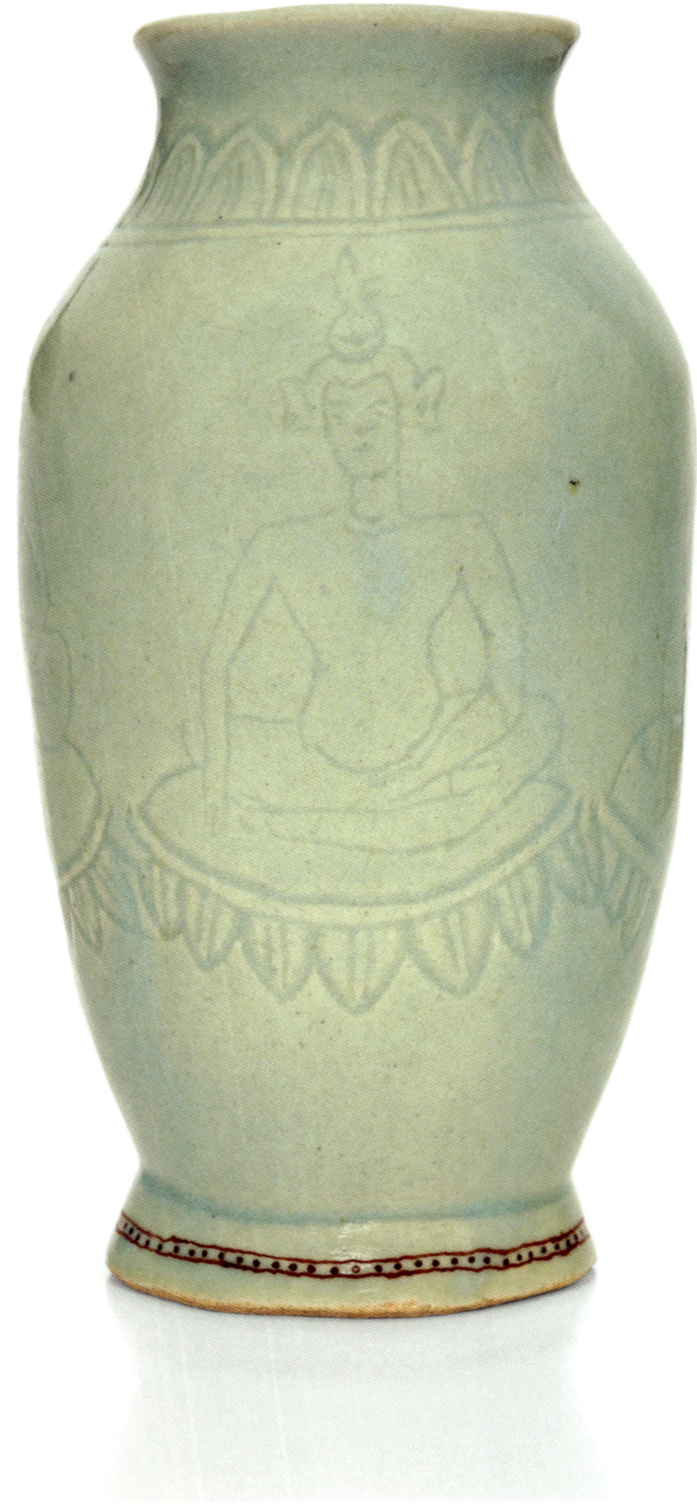

There is a Buddha that usually stands in my room. I was looking for such an image for a long time, and I found it in a high street in Kensington, at a price I could afford. So it's been with me for a long, long time. In bad times you look closely at this thing and its faint smile seems incredibly sustaining. And when the really bad times hit, you look at this image and hope to be sustained by it, and then it's just a piece of bronze and it's totally dead. You realise it's what you bring to this thing that makes it do something for you, or not.

I was wanting to make more of a glaze, and when it came to the bone ash I realised there was very little bone ash, too little. The next ingredient that I needed was tin oxide. And I accidentally put in more tin oxide than I normally would. Now it has too little bone ash and too much tin oxide. So I didn't know what it would do, but this is what it's done. And what an interesting colour, sort of a neutral-ish colour that sometimes can look greenish, sometimes pinker. But the glazed plate wants something, how can I say, not just plain, it wants some scratching and then a drawing, it needs something for that glaze to show up and catch the light.

Inspiration can come from the tiniest thing. I like shards, broken things, because they hint at something. And sometimes, if you have a perfect piece, you might not find it as interesting as the fragment.

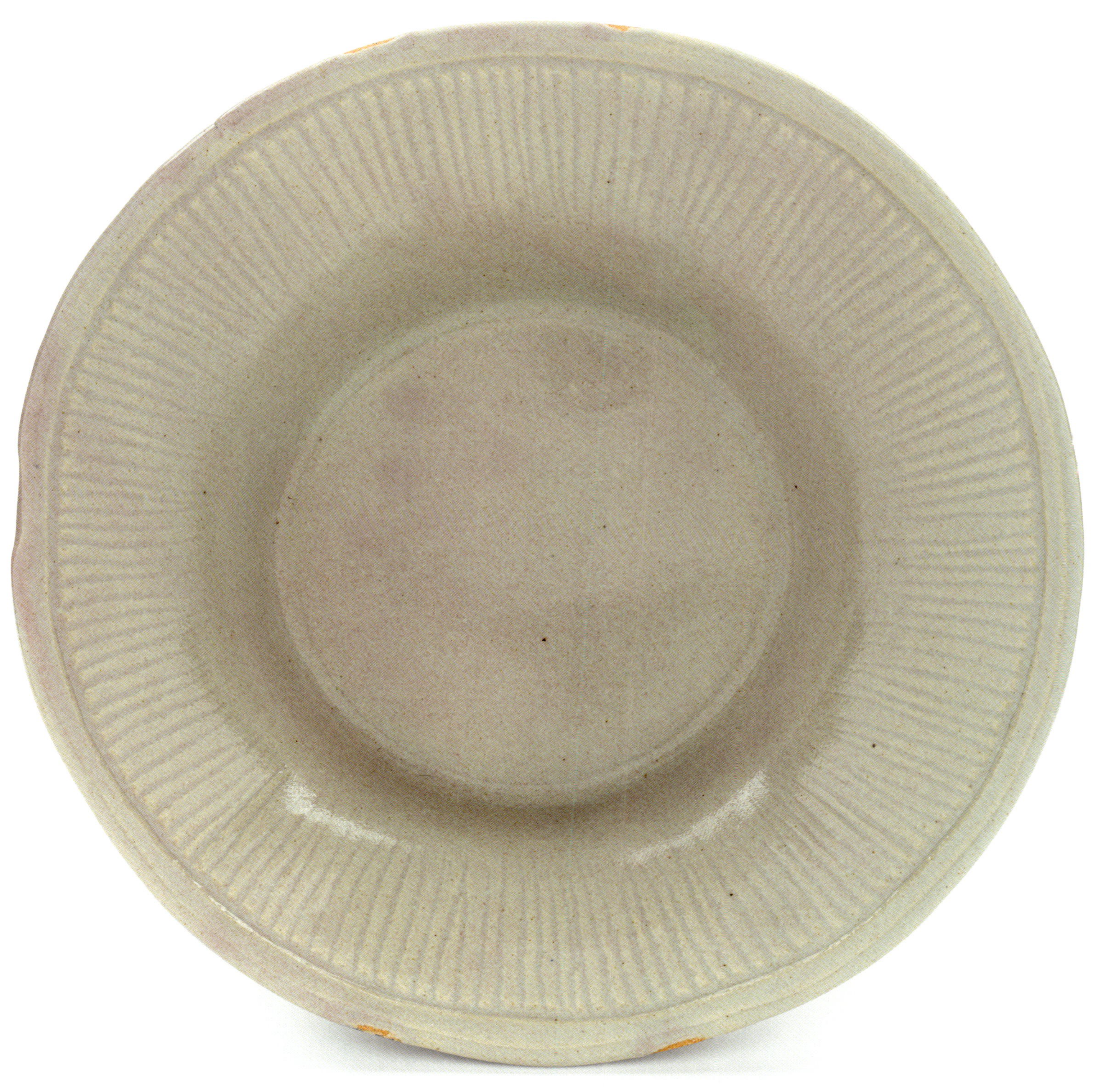

2 August 2020

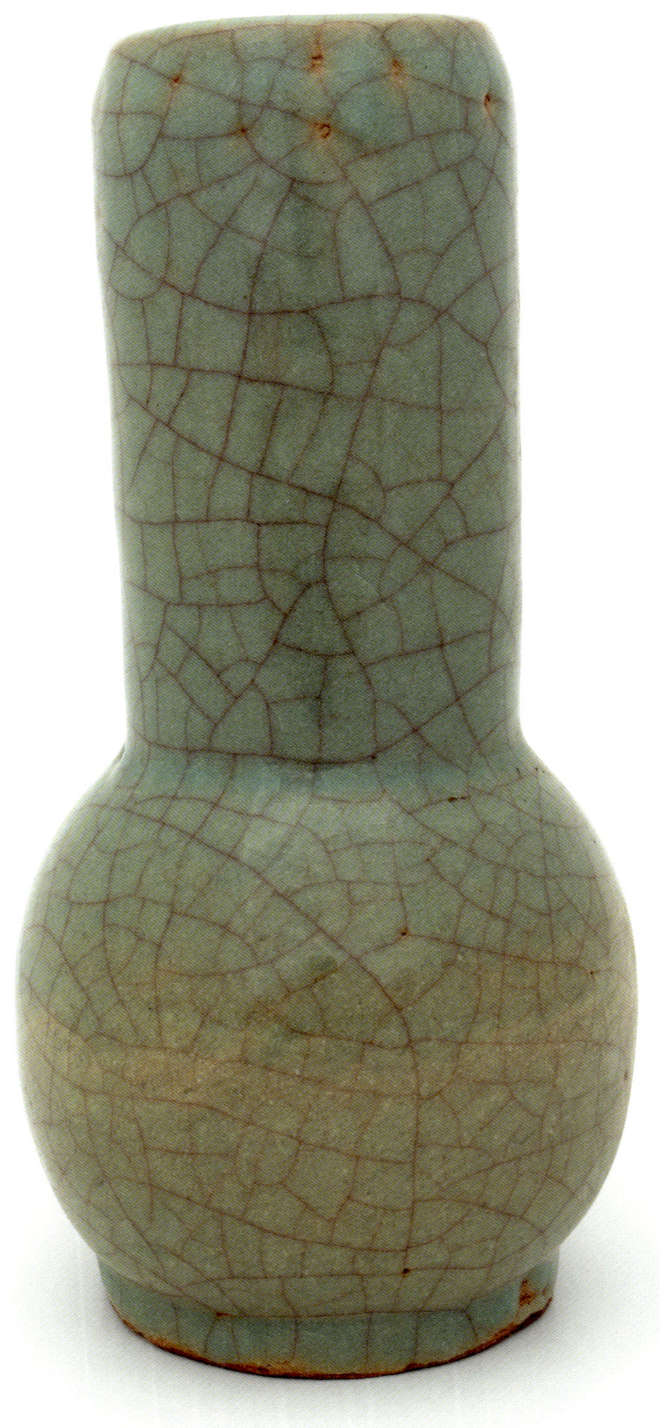

1989

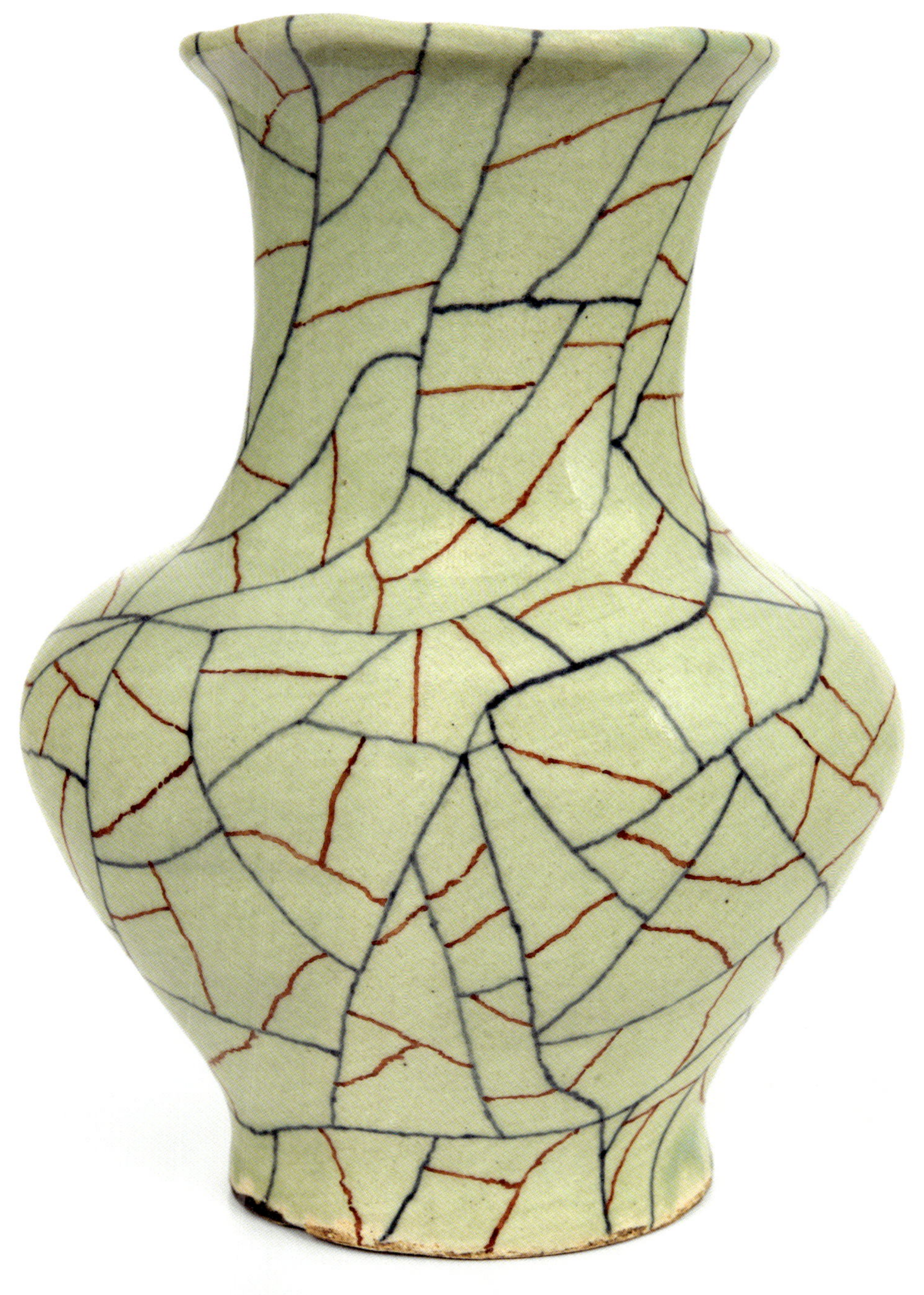

29 June 2016

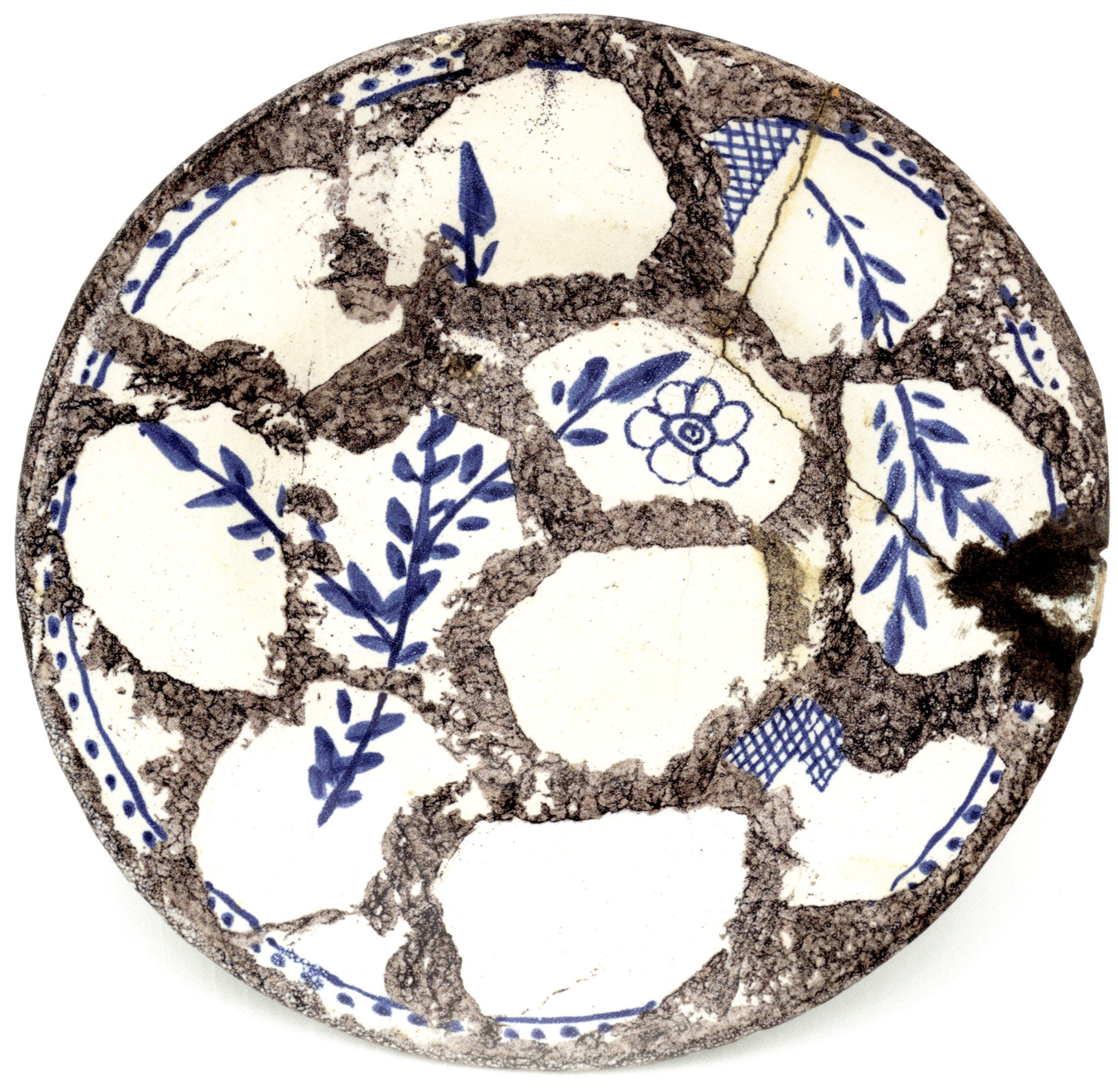

31 October 2001

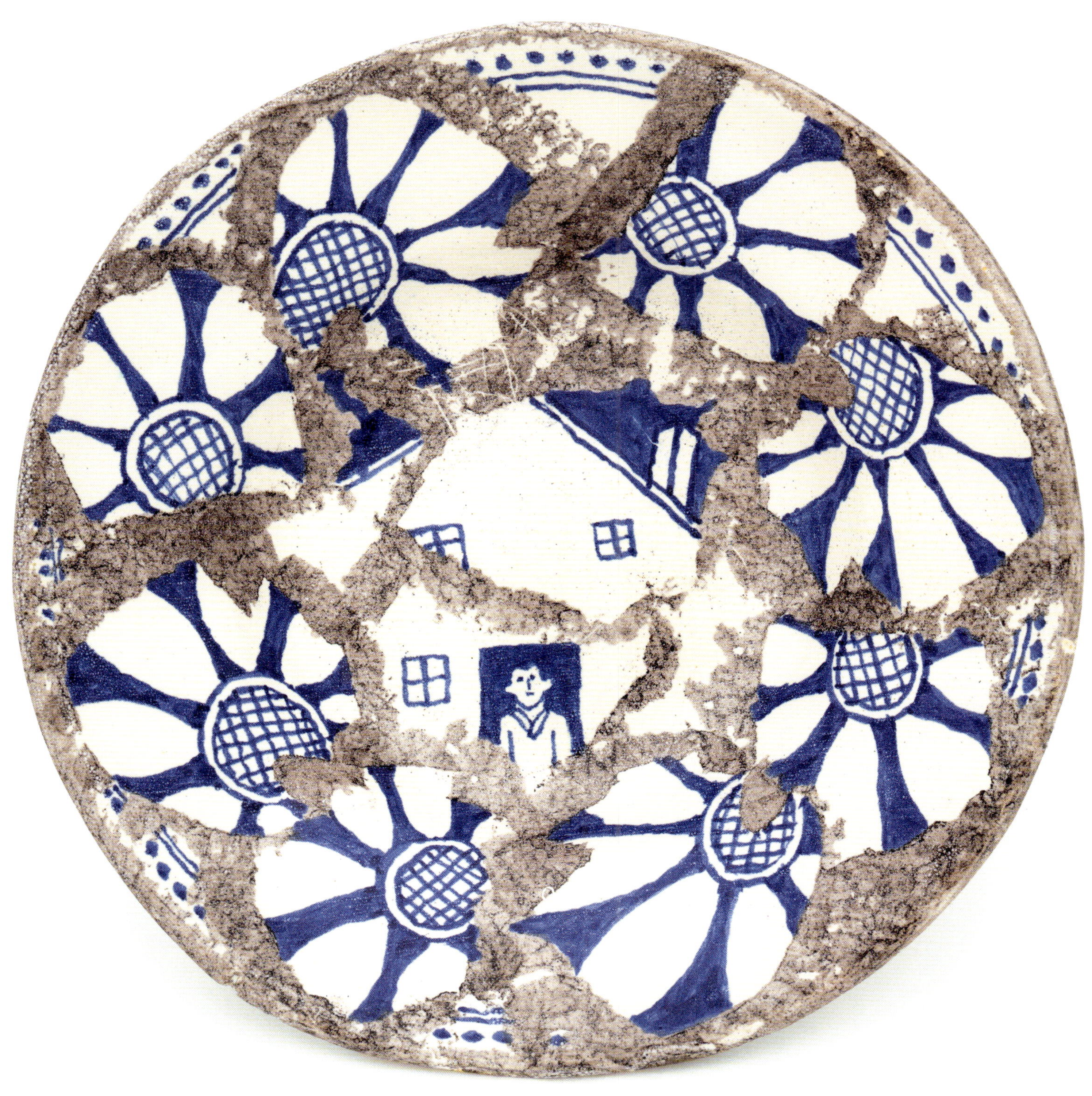

31 October 2001

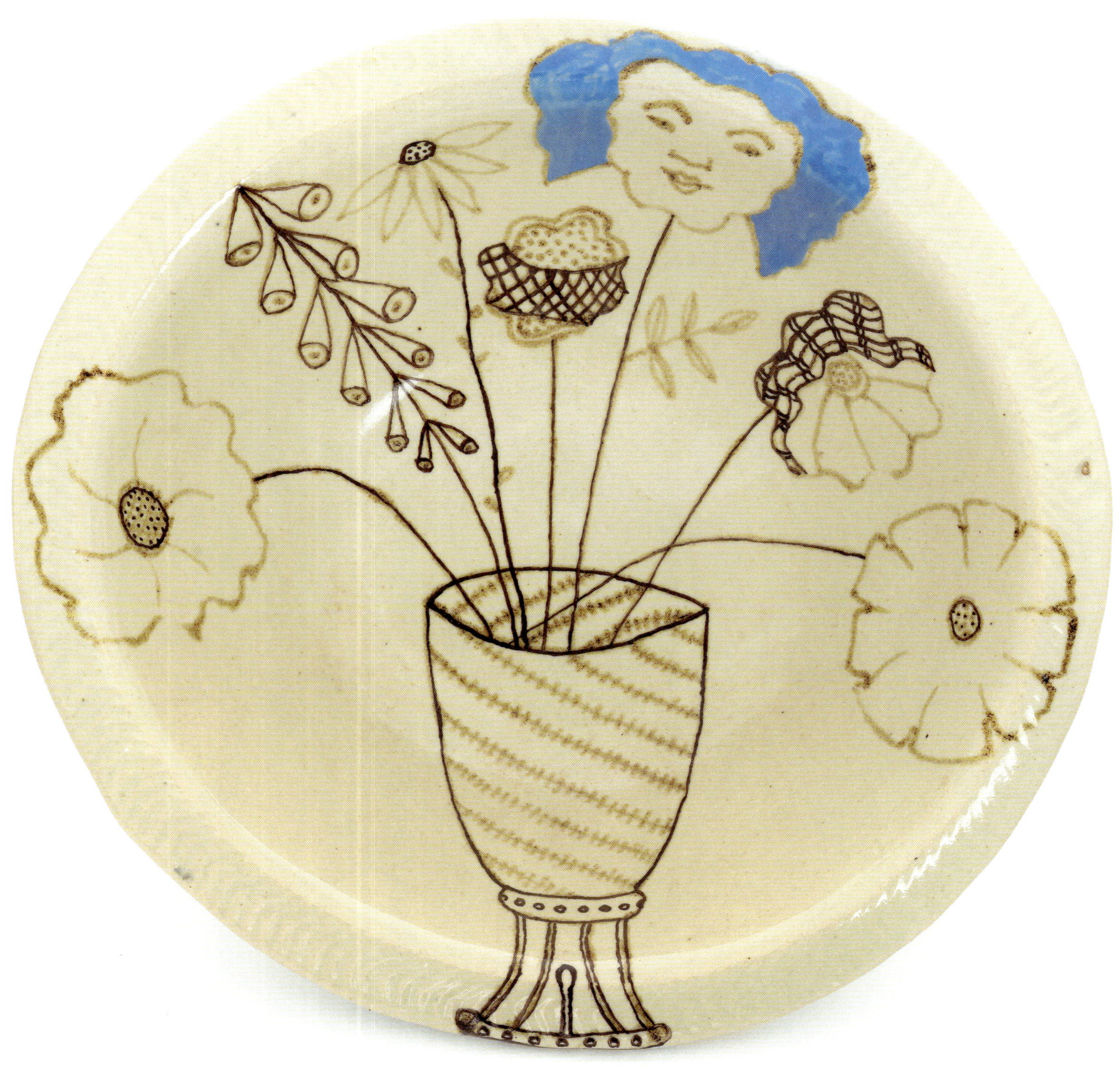

30 August 2017

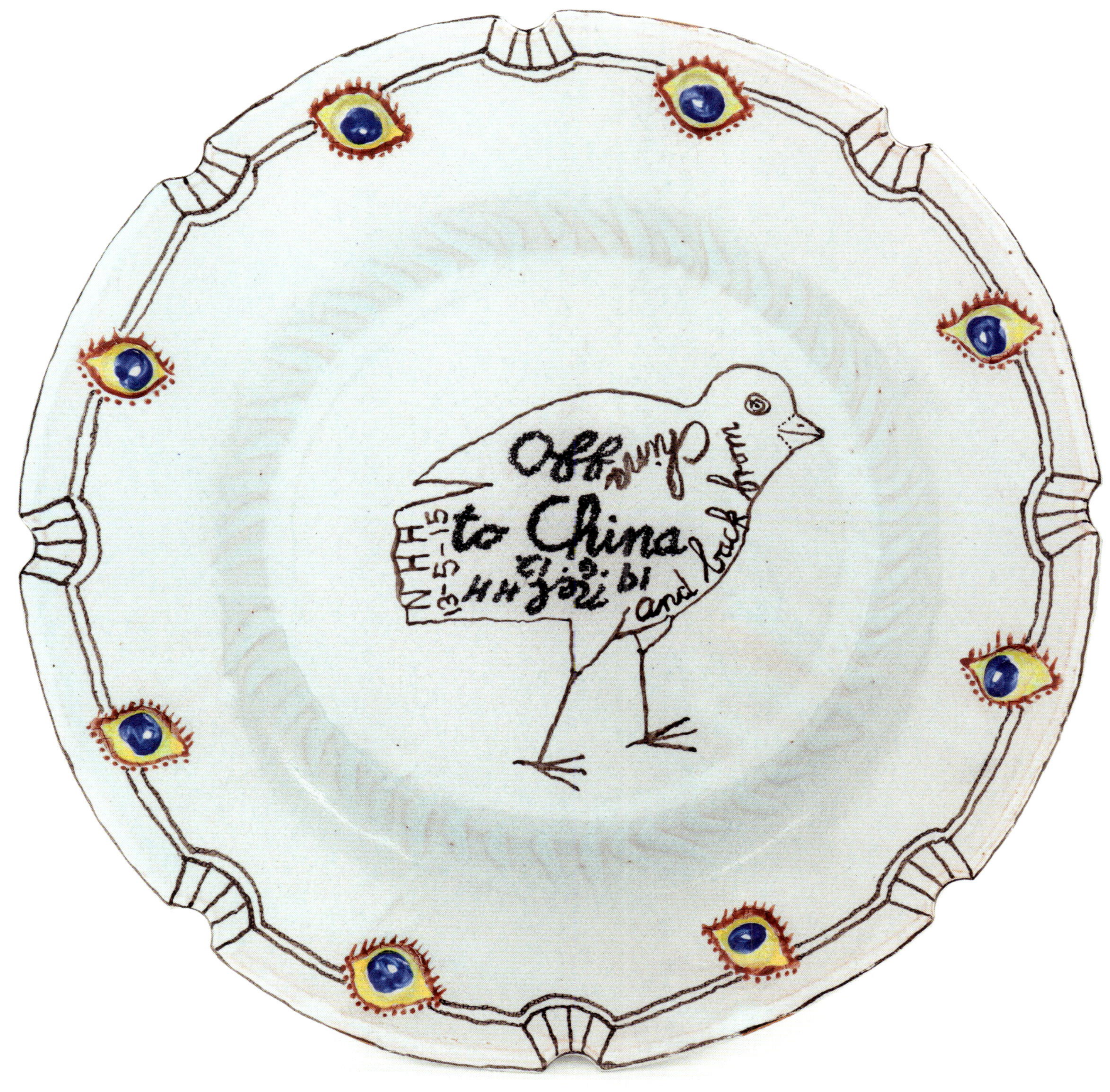

13 May 2015

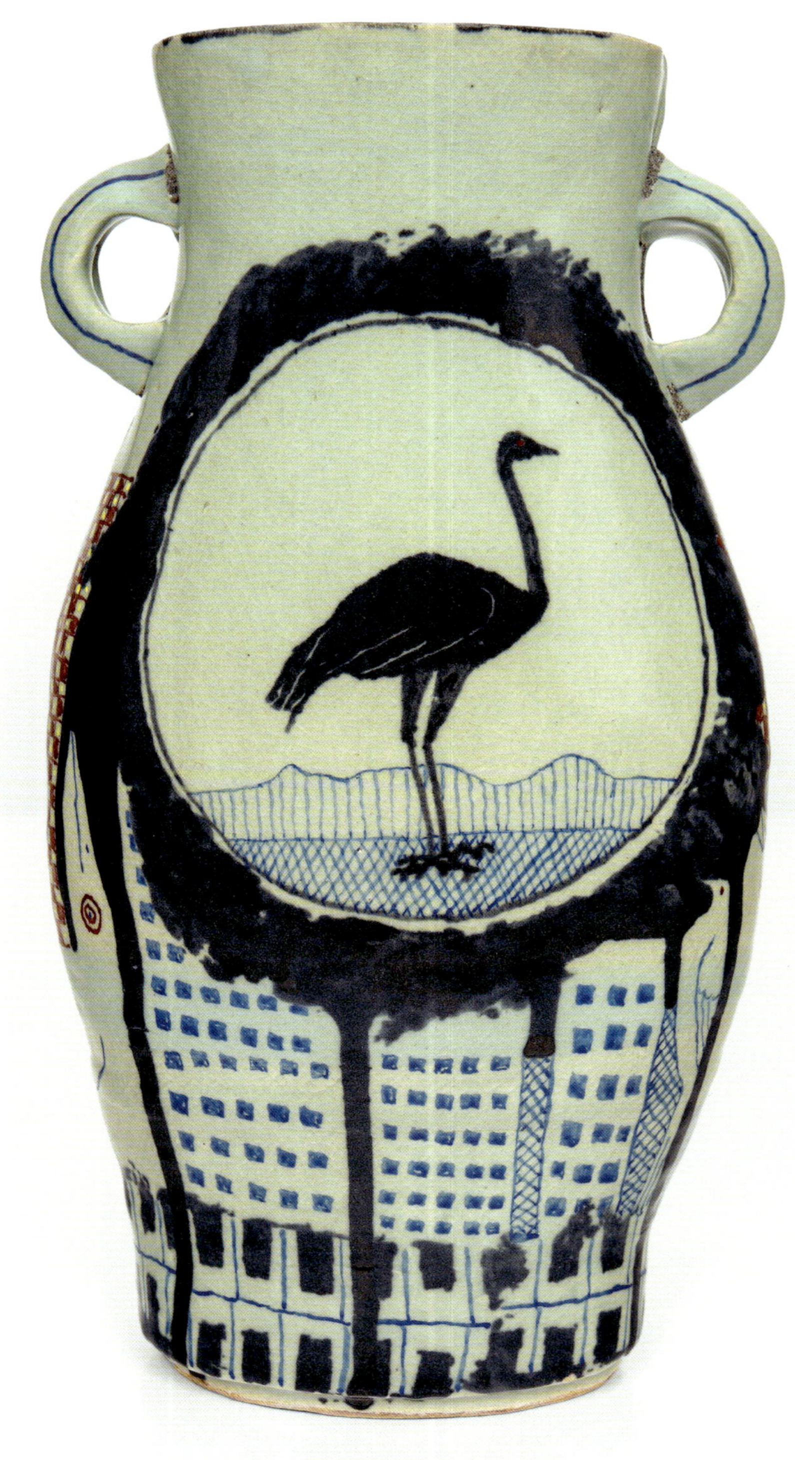

21 December 2015

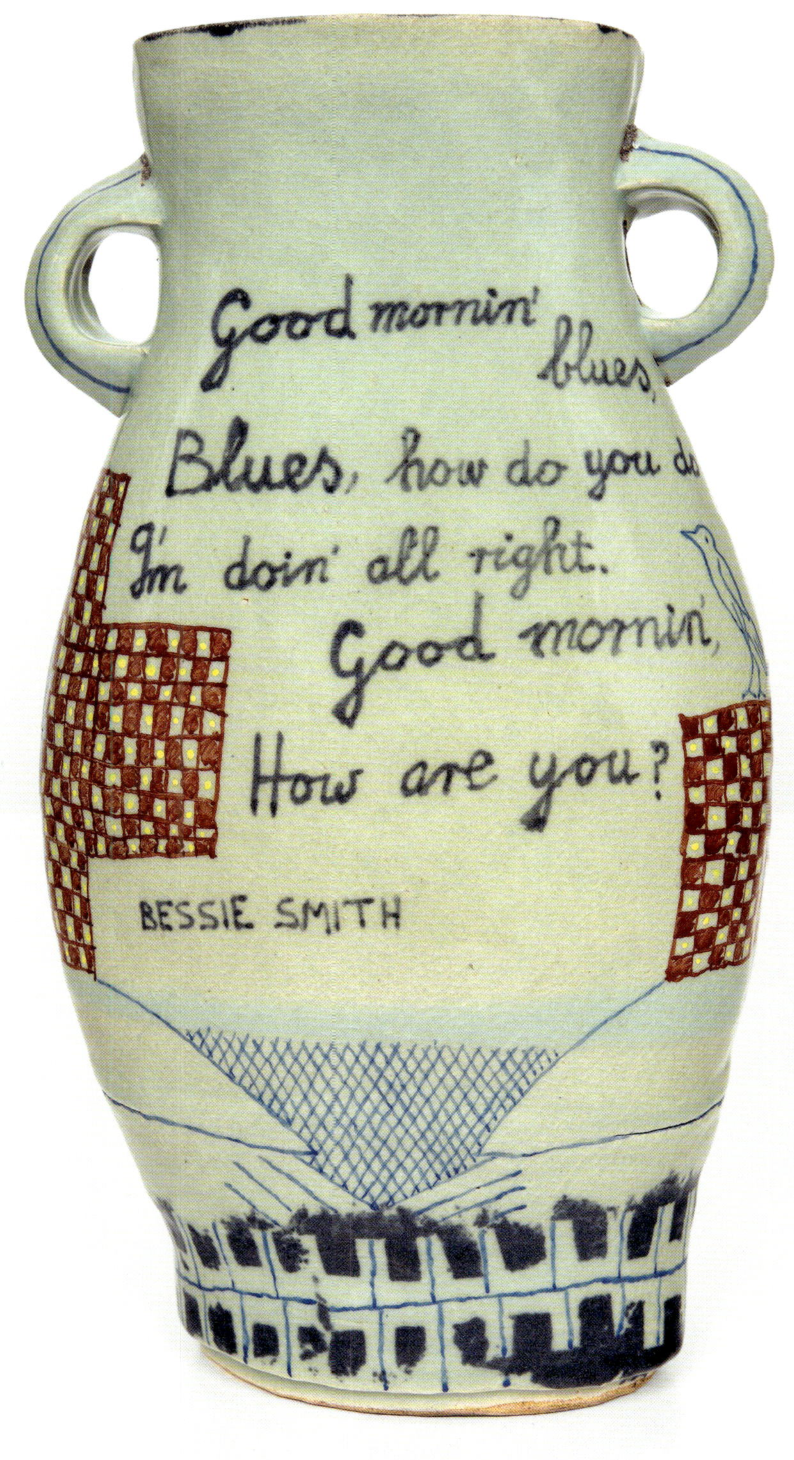
Good mornin' blues,
Blues, how do you do
I'm doin' all right.
Good mornin',
How are you?
BESSIE SMITH

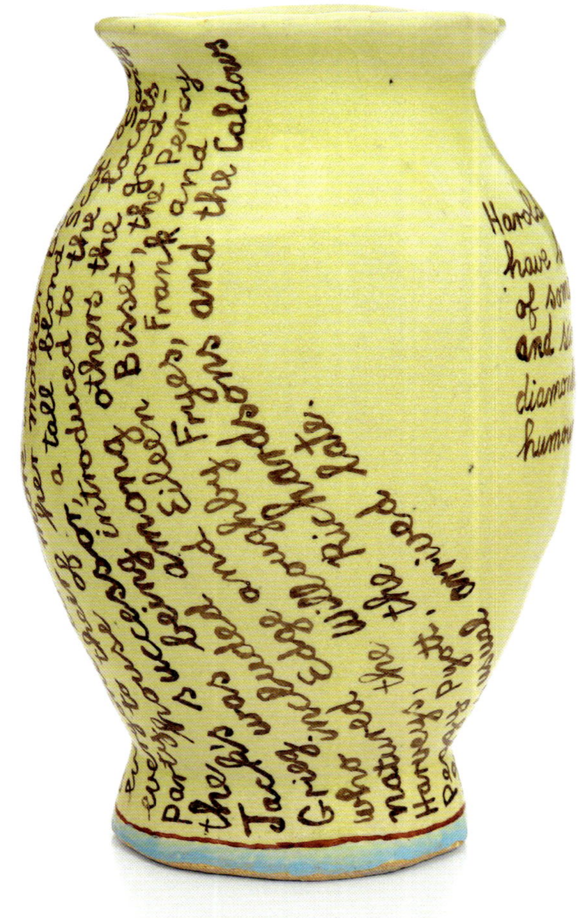

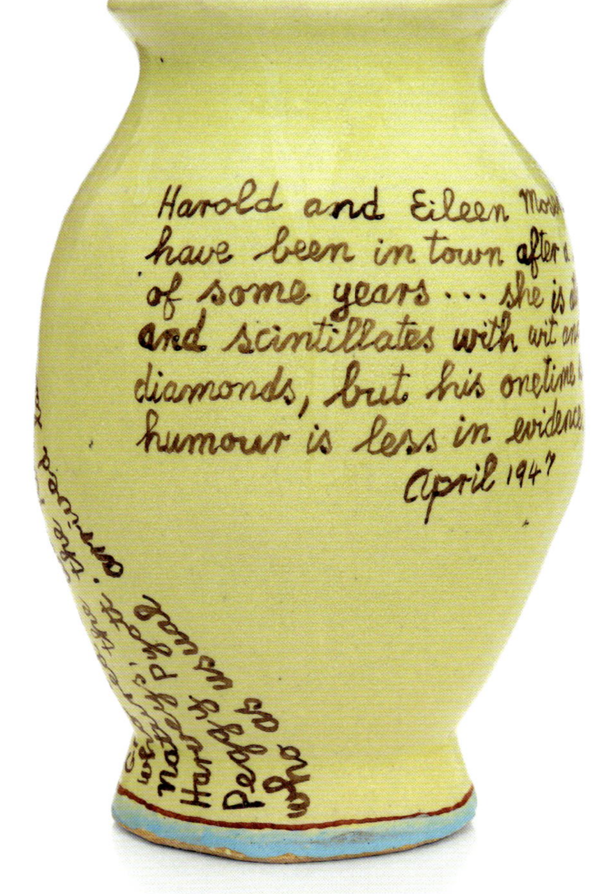

6 February 2017

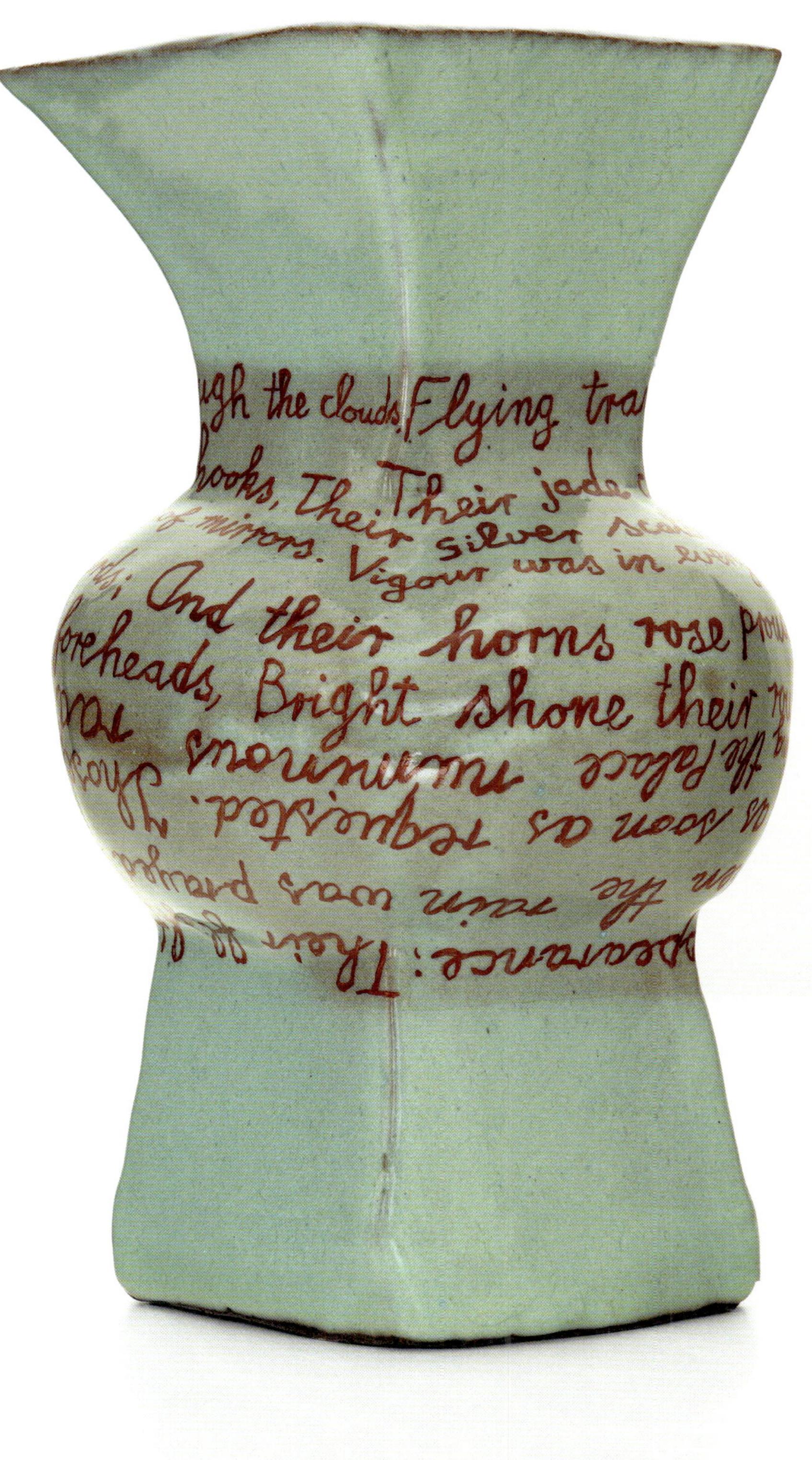

8 January 2015

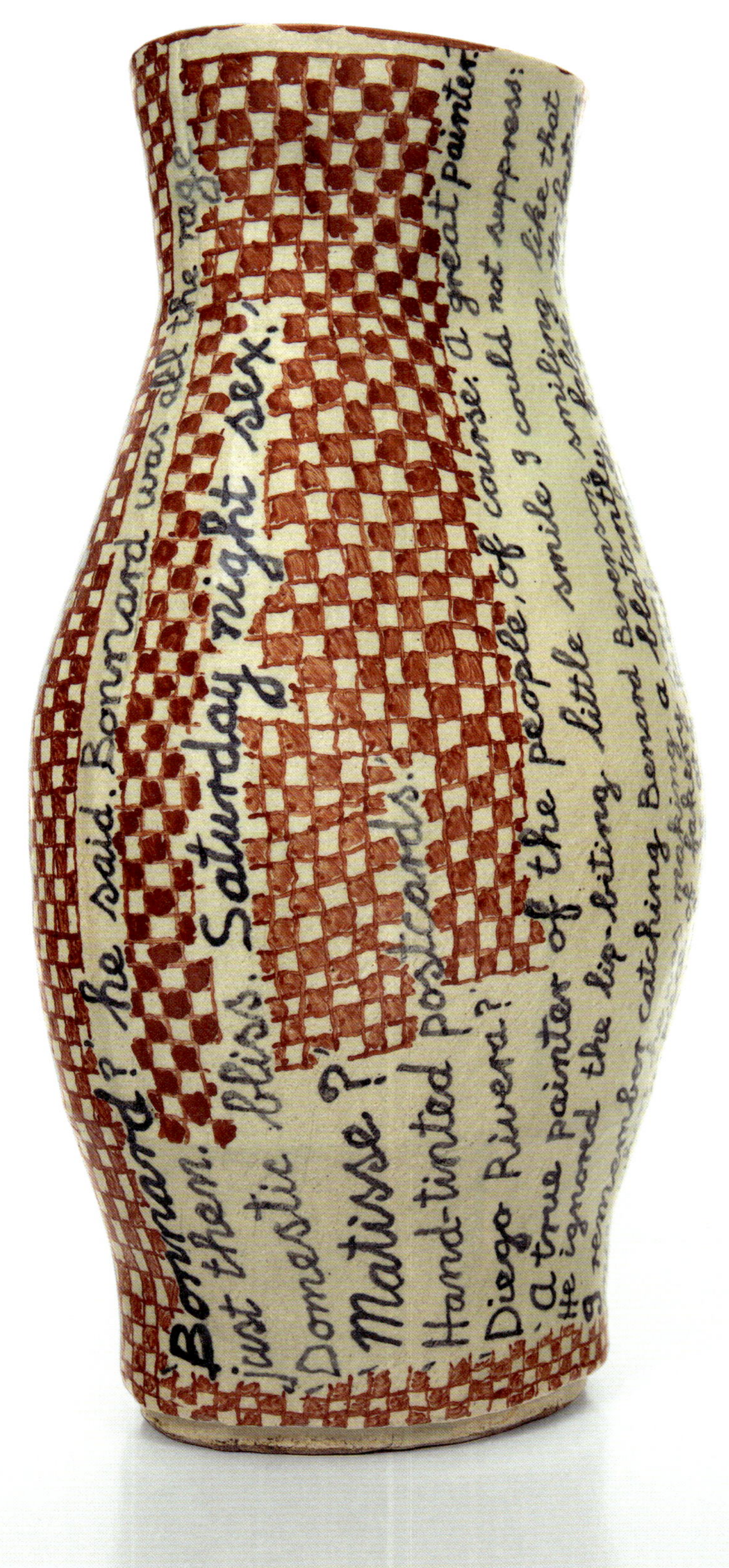

22 February 2016

I can't bring myself to do paintings because I can't imagine a reason for their existence. I suppose, in quite a Protestant way, if something has a use I can do it. I'm quite happy to have vases that I never put flowers in – I just like them. But I like the thought that if you want to you can put flowers in them, and some would be best with flowers – they'd be completed. But I get so involved with them, sometimes I think, 'What's that all about, they're just fucking vases.'

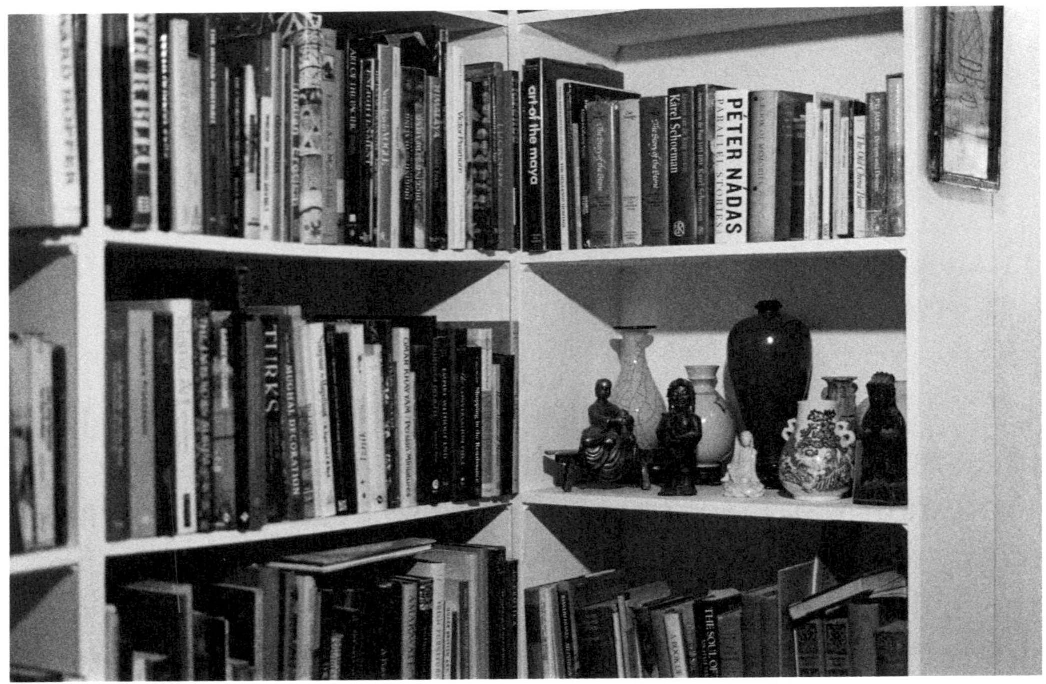

From an existing piece, historic or mine, a new shape or pattern or colour inspires me. It could be an Imari plate from a good period, late seventeenth or early eighteenth century with a blue outside and the iron-red and gold in addition to the blue on the inside, and a small Ming-period peasant bowl with a blue outside and blue-and-white inside. I find little aspects of things able to seed another whole batch of things.

My collection of rubbish is a study collection, it's got to do with things that are inspiring in some way. It's a reference library and it's got better things and rubbish things, and they're mixed together.

I can't help but feel that things are like living entities. That's how they seem to me – like living things. Like the stones I carry – for me they are alive. What kind of life they have I don't know, but they seem alive as I suppose everything could be alive. It's got a life, this piece of wood, or whatever.

I find books very valuable, but they can only go so far, and at the end of the day you've got to have something in your hand that you can turn over and feel the surface of, and check out the this and the that. You actually need that physical contact. And I have sometimes acquired goodish and okay things, and then I've got things that are absolute rubbish, but there might be some little thing about them that is sort of intriguing, to put it that way.

Things are lost along the way from wars, naughty children or jealous rivals; they need constant replacement. I like things, and early on made things to supply my own needs. And that is how it continues to be. I keep back items from a series and also some unique things. And after a while some can go to be replaced by new things. Of things not made by me, in anticipation of a new arrival, I sometimes clear the way for it by giving away some or all of a related kind in order for the new thing, for a while, to rule alone.

When the choice of what to keep is difficult it pleases me because then I suppose that the batch is okay.

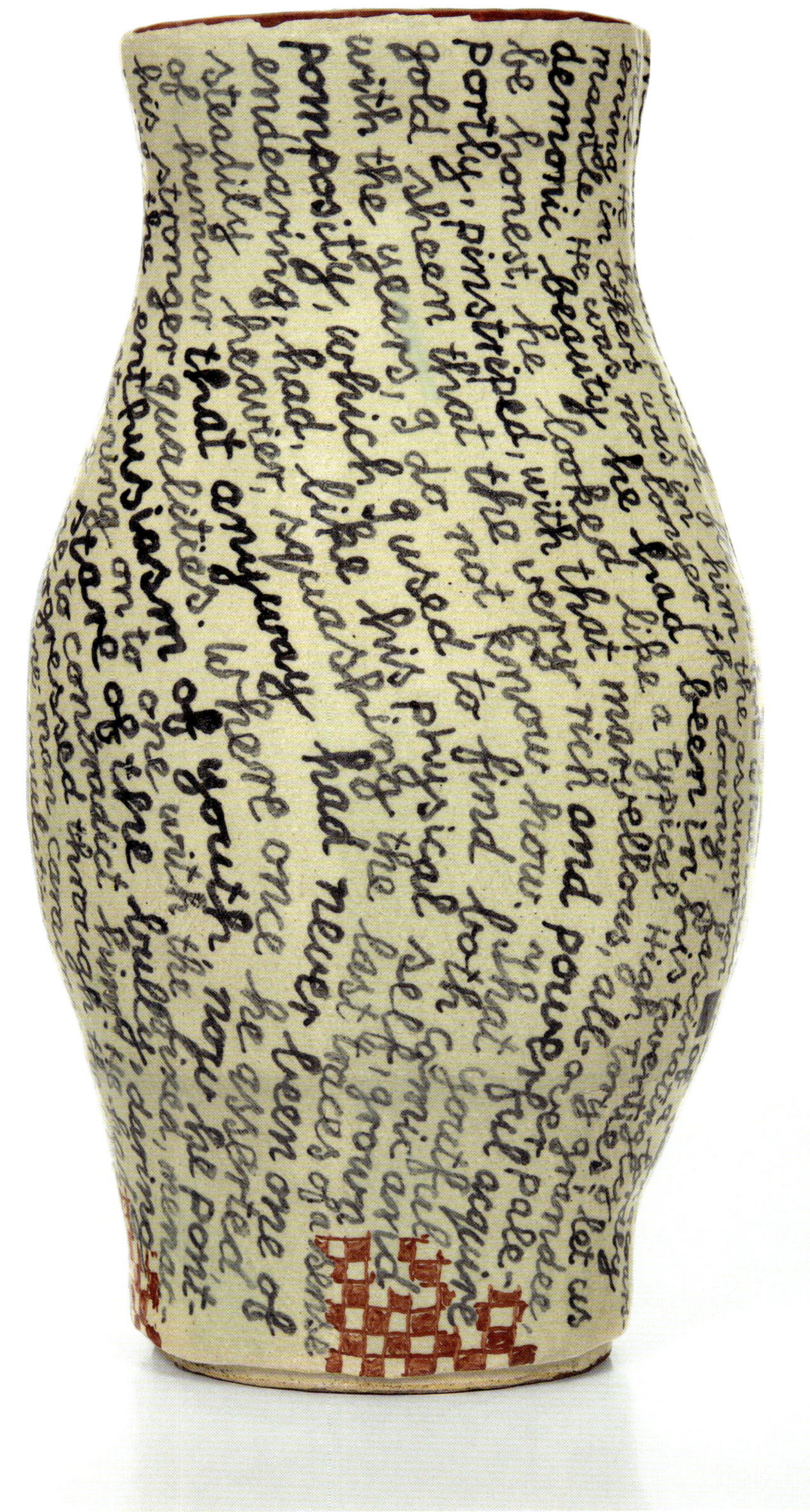

23 February 2016

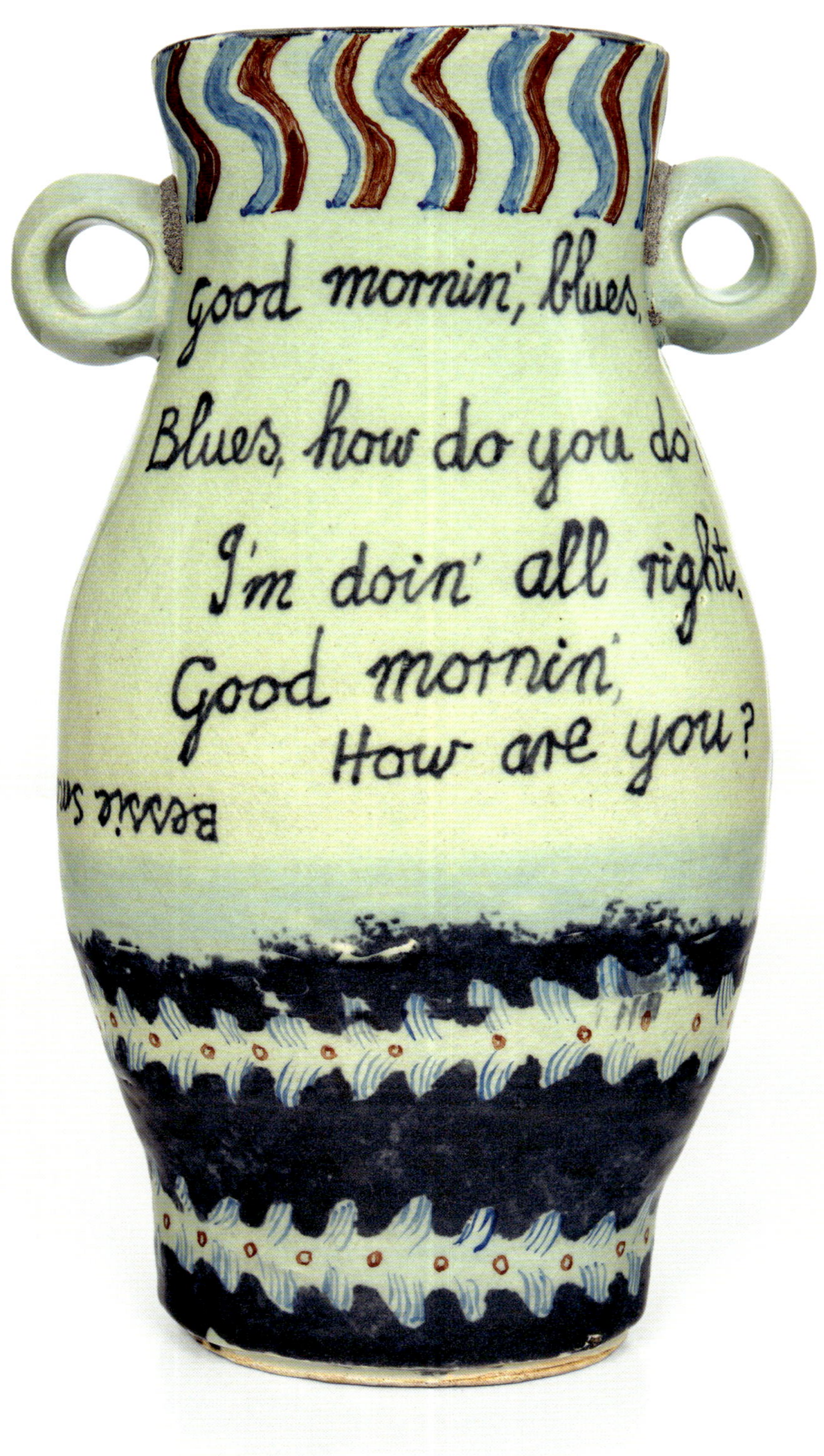

21 December 2015

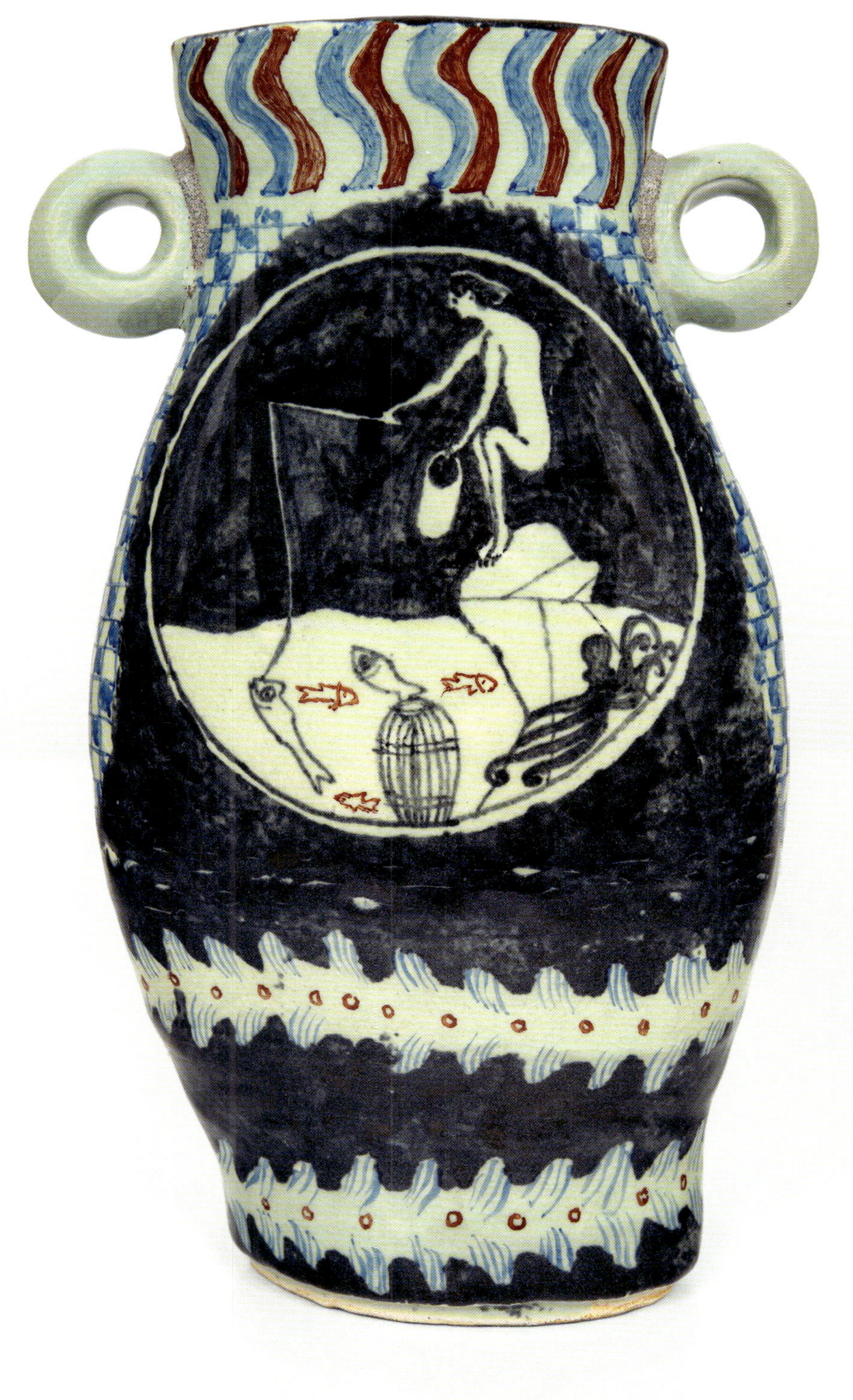

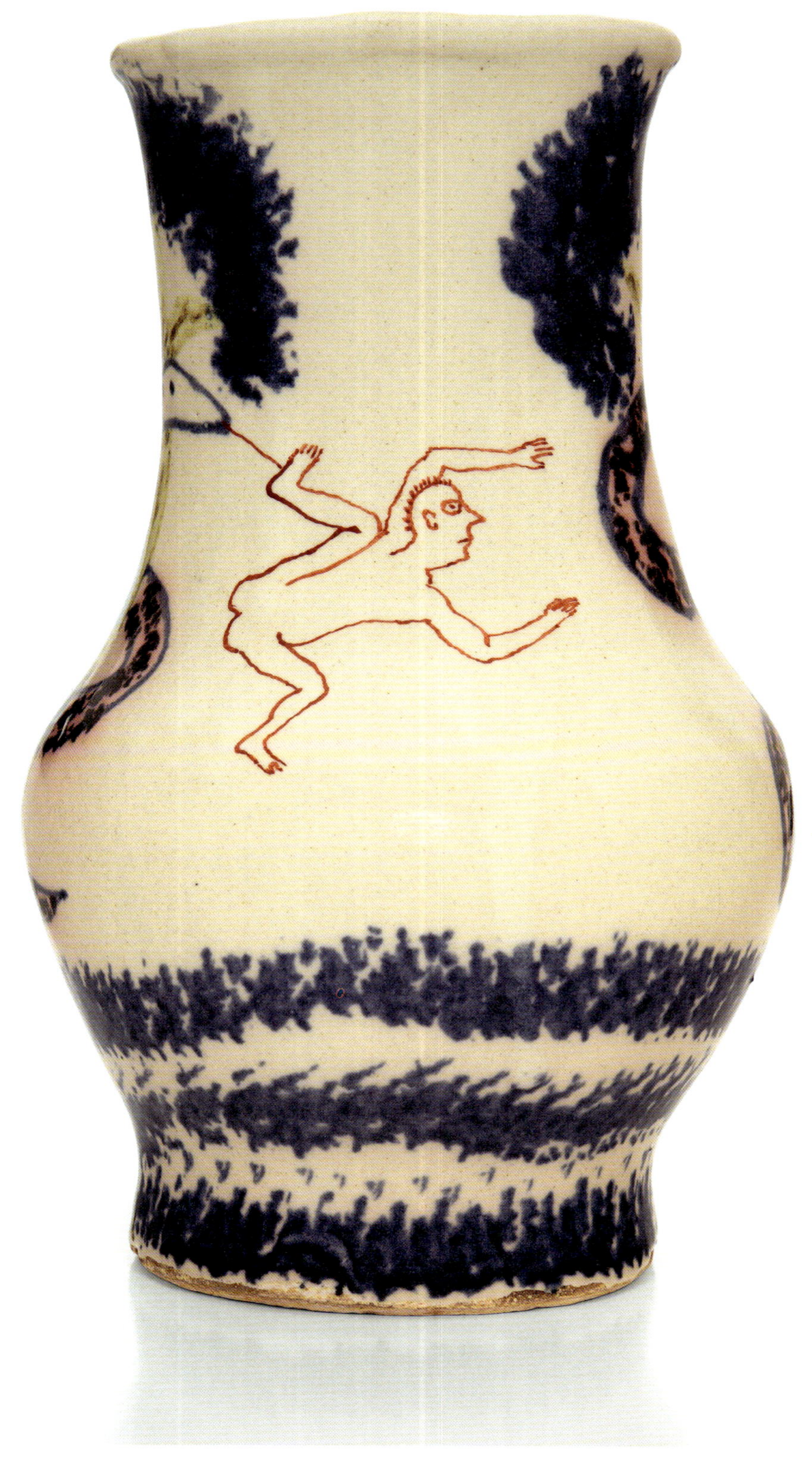

27 January 2017

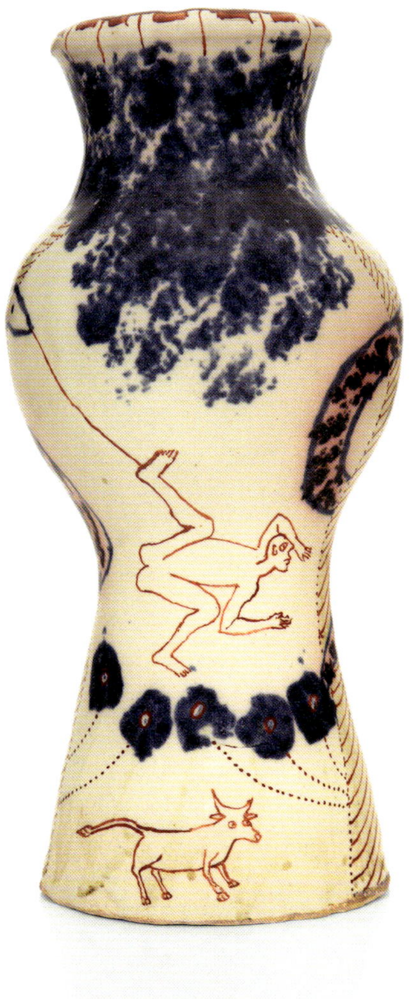

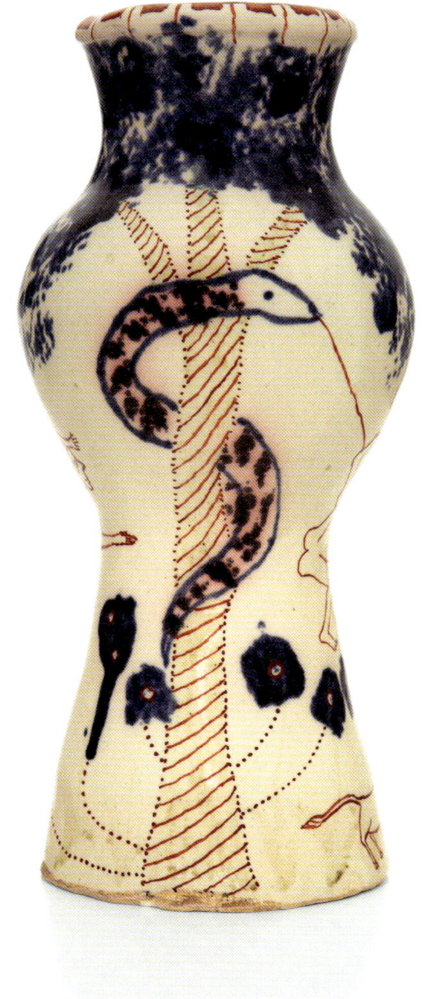

26 January 2017

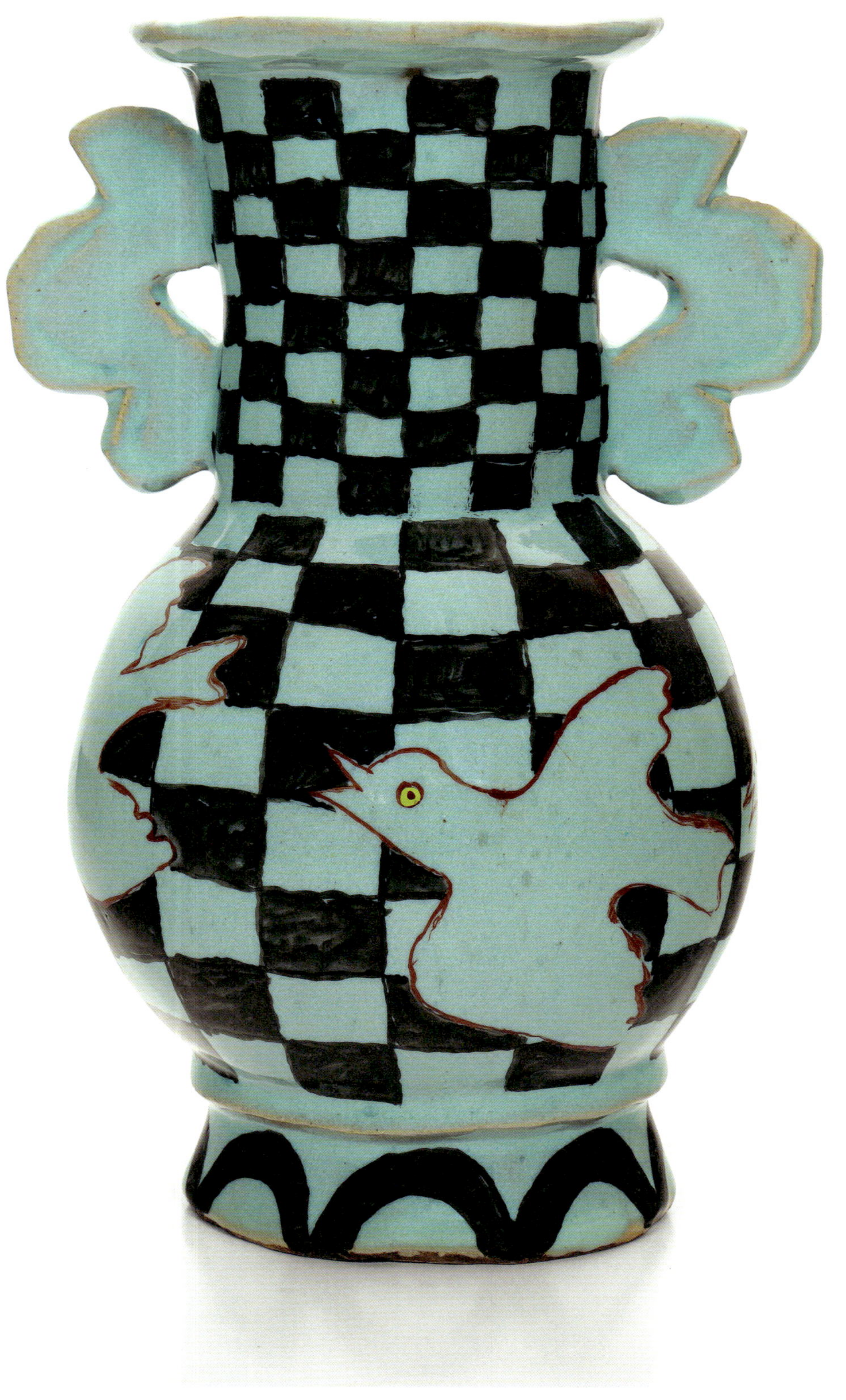

19 September 2019

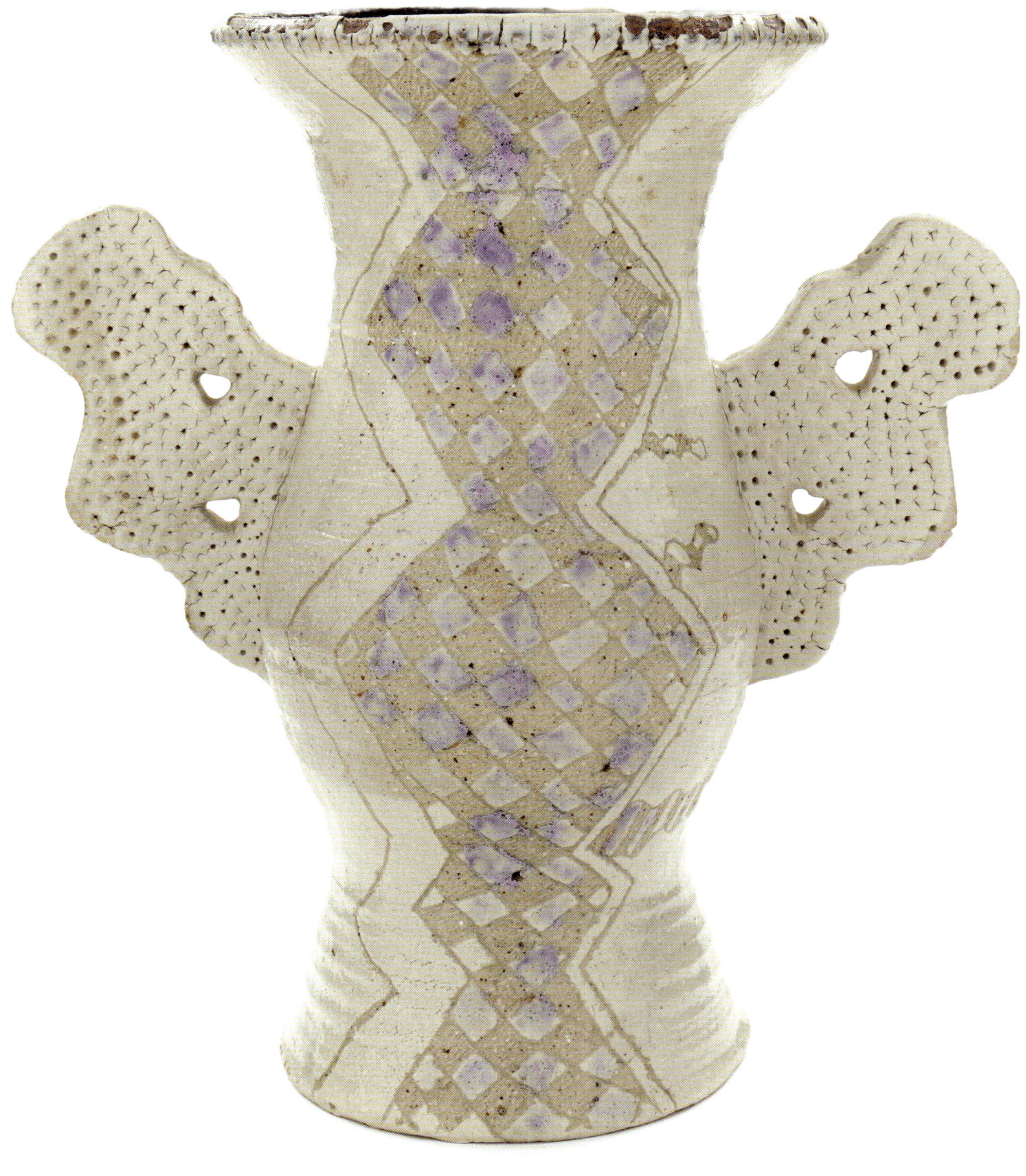

1980s

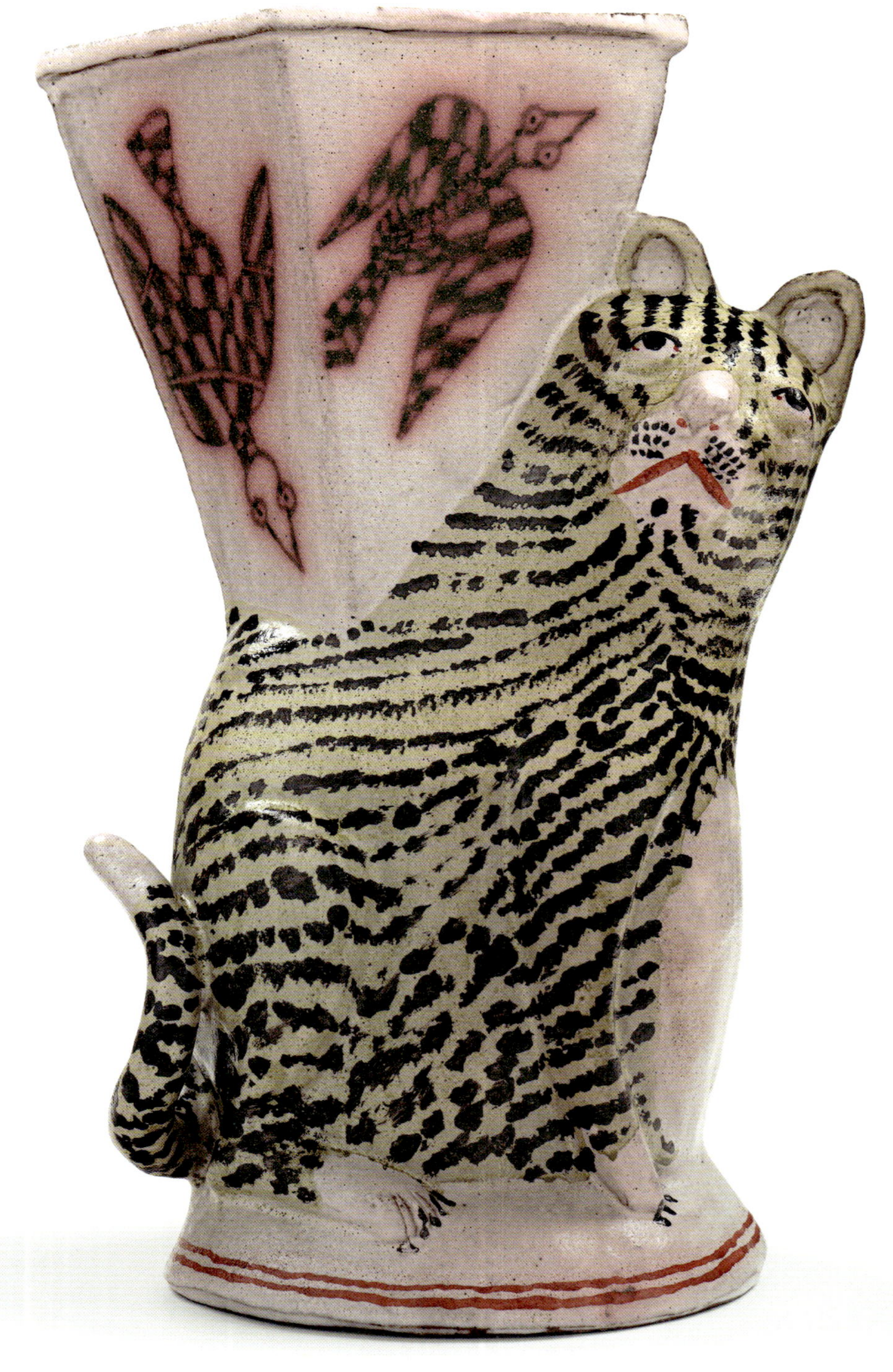

30 June 2021

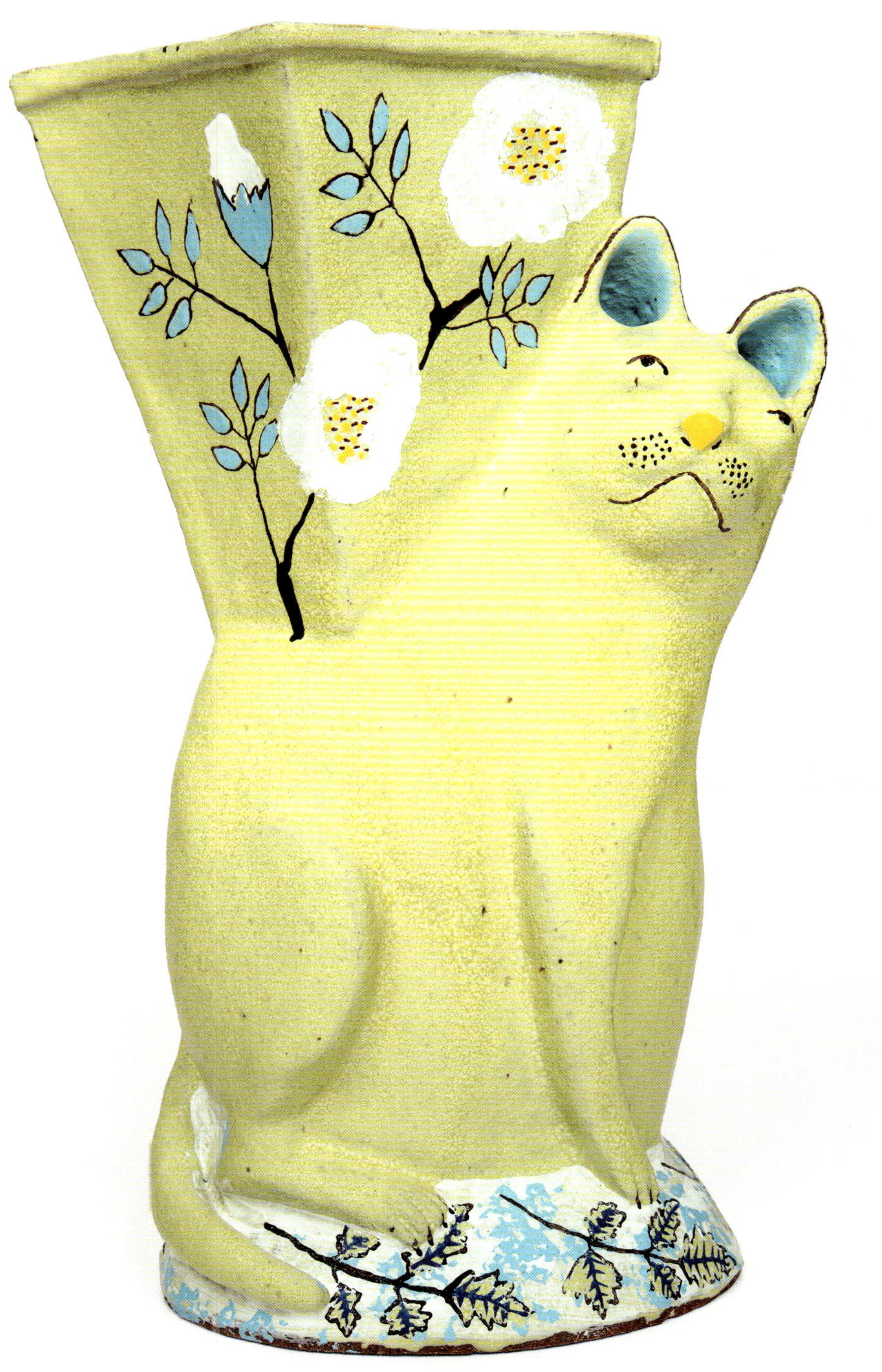

15 April 2016

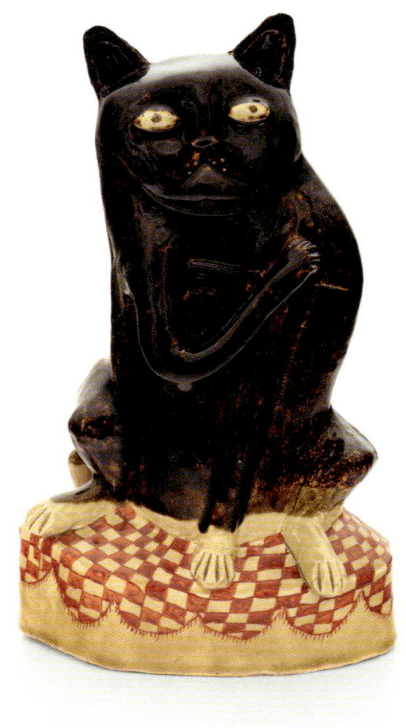

12 August 2018

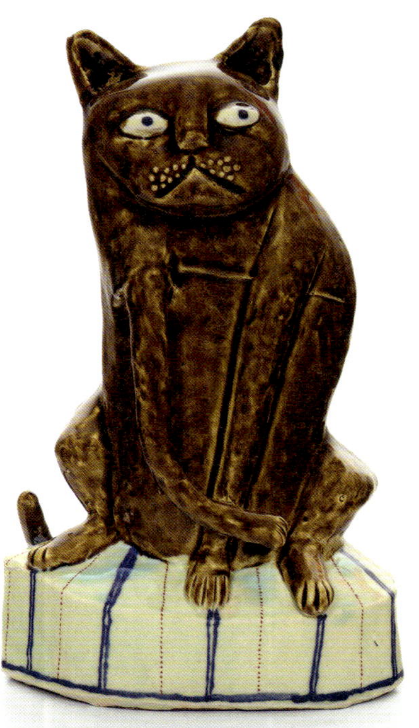

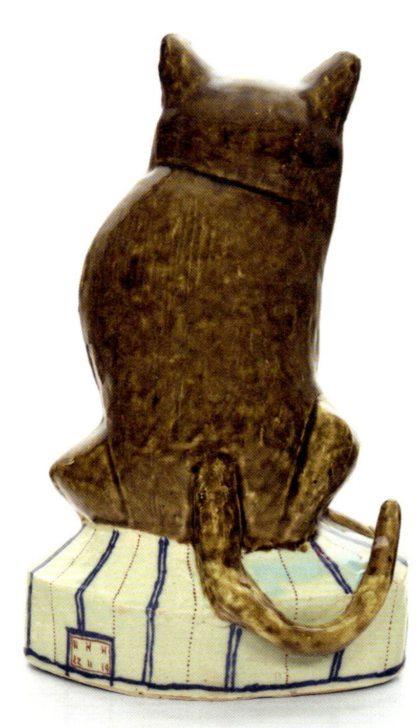

22 November 2019

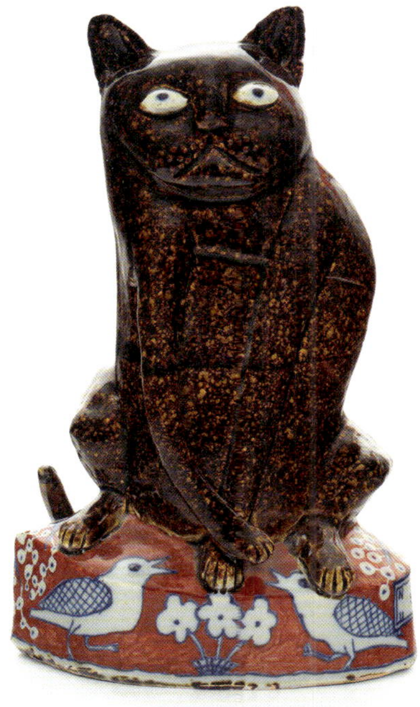

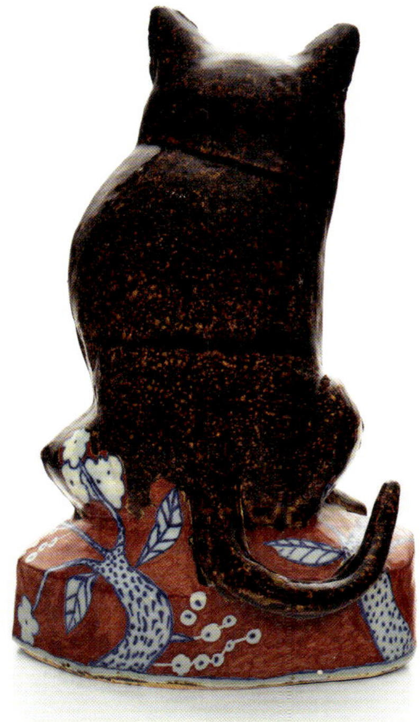

5 November 2018

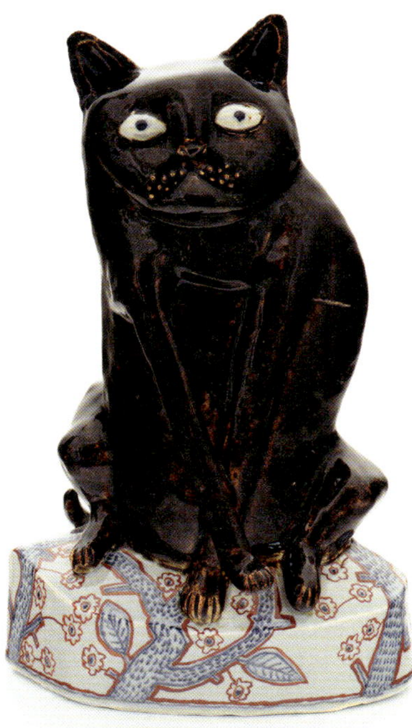

14 September 2018

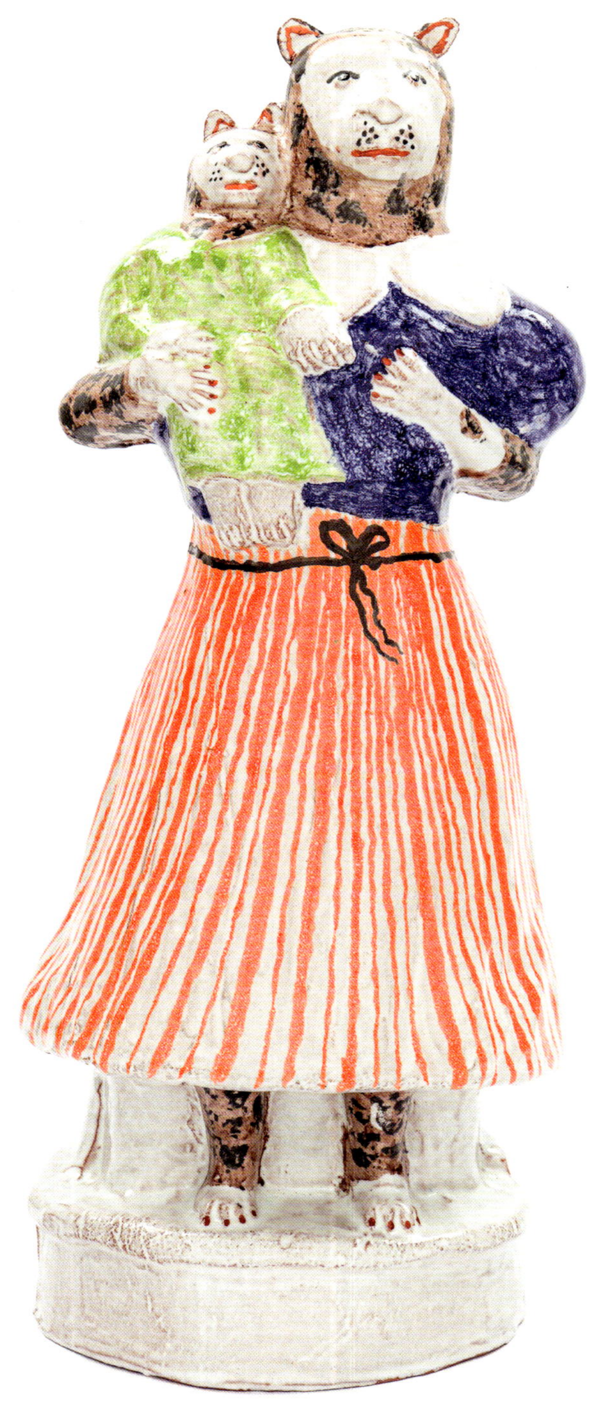

18 May 2021

I like to do people, but people are so in your face, so I do it in the form of a cat. Going right back, people made images of animals, didn't they?

With this cat mother and child, I am paying due homage to an image that has beguiled me for a long time. During the 1960s a friend told me of a Staffordshire pottery figure, quite small, costing £6, of a cat mother and child. I bought it and still have it. It dates from the 1830s to 40s and was meant as a mockery of the snooty, catty nursemaids employed by the rich, with dislike extended to their charges as well. This figure was not popular and is rare as a result. Rather than humans looking cat-like, mine are cats behaving a little like humans and there is no mockery, just wonder at the bond between mother and child. This piece came to mind because I have recently had fairly constant contact with two small boys, pre-walking, pre-talking. Seeing their mothers hold them and, more importantly, holding them myself – it is simply that feeling that I wish to show. The last plate of Goya's *Disasters of War*, titled *Esto es lo verdadero* (This is the truth), was also in my mind.

These two suburban cats find that, in spite of living in a troubled world (the black lines below them), they can still enjoy the moon.

Other cats have supped, washed up and hung out the cloths to dry. Stepping into the yard they are simply transported by a supermoon.

Another cat is interrupted while reading, which I suppose to be myself behaving politely.

The fat cats have their origin in my being fed up with a terrible neighbour. The first ones had a stoneware glaze, and one, in earthenware, seems to have been snapped in a frowsty bedroom of the famous bed by Tracey Emin.

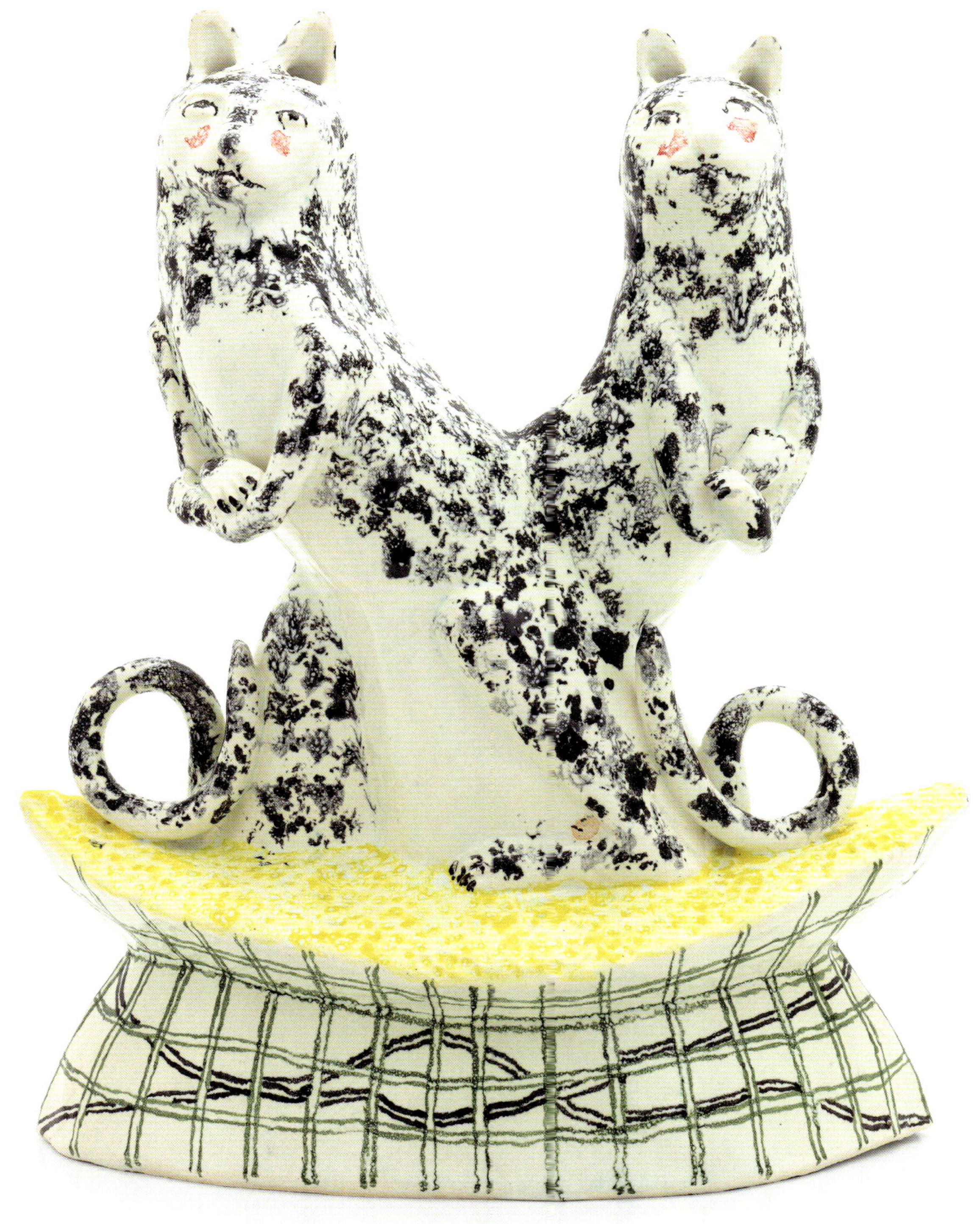

20 April 2021

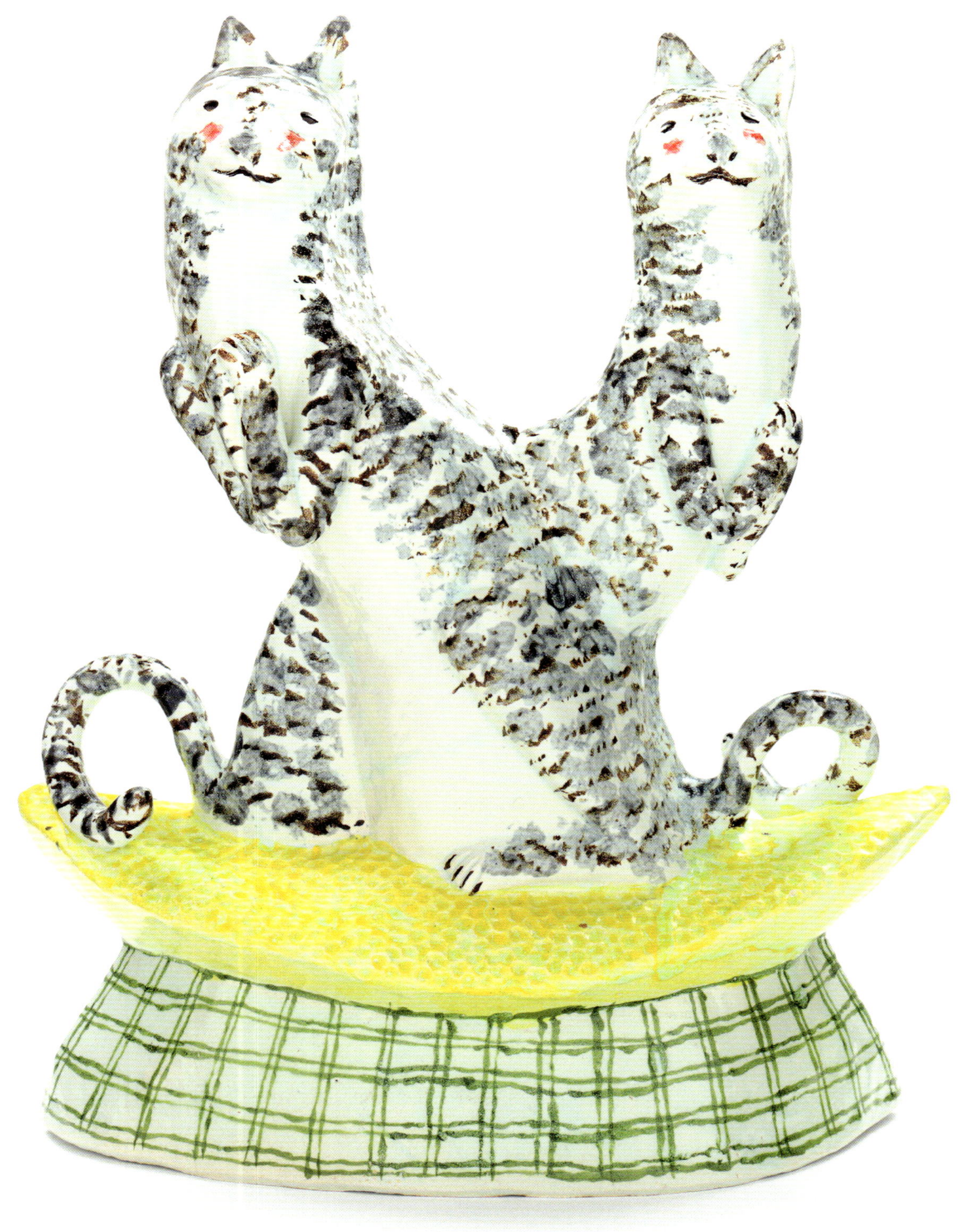

23 March 2021

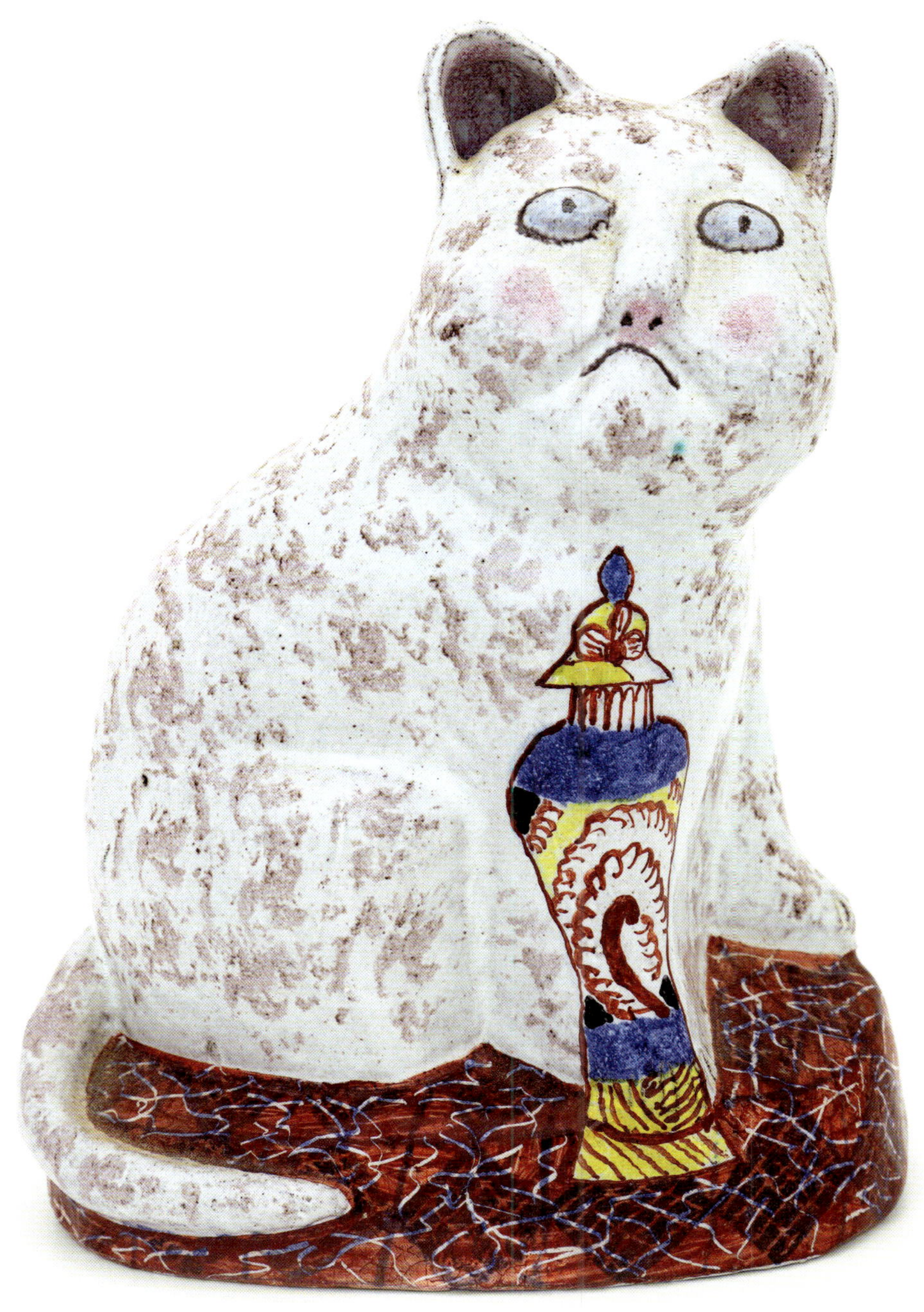

1 December 1995

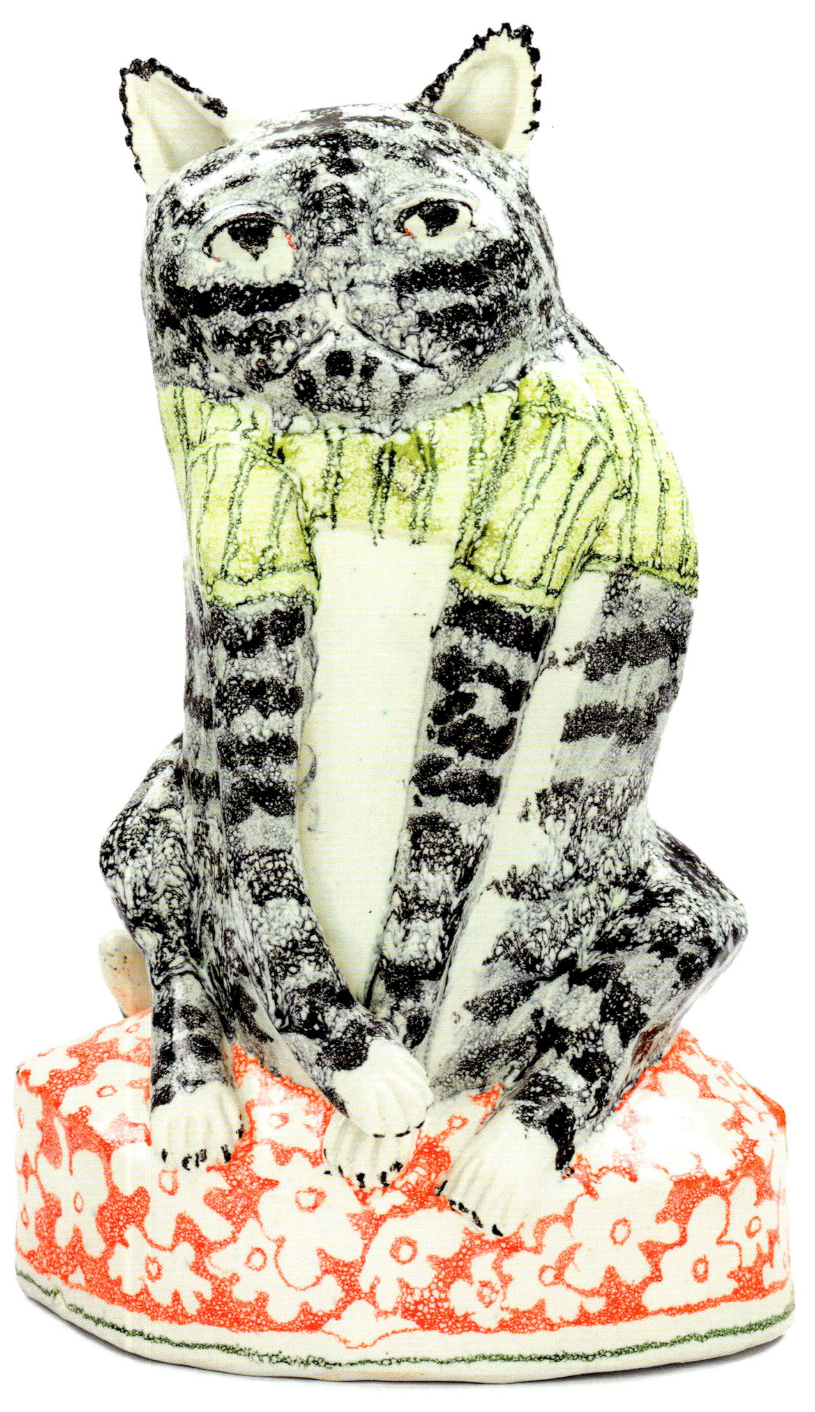

14 January 2021

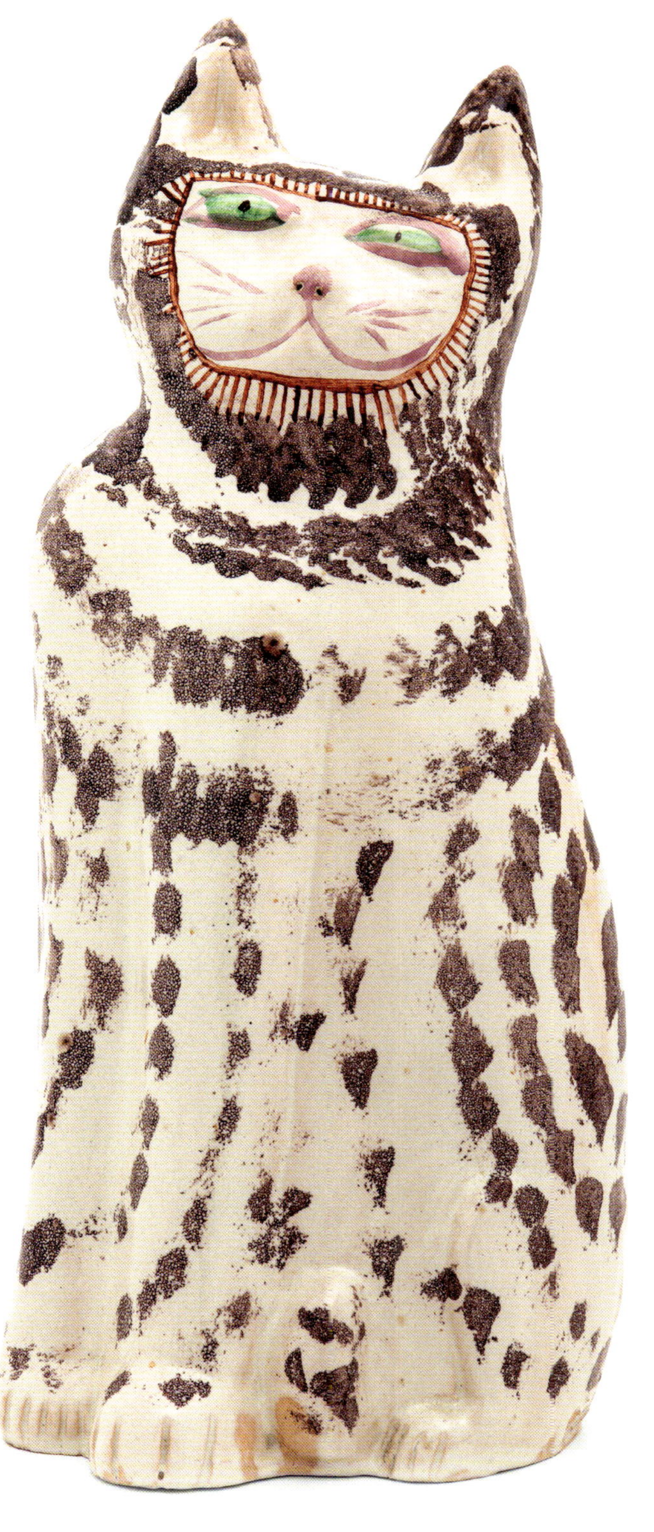

c.1991

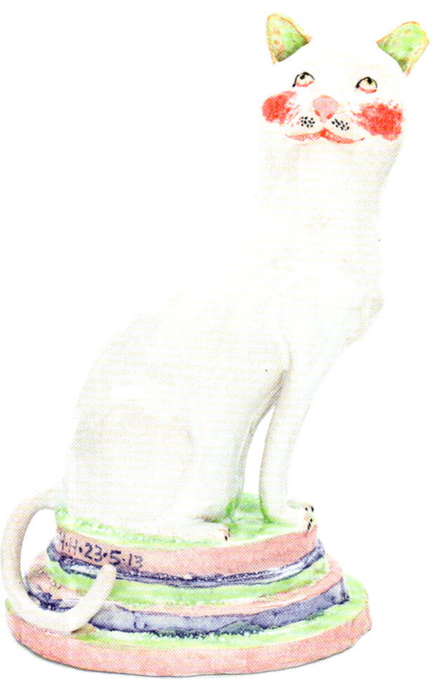

23 May 2013

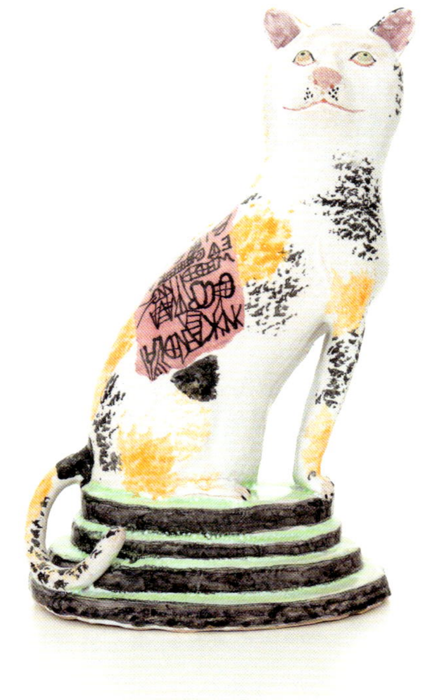

2 May 2013

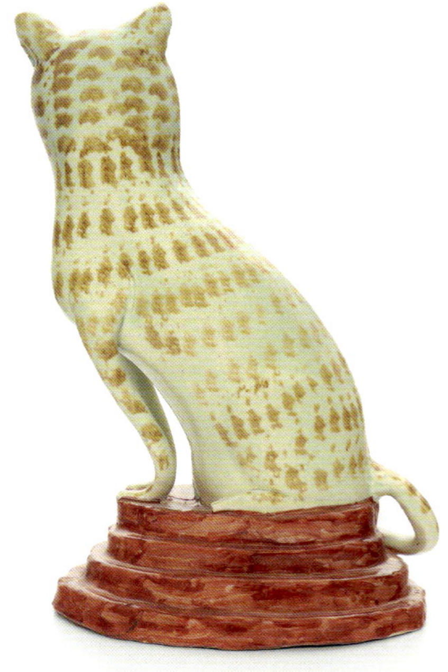

25 November 2019

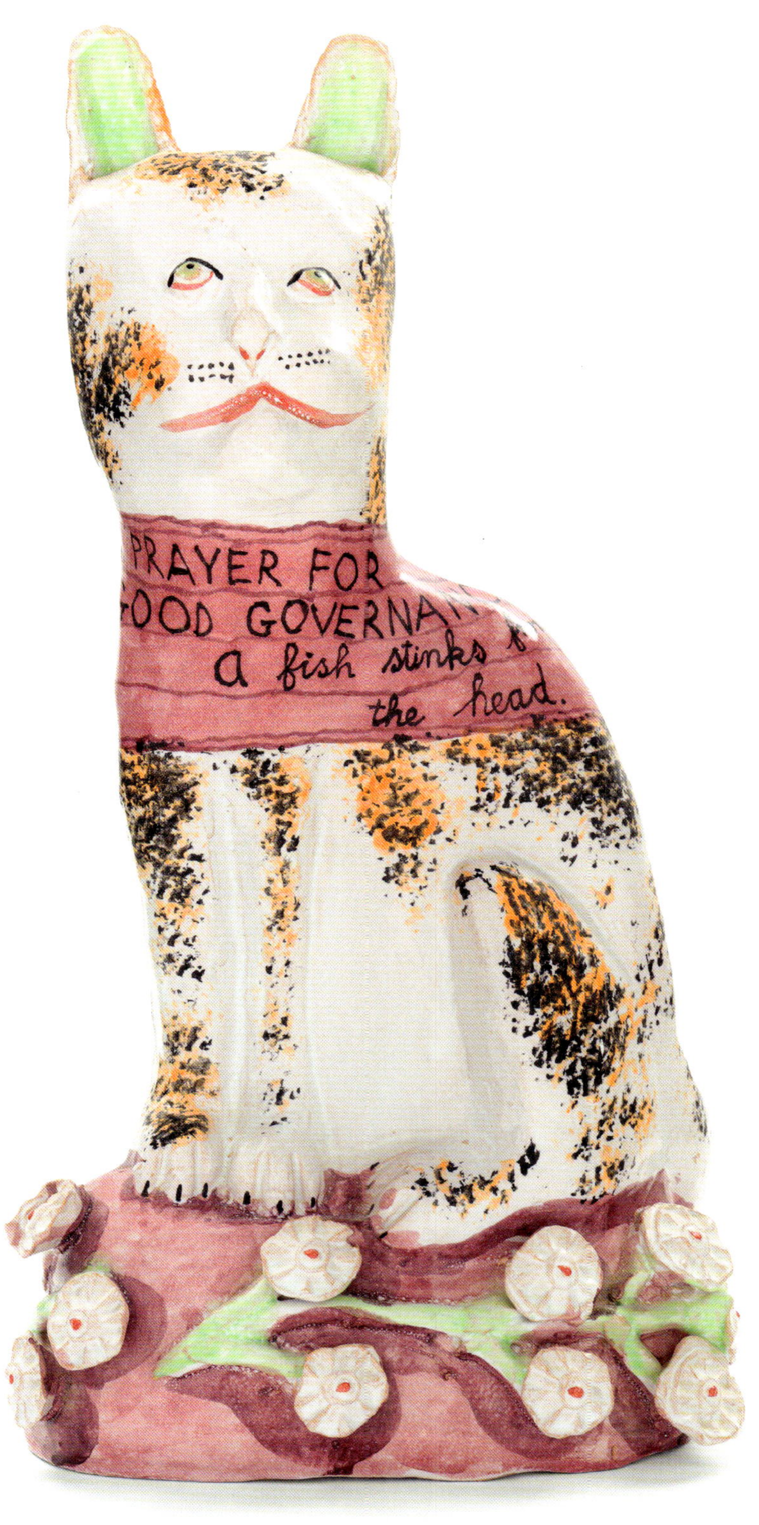

3 April 2013

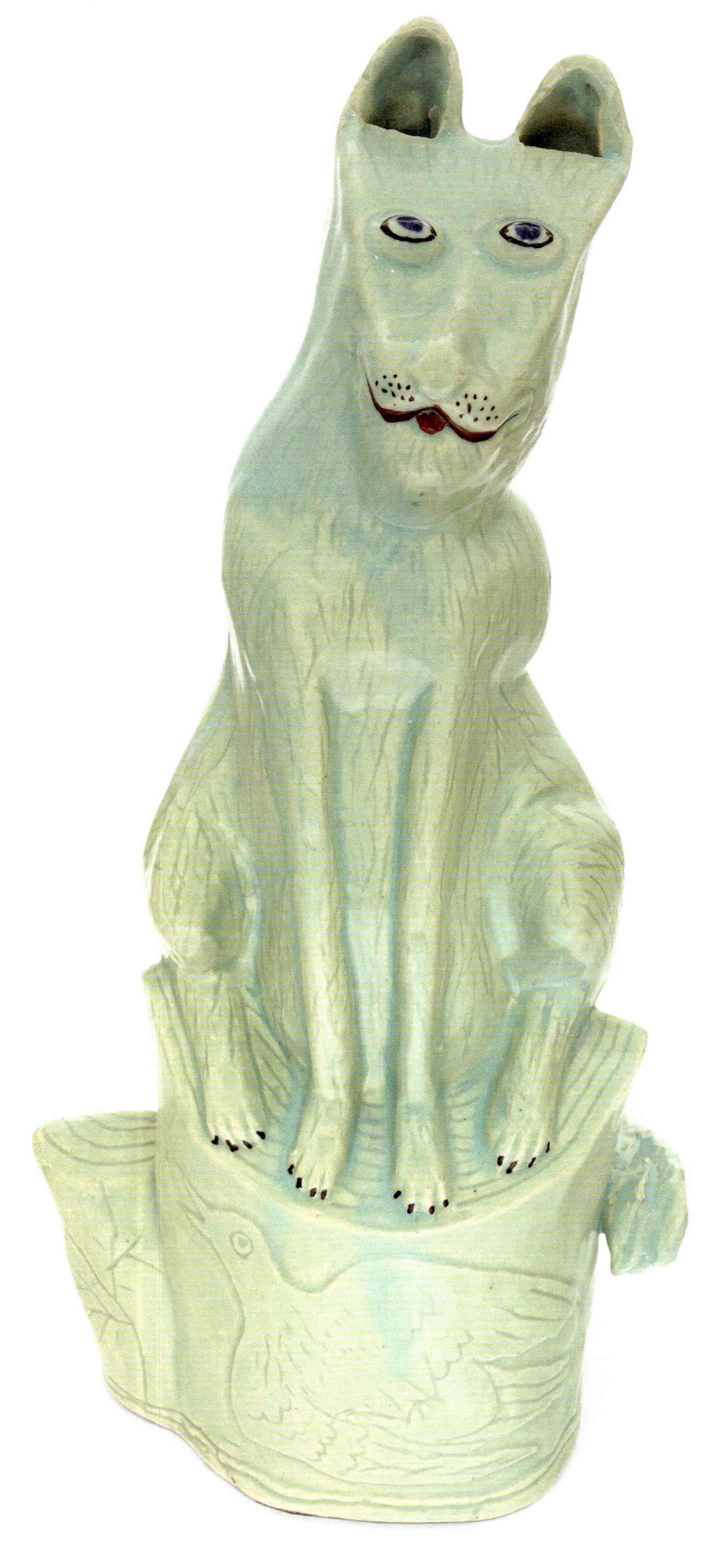

27 May 2019

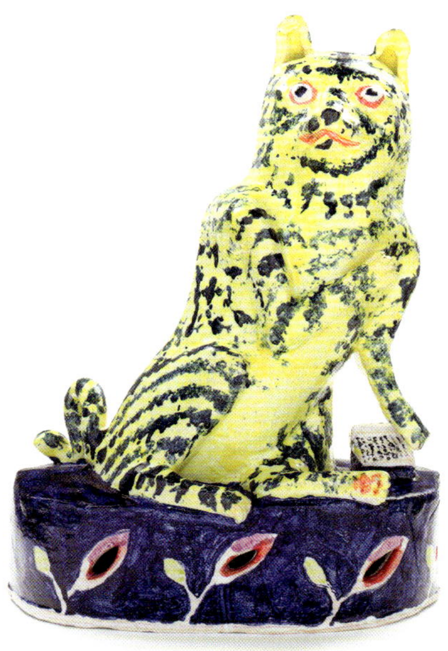

22 March 2021

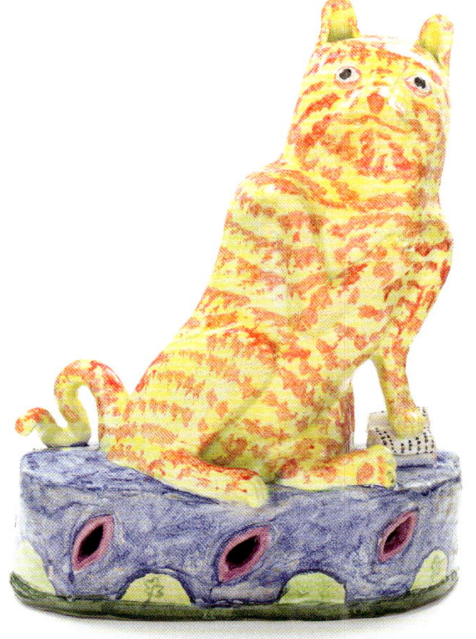

17 March 2021

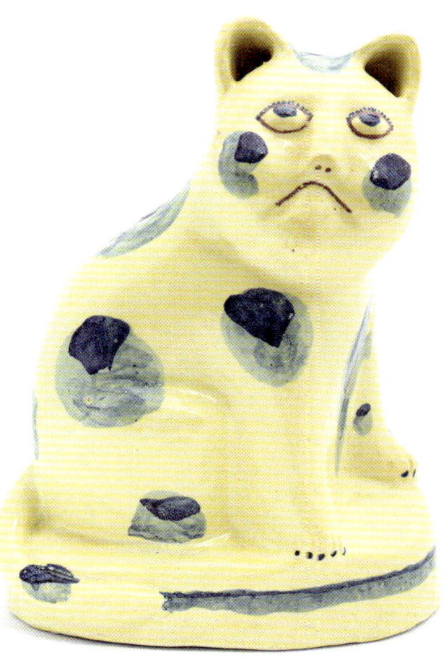

3 December 1996

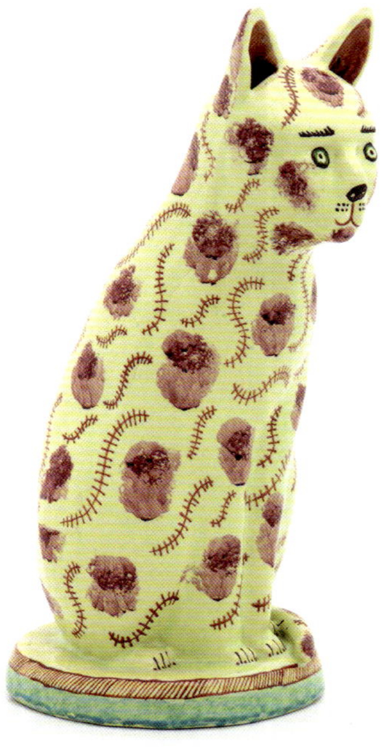

9 November 2006

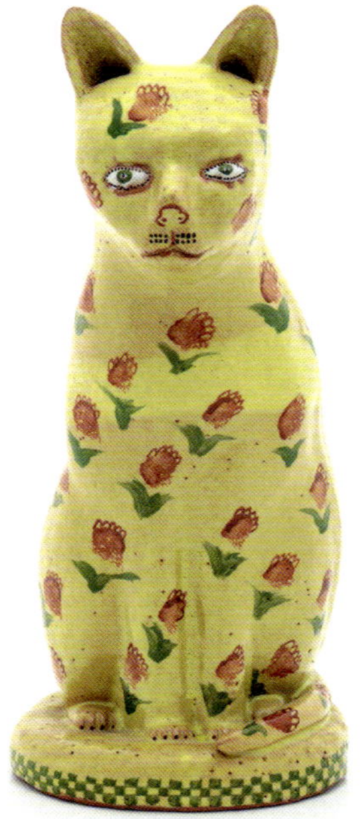

16 December 2007

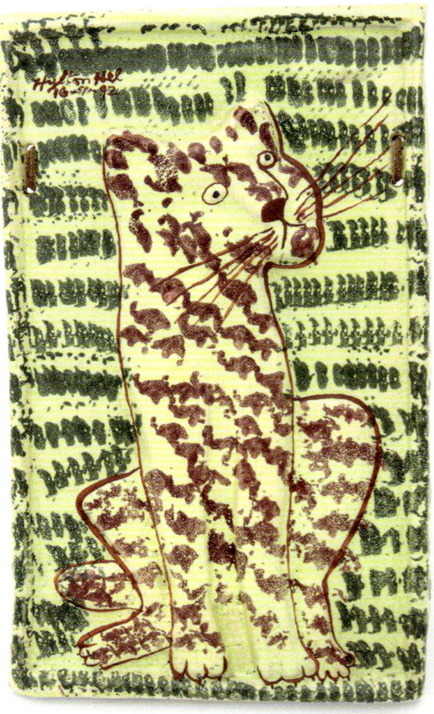

16 July 1992

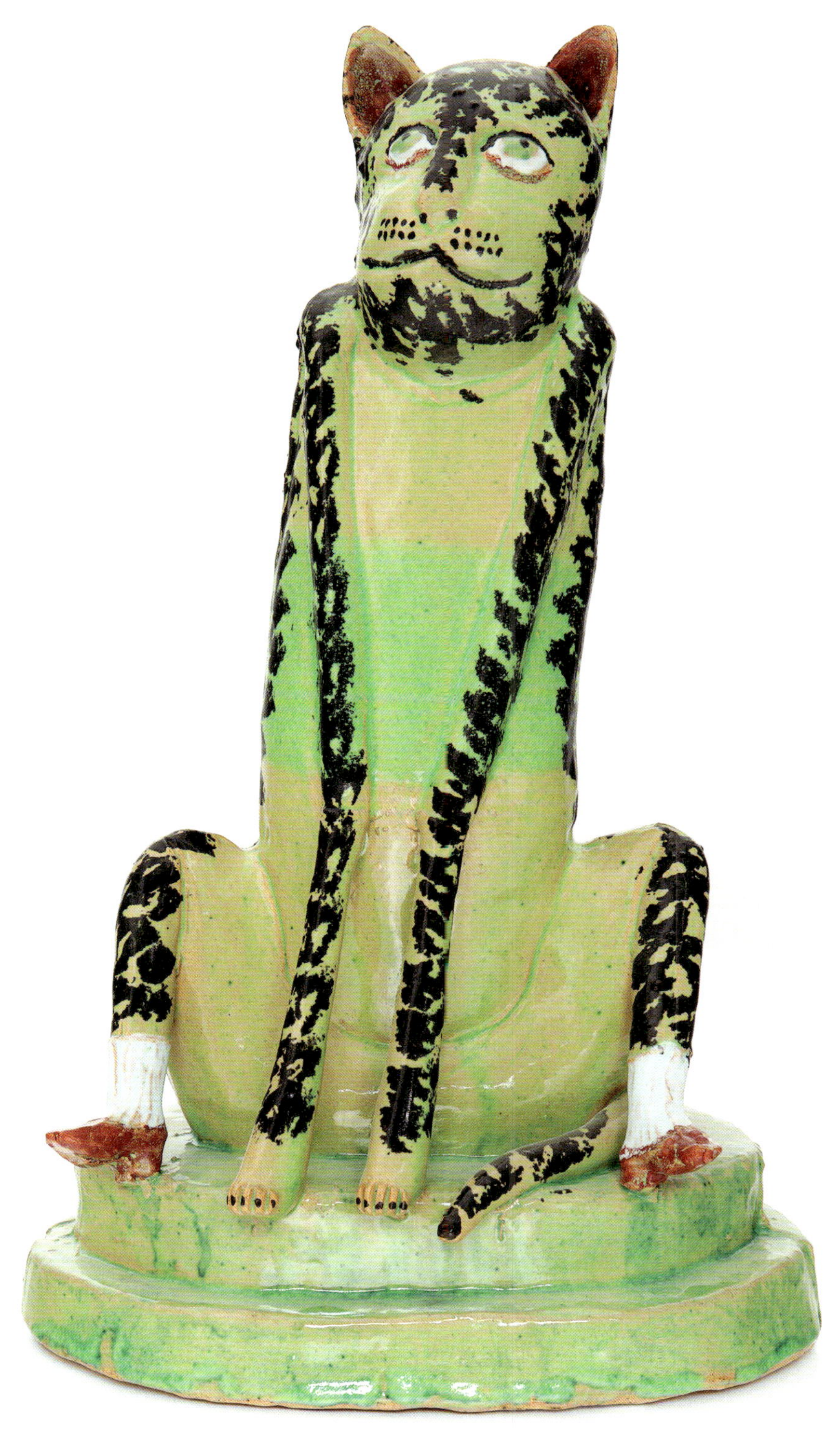

19 February 2013

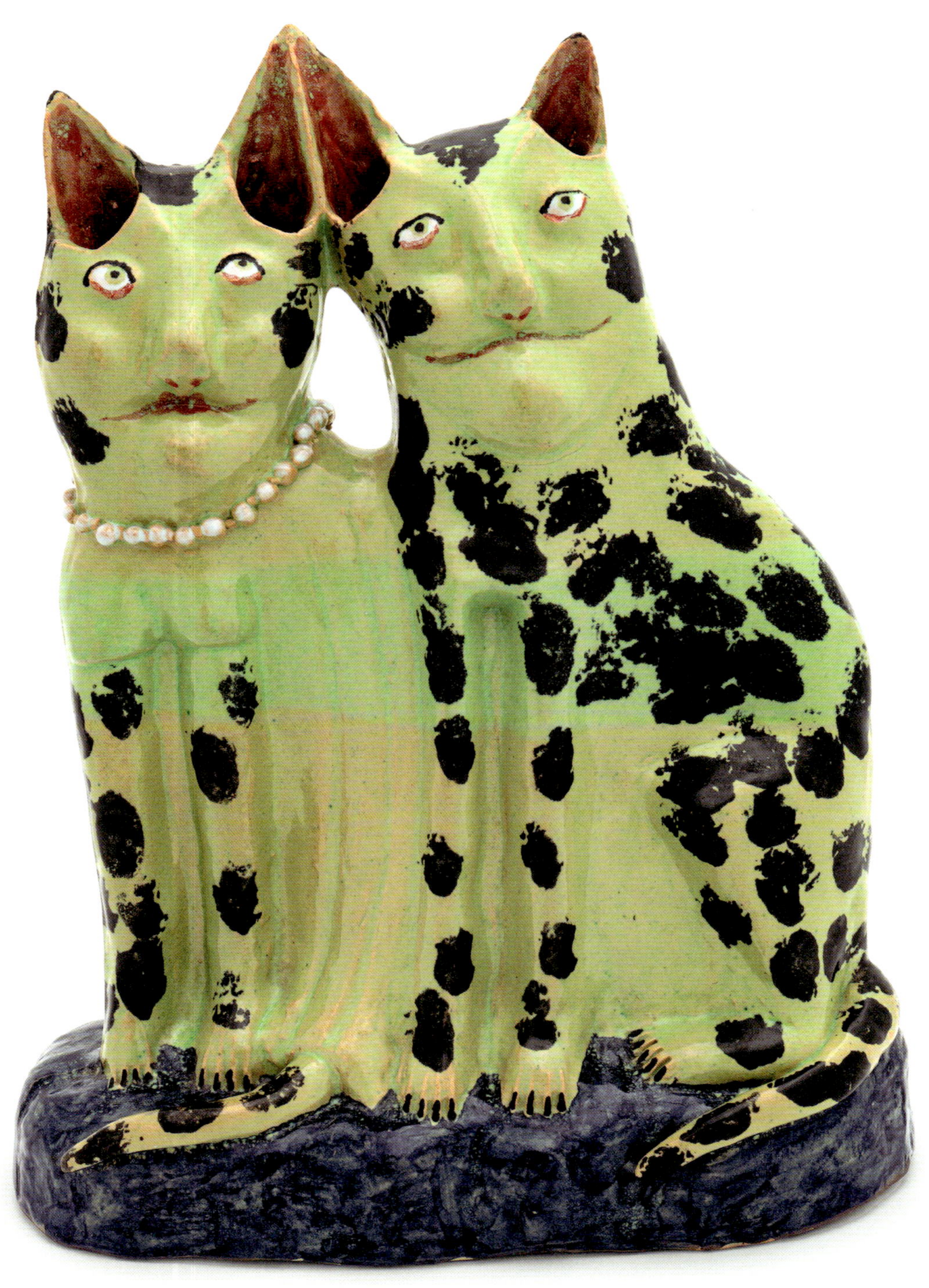

8 March 2013

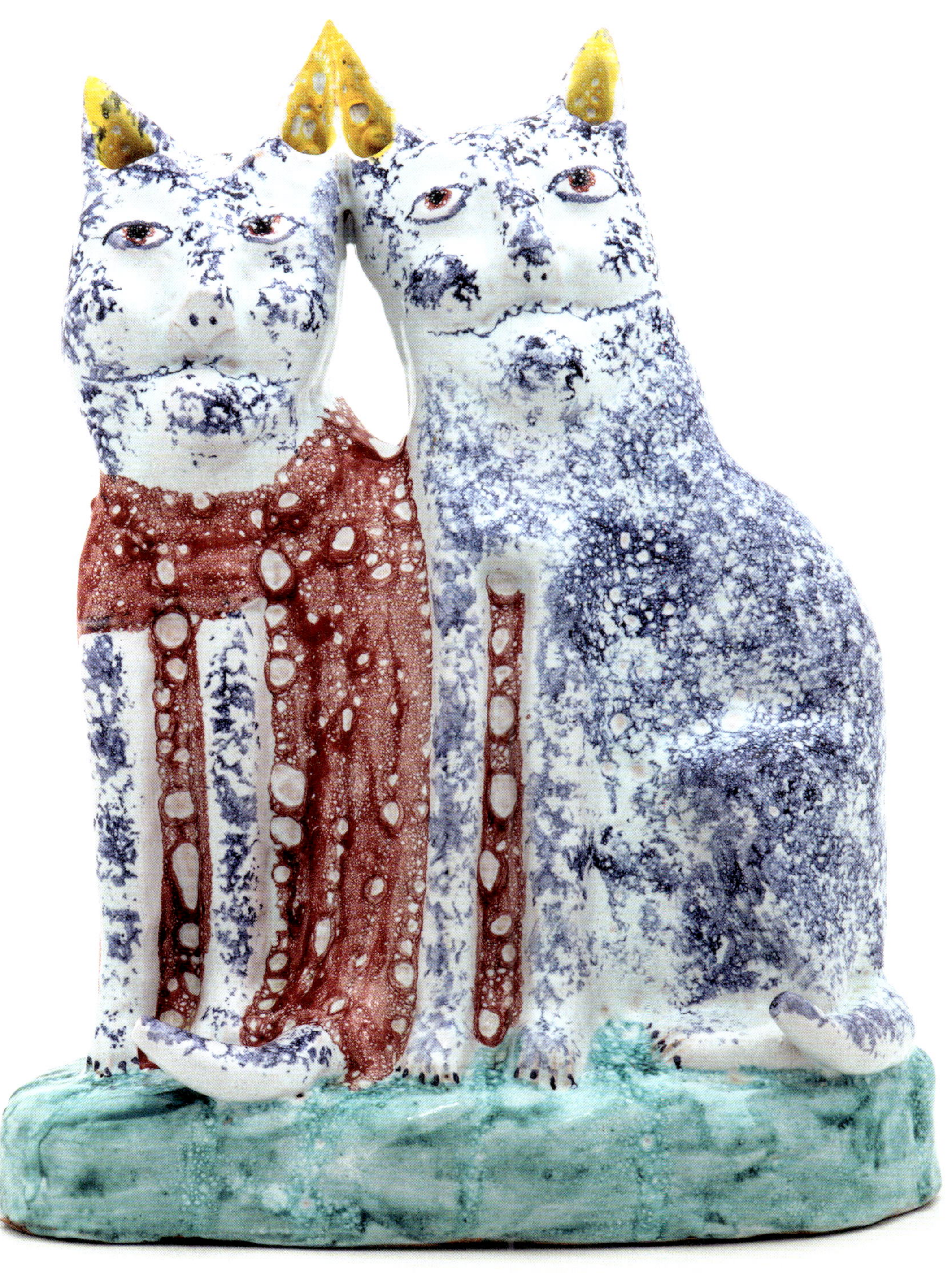

16 February 2012

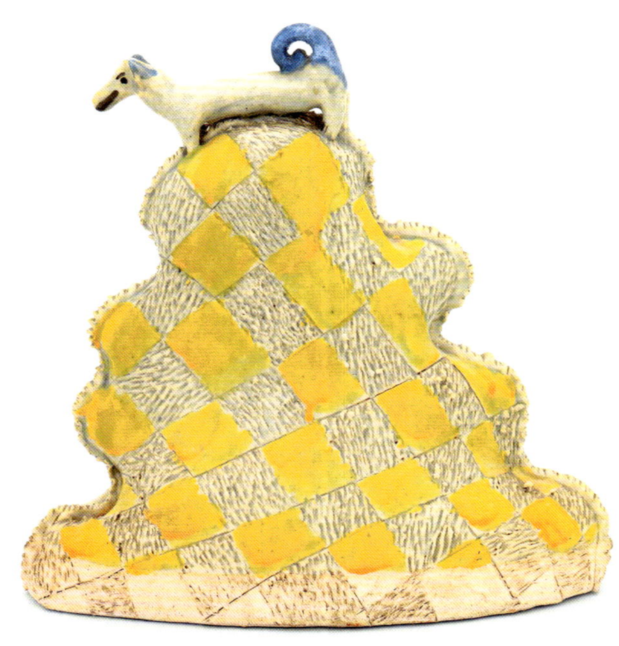

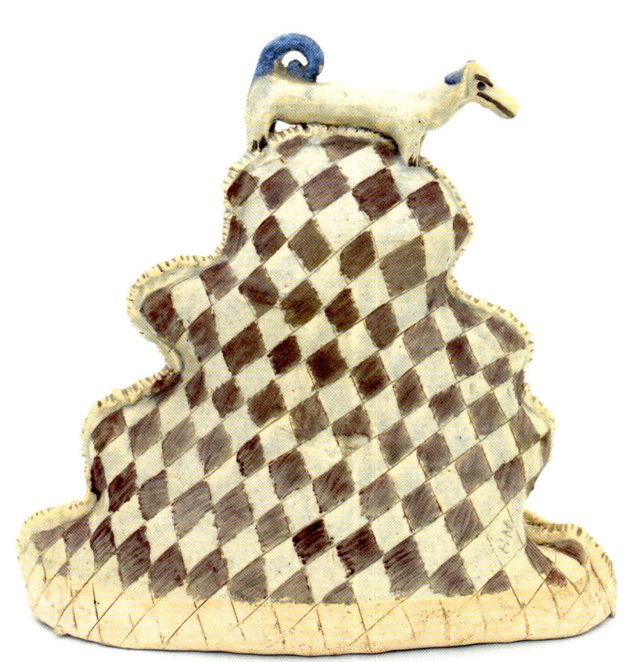

1970s

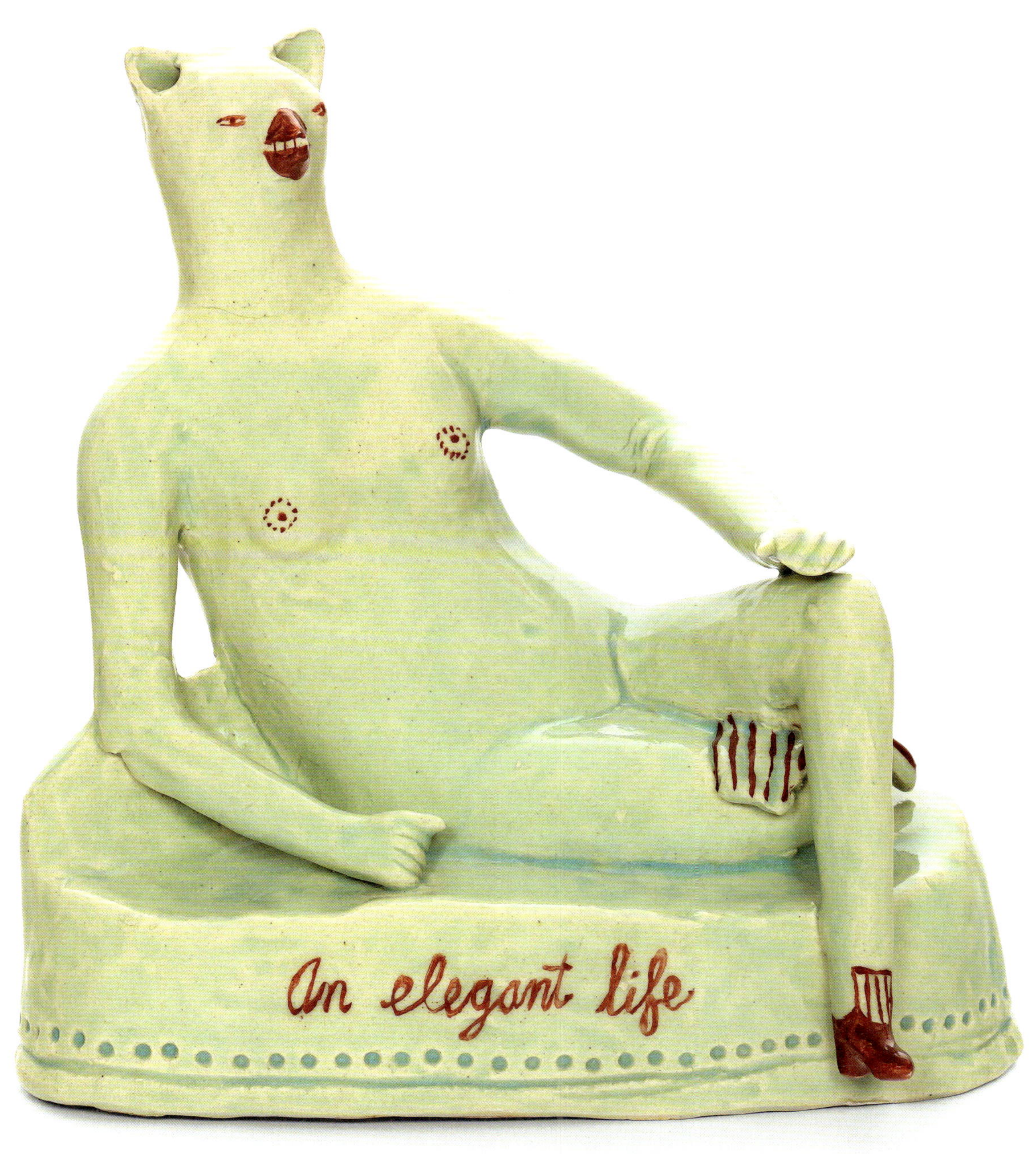

25 November 2019

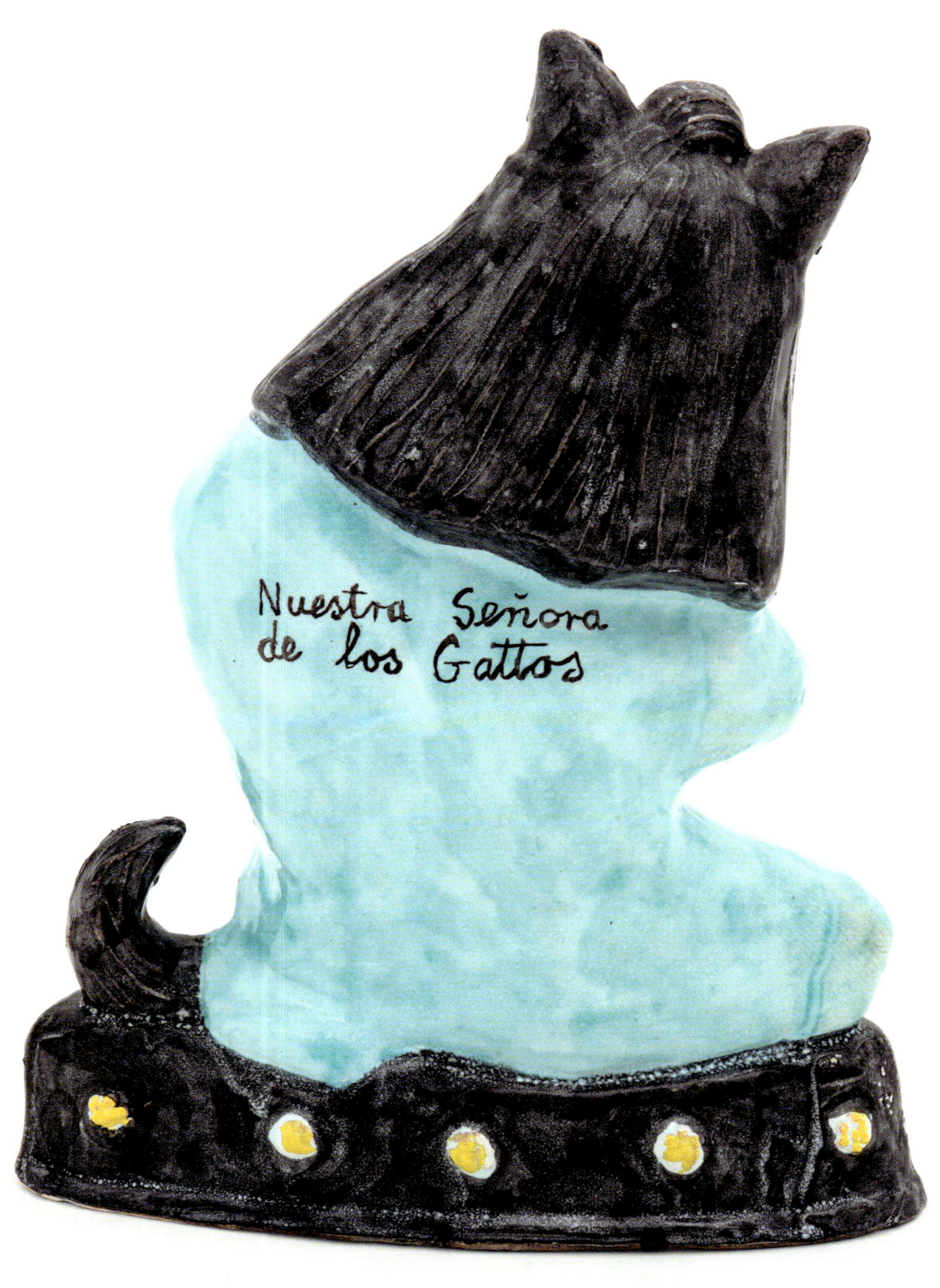

22 November 2010

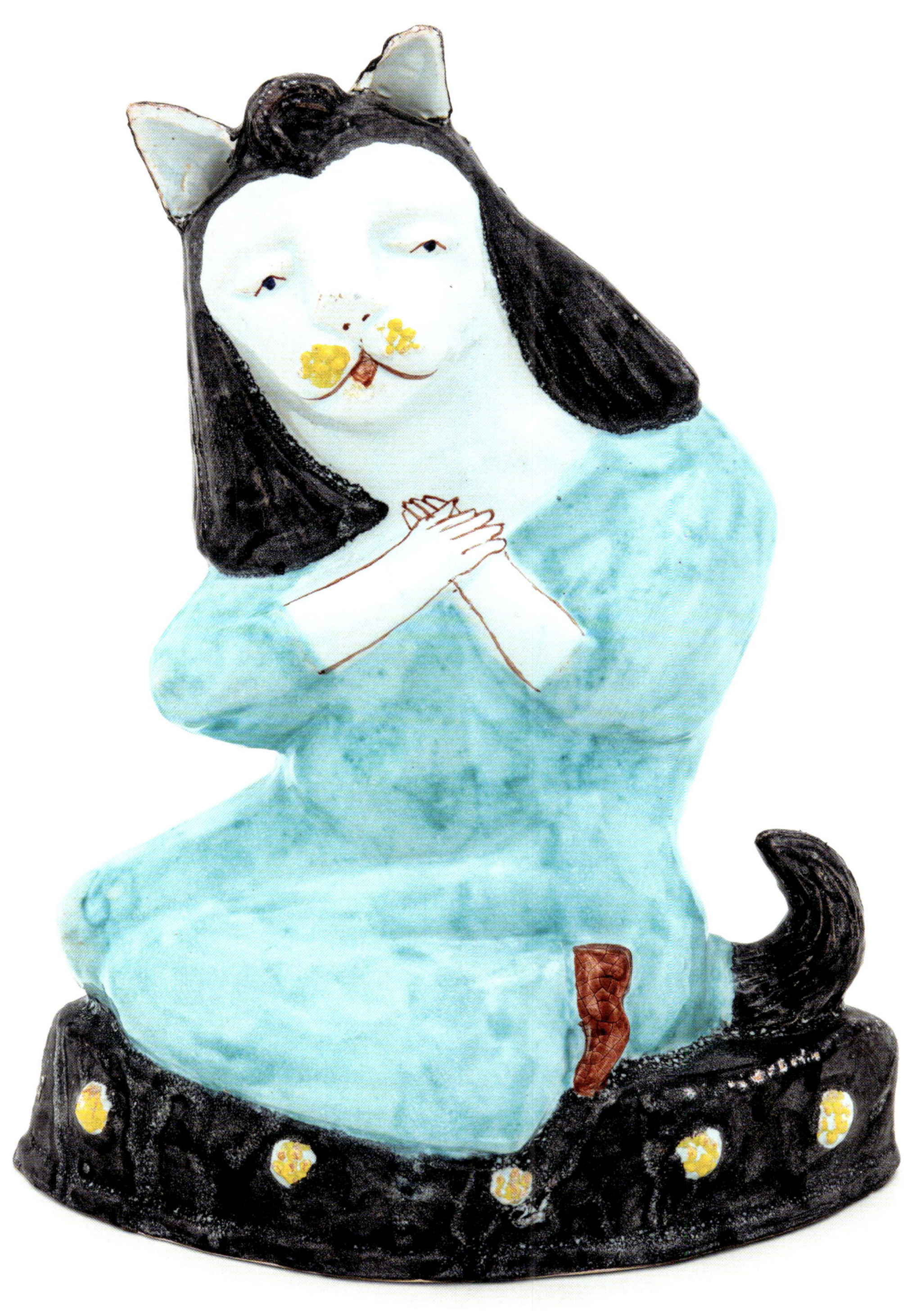

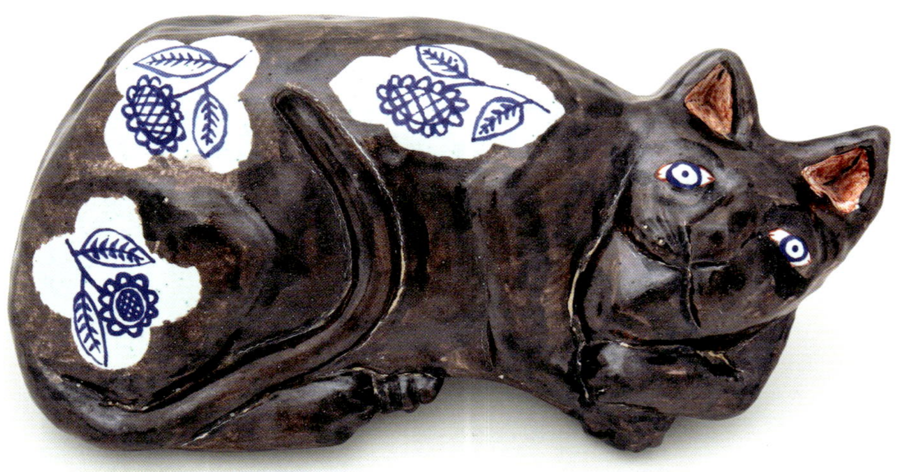

5 February 2003

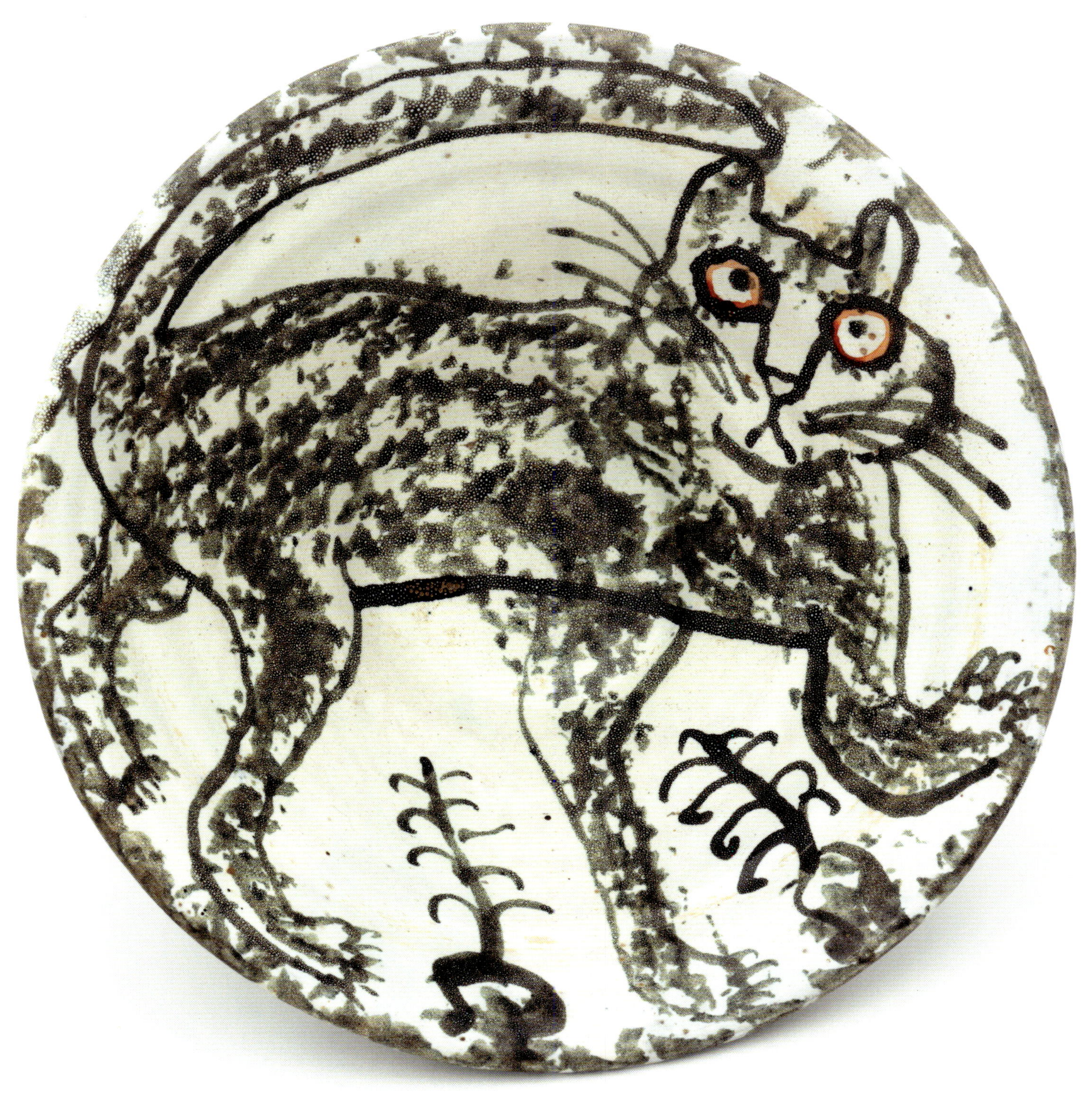

Late 1980s

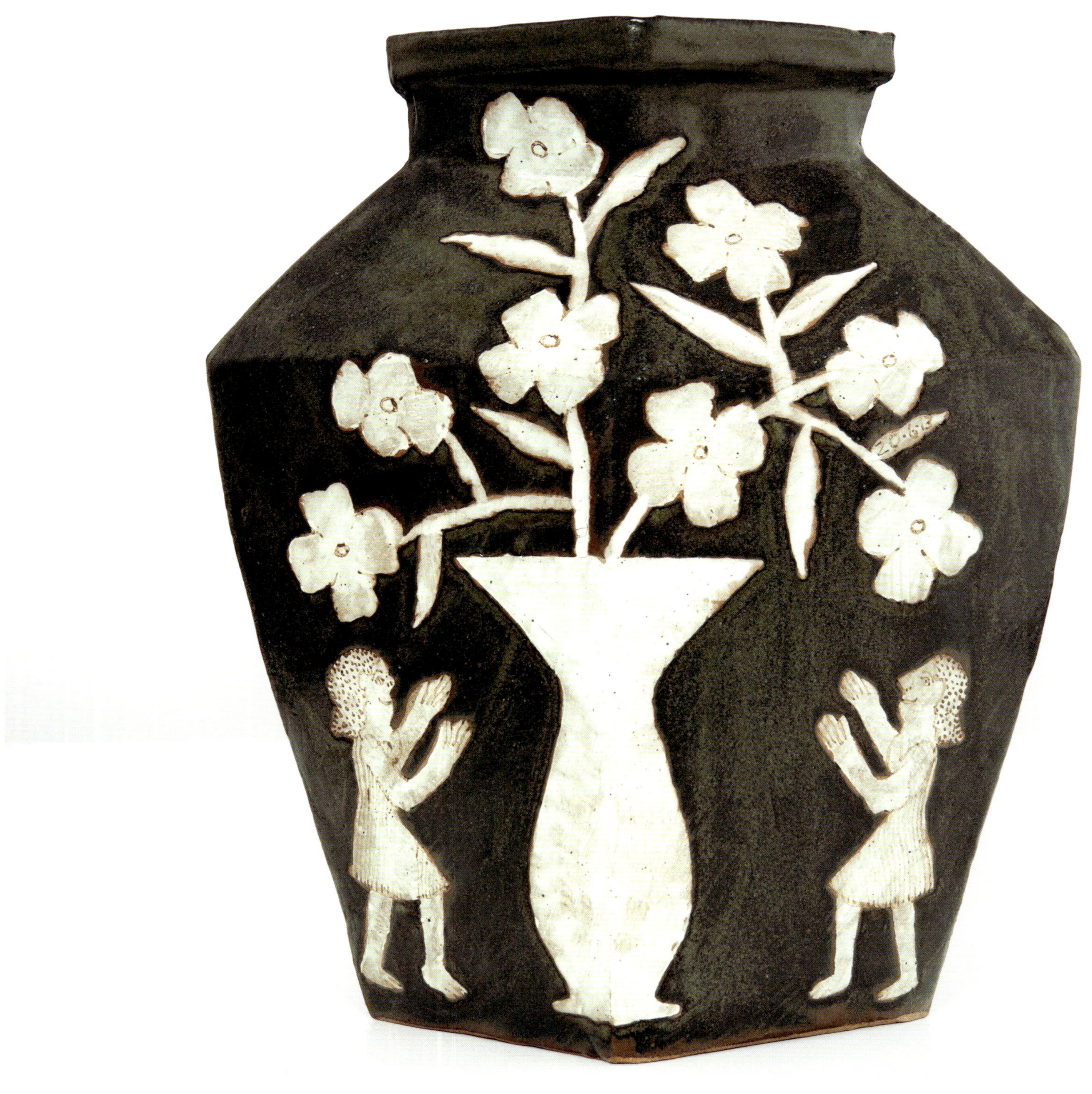

24 June 2013

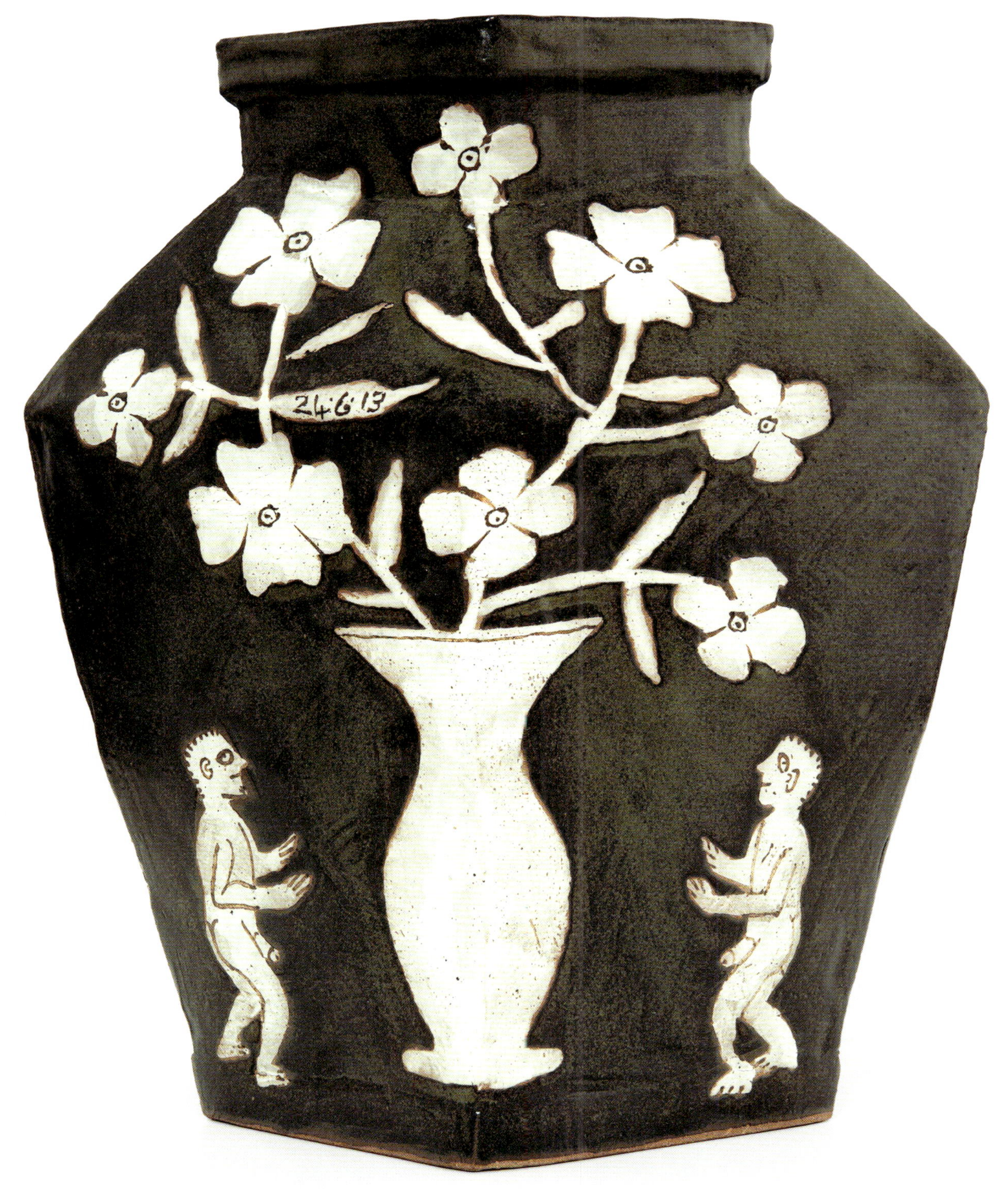
24.6.13

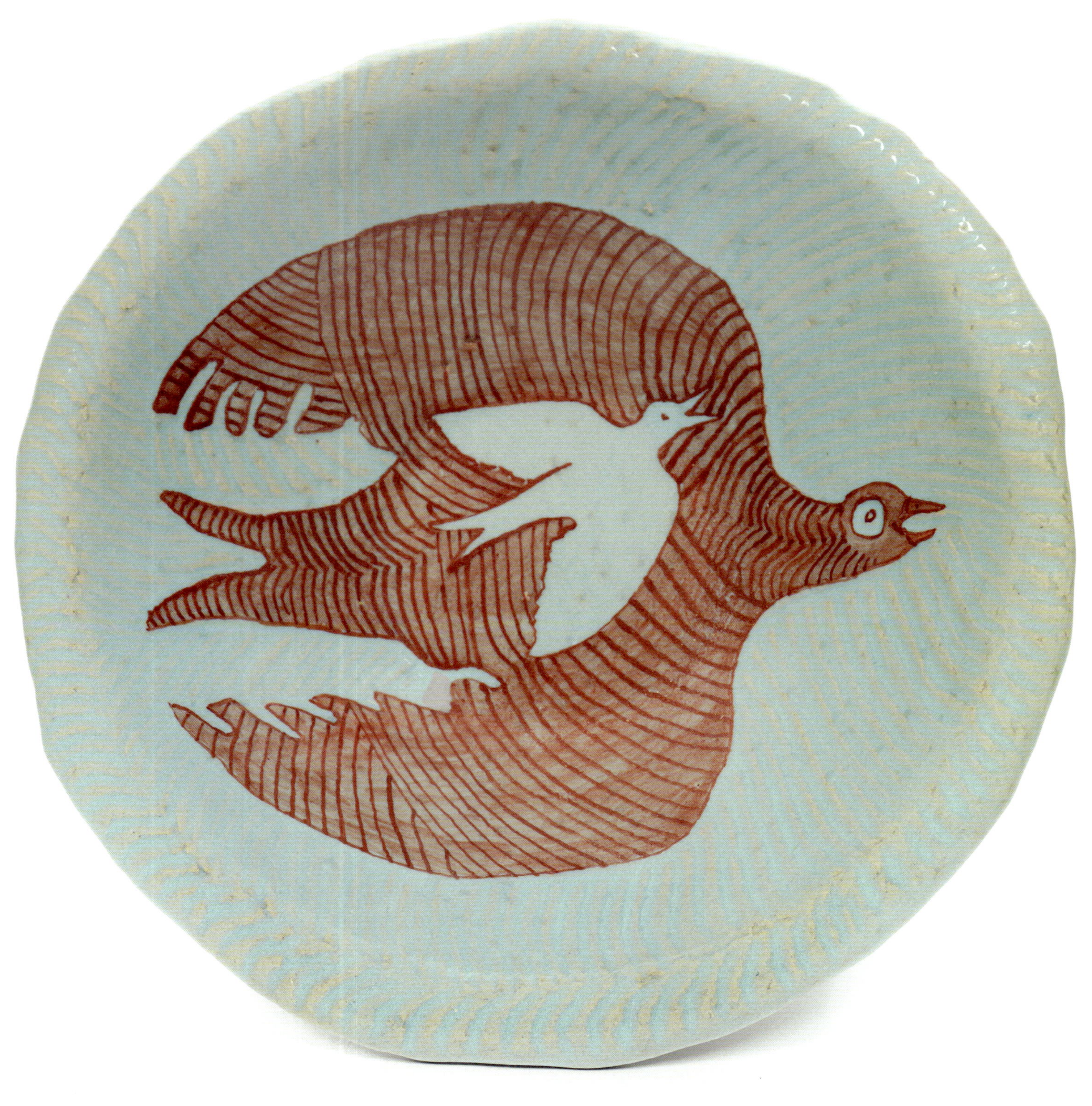

29 September 2019

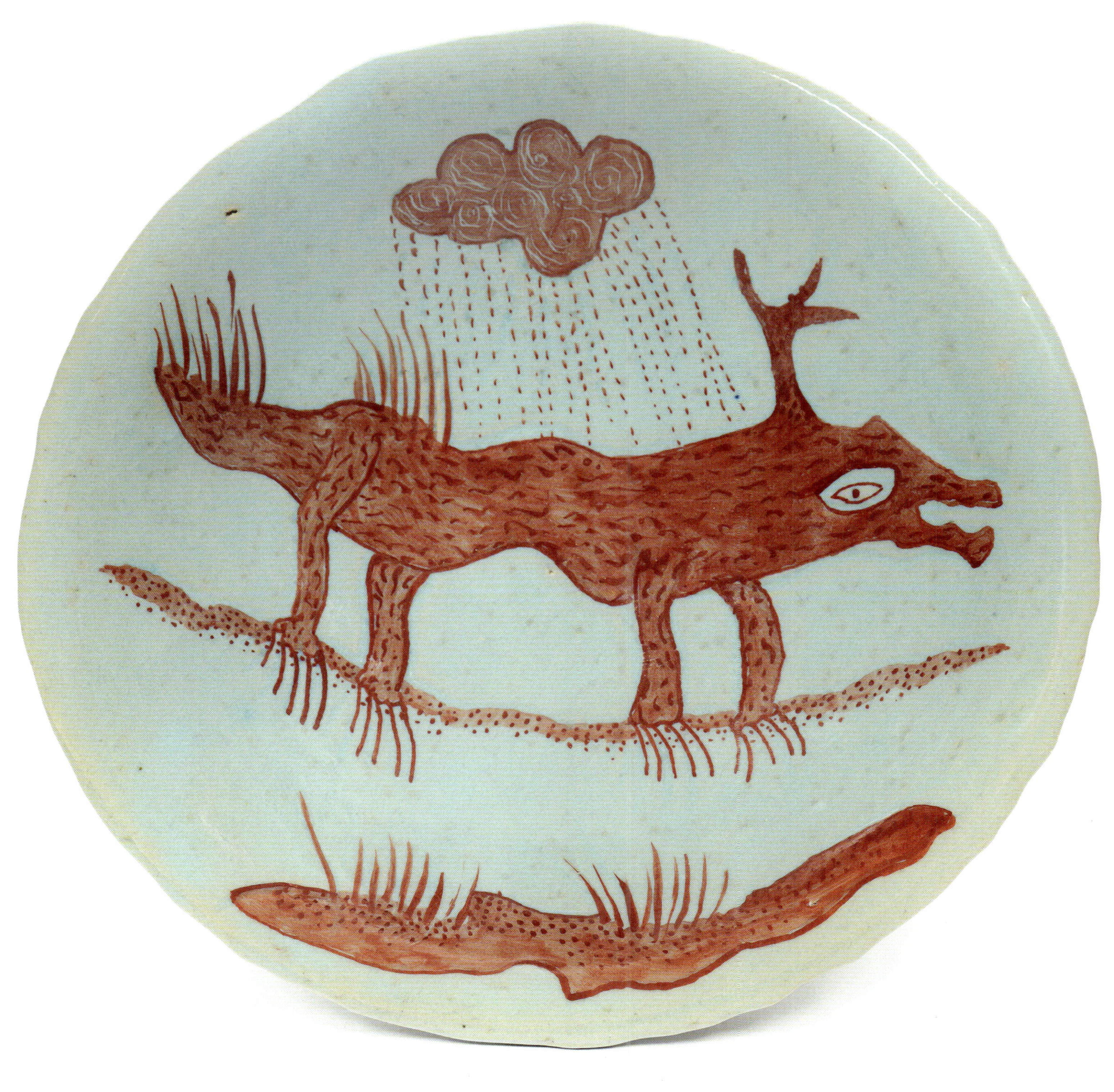

26 September 2019

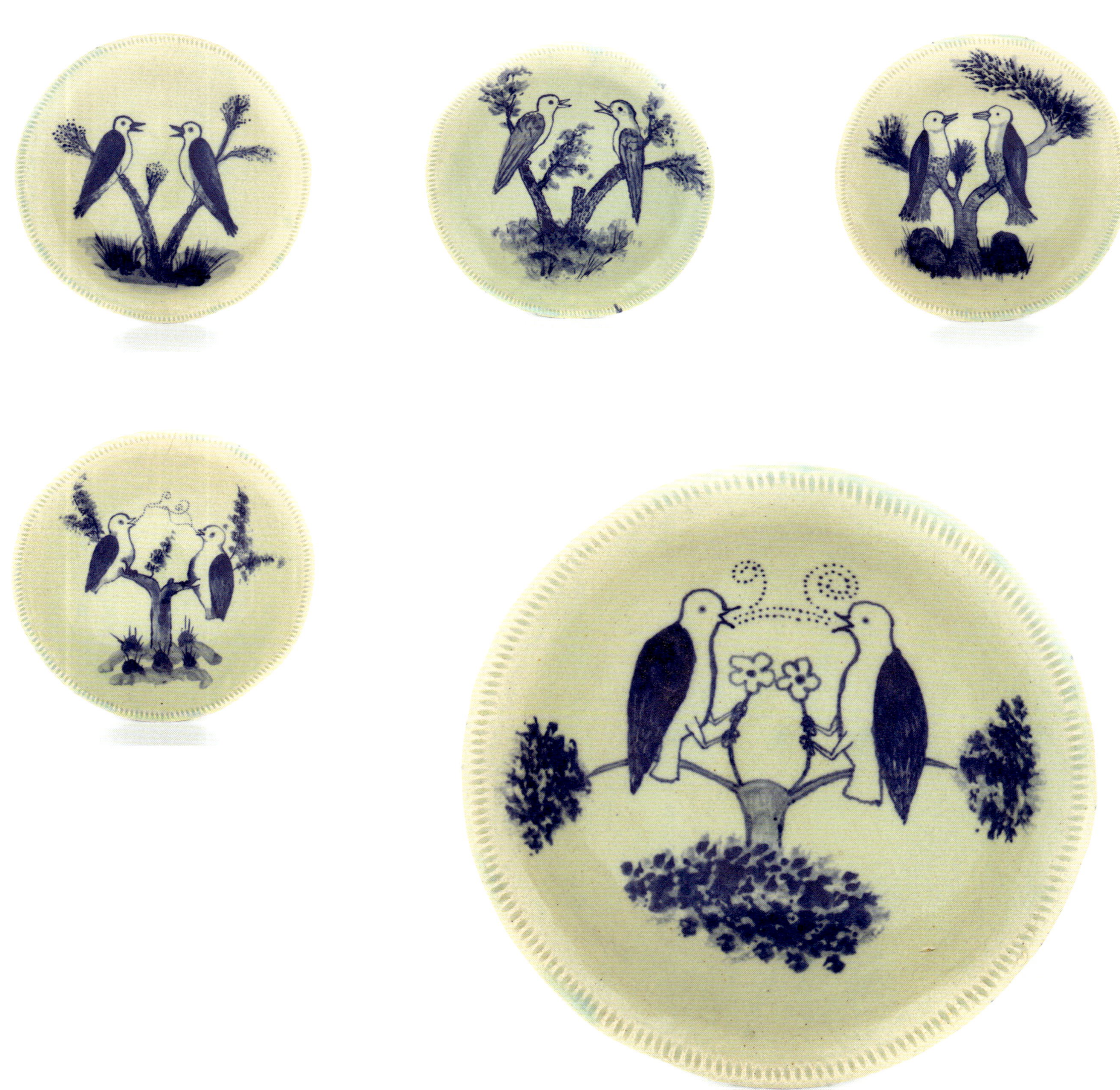

12 February to 4 March 2020

There's a dark colour that I've used recently, a mix of black iron and cobalt carbonate. In Beijing in 2019 I bought a vase with a little handle on the side and a chip out, and it's got a very impure cobalt – that was the inspiration for this mix of colour.

I used the birds from one of those blue and white things I bought in a bundle. There's one with two birds, and so it was interesting for me to make these things with two birds. They're all different, but it's that idea – I'm looking for an idea like that, one thing, to inspire the series.

I was thinking about ancient Japanese images from temples, where you have a monk or such and there's like a little iron thing that's coming out of the mouth, with a little figure at the end, like a speech bubble for the sculpture. And so, for some of them, I made the singing visible.

These funny little things are in the head while you are working, and respond to the immediate stuff you are working with. It could be green paint off the brush, which otherwise you might twist and turn to make into a tree with leaves, but just that green, as it were, strives to exist in its own right. How could it best manifest itself? I suppose I'm trying to make things that just exist, as if they've always existed, and a reluctance to say, 'These hands totally made that.' In other words, calling something into existence without actually being there for every little something of its manifestation. To have something come into being without, as it were, totally controlling it.

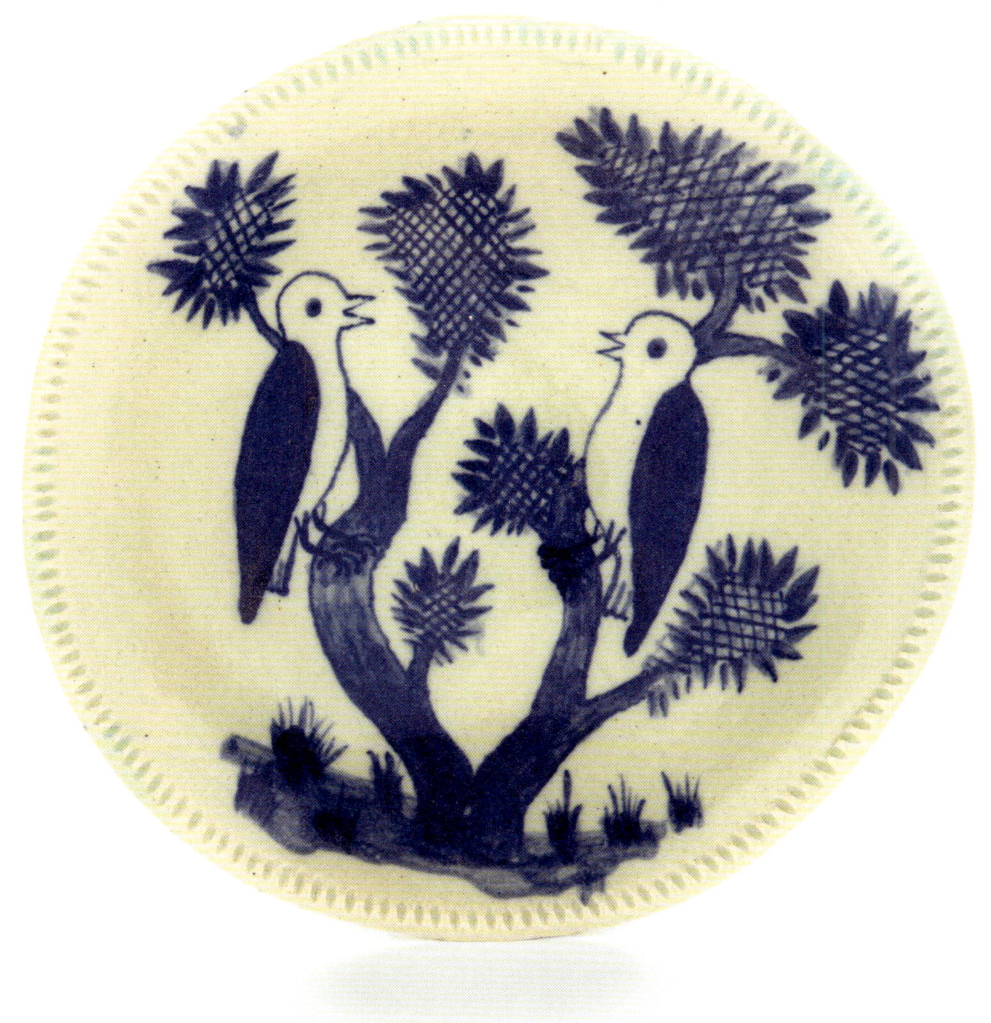

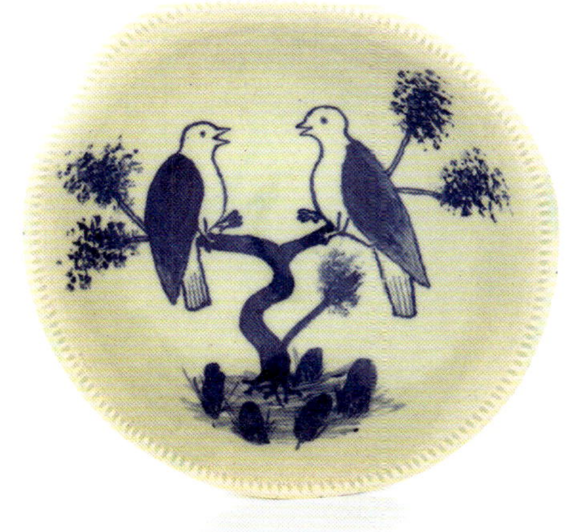

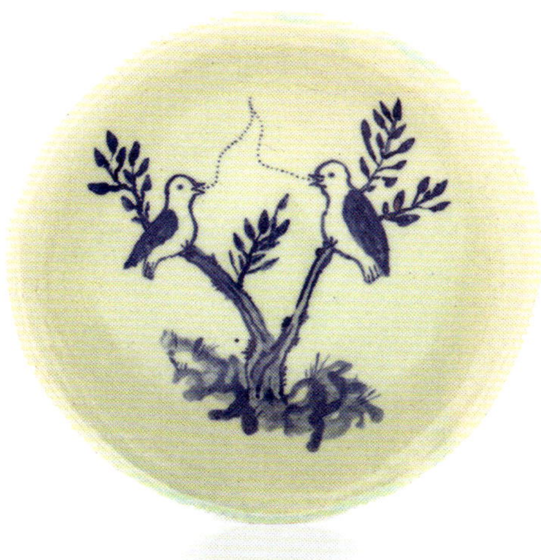

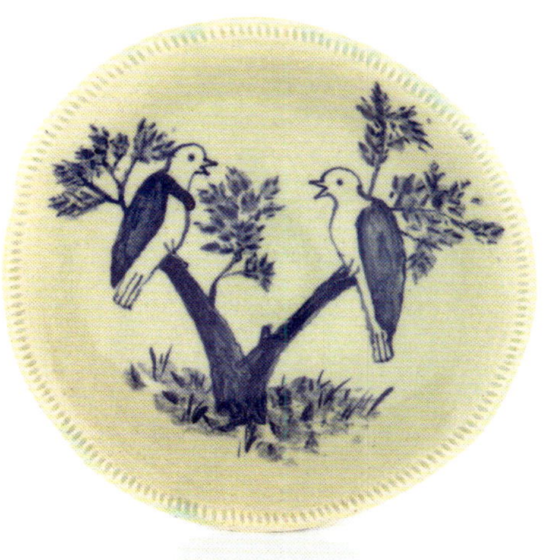

12 February to 4 March 2020

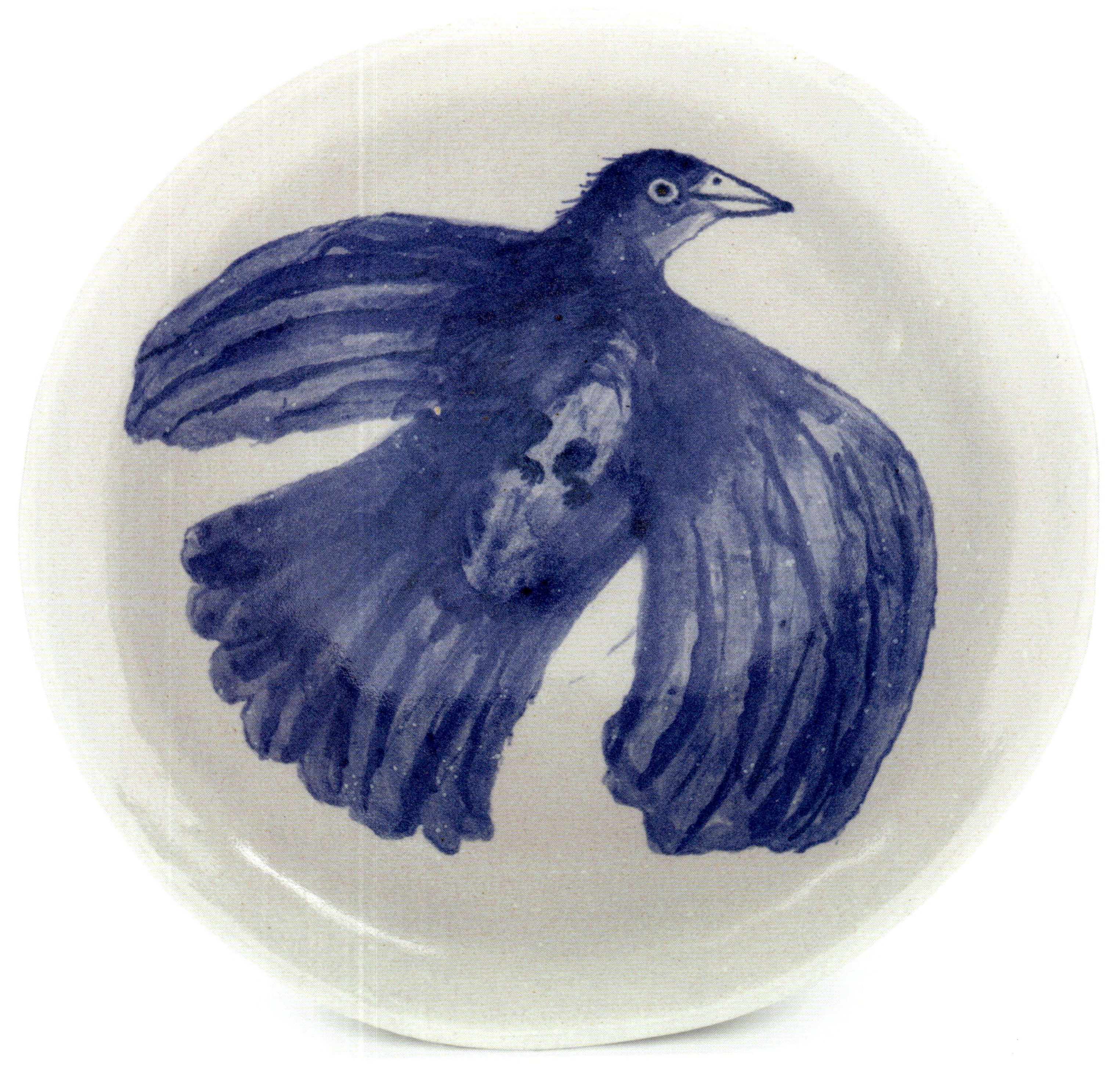

17 November 2020

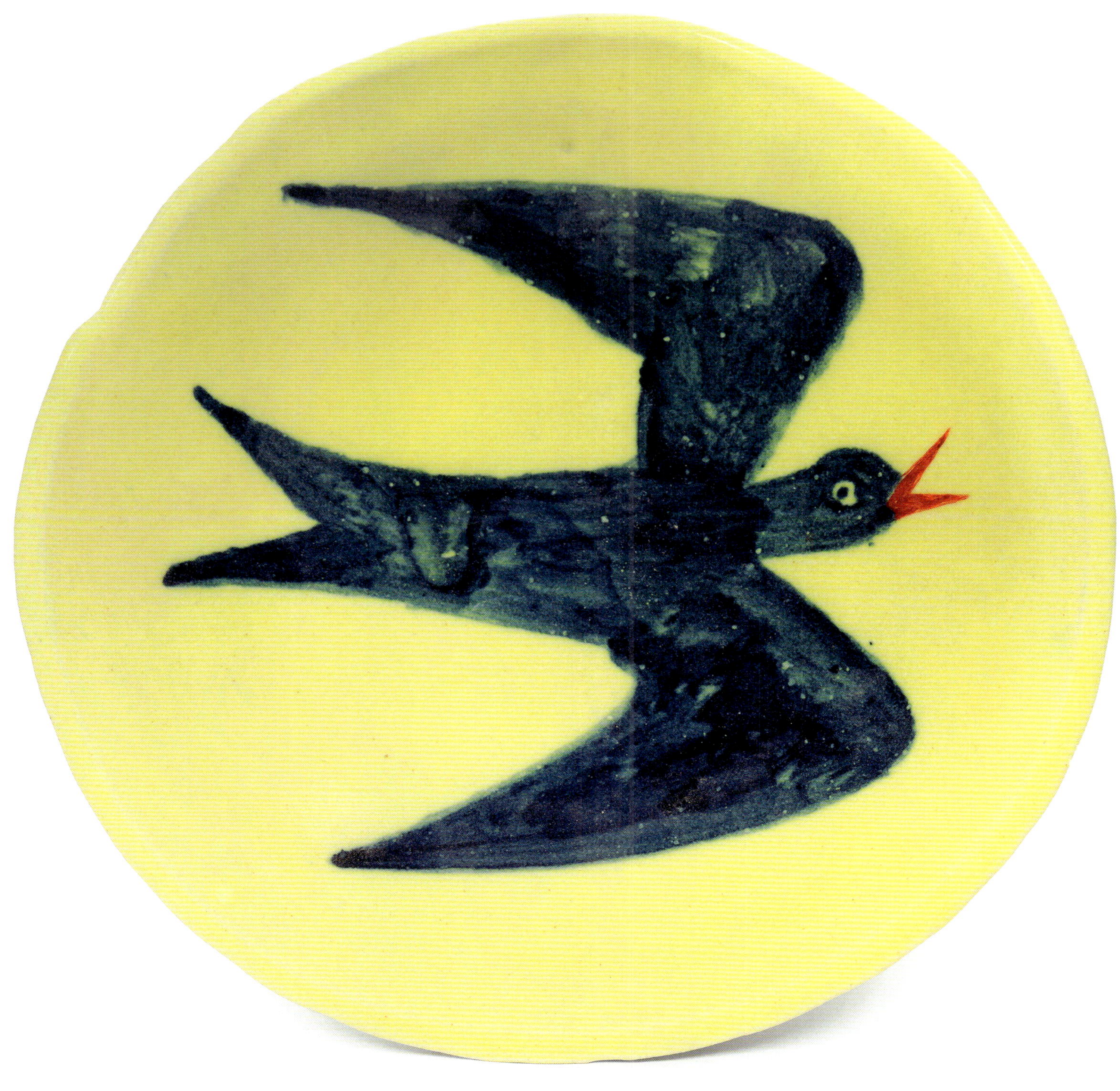

18 September 2019

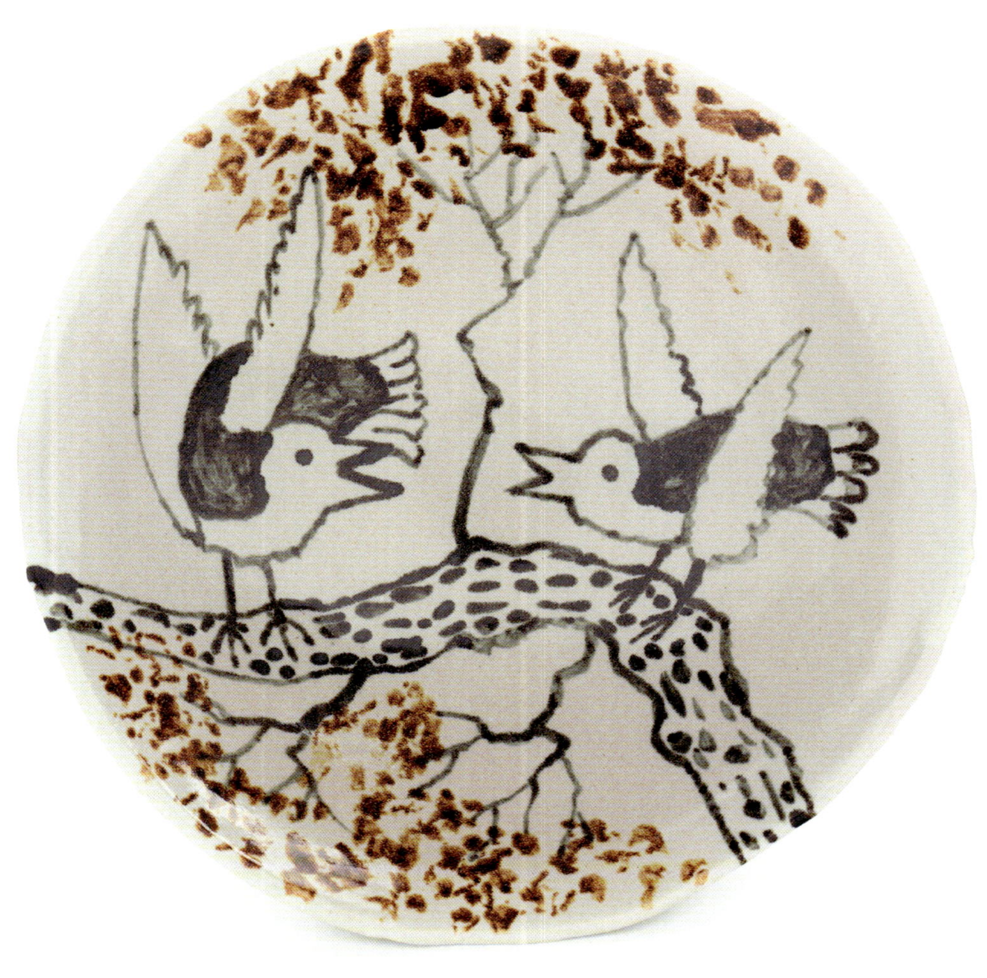

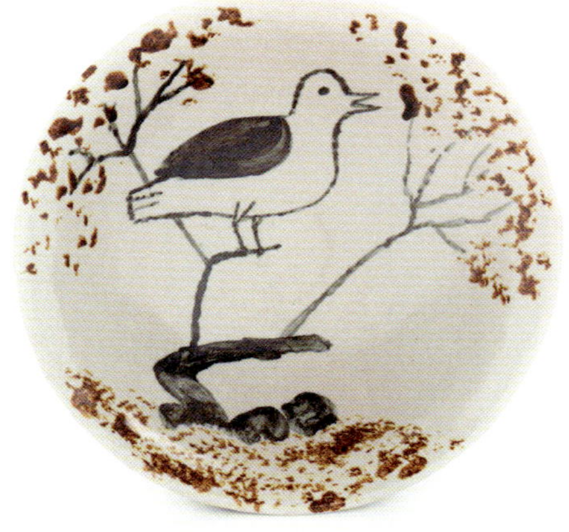

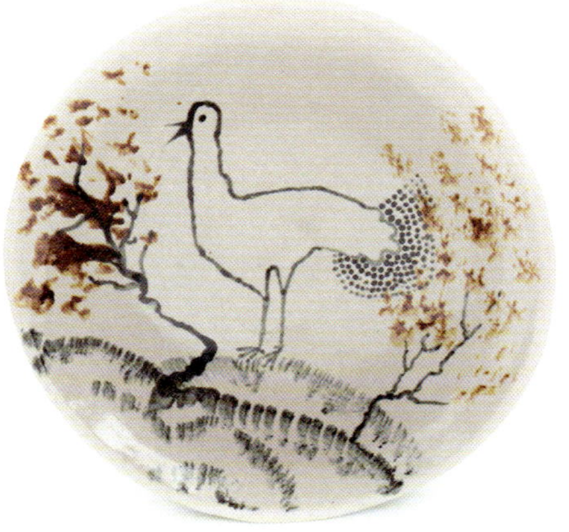

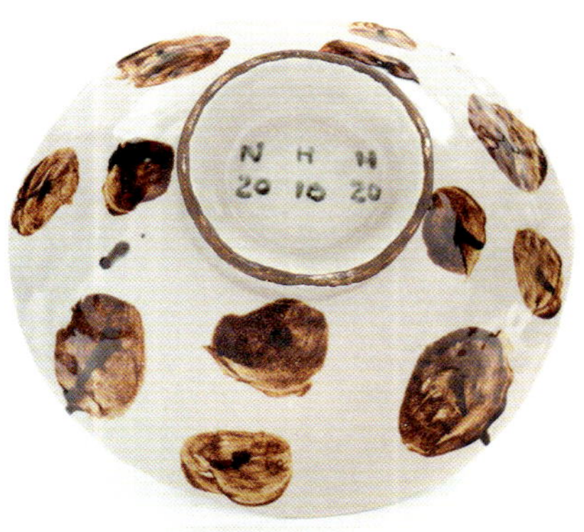

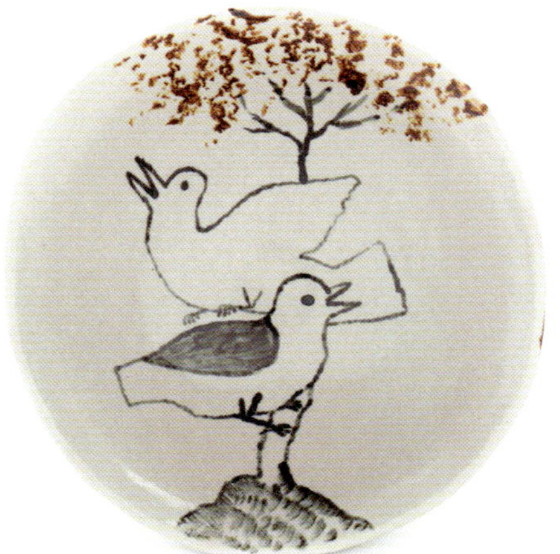

20 October 2020

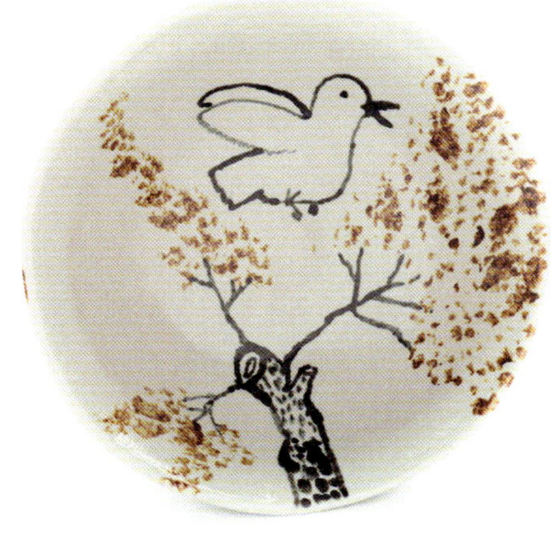
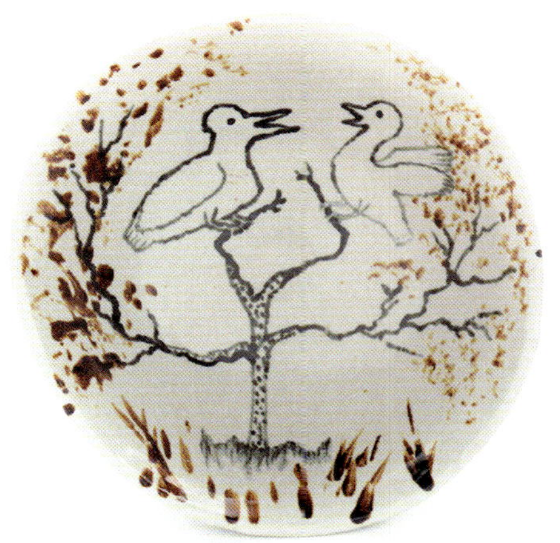
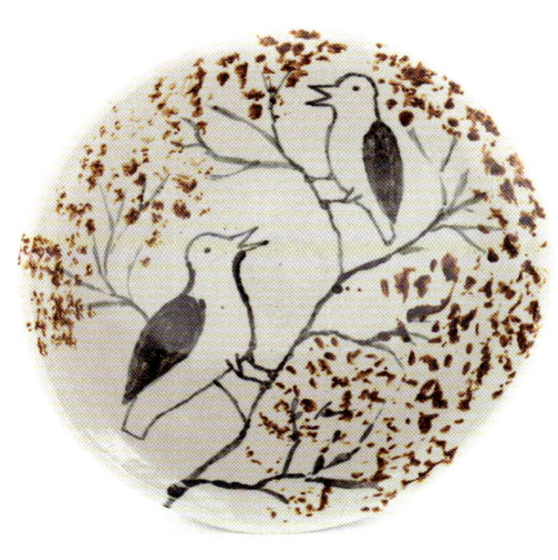
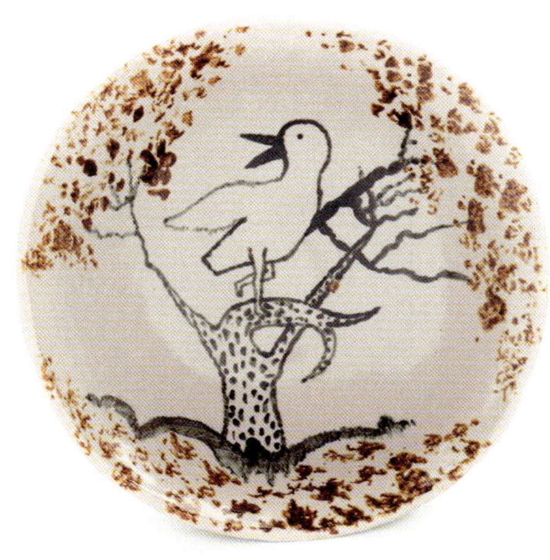
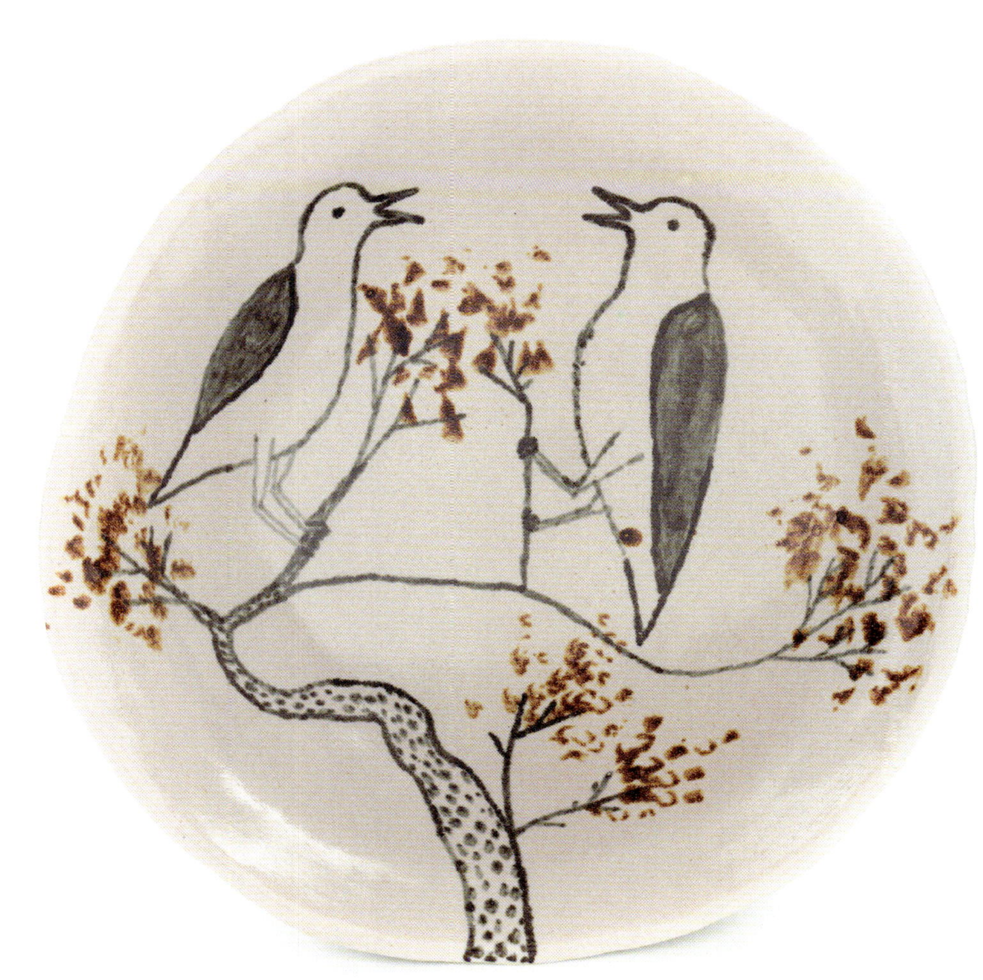

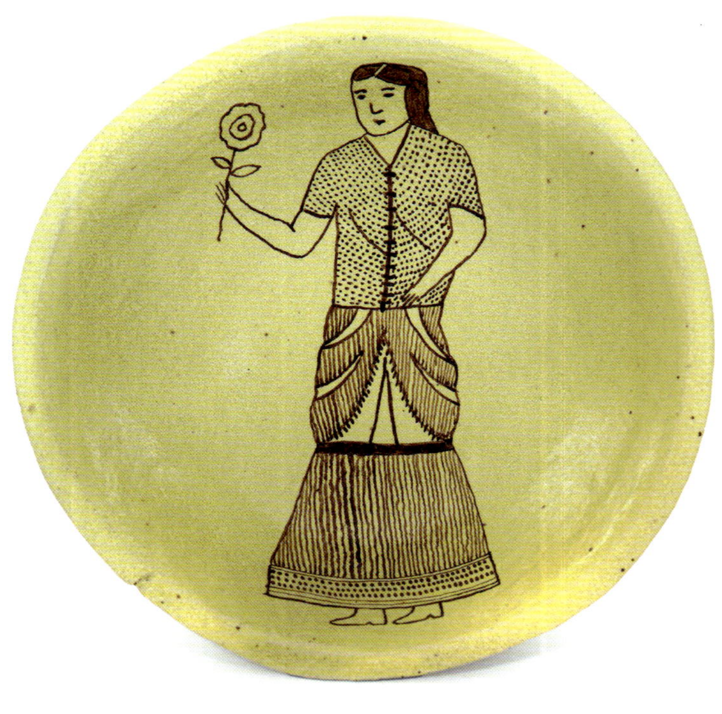

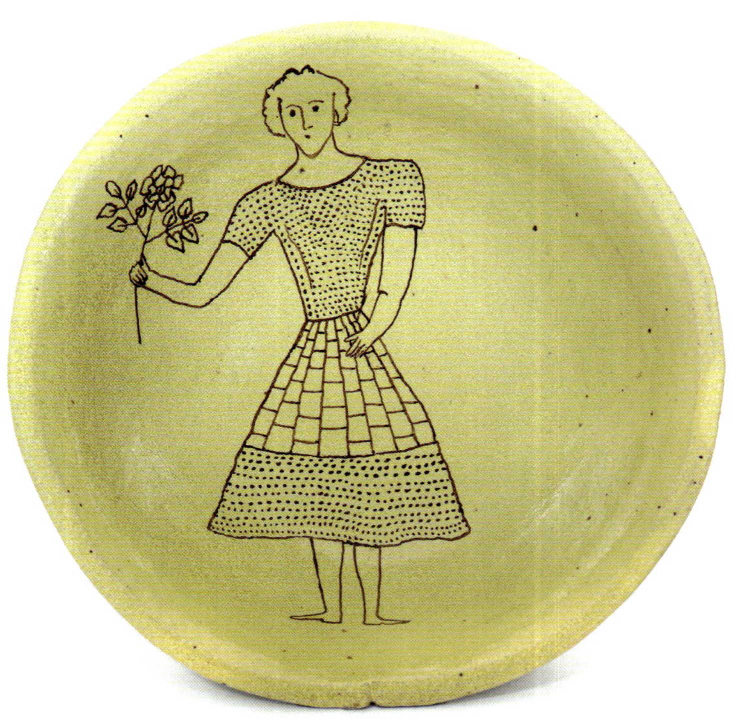

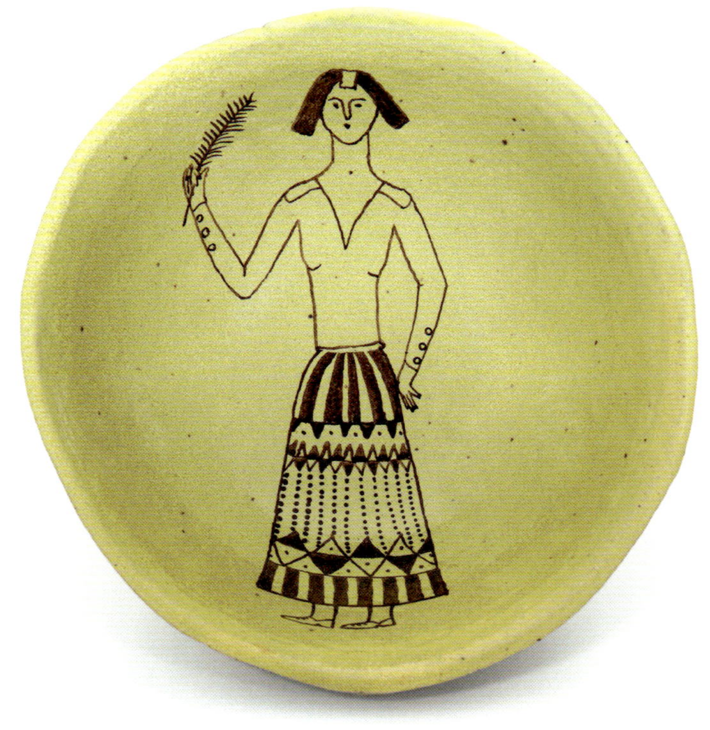

23 March 2016

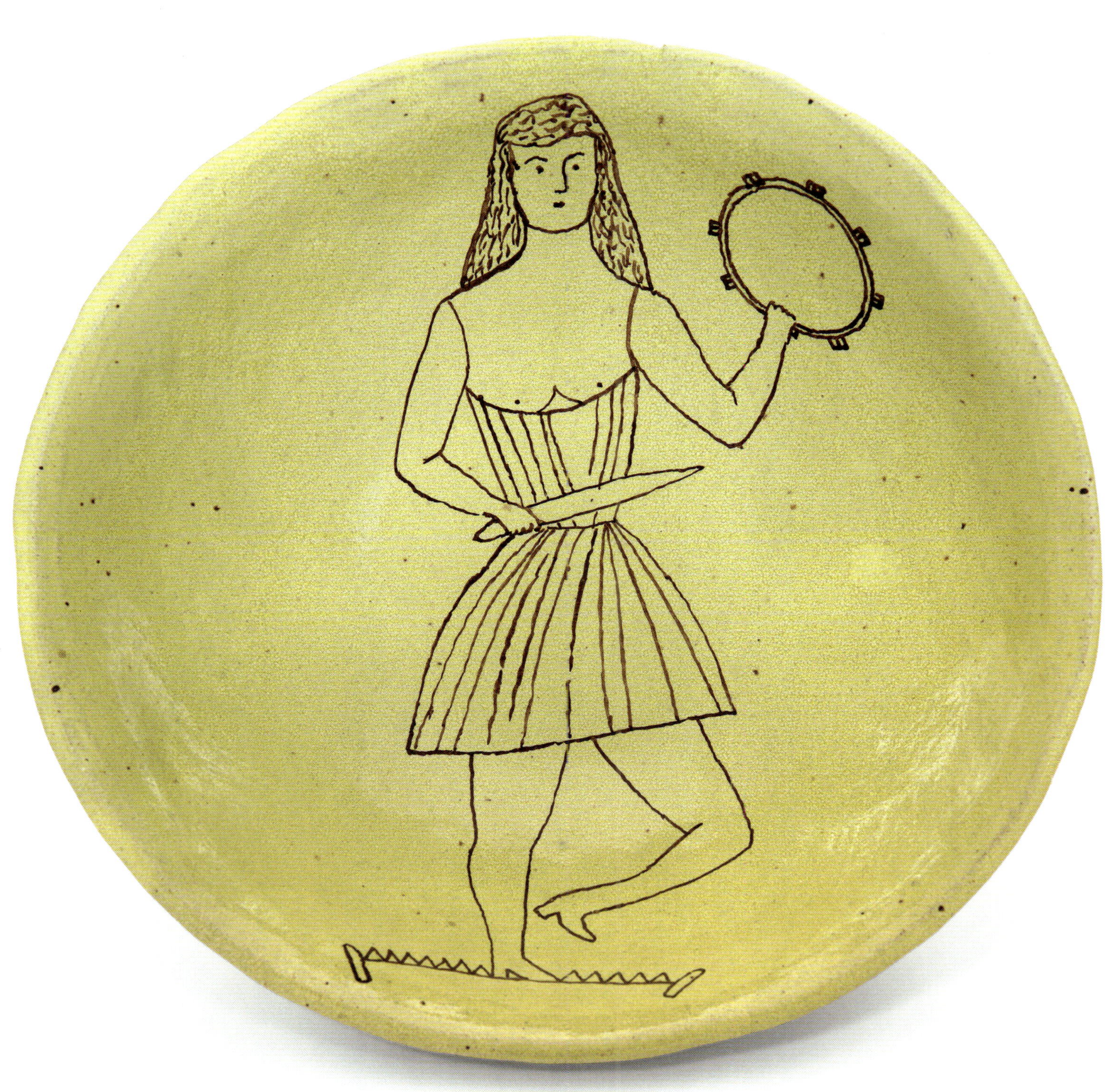

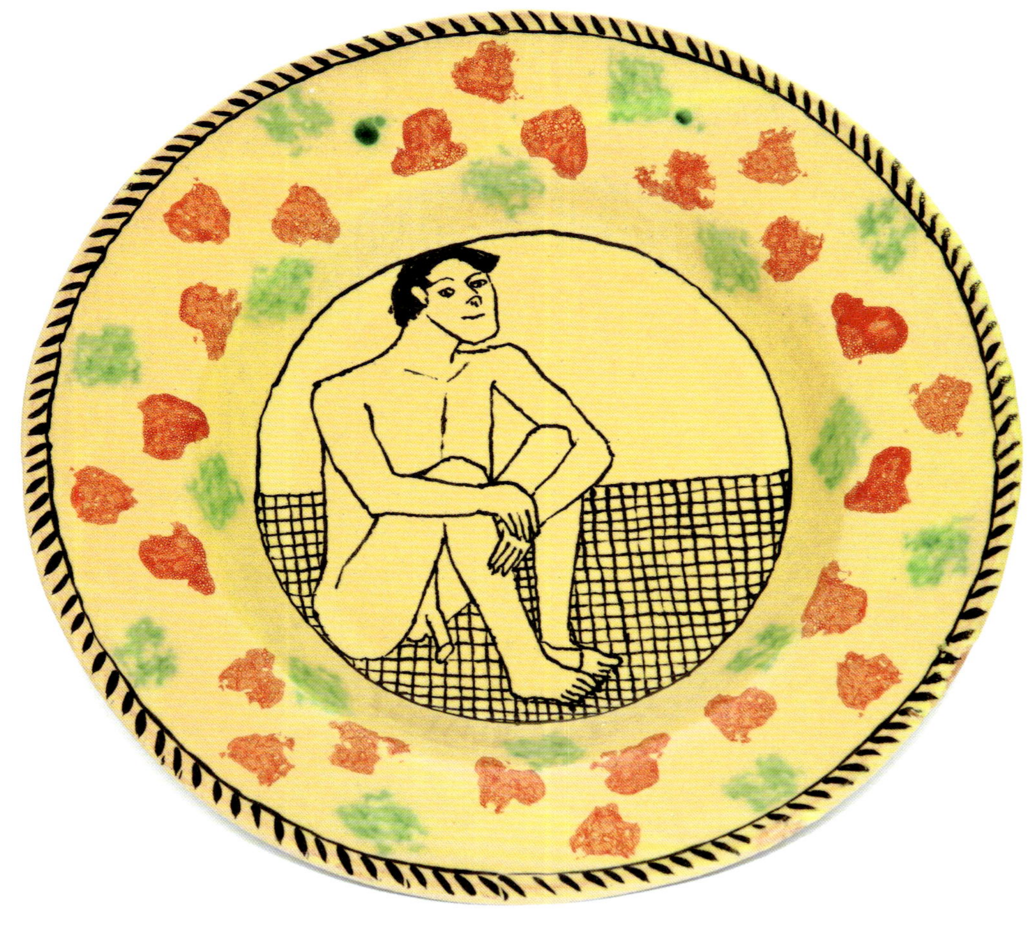

8 October 2012

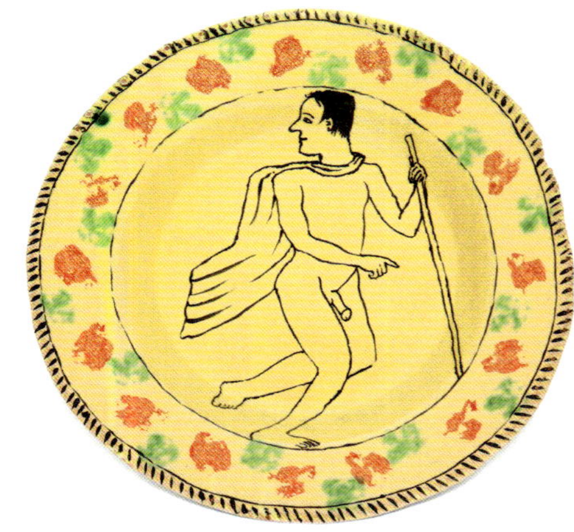

2 October 2012

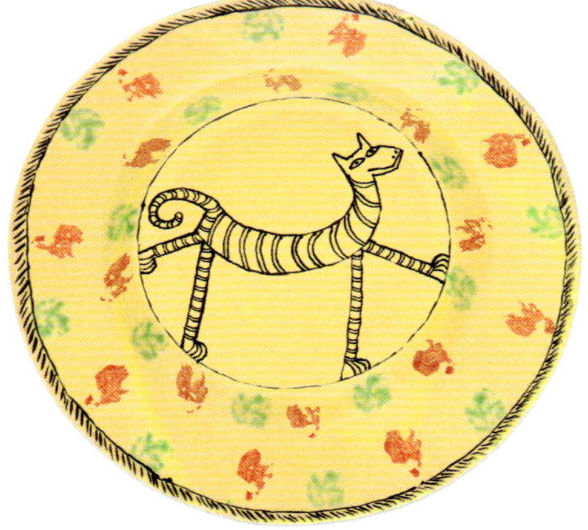

8 October 2012

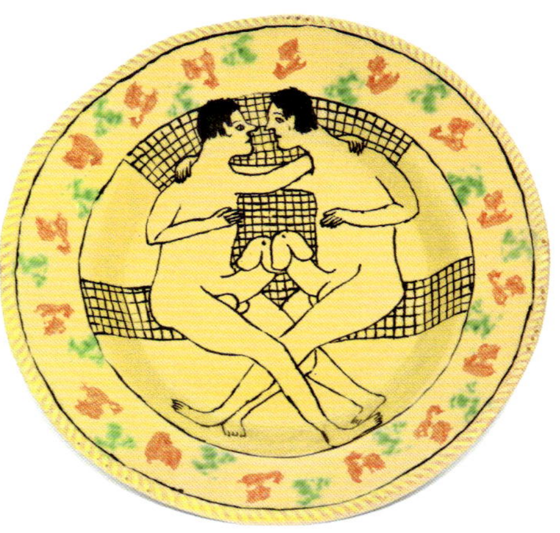

2 October 2012

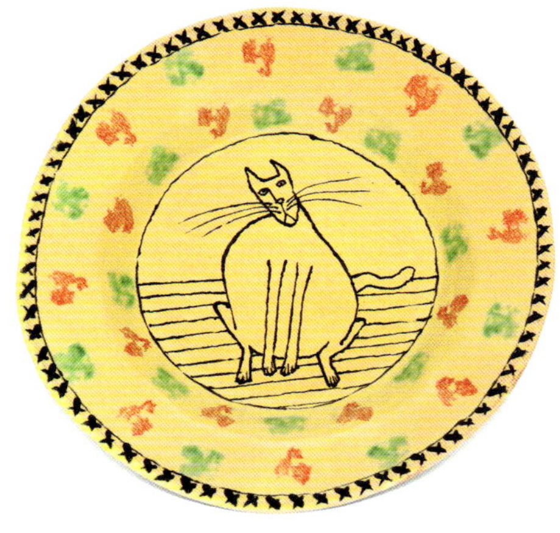

10 October 2012

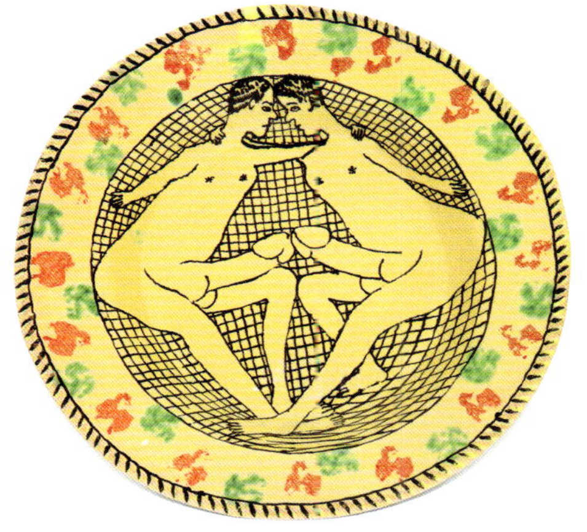

2 October 2012

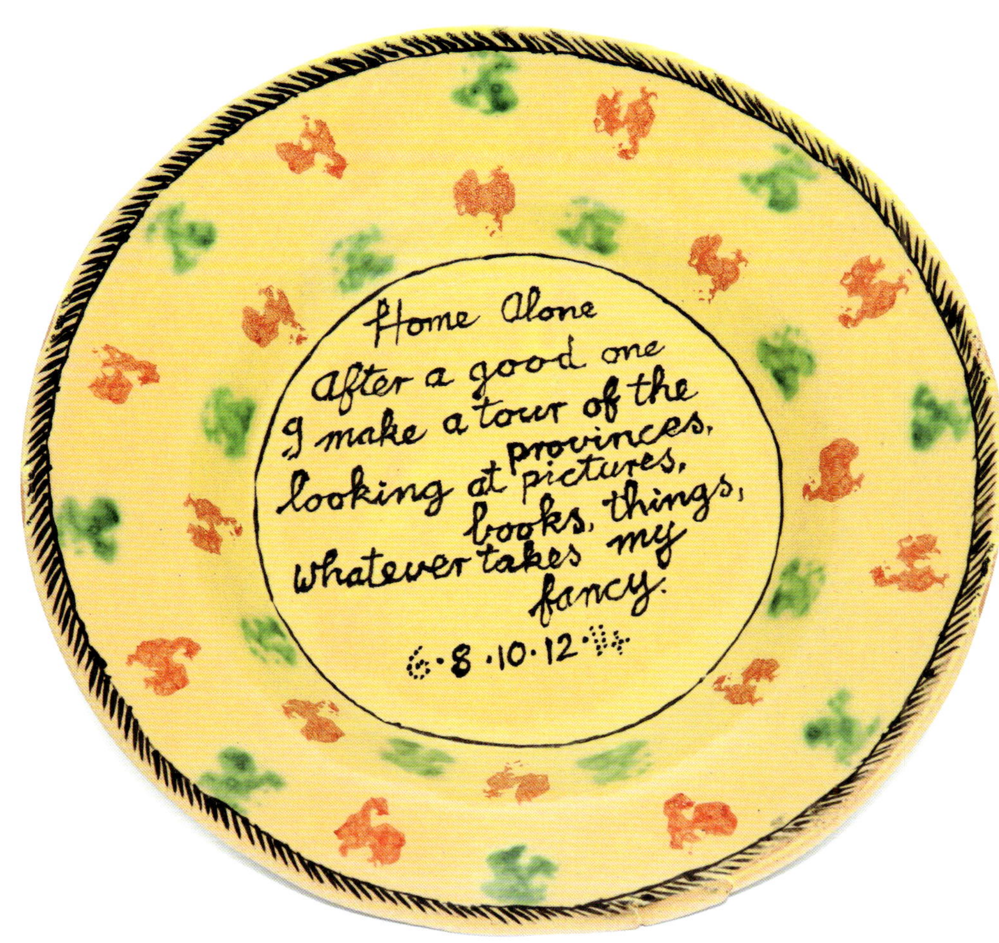

8 October 2012

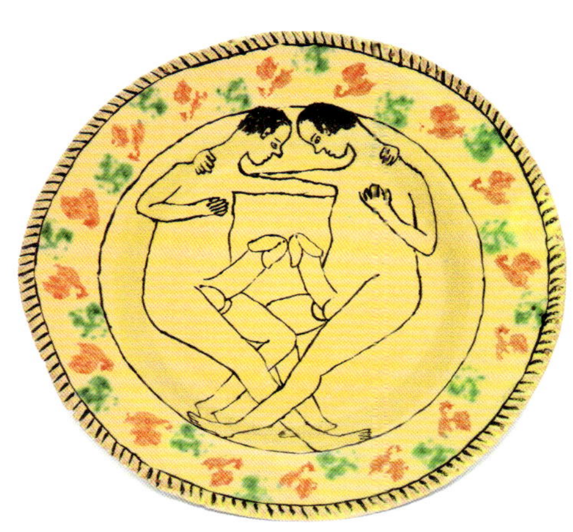

2 October 2012

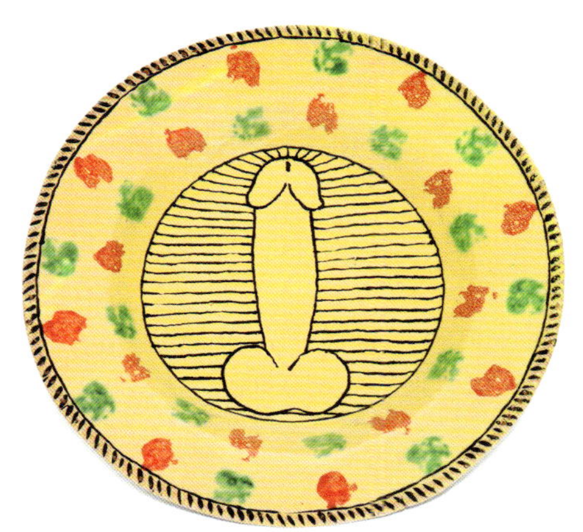

2 October 2012

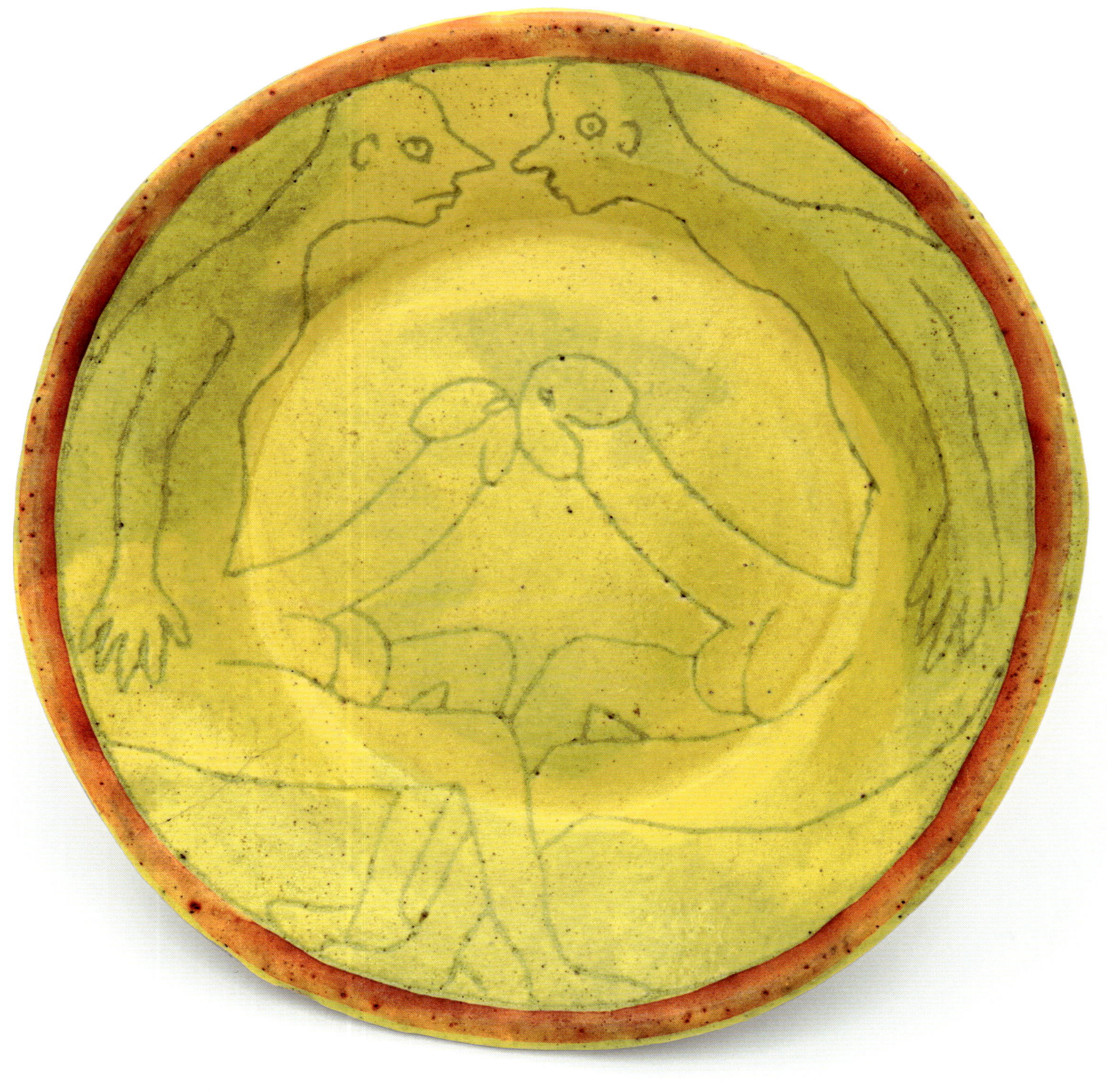

Late 1980s

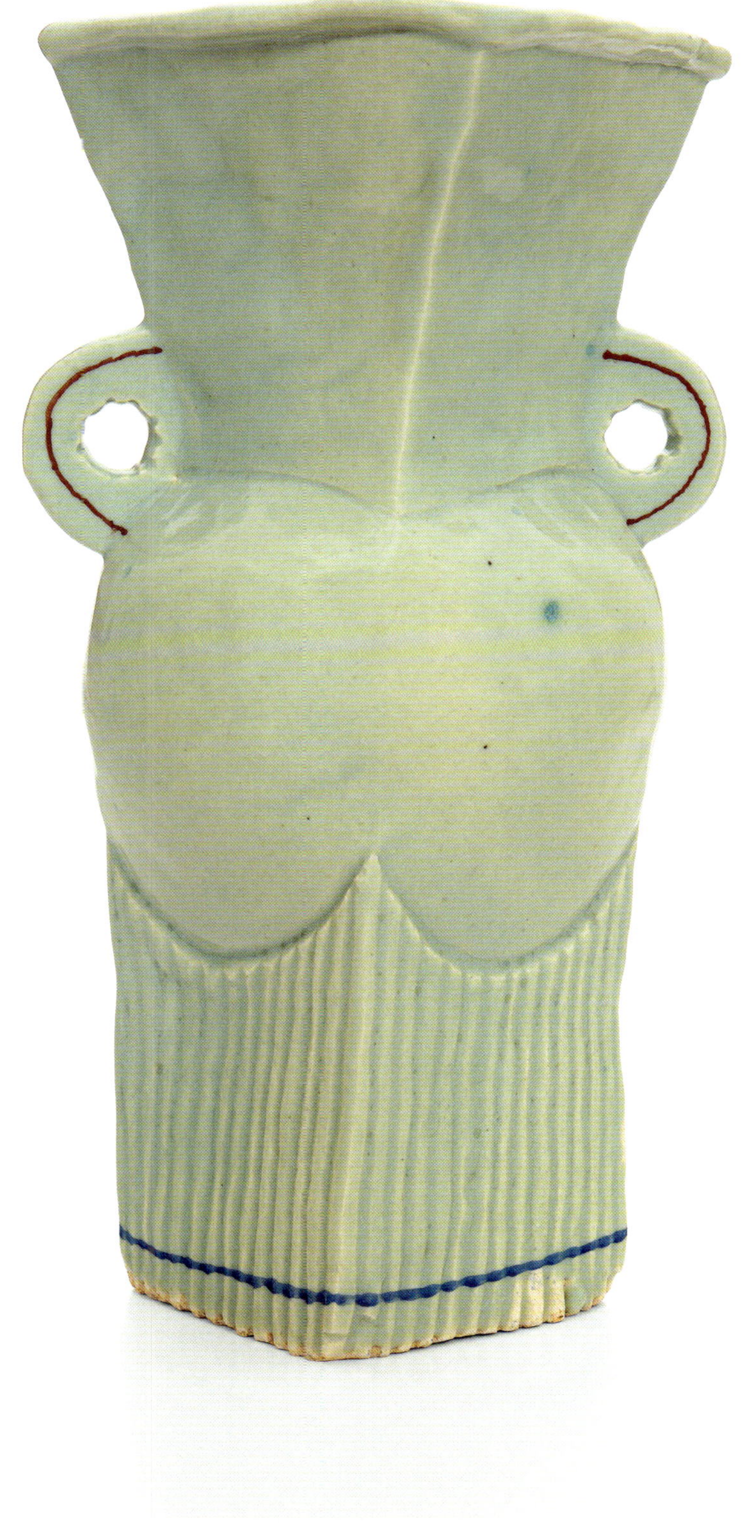

23 February 2017

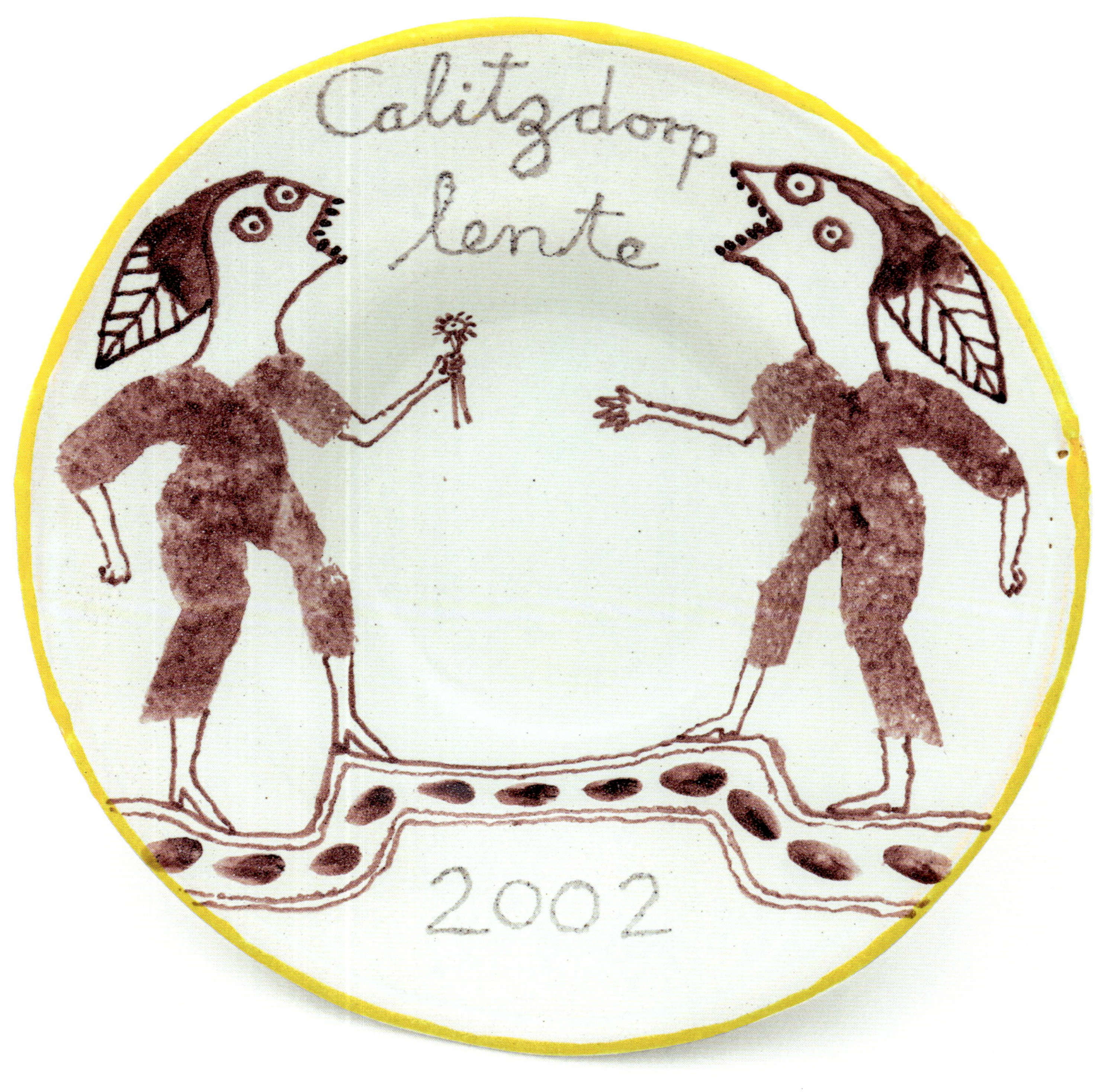

4 August 2002

The Chinese idea of originality is something that makes sense to me. True originality is seen as very rare, so people paint deliberately in styles that have gone before, a landscape by so-and-so in the style of some master of the past, but every now and then you get a truly original painter, and then a new school starts with that. Whereas in the West we expect, demand, originality. It's not something that can just be demanded like that.

The Europeans used a Roman technique for glazing, and they made things mostly with an iron-bearing clay so it would have a reddish colour. They put raw lead oxide onto the wet clay, let it dry and then fired it, and the lead combined with the clay and formed a glaze. And that's how it was until the Moors came into Spain and they brought techniques and things with them from the Middle East. There was a long period of exchange... They brought this technique of opacifying the glaze with tin oxide – you get a white surface, and then you can use colours on that. The blue colour is the strongest in ceramics, any temperature that the clay will take, the cobalt can take, which makes that blue colour very persistent. That's why it's used, because it's the most reliable colour to use, and for things which have to go through intense heat, that colour stays.

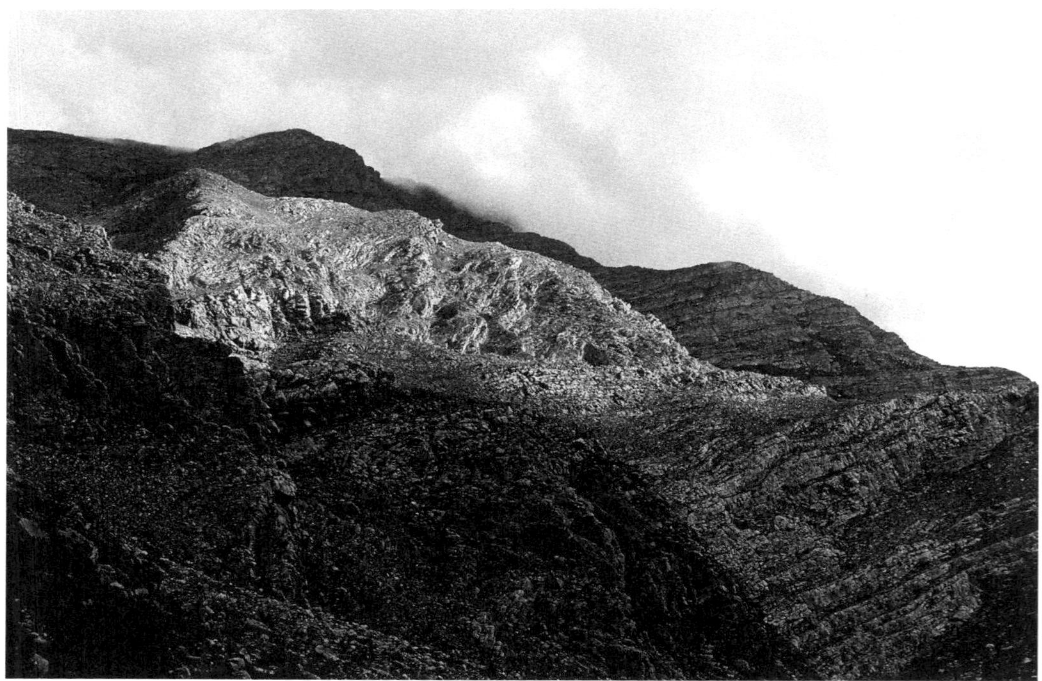

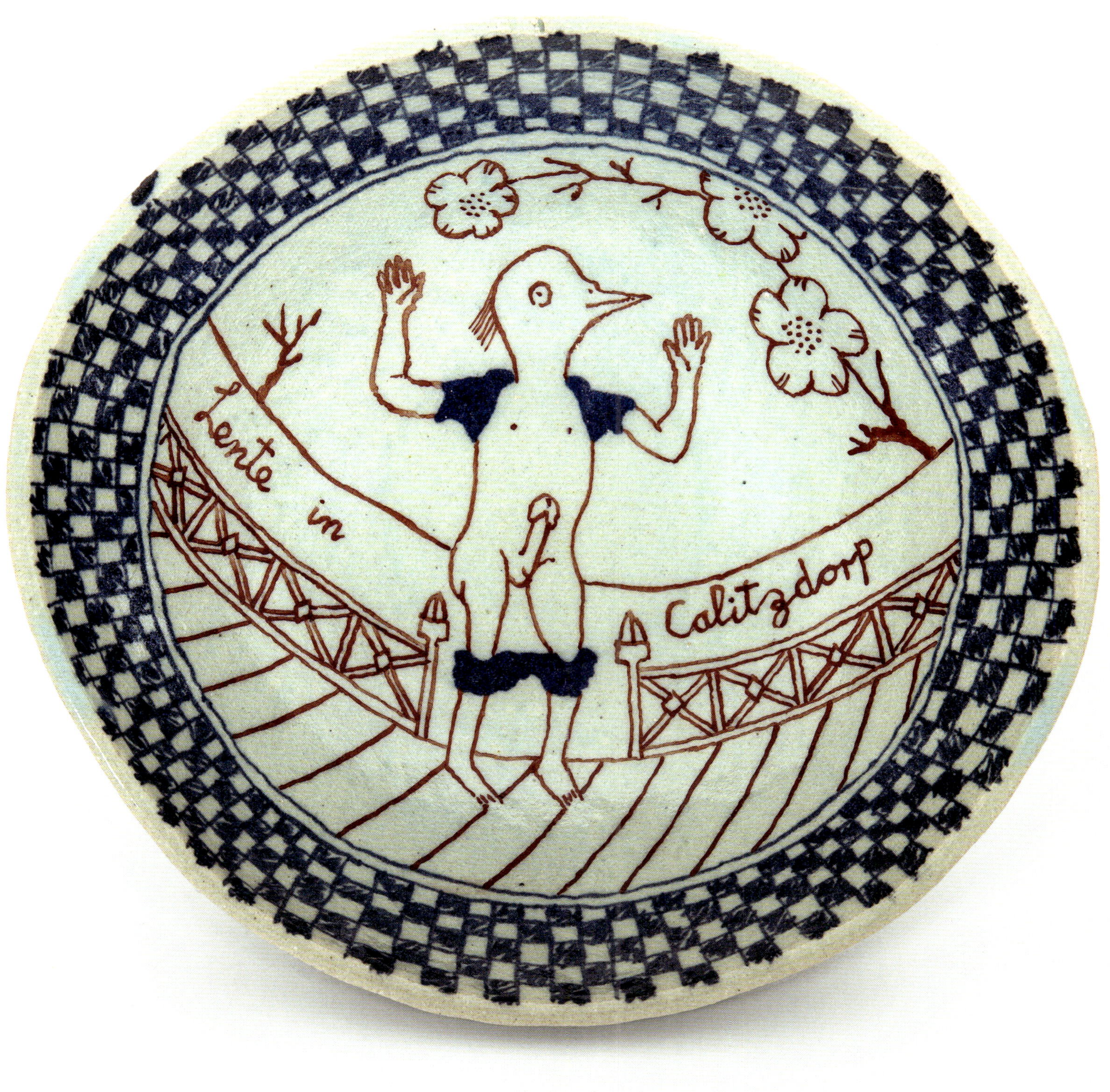

11 August 2015

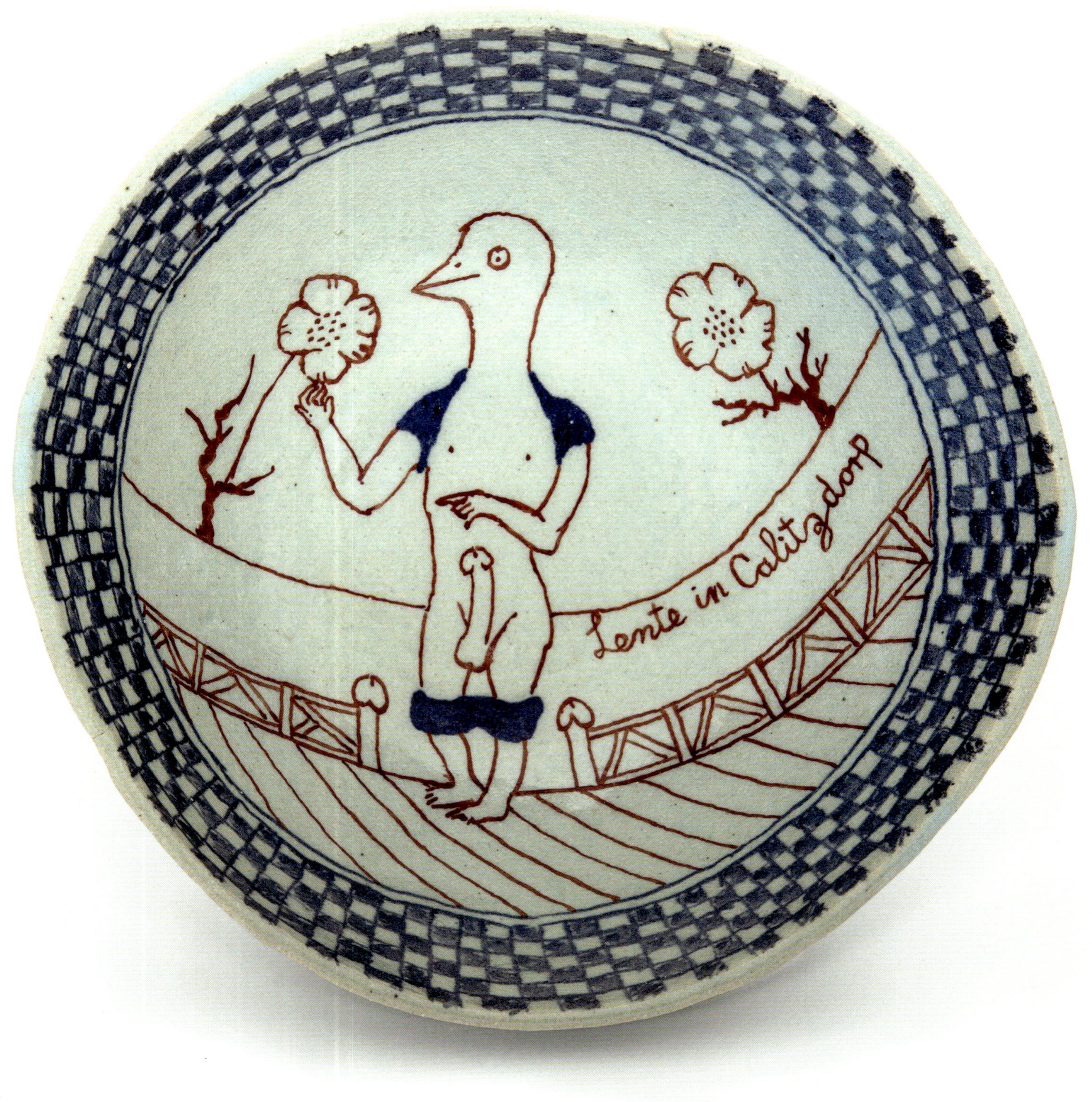

11 August 2015

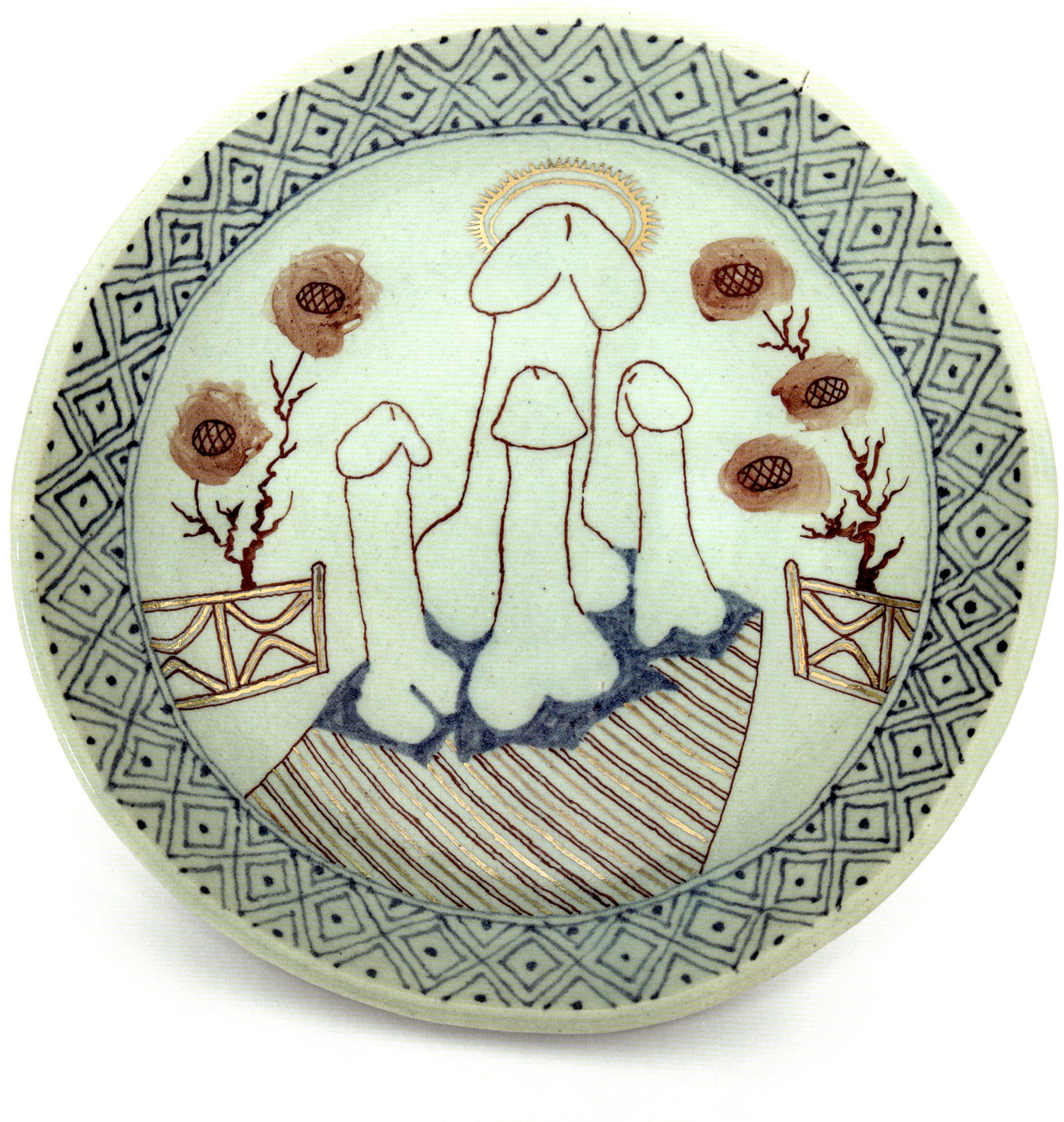

24 August 2015

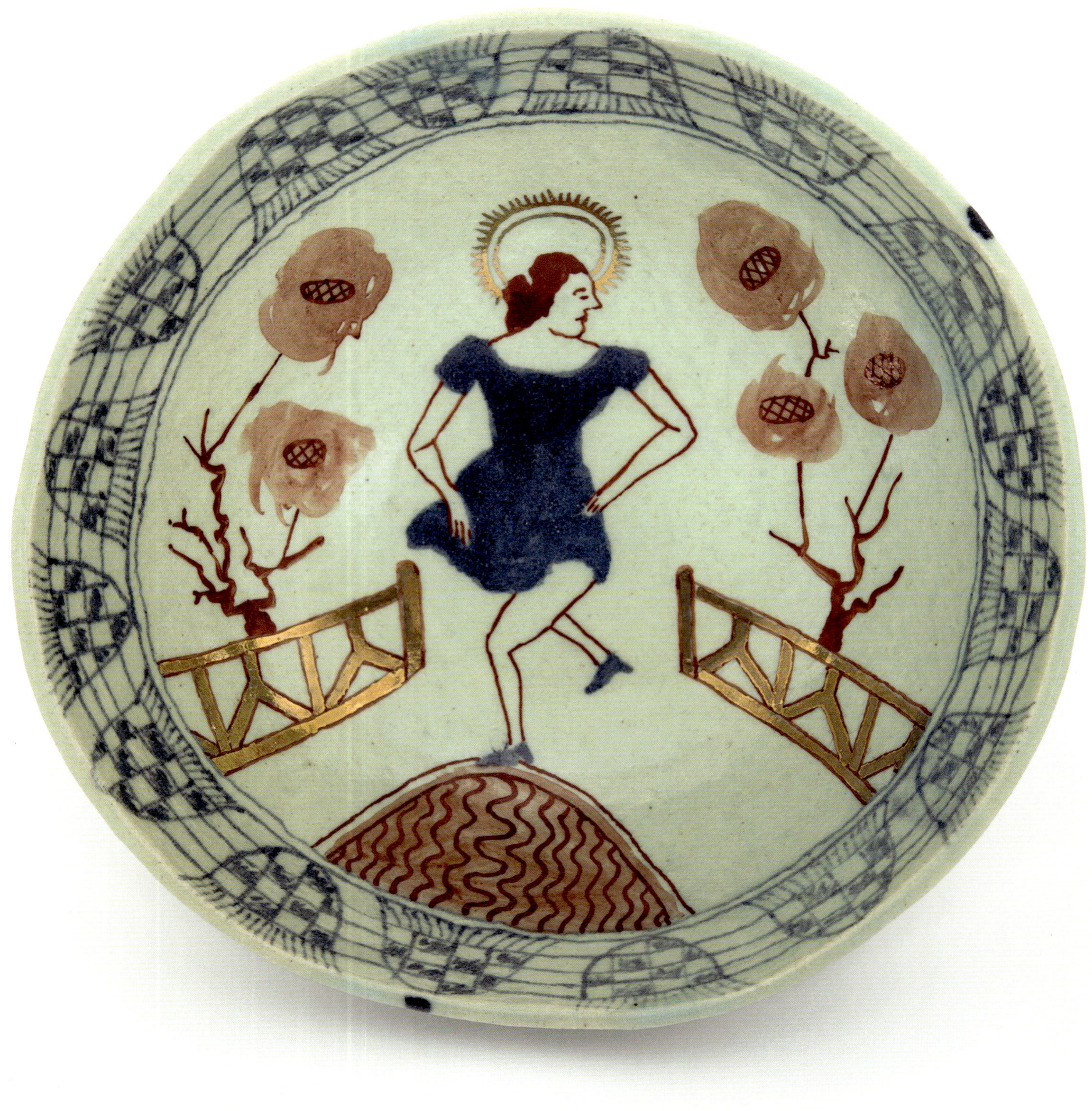

24 August 2015

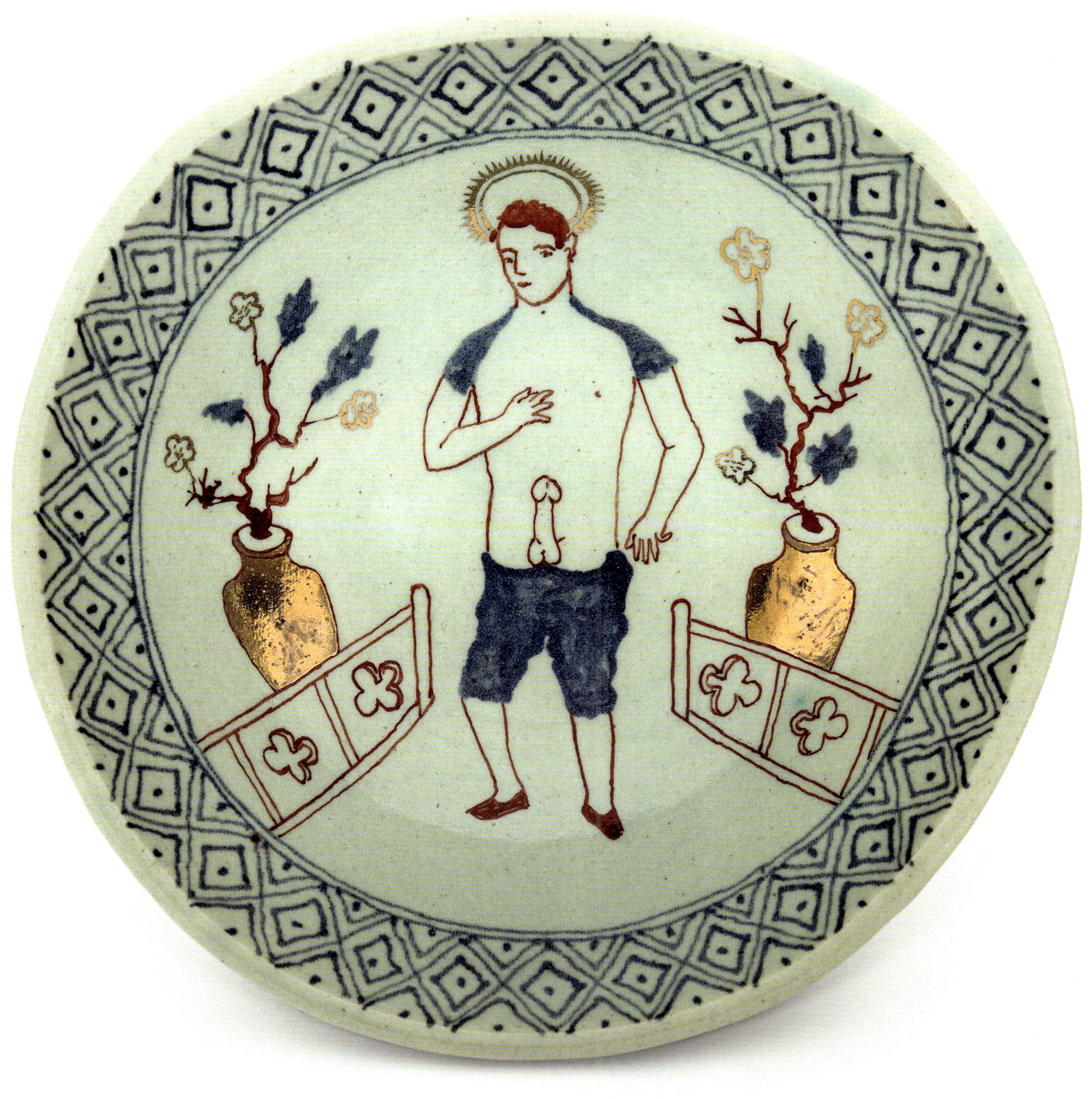

24 August 2015

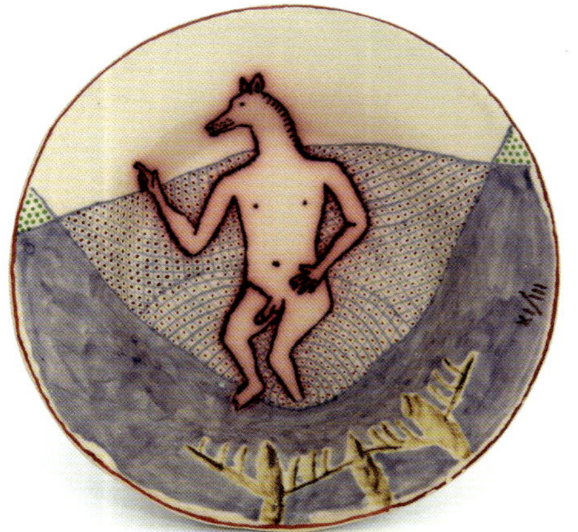

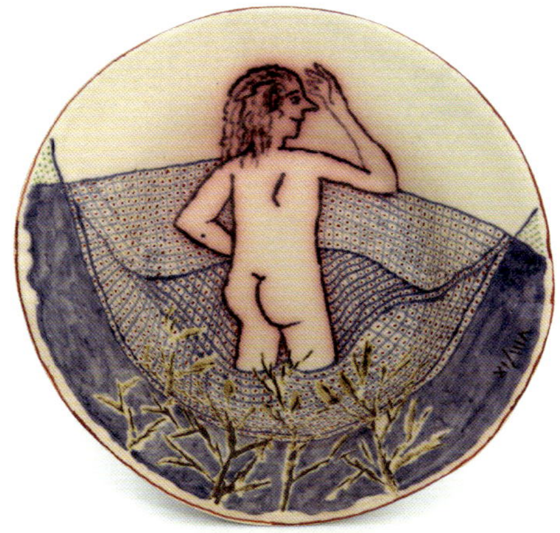

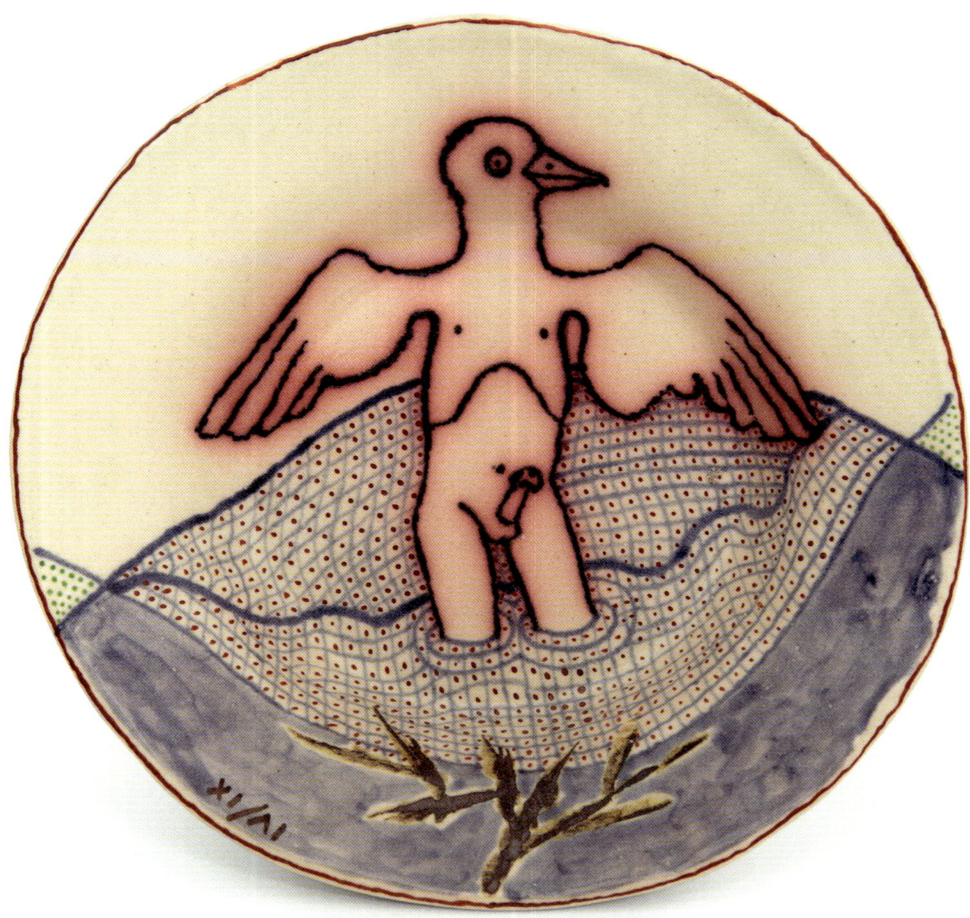

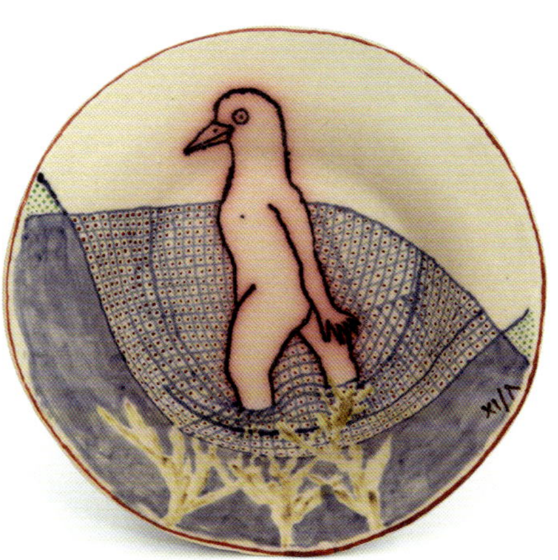

26 January 2017

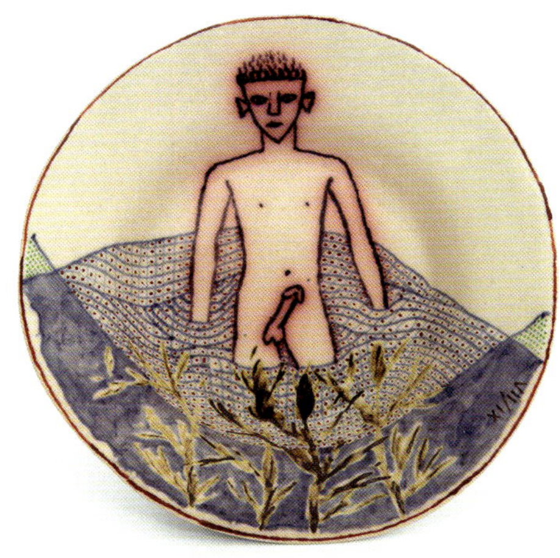

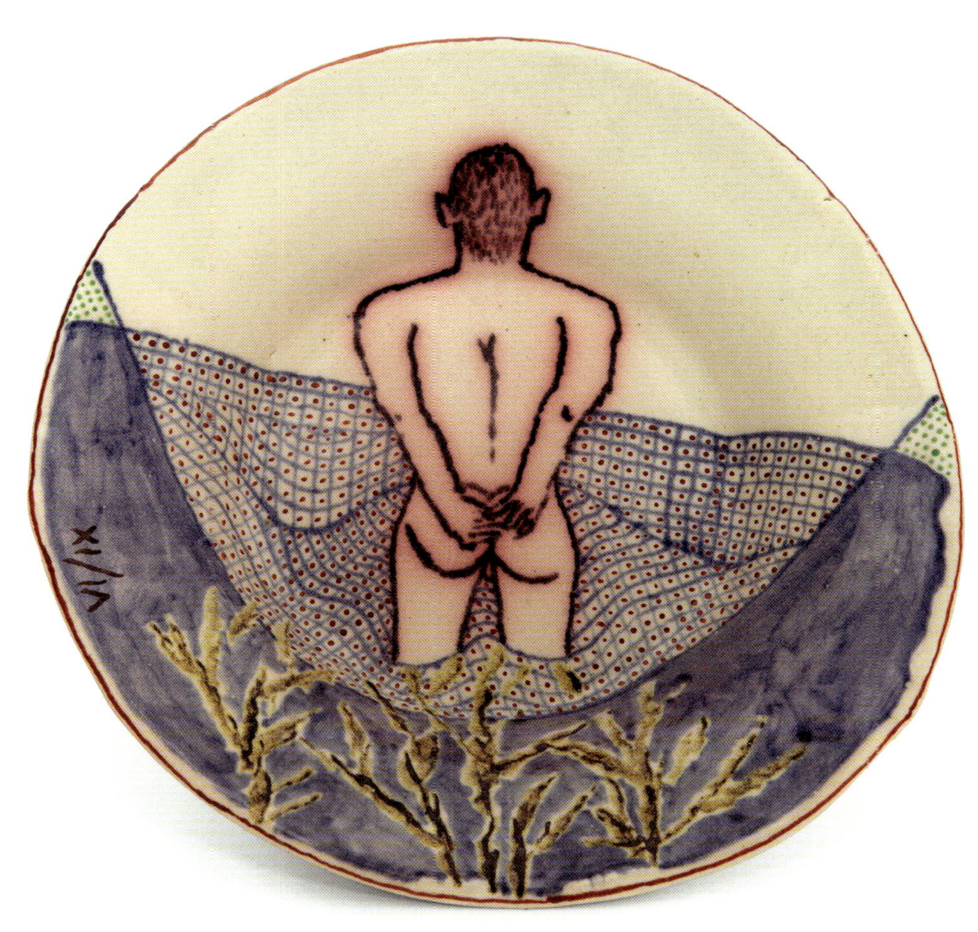

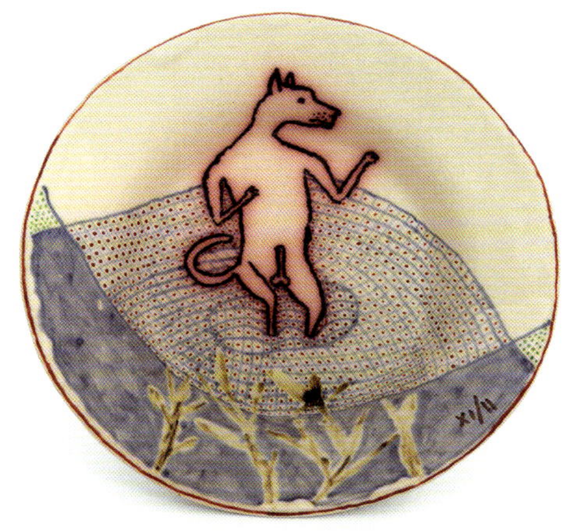

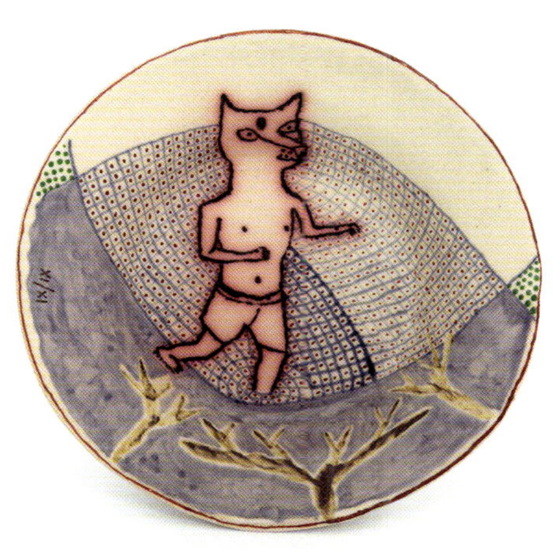

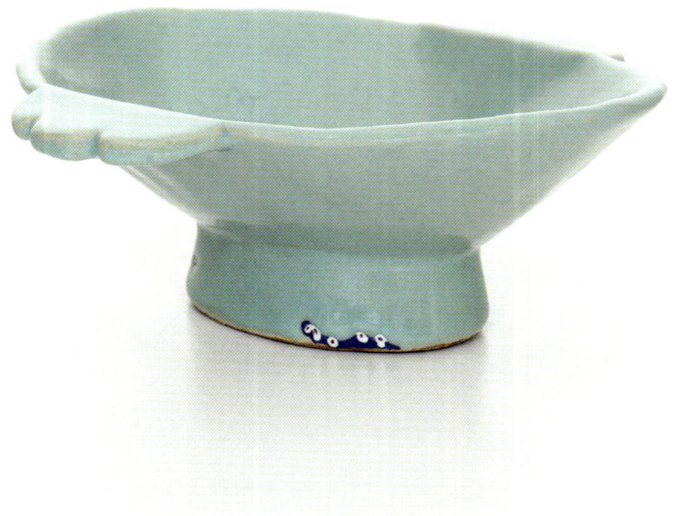
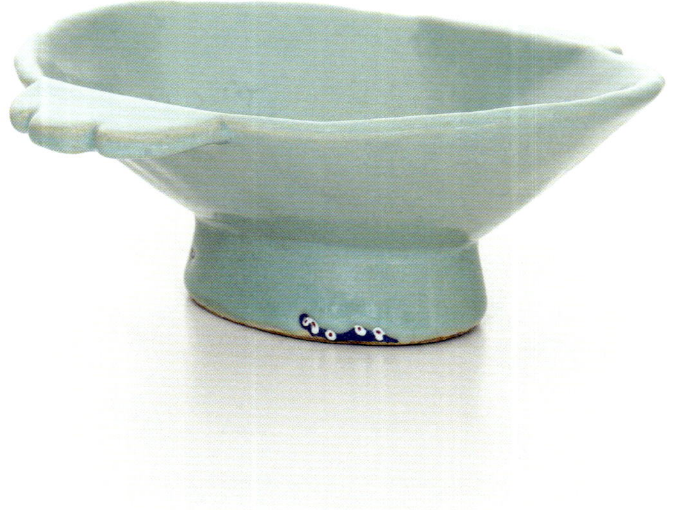

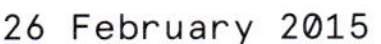
26 February 2015

1 April 2015

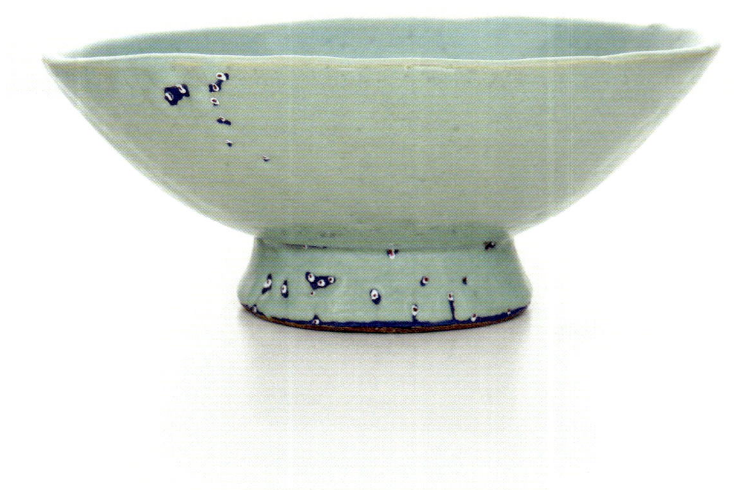

26 February 2015

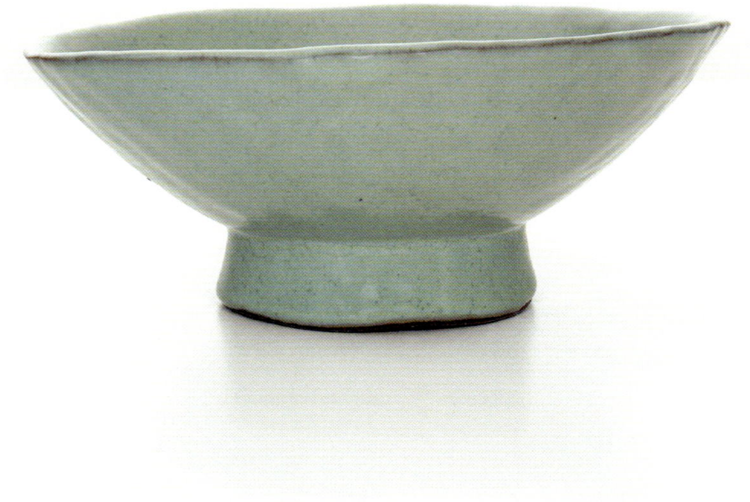

23 December 2014

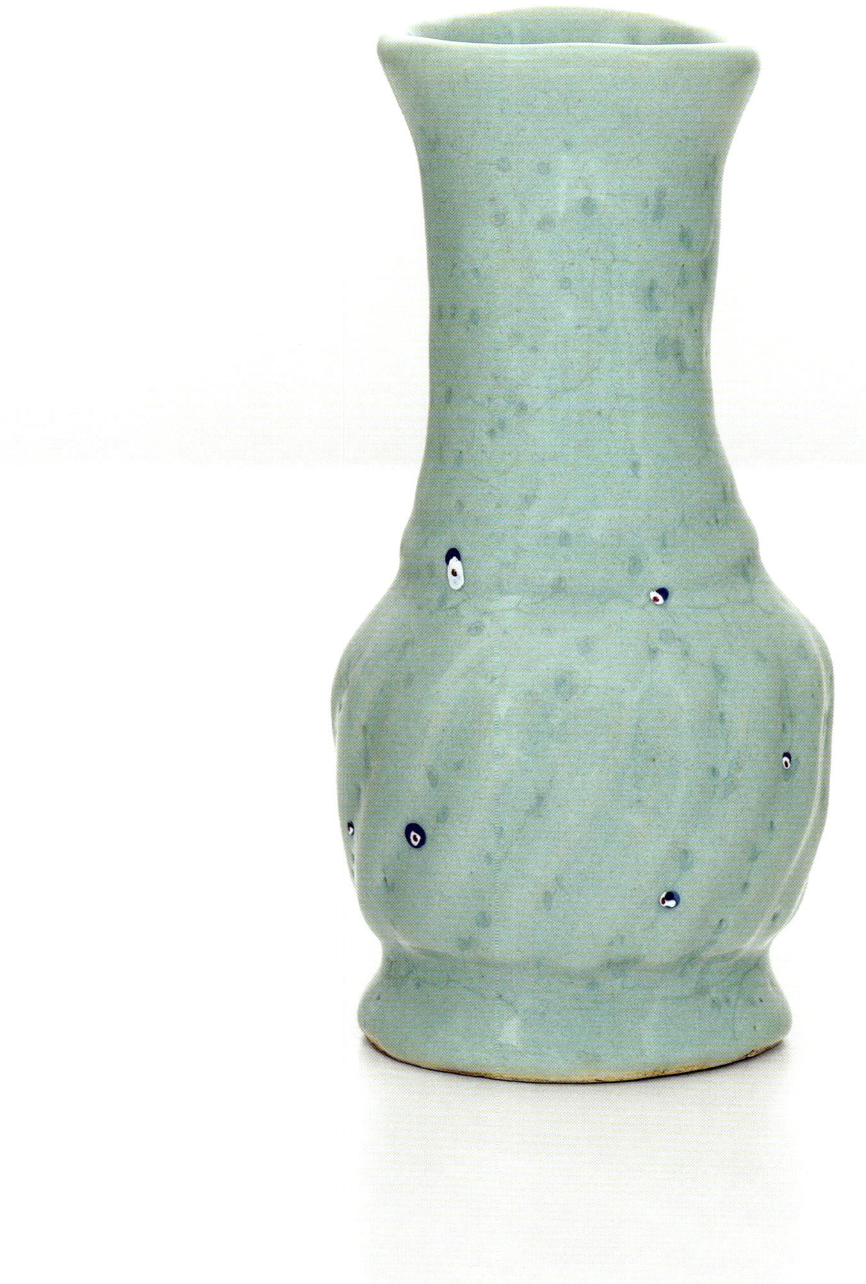

26 February 2015

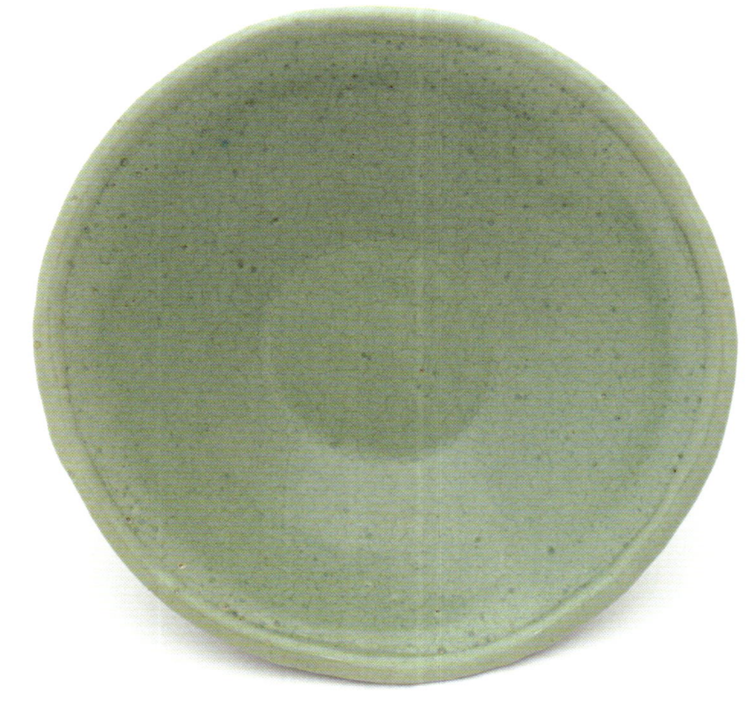

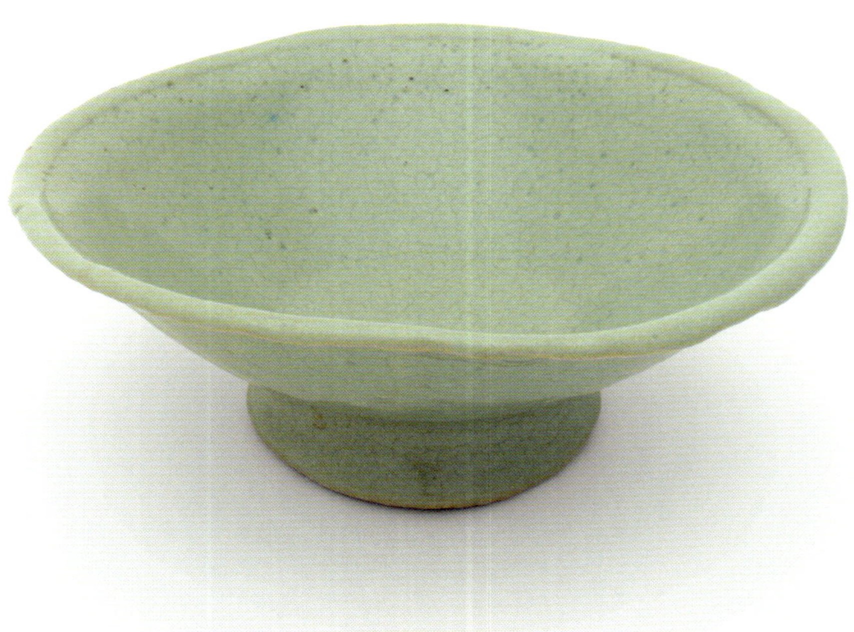

28 November 2014

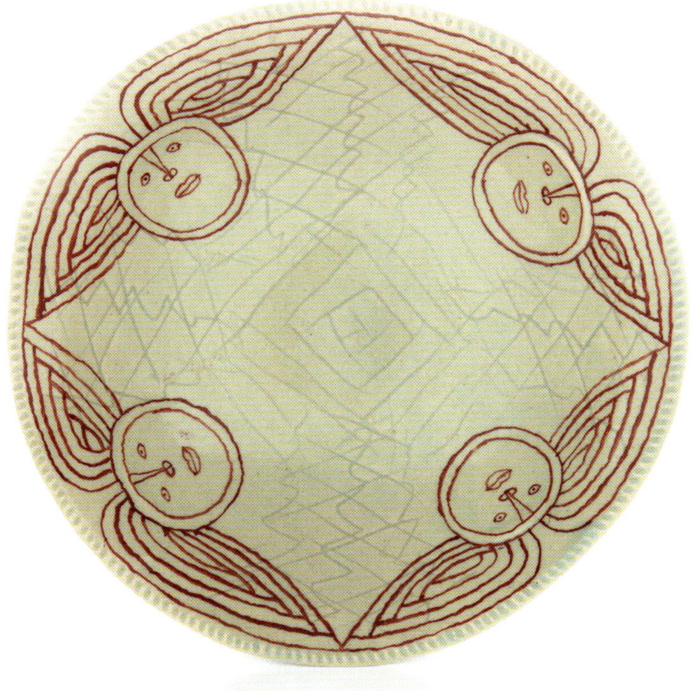

3 February 2020

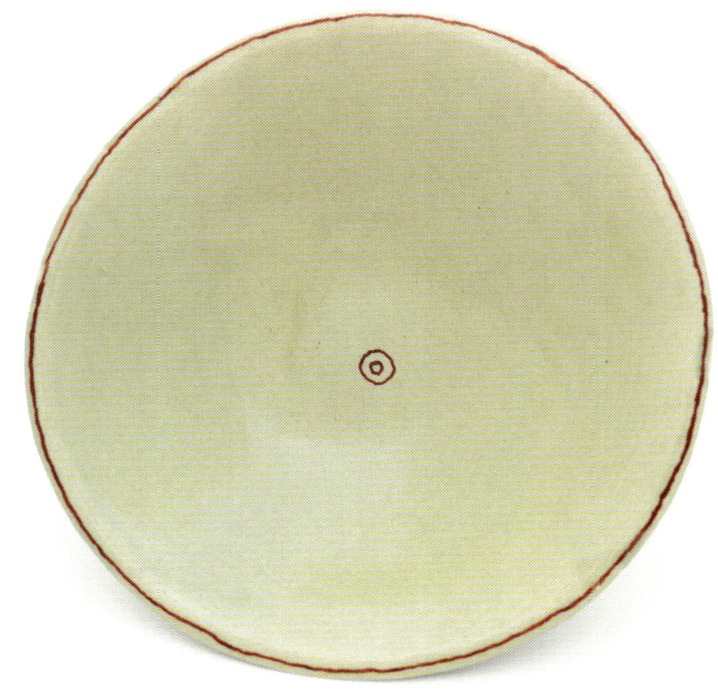

24 July 2016

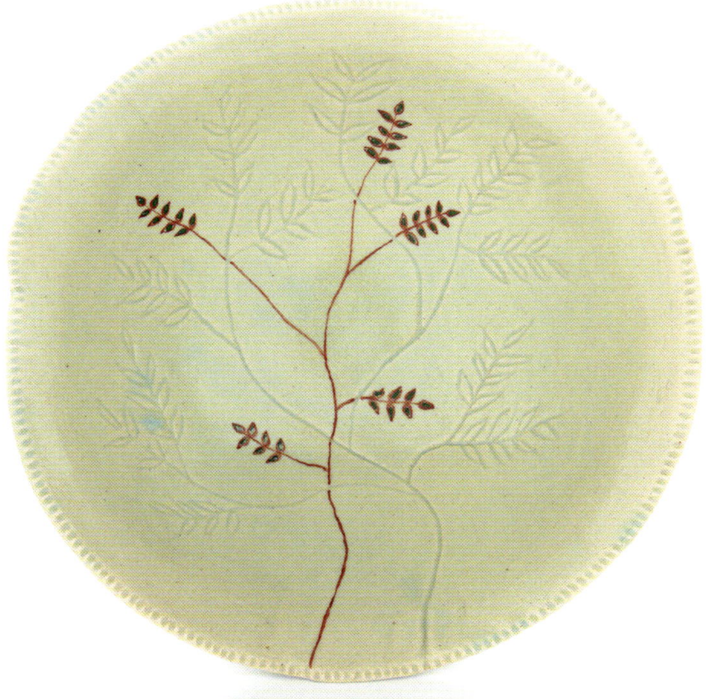

4 February 2020

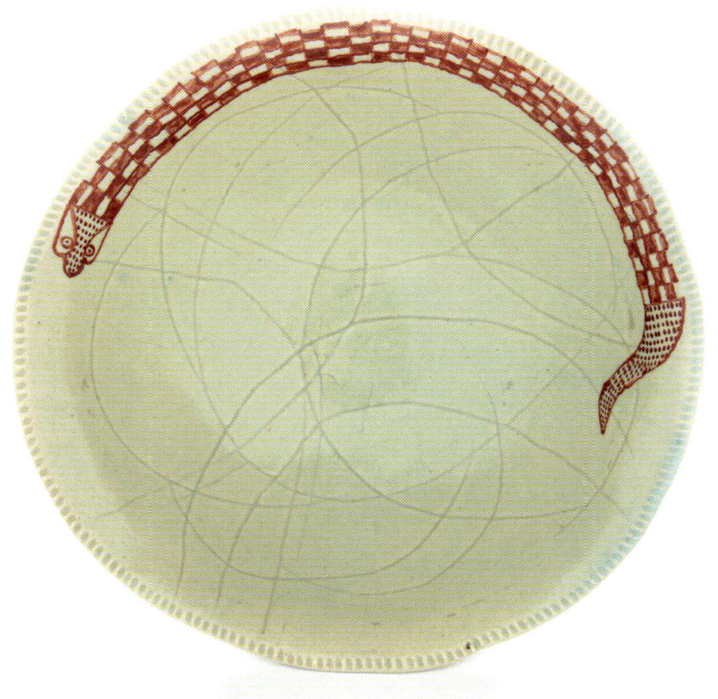

4 February 2020

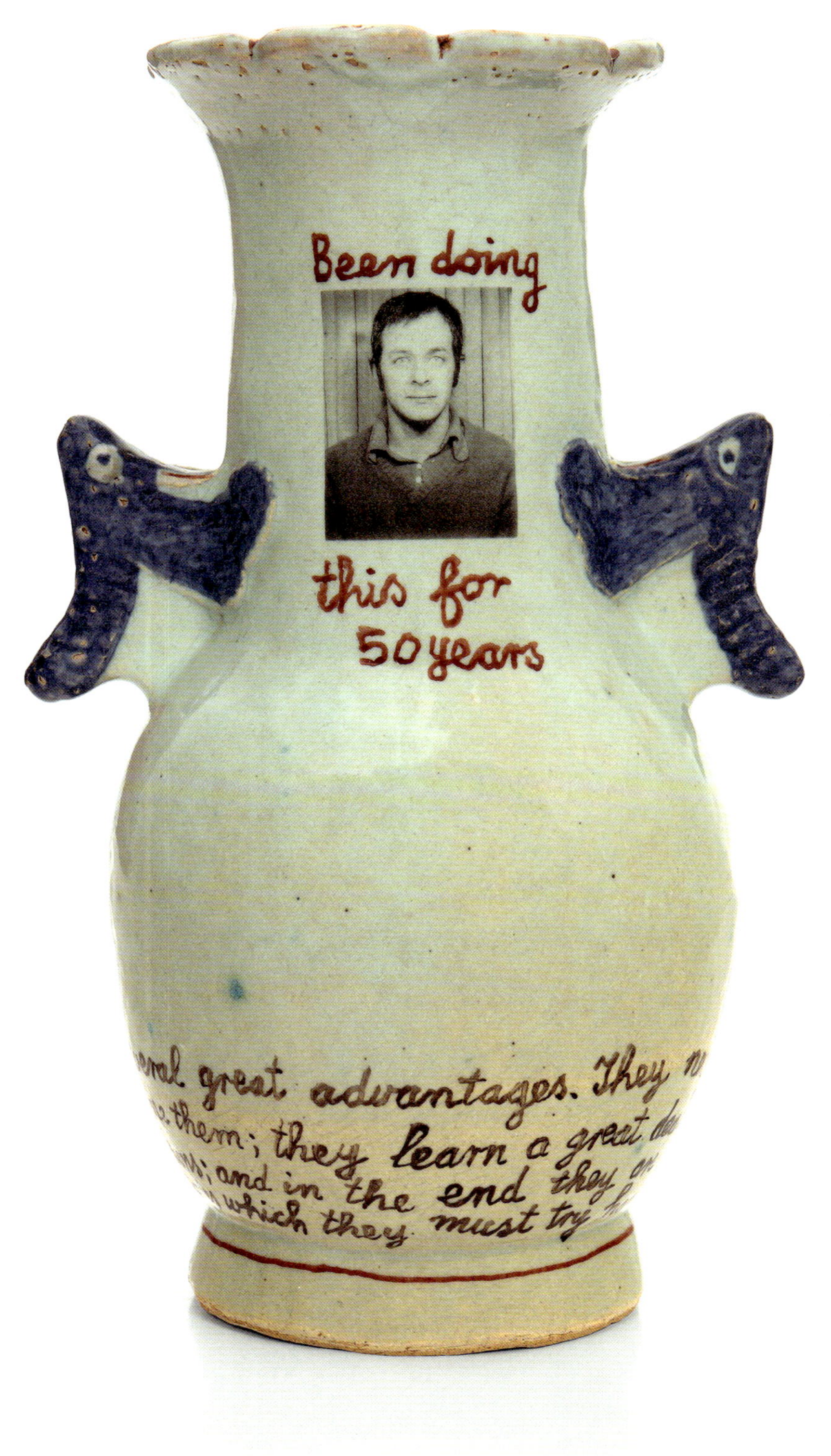

24 March 2017

It's a strange sensation to be old, which one never expected; you can't really imagine it, you just find yourself there. You think, 'Why do I do it, why do I keep working?' I do it because it's the thing that comes most naturally, somehow I'm happy doing it. I like to see the transformation from this to that to that. And opening the kiln is a shock of a kind.

Most of what I make are plates. The same shape over and over, but like people each one is different. That means I don't have to think too much about the shape and can concentrate on the thing that mostly gets me going, namely colour alone or combined with other colours, lines, blotches.

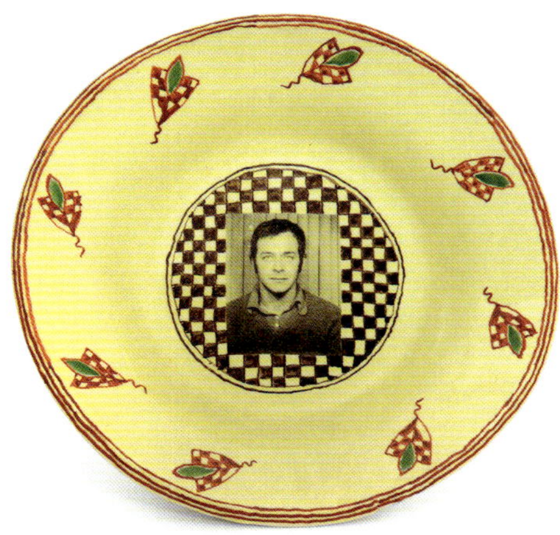

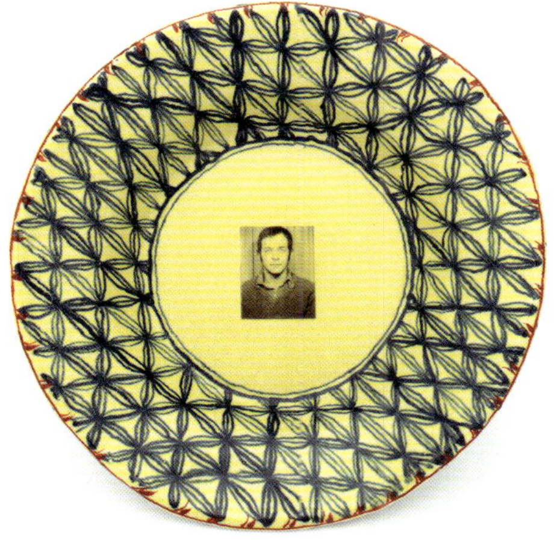

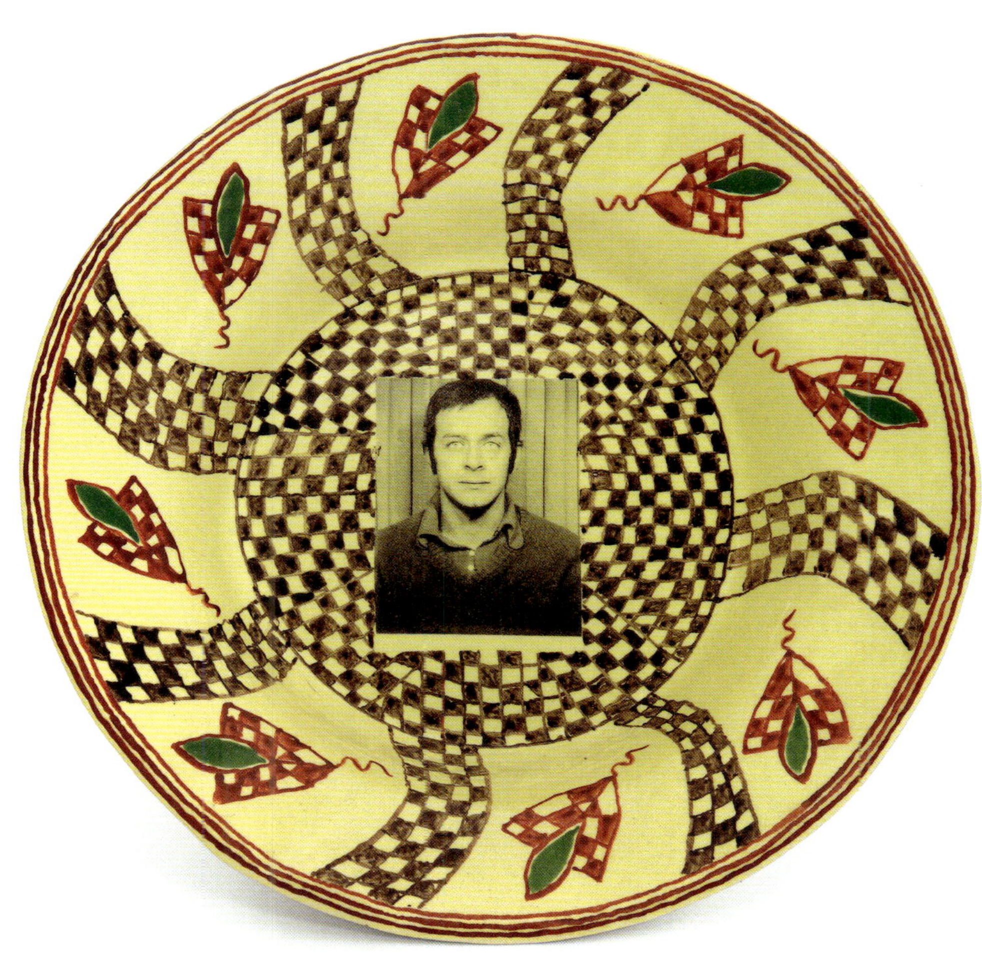

31 March 2017

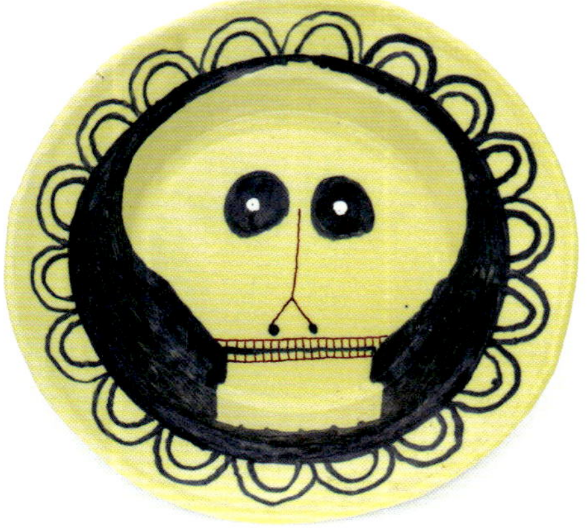
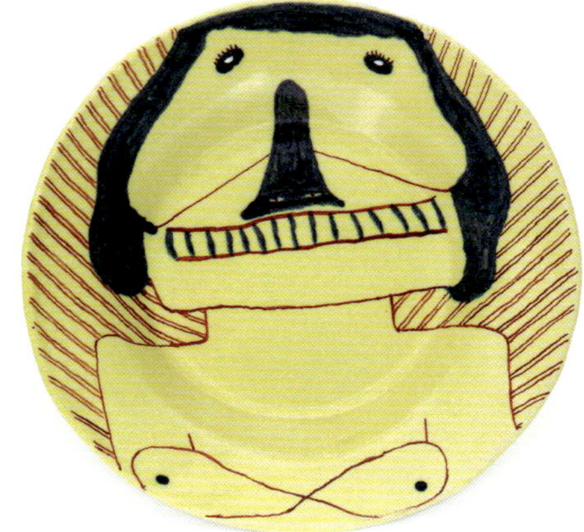
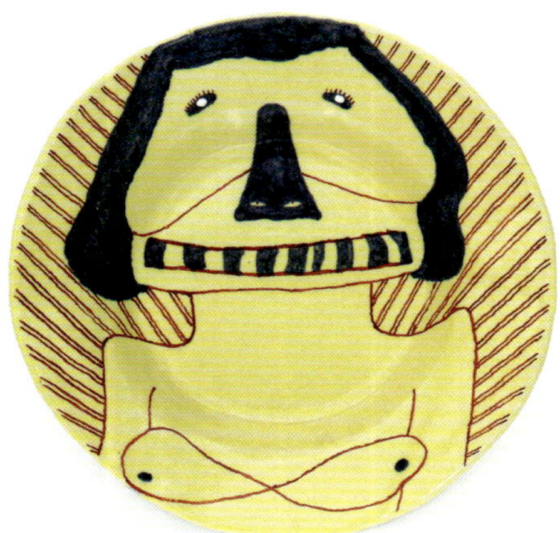
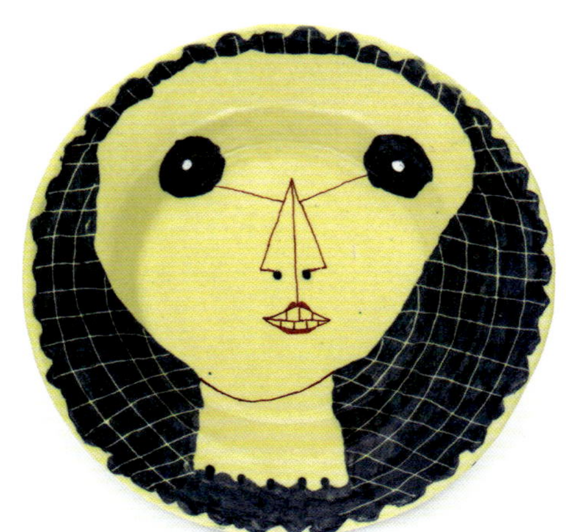
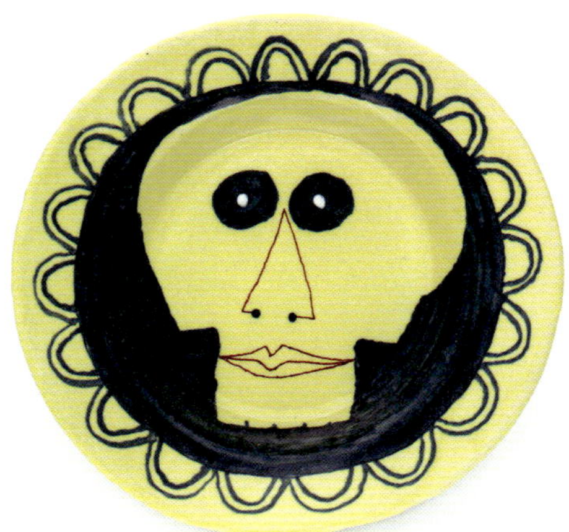

13 July 2017

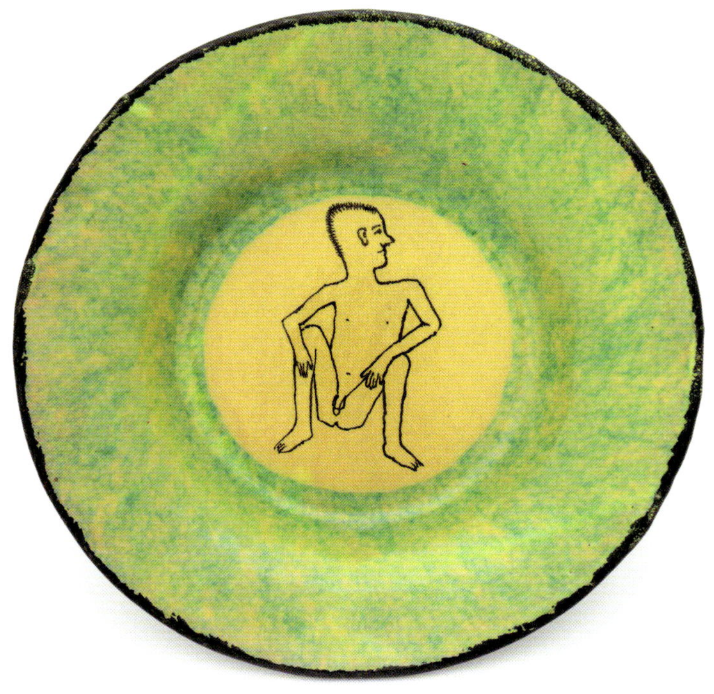

11 November 2012

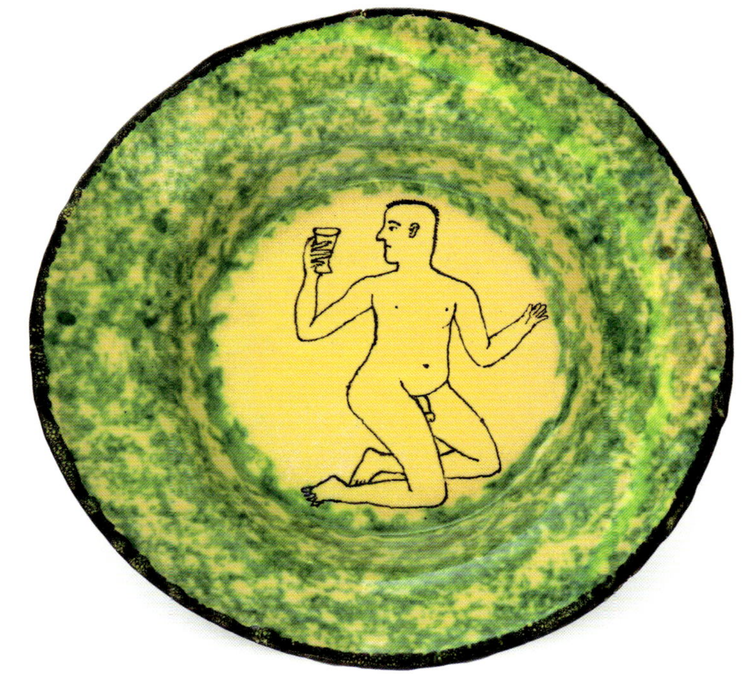

11 November 2012

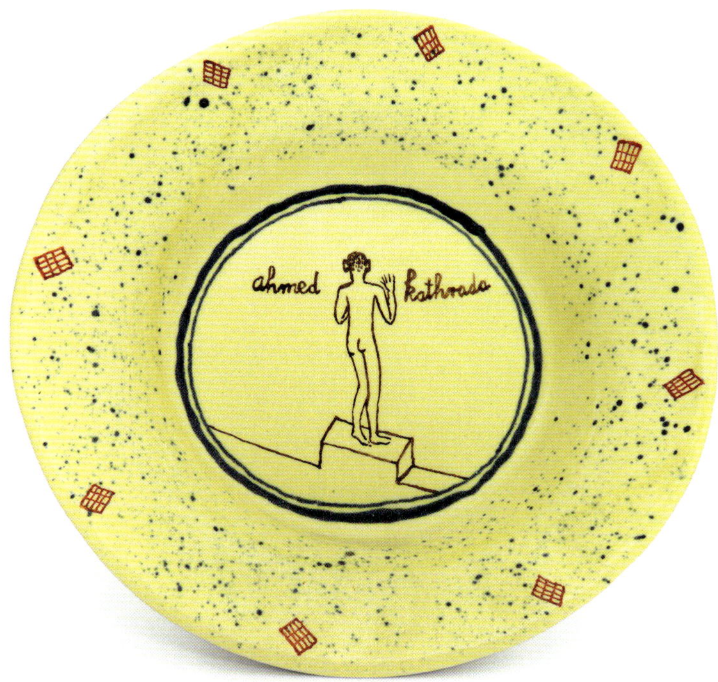

29 March 2017

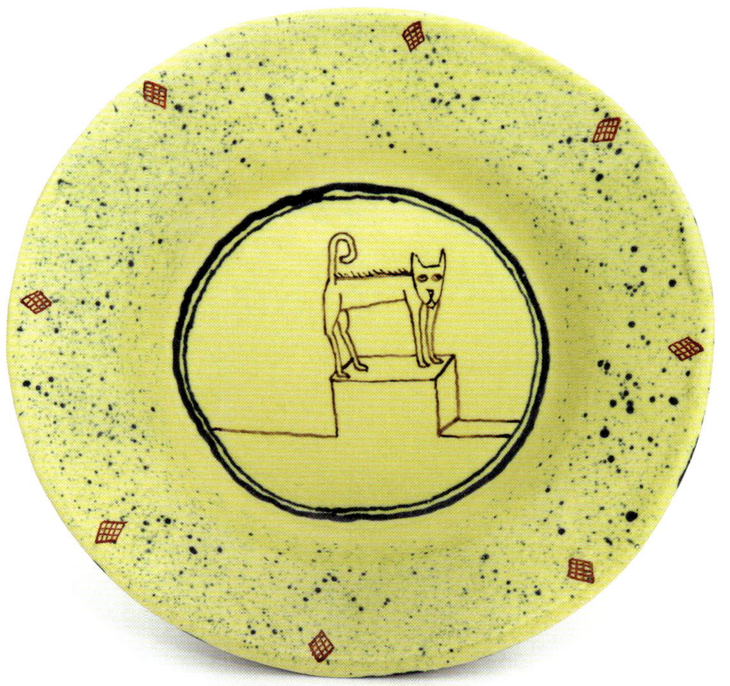

29 March 2017

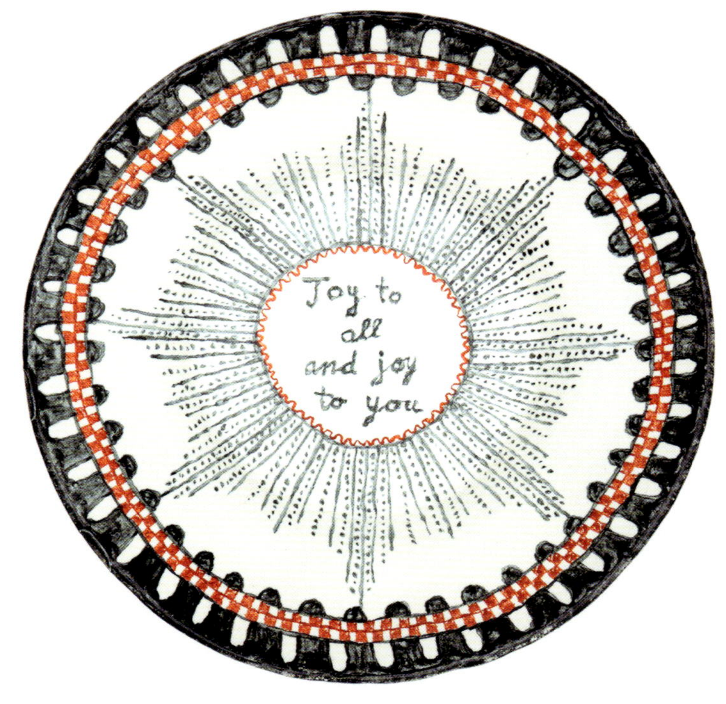

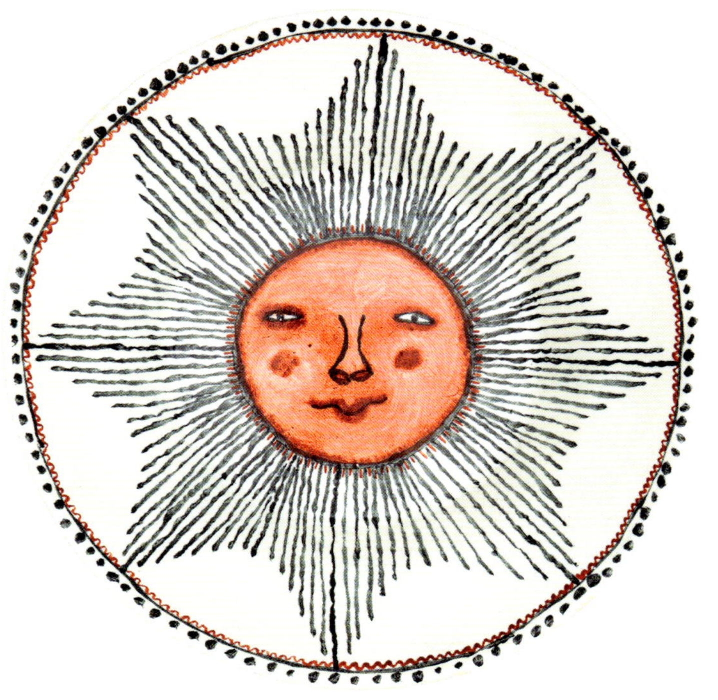

24 to 30 July 2020

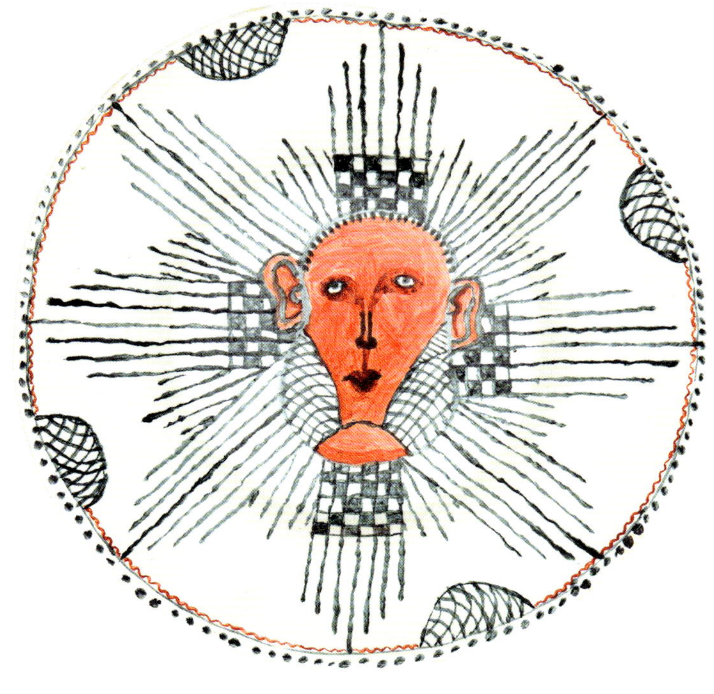

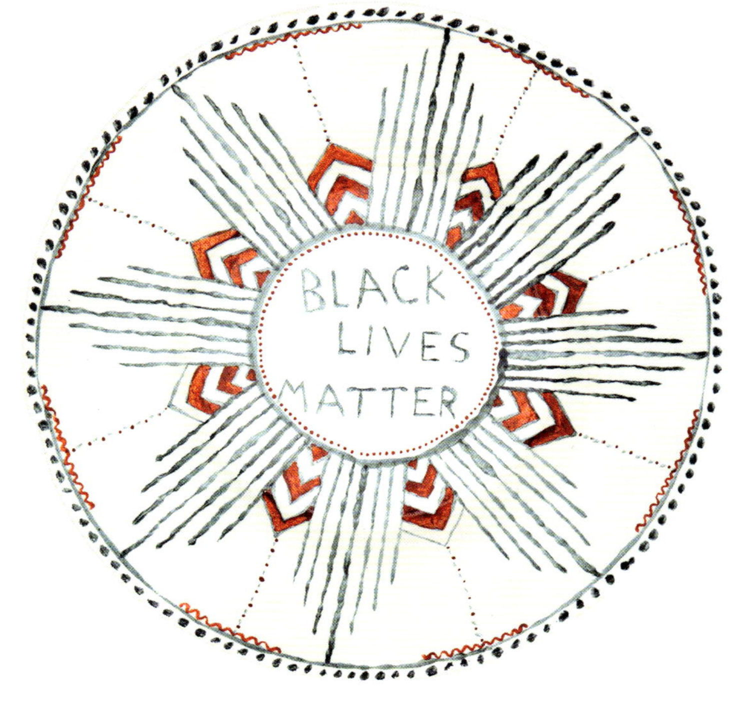
BLACK
LIVES
MATTER

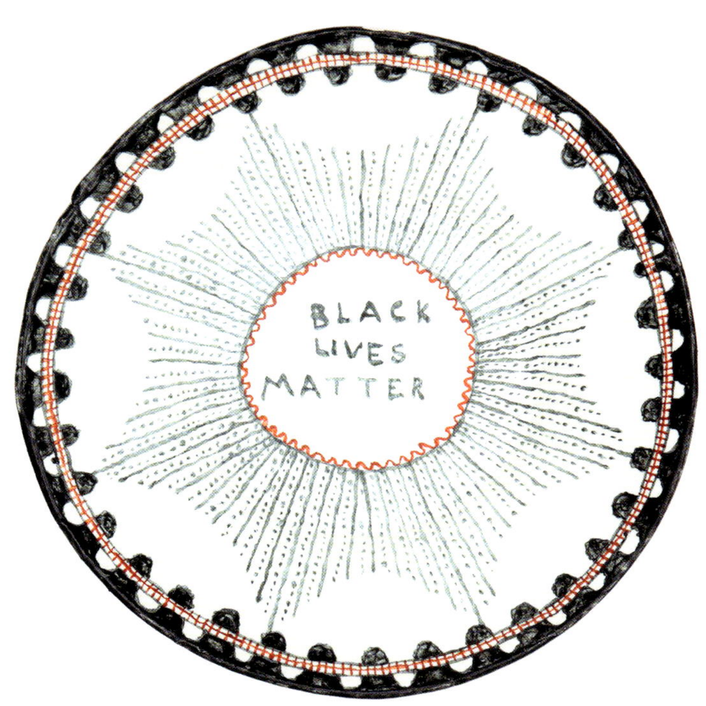
BLACK
LIVES
MATTER

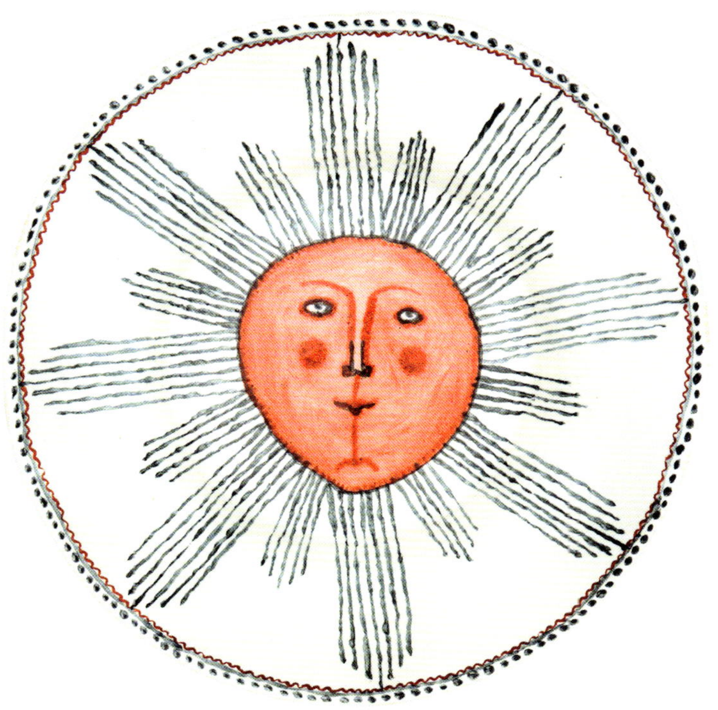

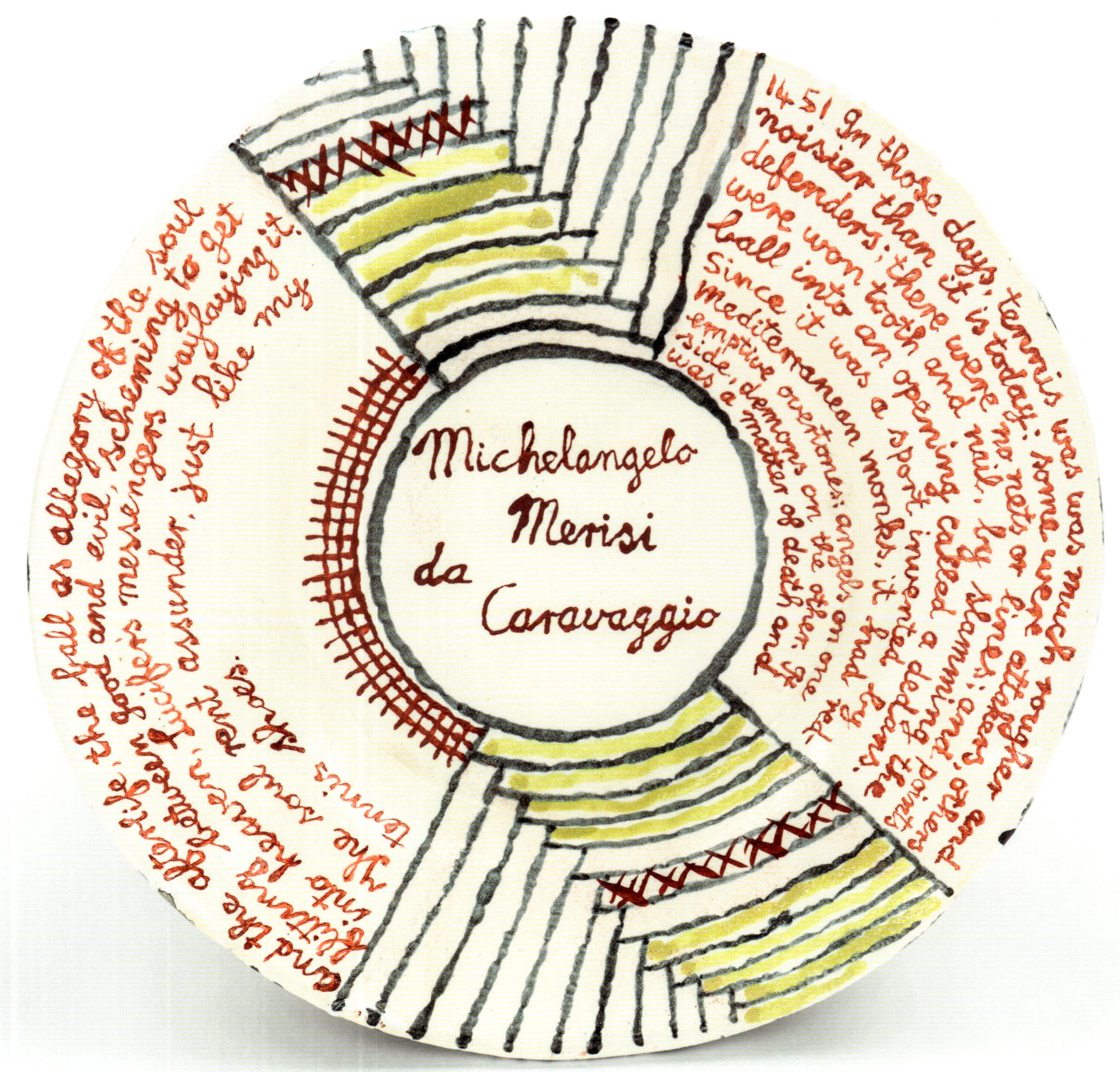

12 to 14 August 2020

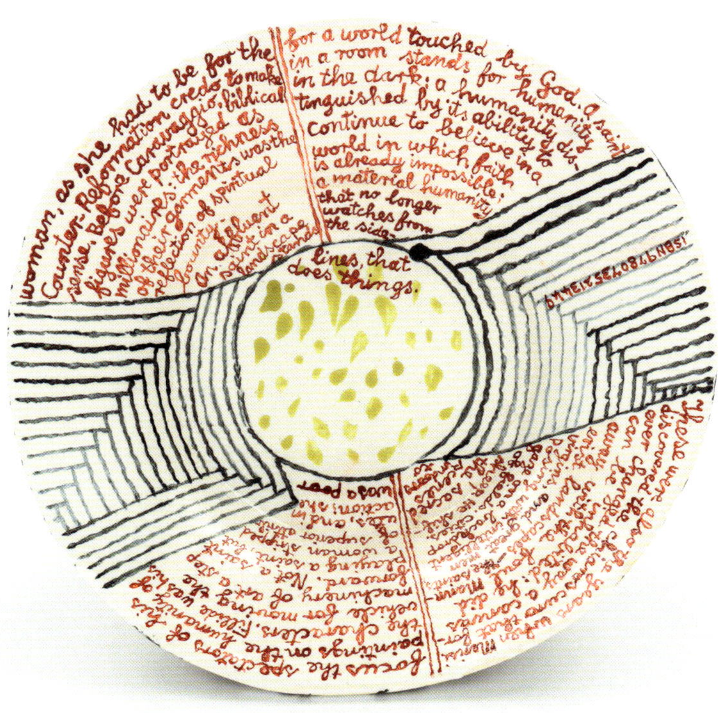
for a world touched by God. A saint
in a room stands for humanity
in the dark: a humanity dis-
tinguished by its ability to
continue to believe in a
world in which faith
is already impossible,
a material humanity
that no longer
watches from
the side.
lines that
does things.

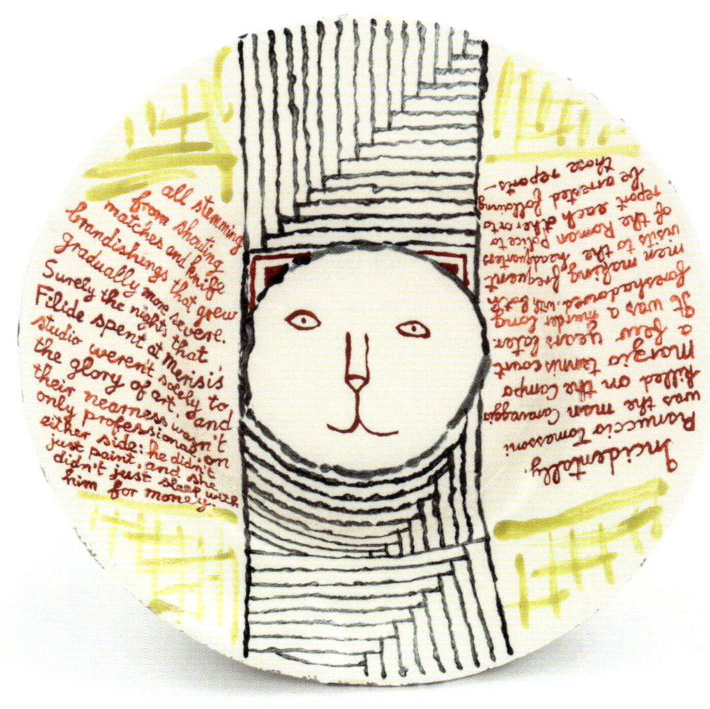

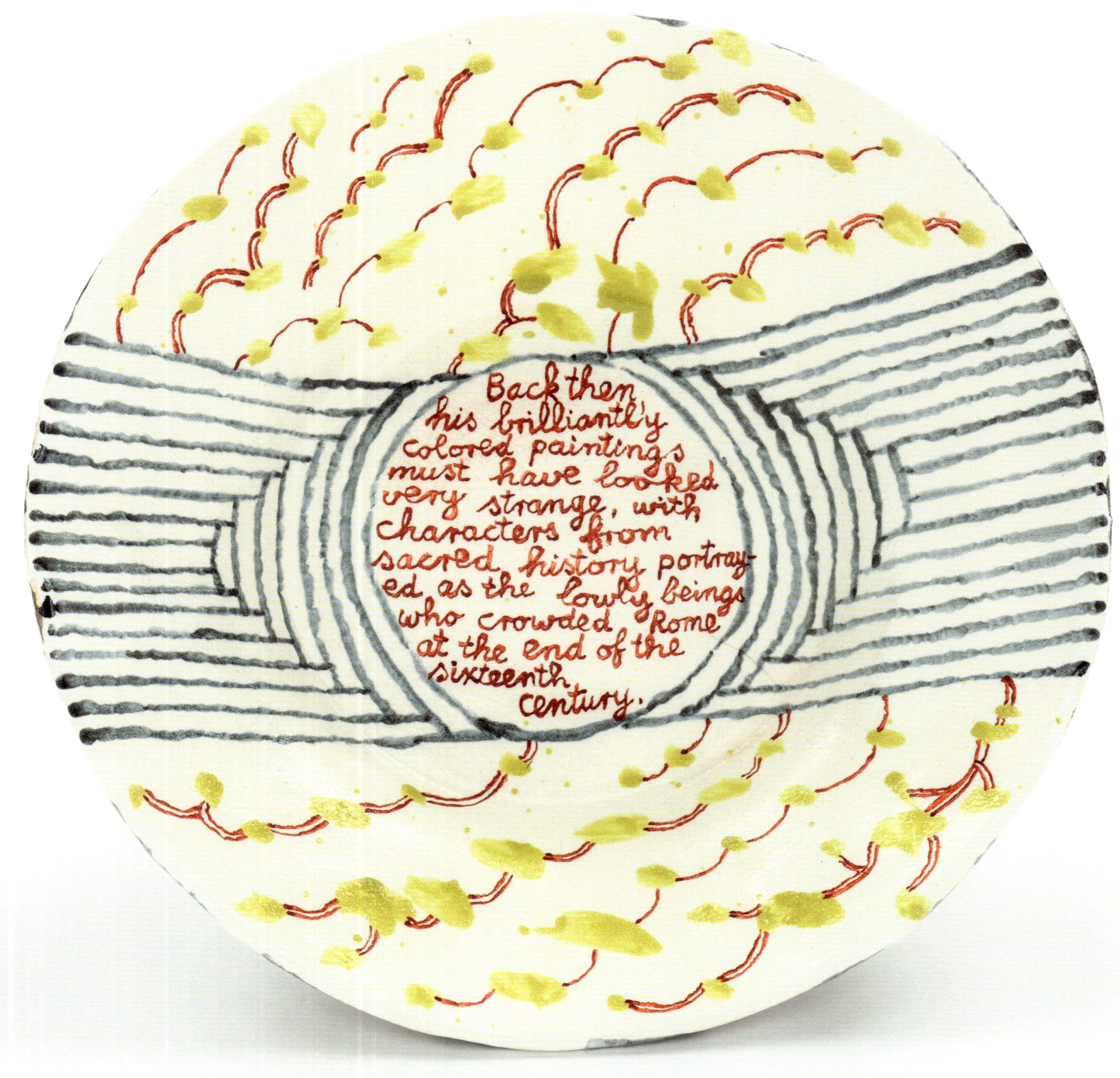

12 to 14 August 2020

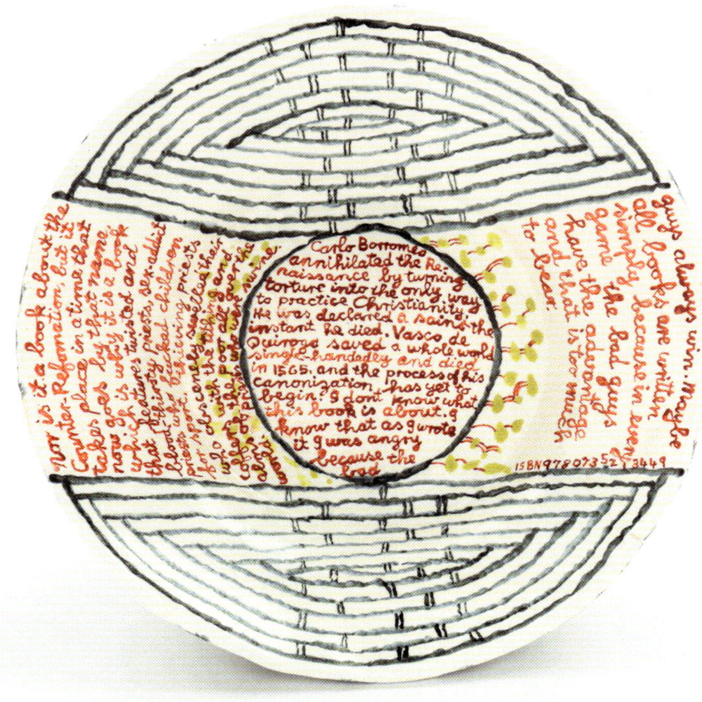
Carlo Borromeo annihilated the Renaissance by turning torture into the only way to practice Christianity. He was declared a saint the instant he died. Vasco de Quiroga saved a whole world singlehandedly and died in 1565, and the process of his canonization has yet to begin. I don't know what this book is about. I know that as I wrote it I was angry because the bad

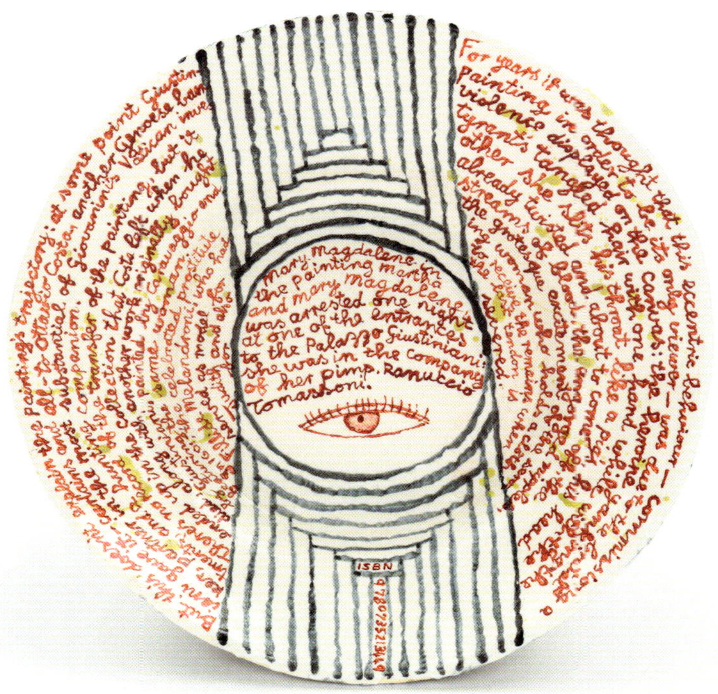
Mary Magdalene in the painting Martha and Mary Magdalene was arrested one night at one of the entrances to the Palazzo Giustiniani. She was in the company of her pimp, Ranuccio Tomassoni.
ISBN

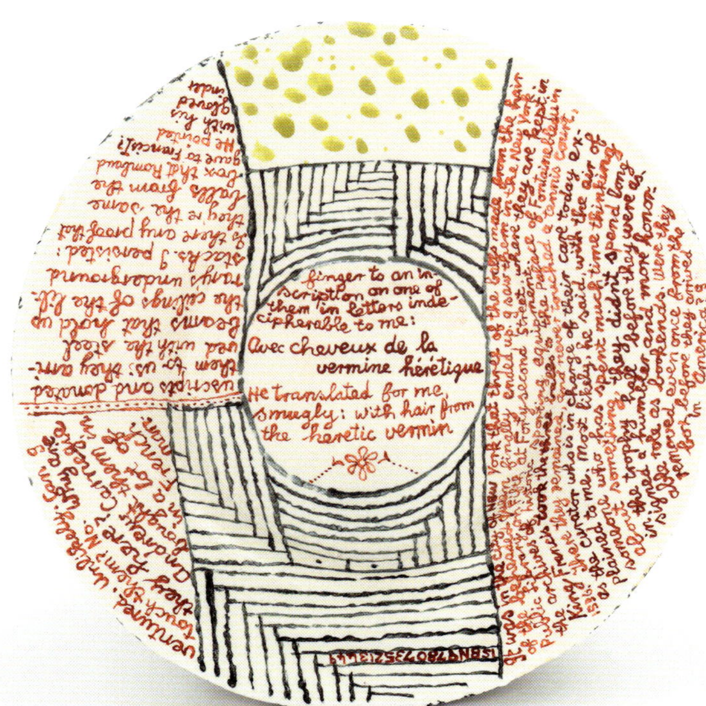
finger to an inscription on one of them in letters indecipherable to me:
Avec cheveux de la vermine hérétique
He translated for me, smugly: with hair from the heretic vermin

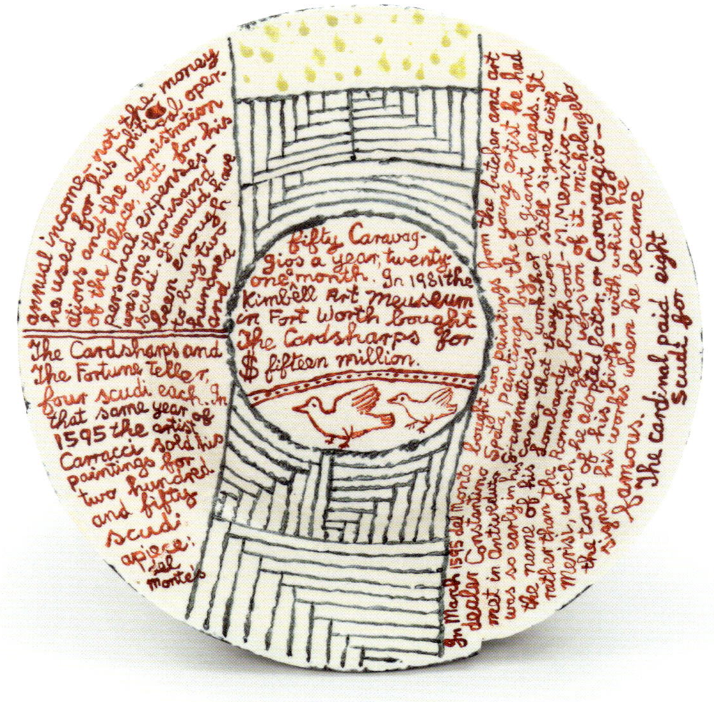

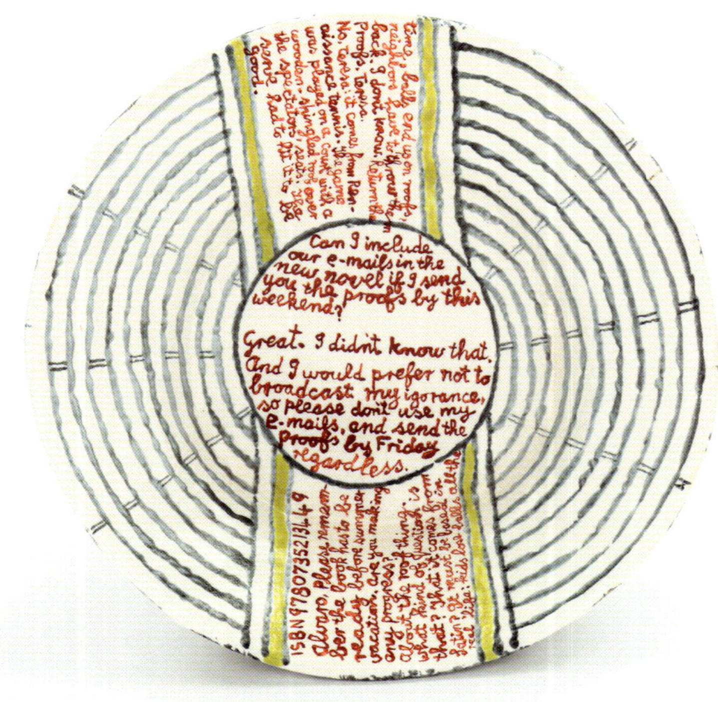

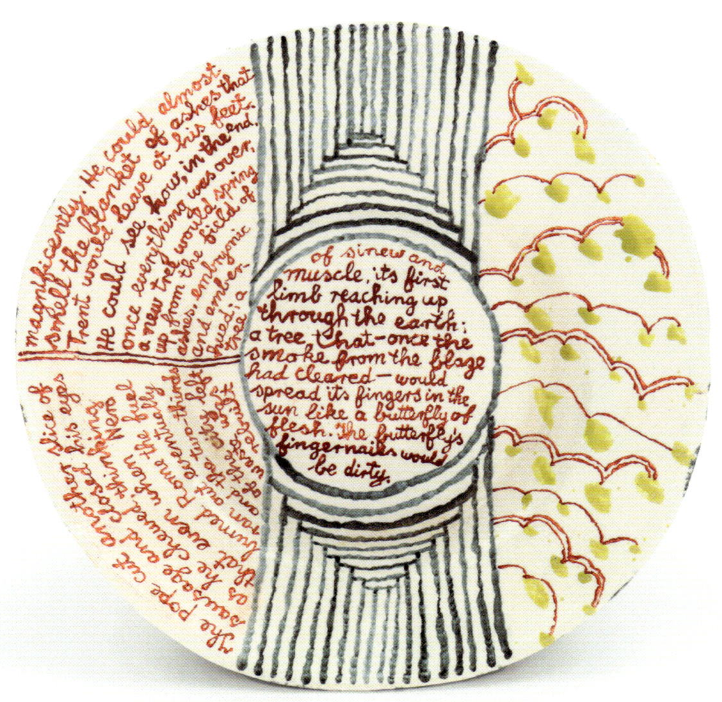

12 to 14 August 2020

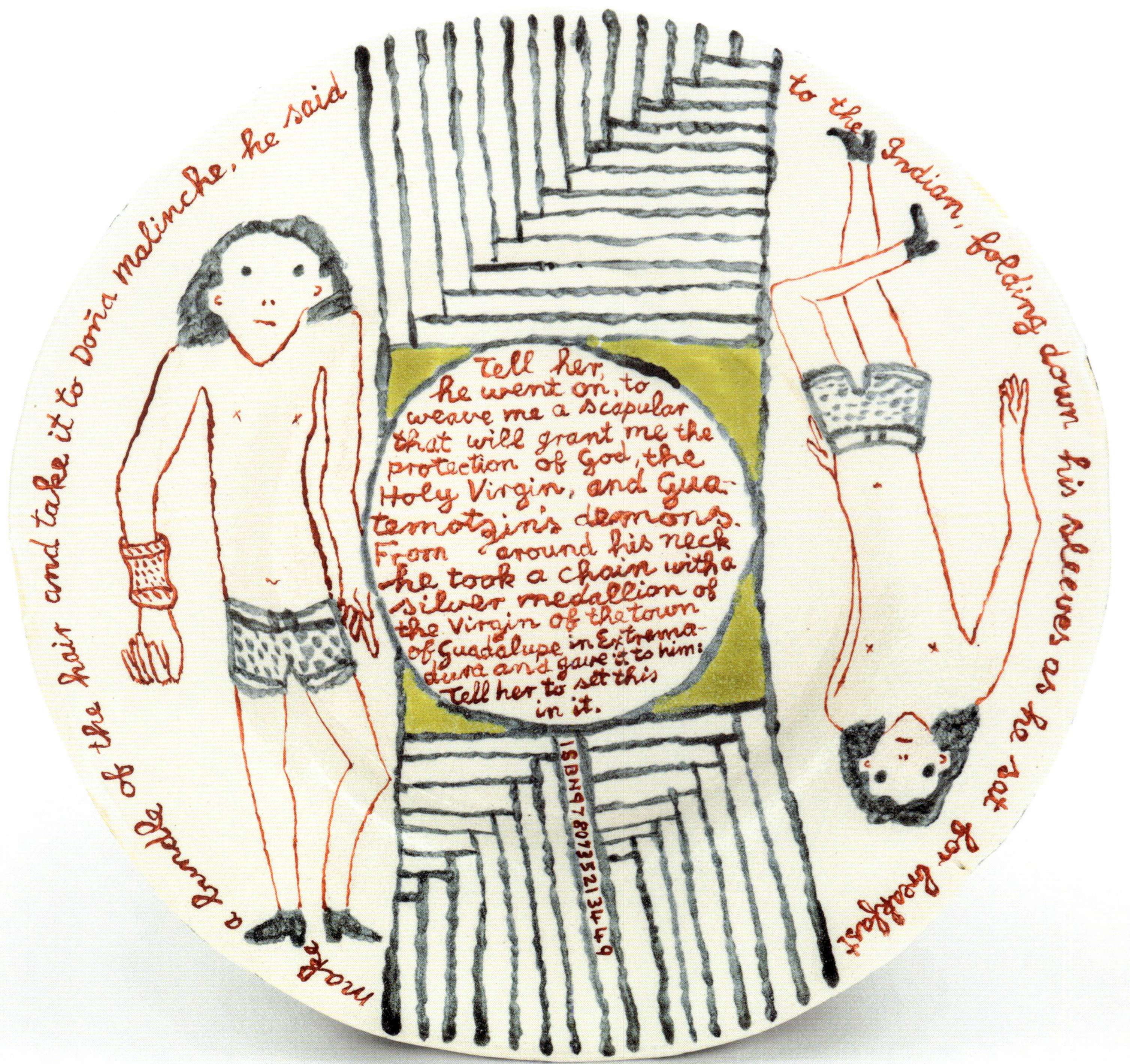
make a bundle of the hair and take it to Doña Malinche, he said to the Indian, folding down his sleeves as he sat for breakfast
Tell her,
he went on, to
weave me a scapular
that will grant me the
protection of God, the
Holy Virgin, and Gua-
temotzin's demons.
From around his neck
he took a chain with a
silver medallion of
the Virgin of the town
of Guadalupe in Extrema-
dura and gave it to him:
Tell her to set this
in it.
ISBN9780735213449

Never has a man
done for any faith what
Hernán Cortés did for Renaissance
Catholicism, and yet five centuries
after the greatest religious feat of all time,
the Vatican continues to look the other way when-
ever his name is invoked. what a provincial brute he
must have been never to receive recognition
for having set
at the feet
of the pope—his right ball—a world complete with all its
animals, plants, temples, and little houses with hun-
dreds of thousands of ladies and gentlmen
inside, cavorting like rabbits, taking
advantage of the fact that they could
run around almost buck naked
in the eternal good
weather.

12 to 14 August 2020

I wanted to use the red colour because it gives a nice optimistic lightness, but I didn't want to make a pattern, because your mind reads a pattern and then that's all it sees. I wanted to make it more complex than simply a pattern. The text is from the book *Sudden Death* by Álvaro Enrigue. The other is sort of abstract, it looks a bit like a watch, you see, so I made it one.

In the West we've got hierarchies of material; oil on canvas is powerful, bronze, as is marble, high up there. For the Chinese it was writing, bits of writing. But there was nothing like it in Western culture, this kind of thing. You see, it starts with writing in this hierarchy, and then old musical instruments, and so forth, and somewhere along the line it comes to pottery.

Modern Chinese has been simplified down to a mere 3,000 characters, something like that, whereas before there were many more. I found often that literate Chinese struggle with old texts because the language has been so simplified. I have a small thing from the eighteenth century with some writing on the side. A Chinese man once translated it for me. He said, 'Last night the autumn wind scattered the chrysanthemum petals over the terrace' ... or something like that.

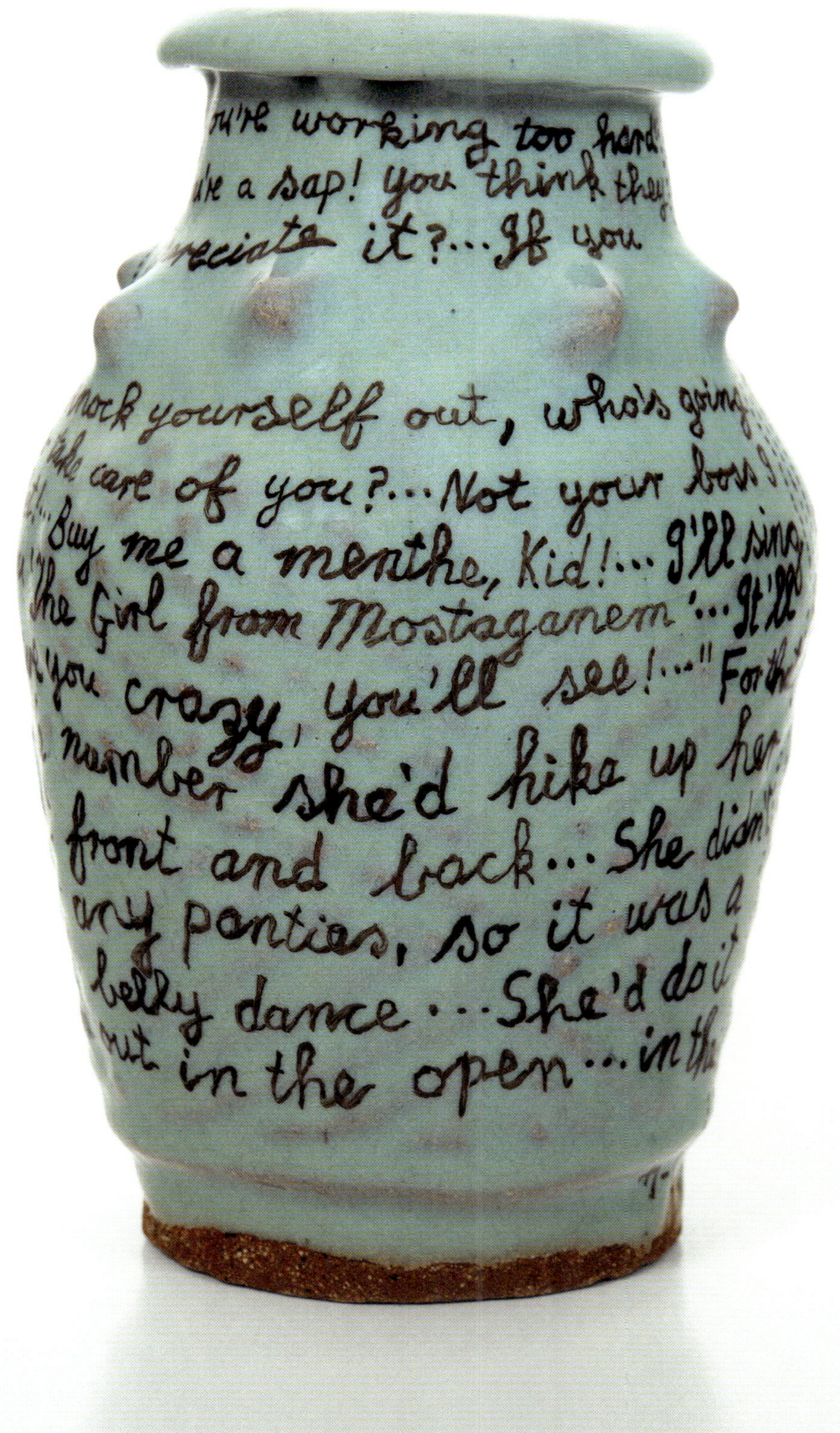

5 February 2016

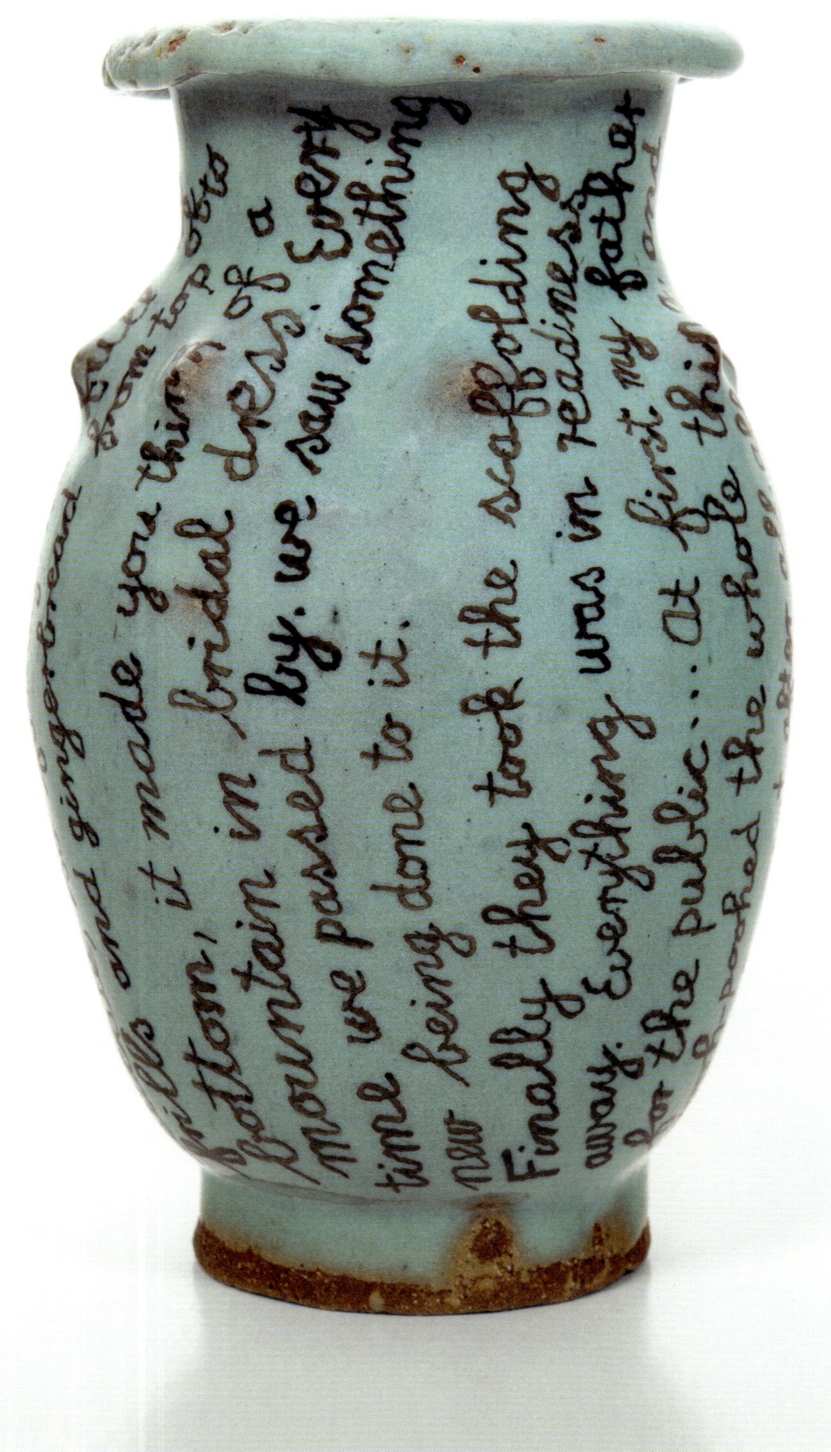

5 February 2016

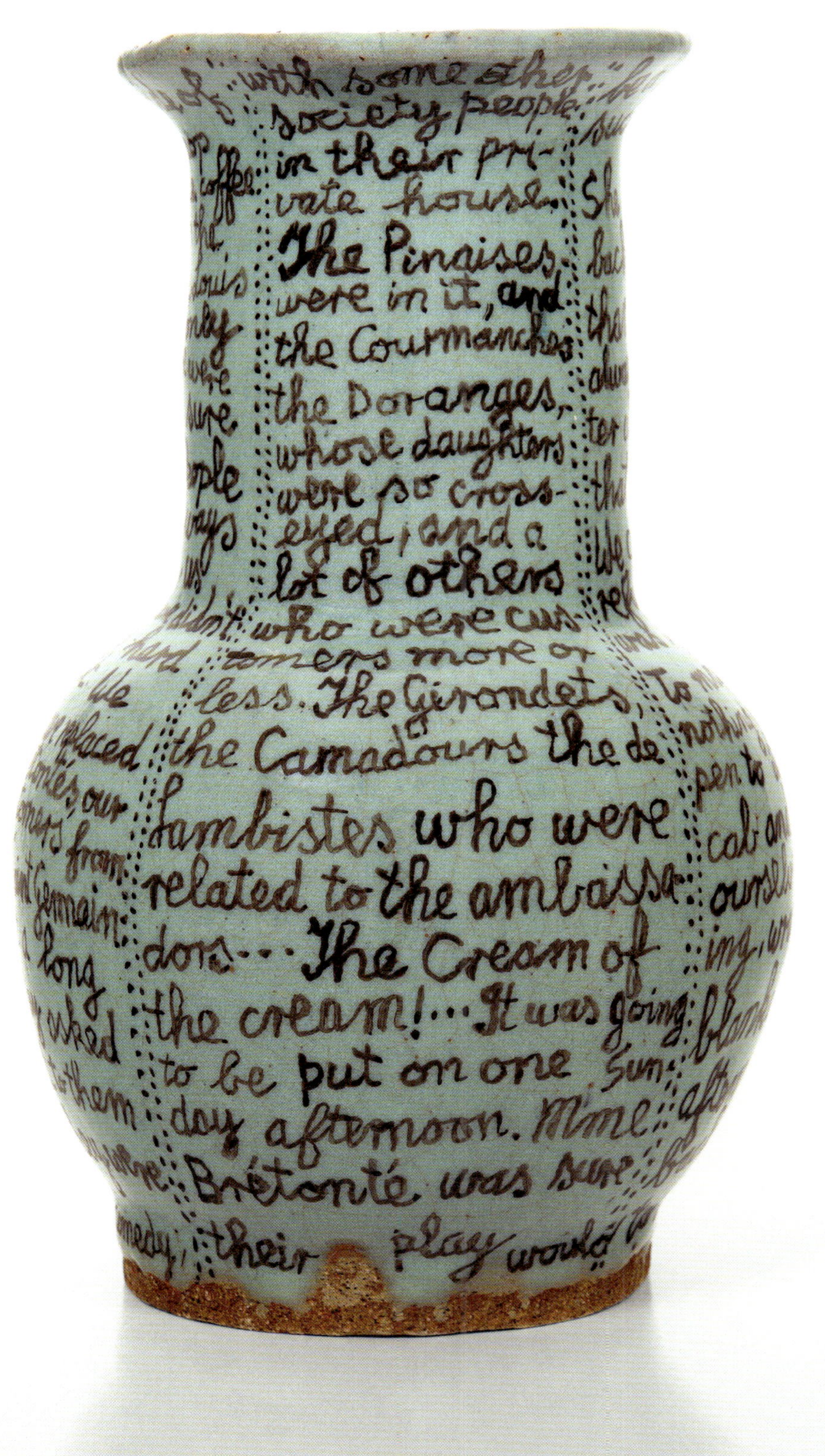

5 February 2016

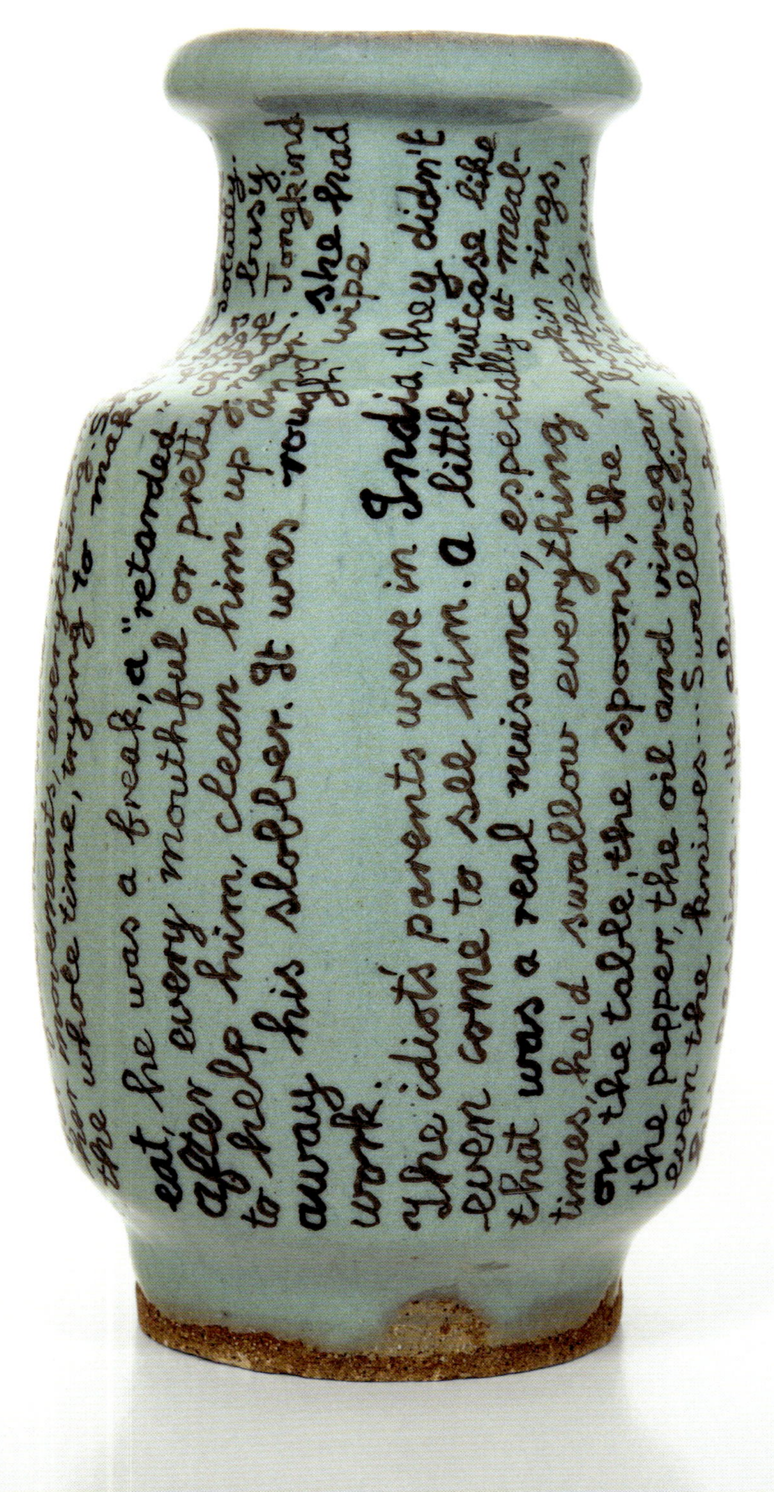

5 February 2016

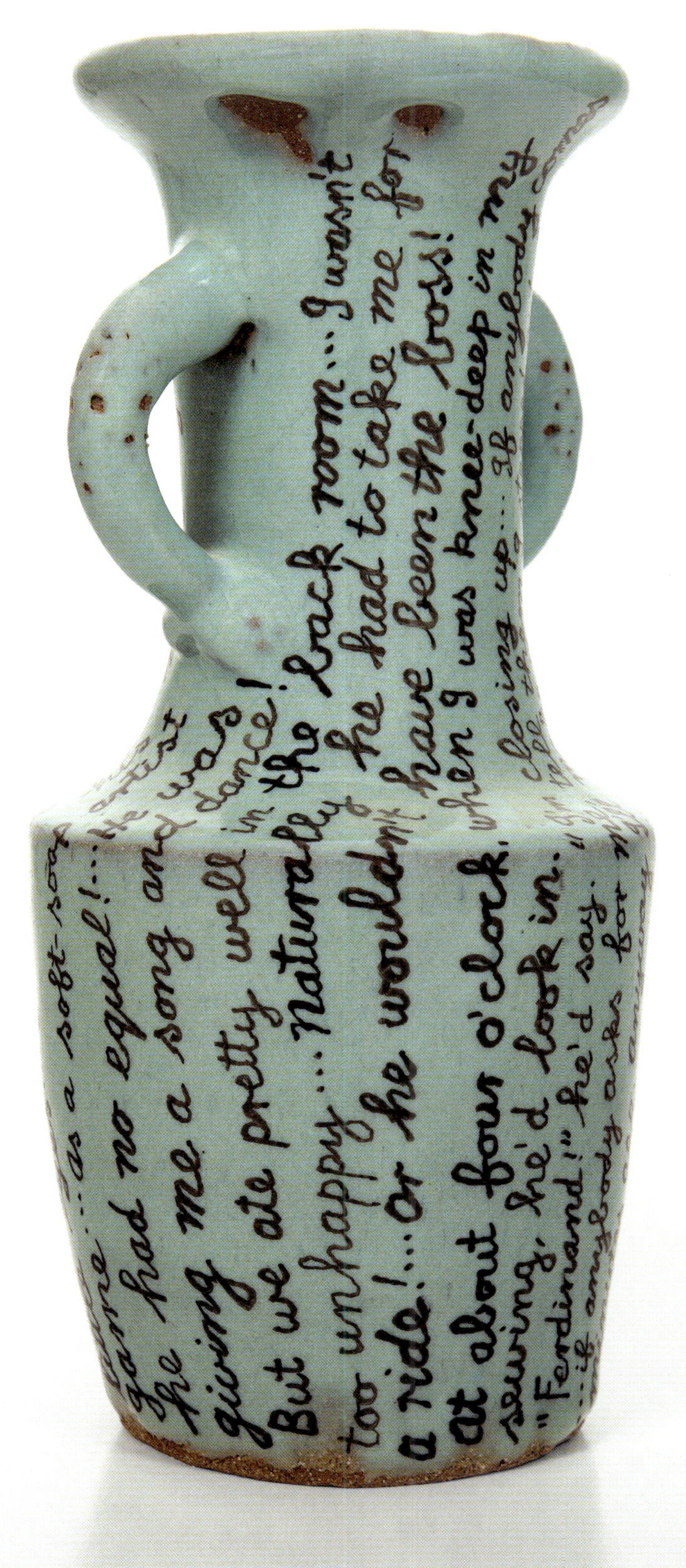

5 February 2016

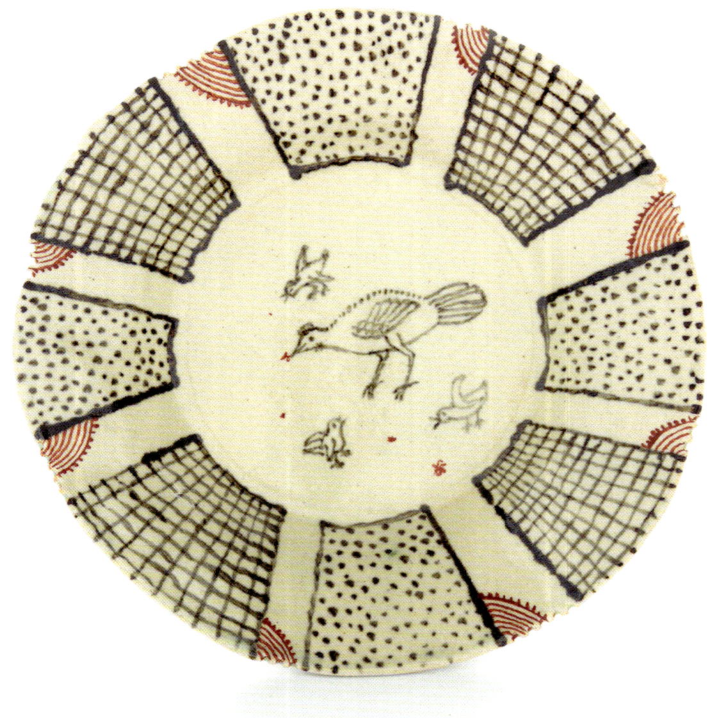

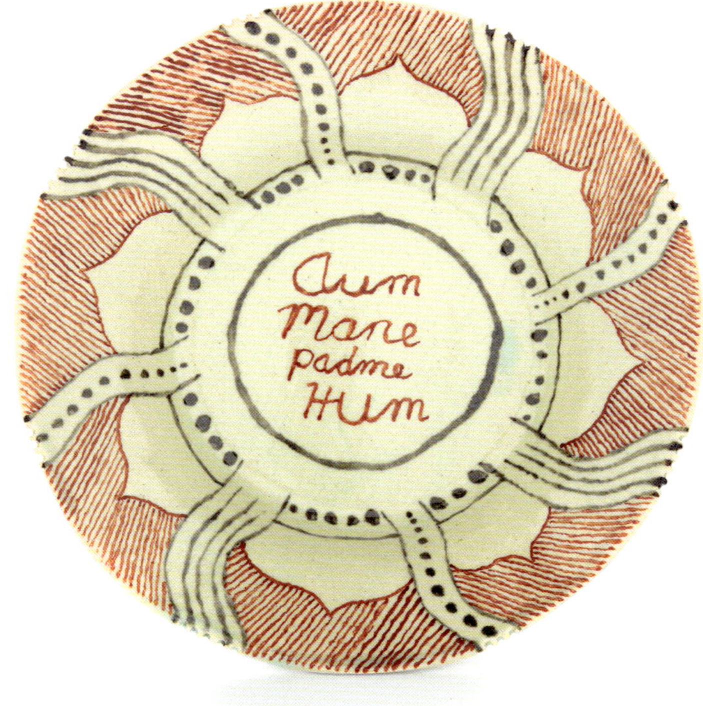

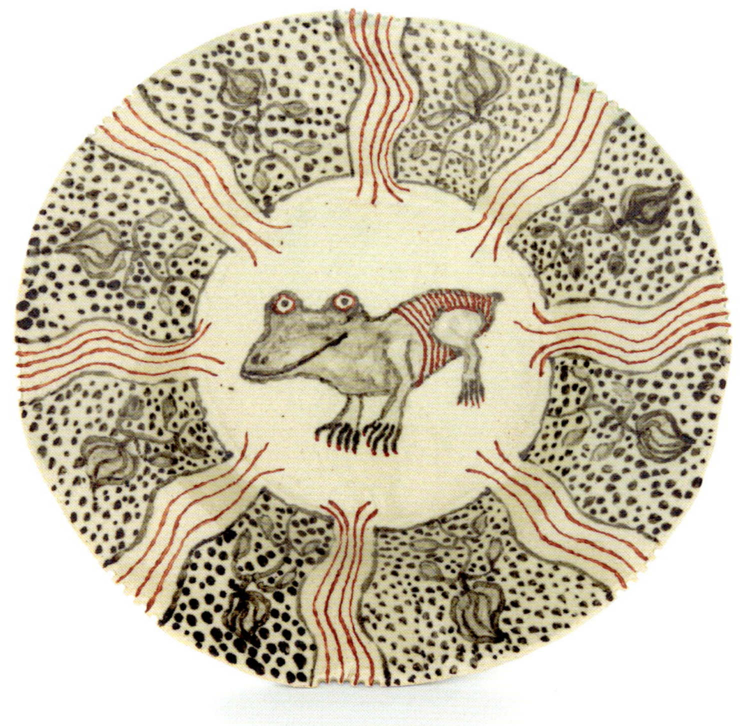

4 to 14 April 2020

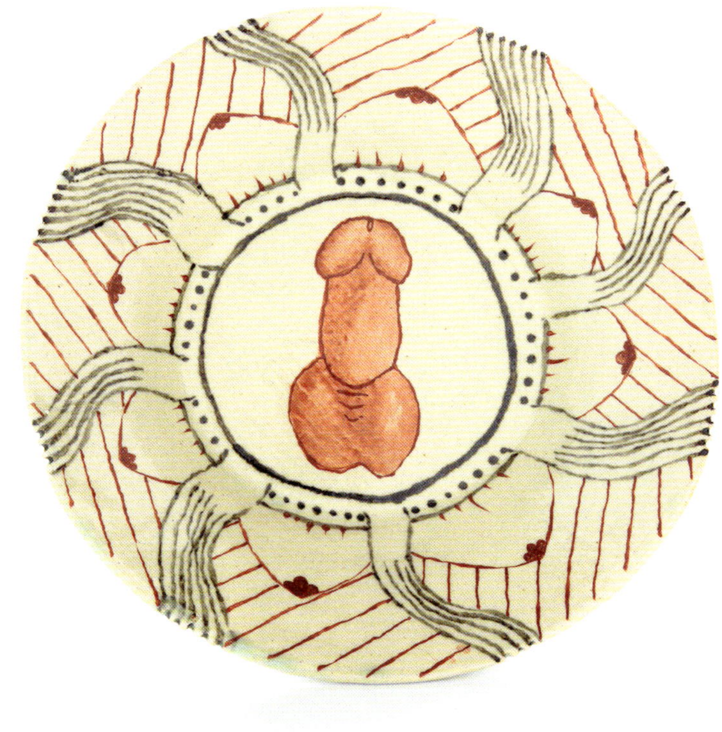

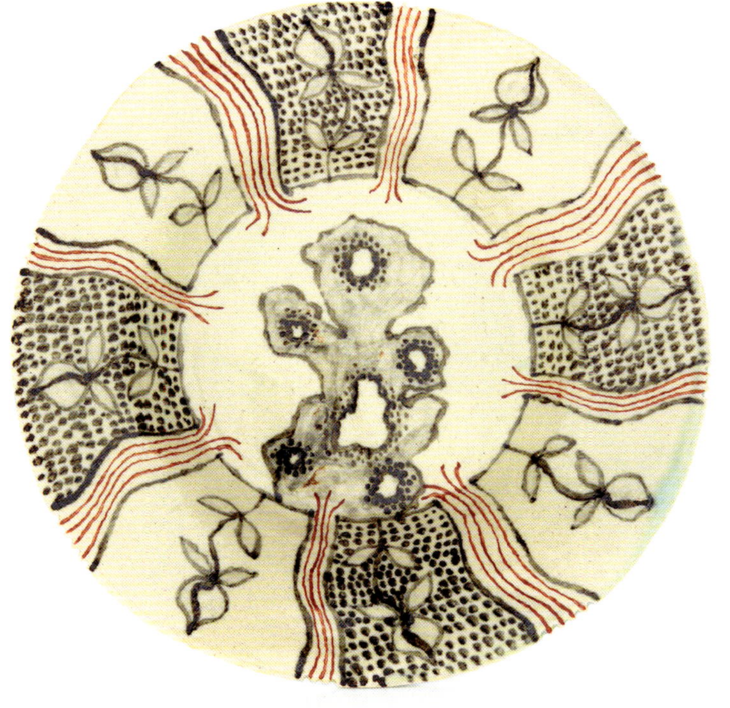

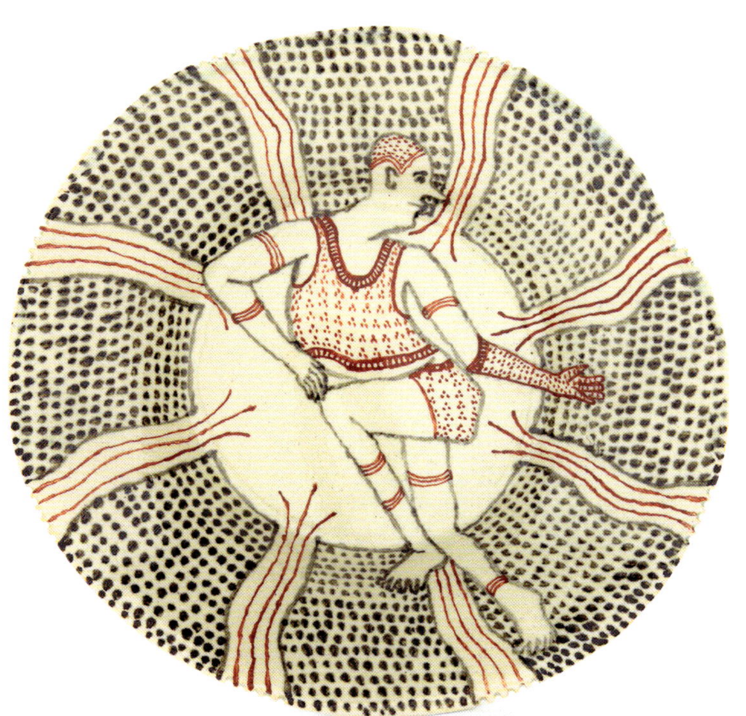

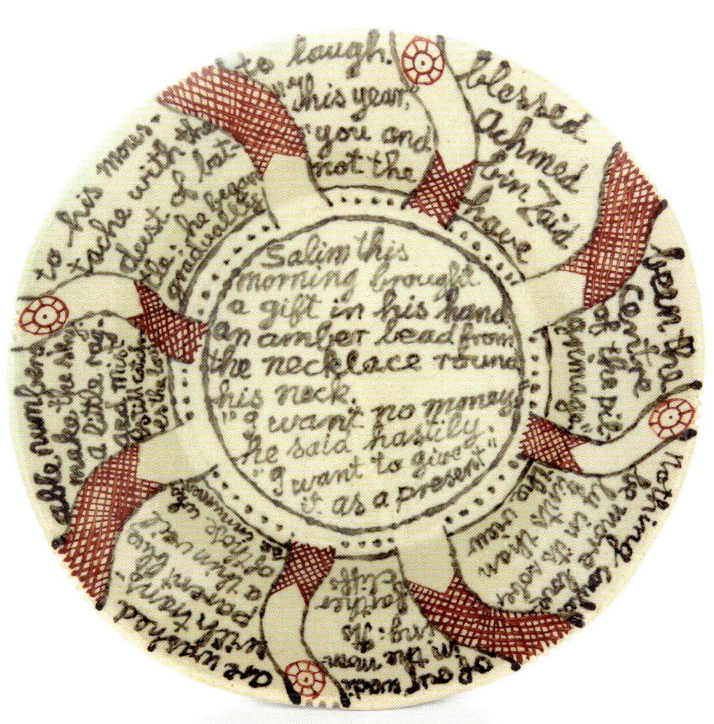
Salim this morning brought a gift in his hand an amber bead from the necklace round his neck. "I want no money" he said hastily "I want to give it as a present".

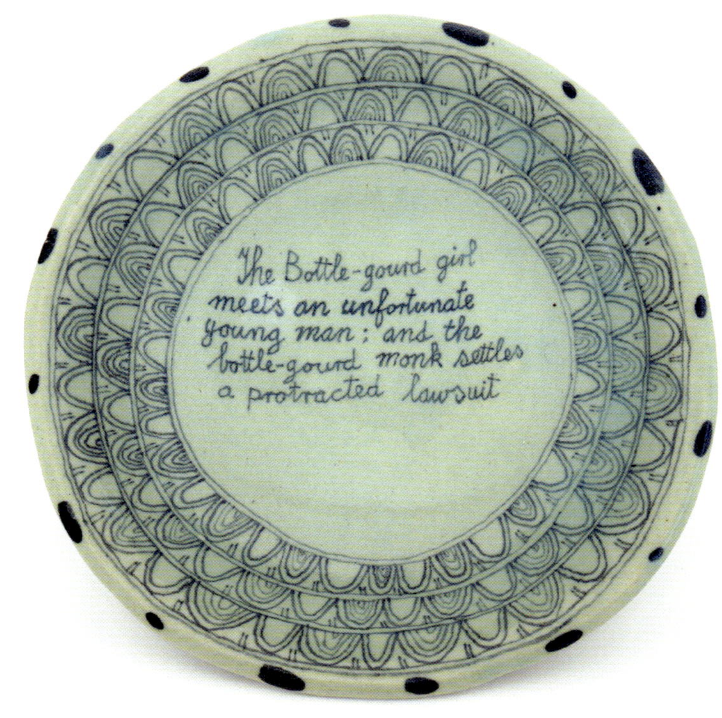

6 October 2015

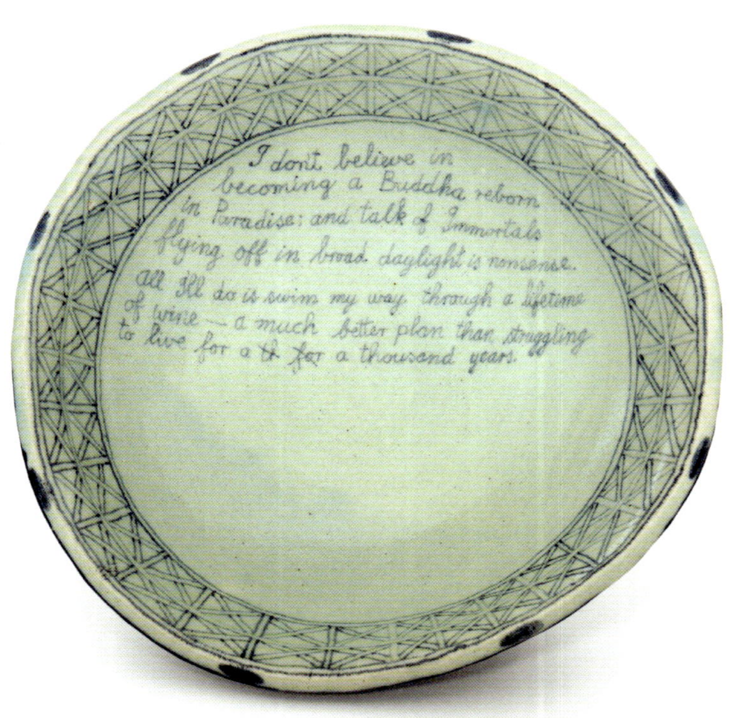

11 September 2015

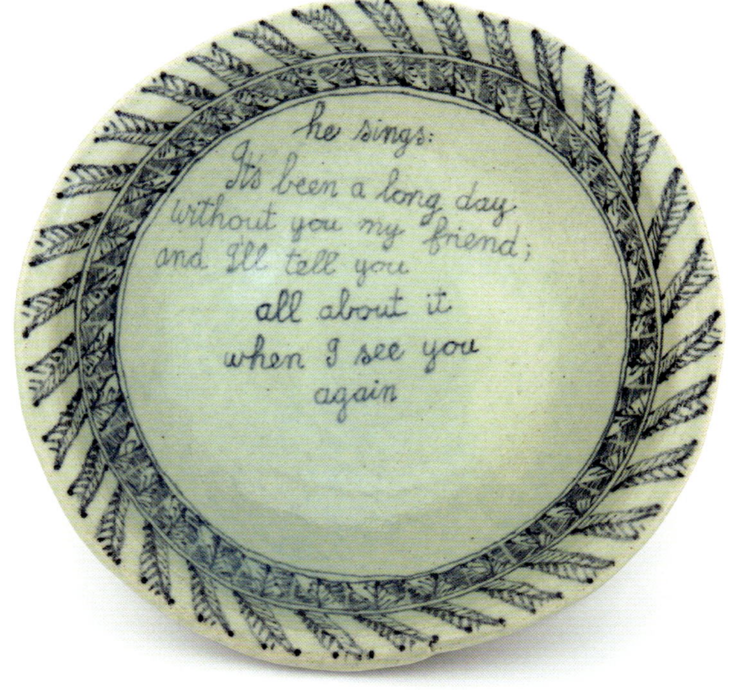

11 September 2015

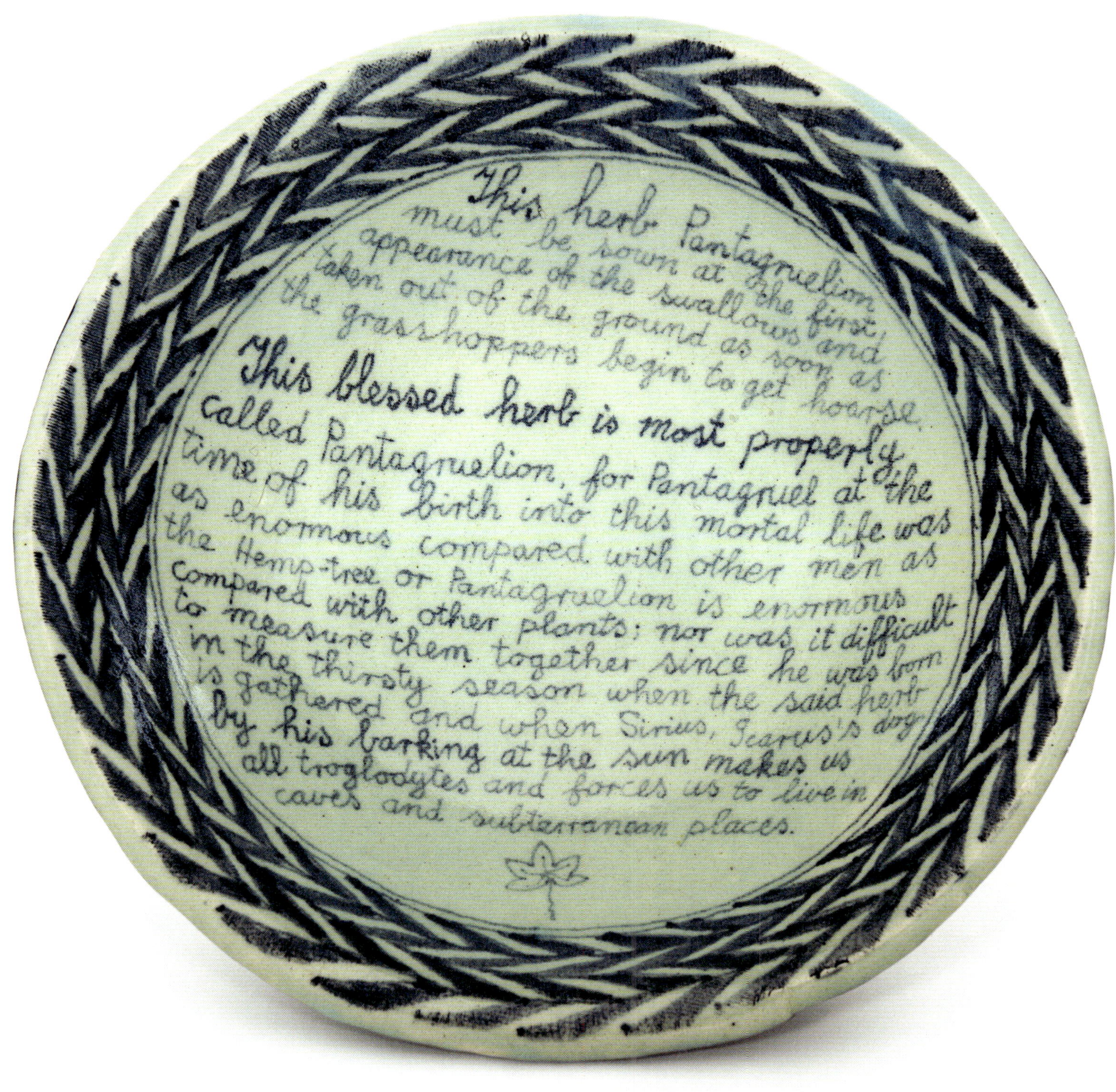

11 September 2015

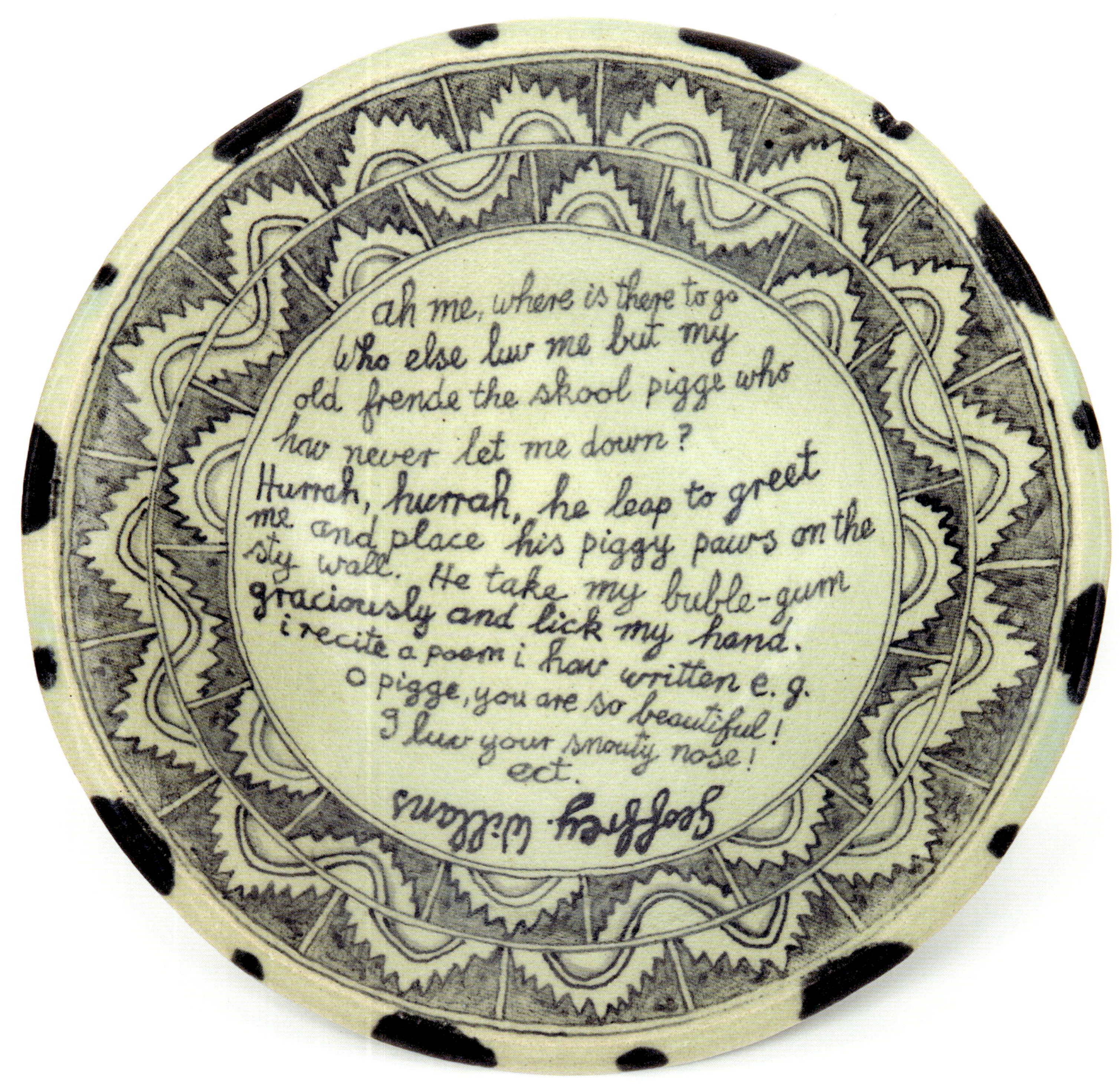

6 November 2015

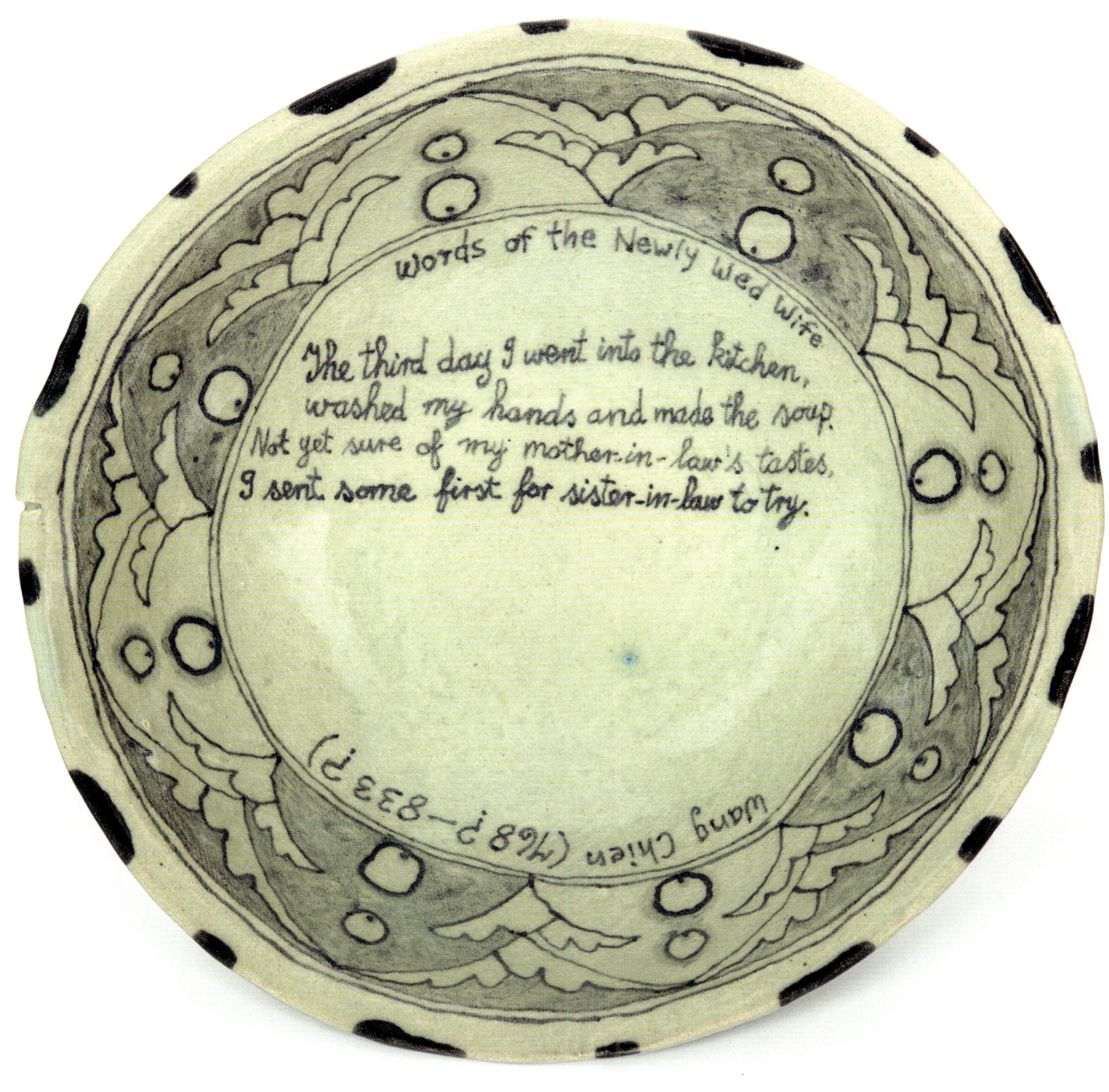

6 November 2015

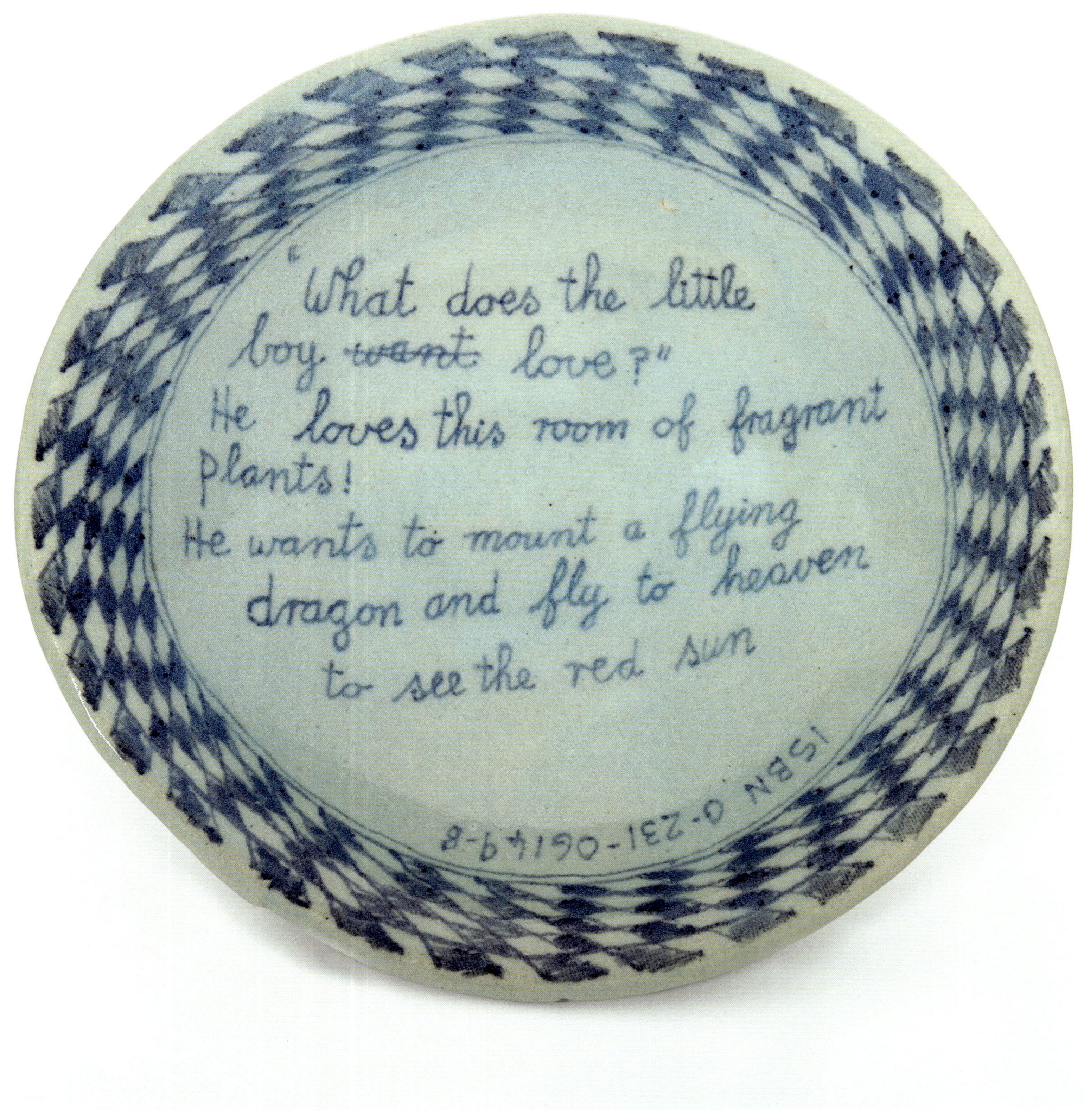

11 September 2015

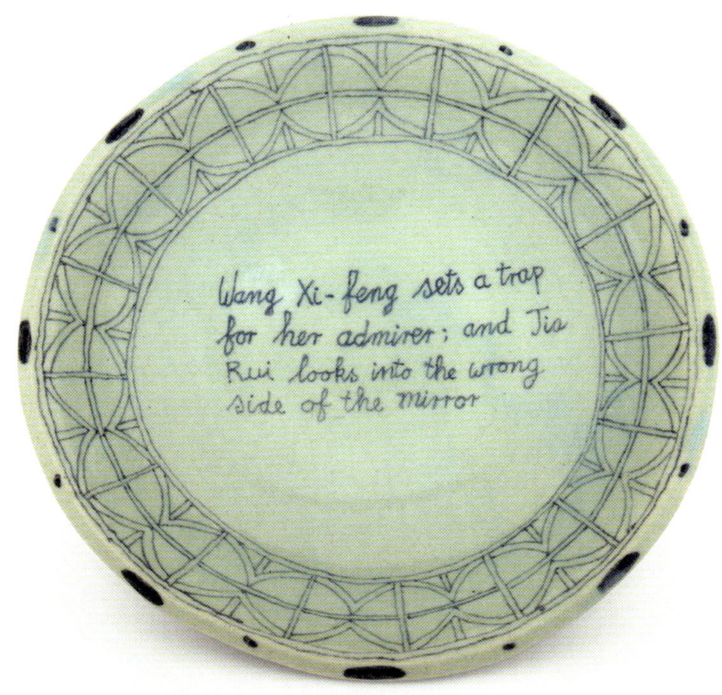

6 October 2015

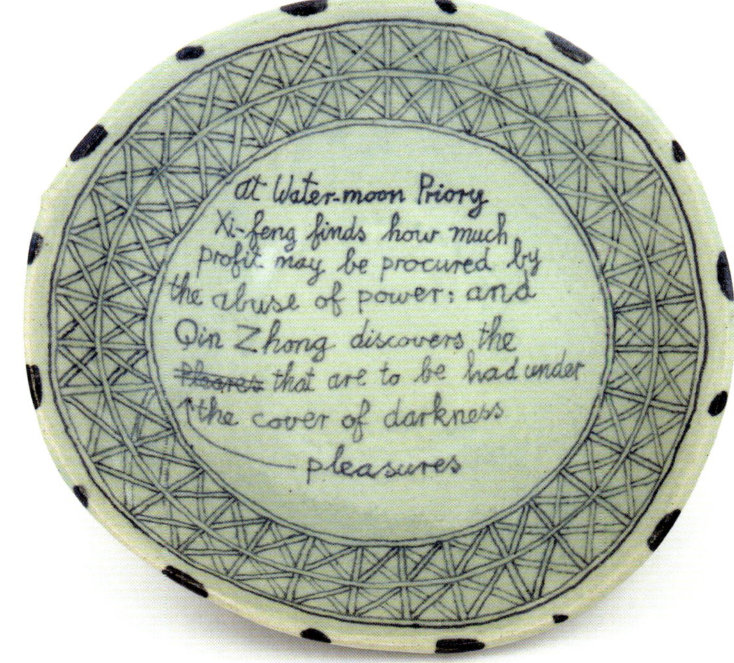

6 October 2015

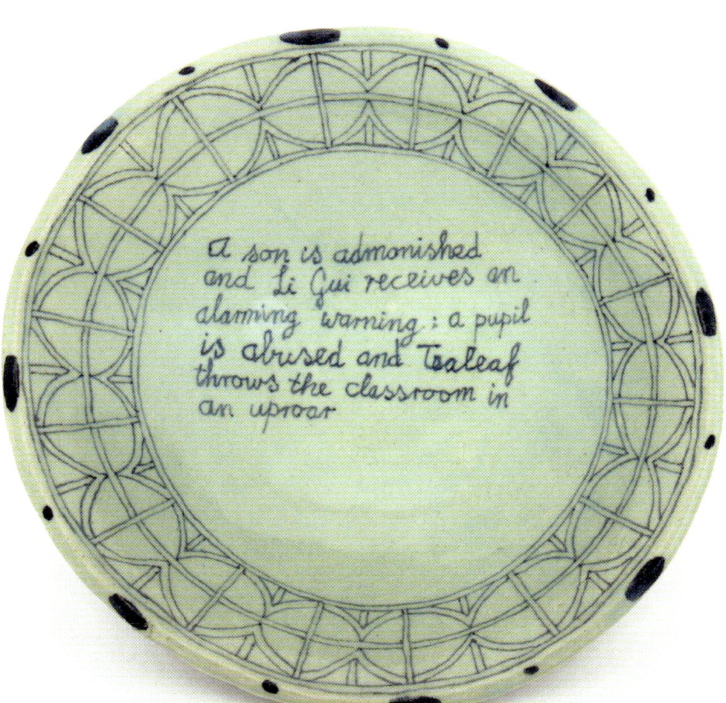

6 October 2015

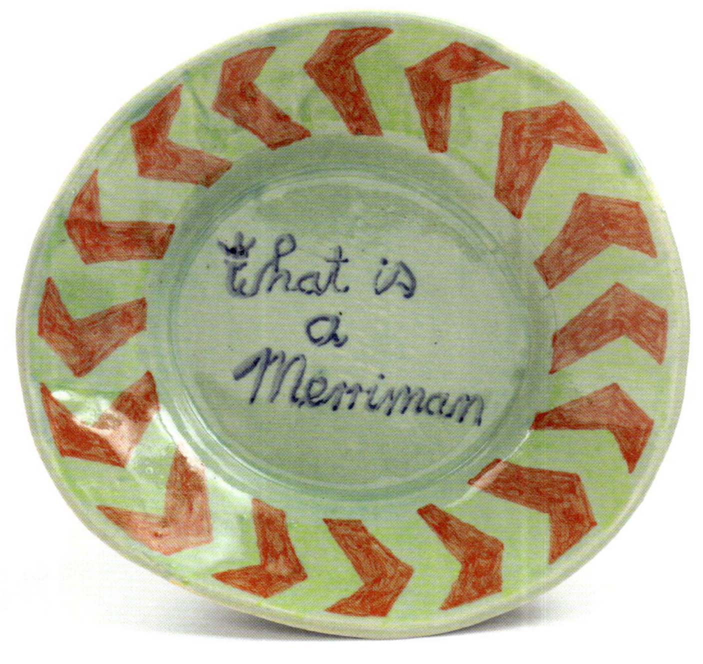

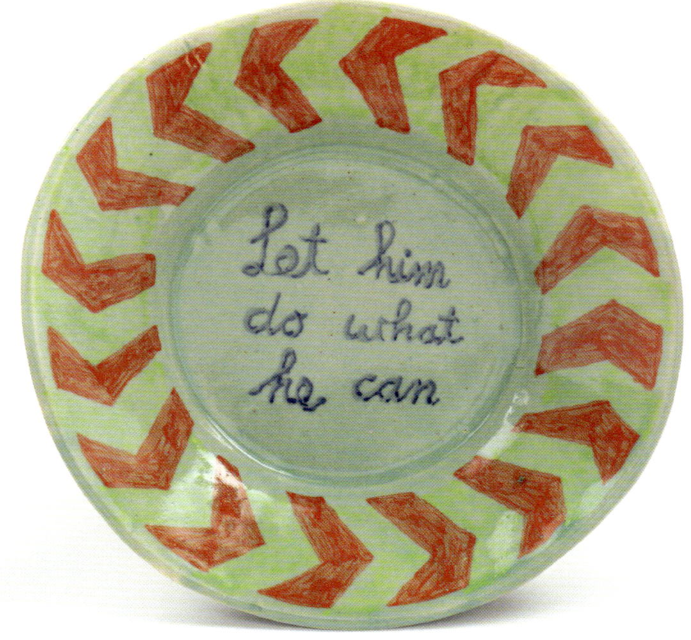

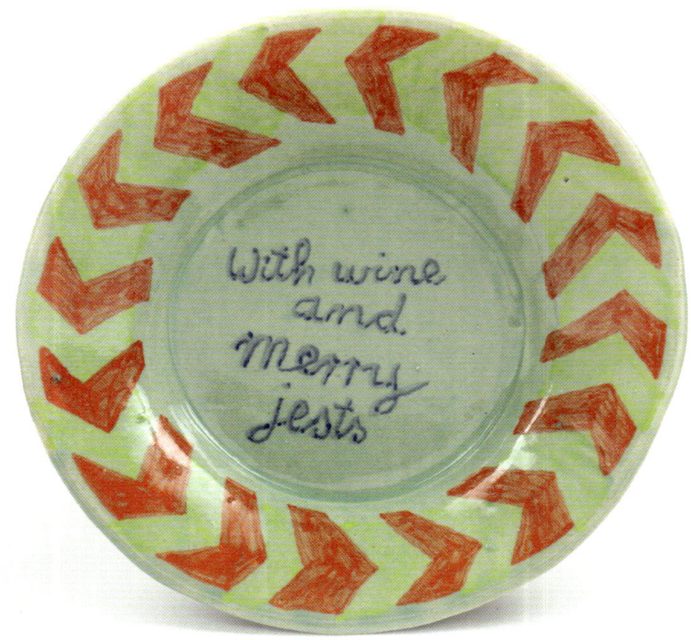

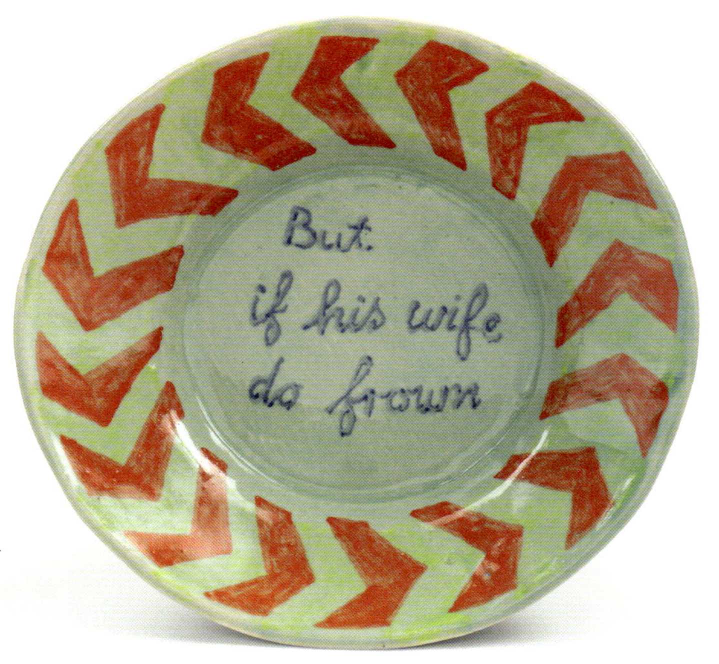

8 November 2021

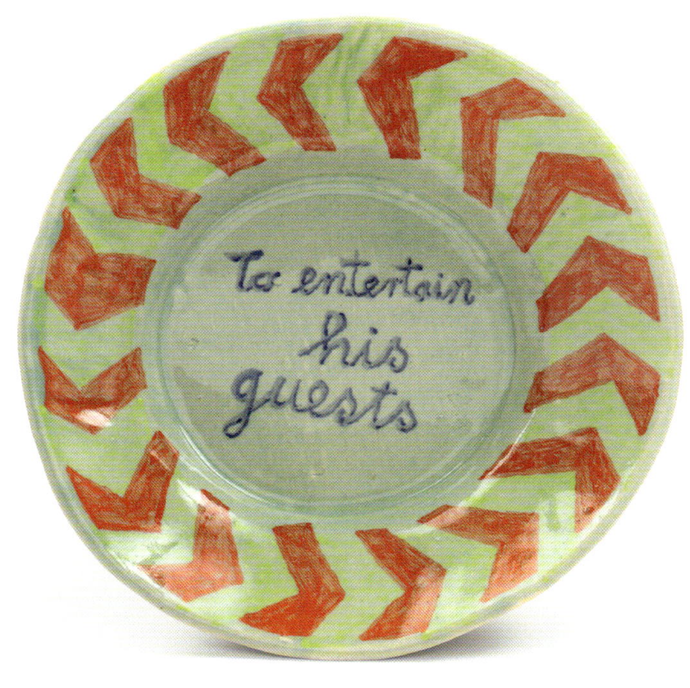
To entertain
his
guests

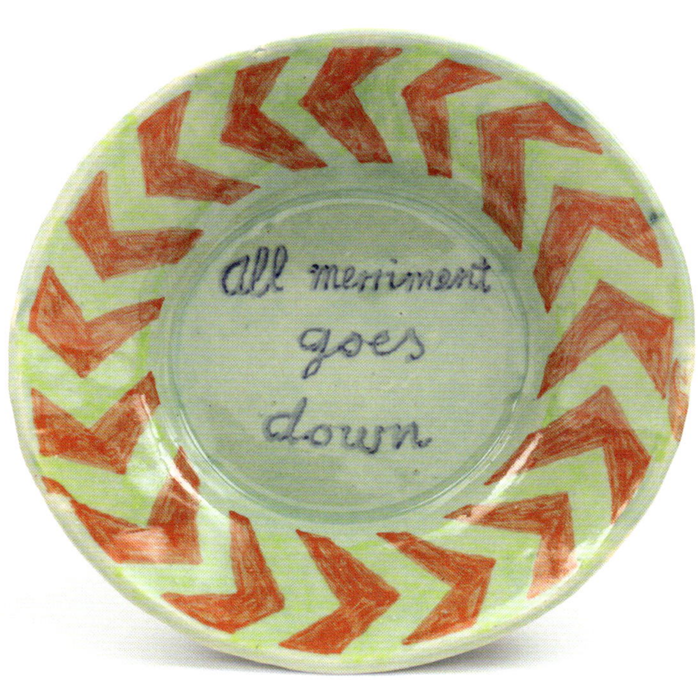
All merriment
goes
down

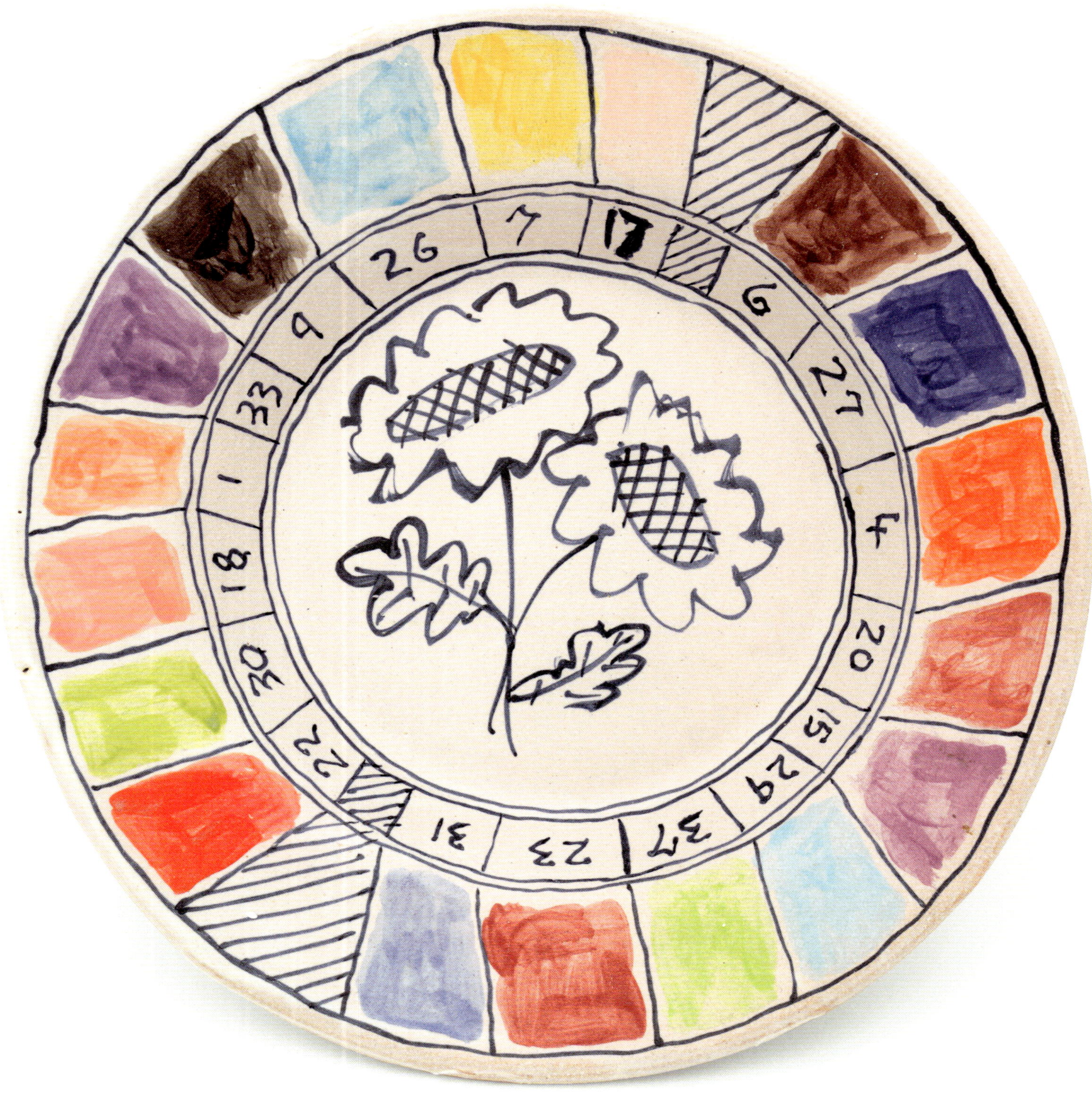

11 November 2011

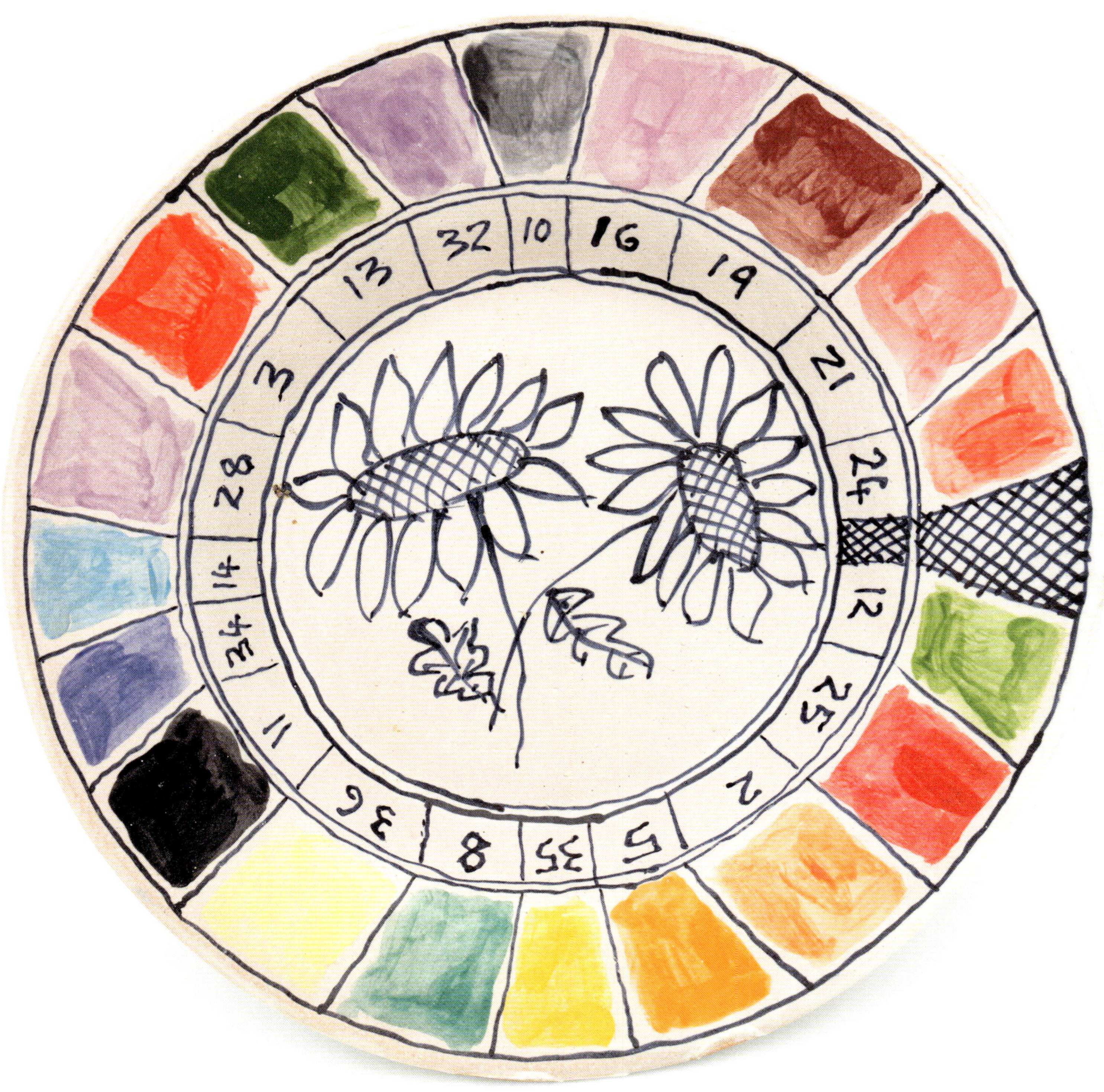

11 November 2011

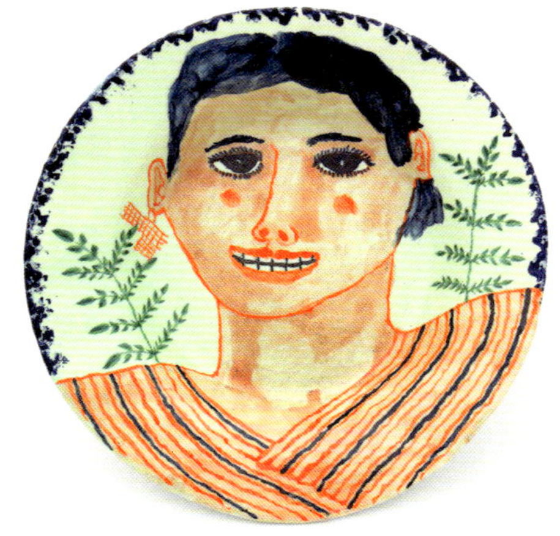

9 May 2024

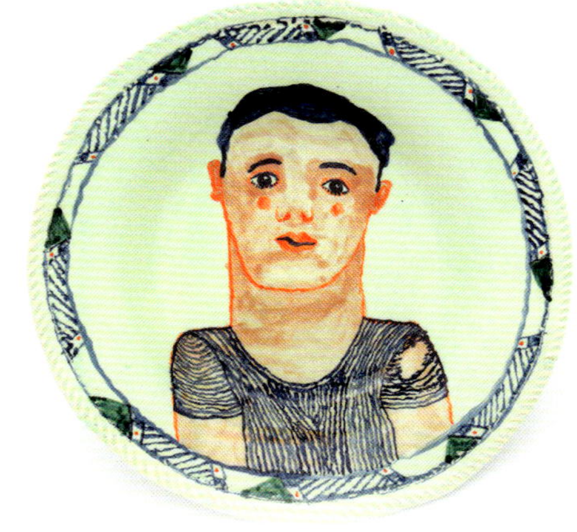

30 May 2024

9 May 2024

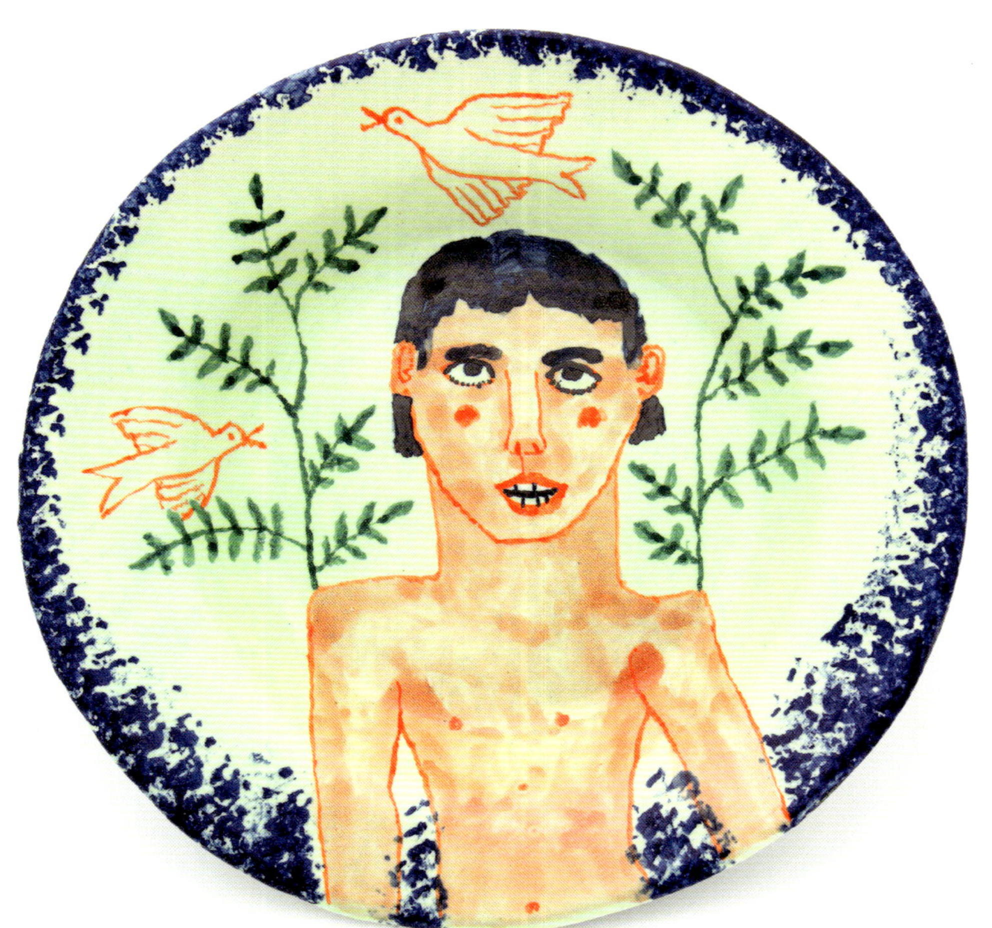

9 May 2024

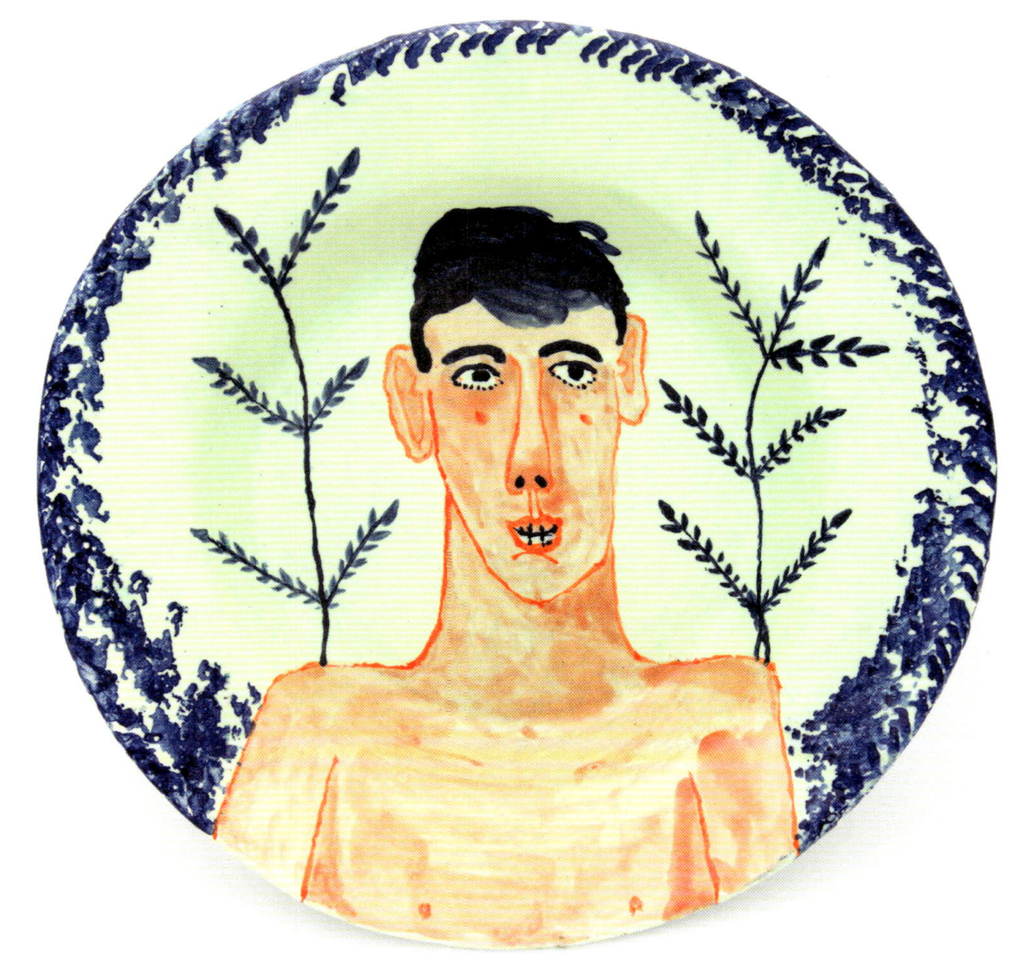

9 May 2024

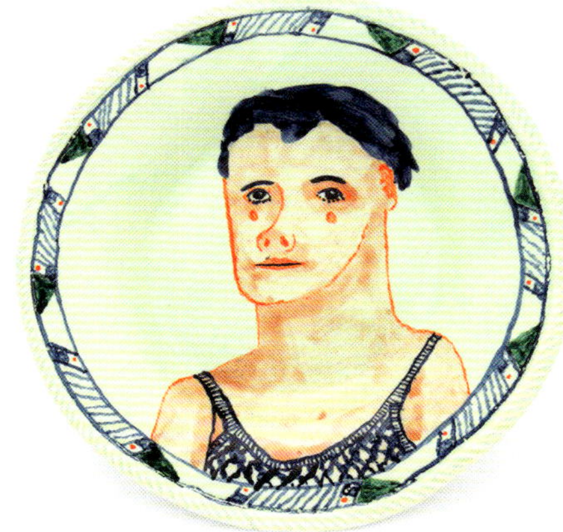

30 May 2024

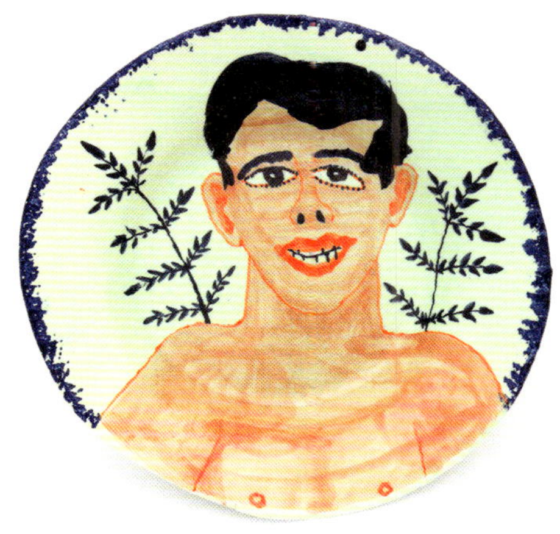

9 May 2024

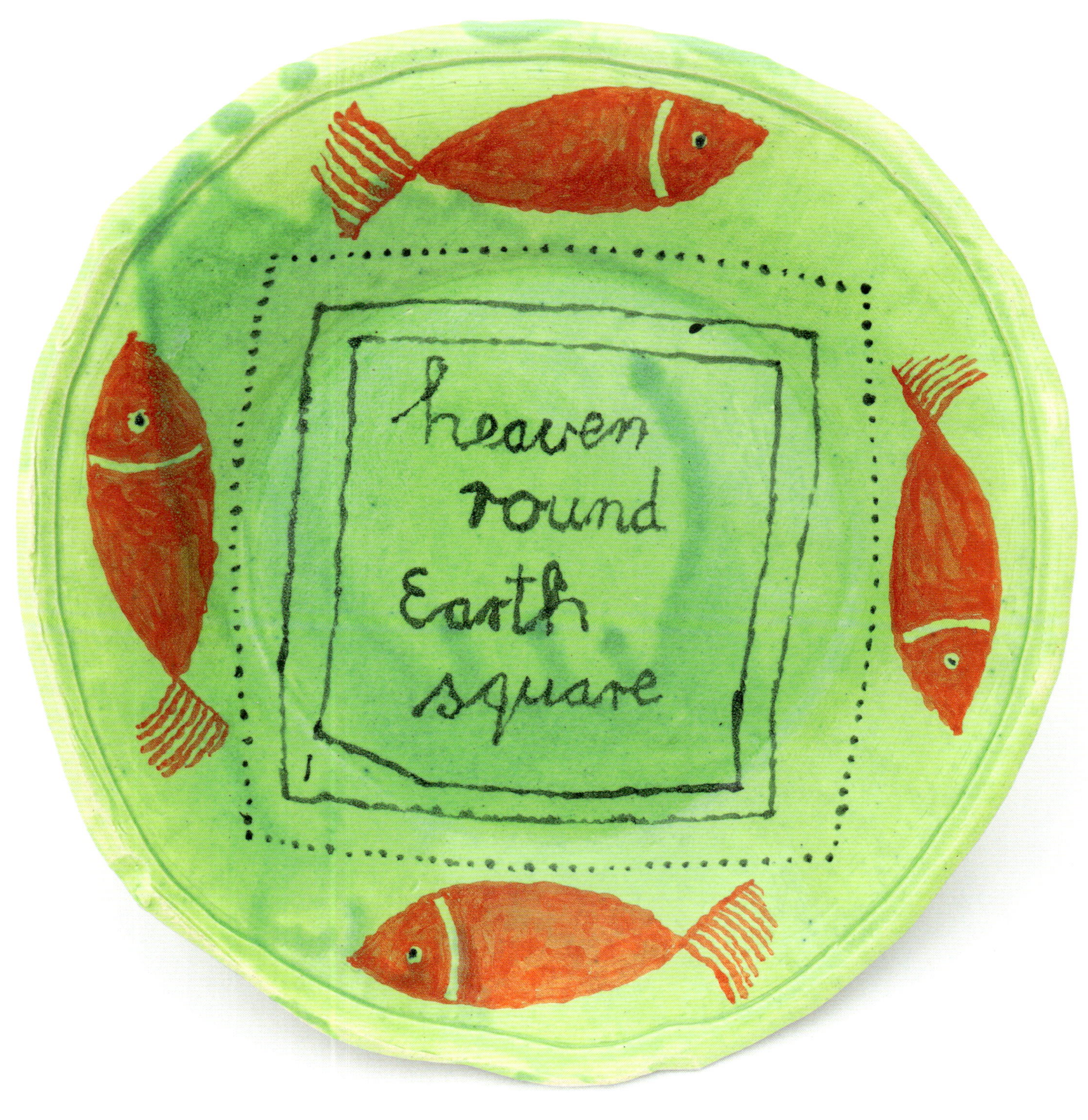

17 August 2023

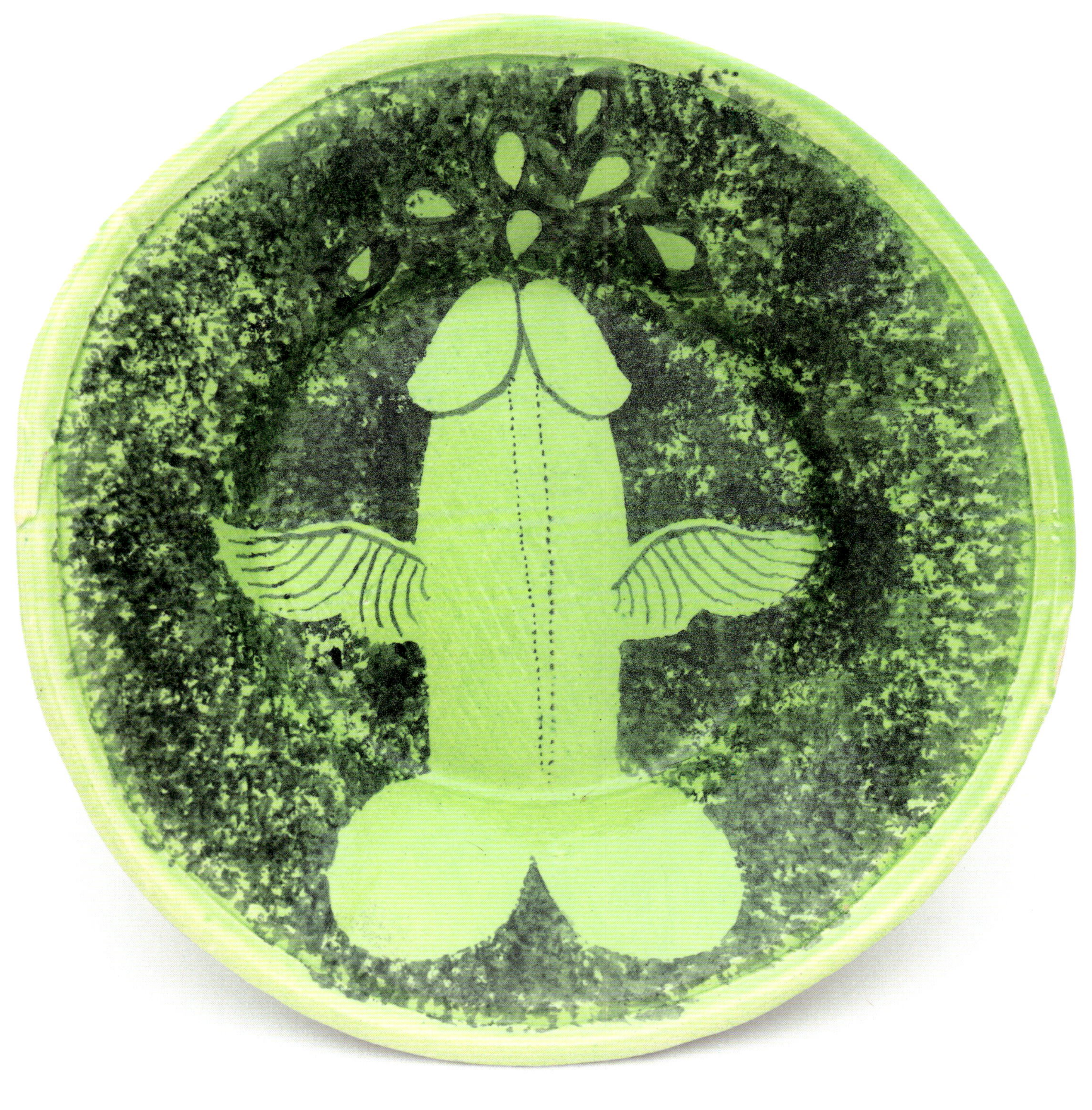

1 March 2014

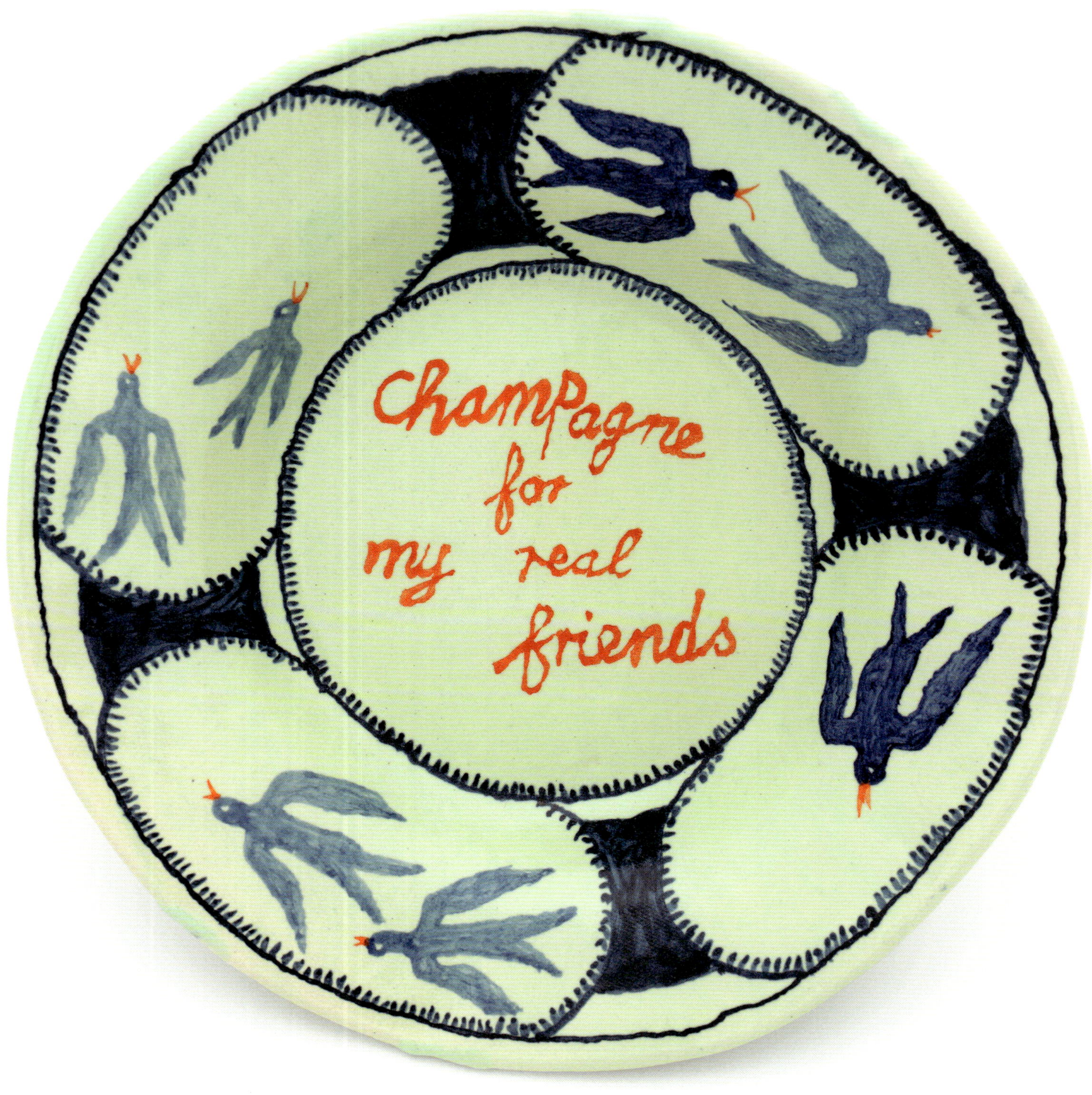

20 July 2024

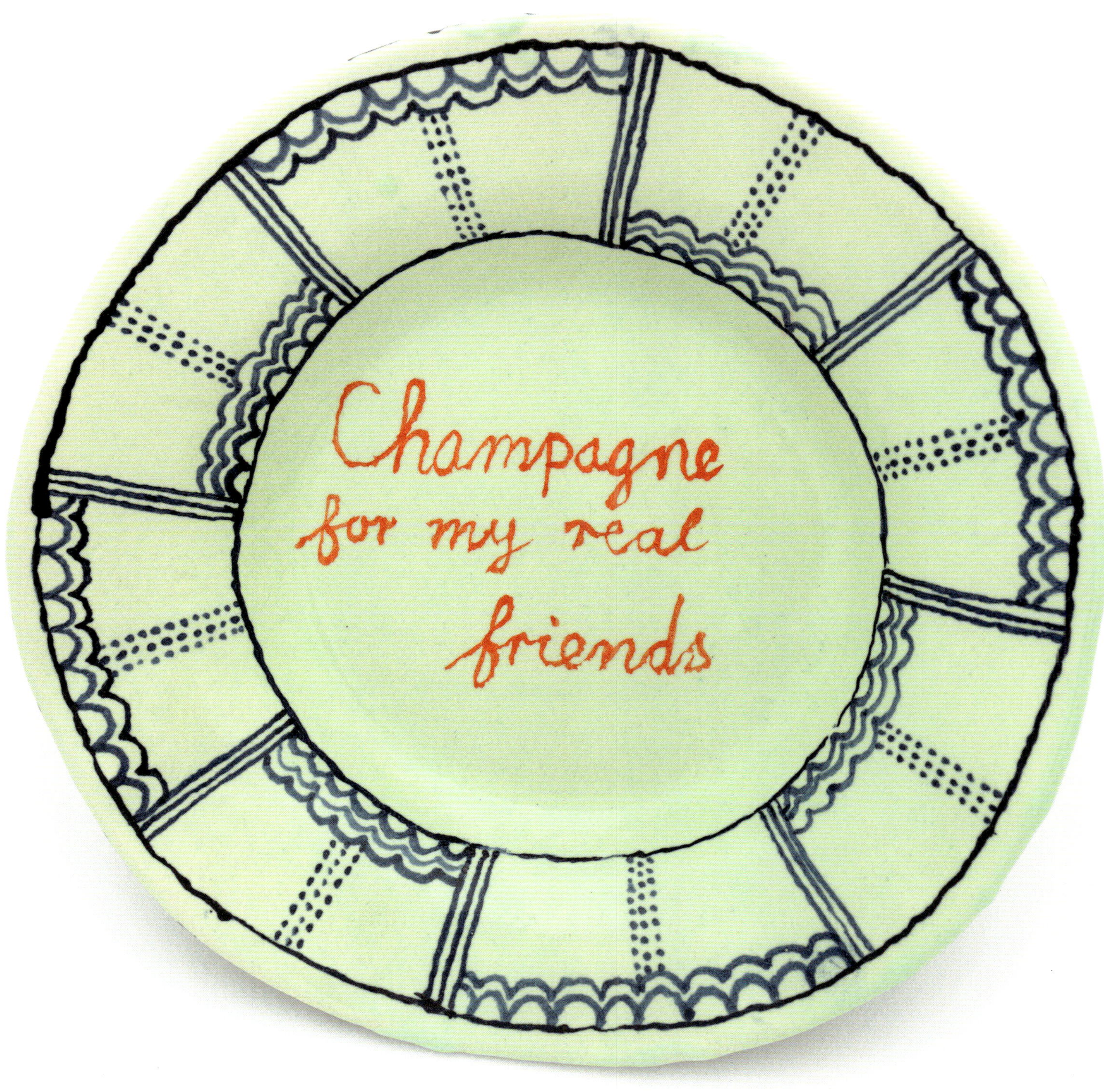

20 July 2024

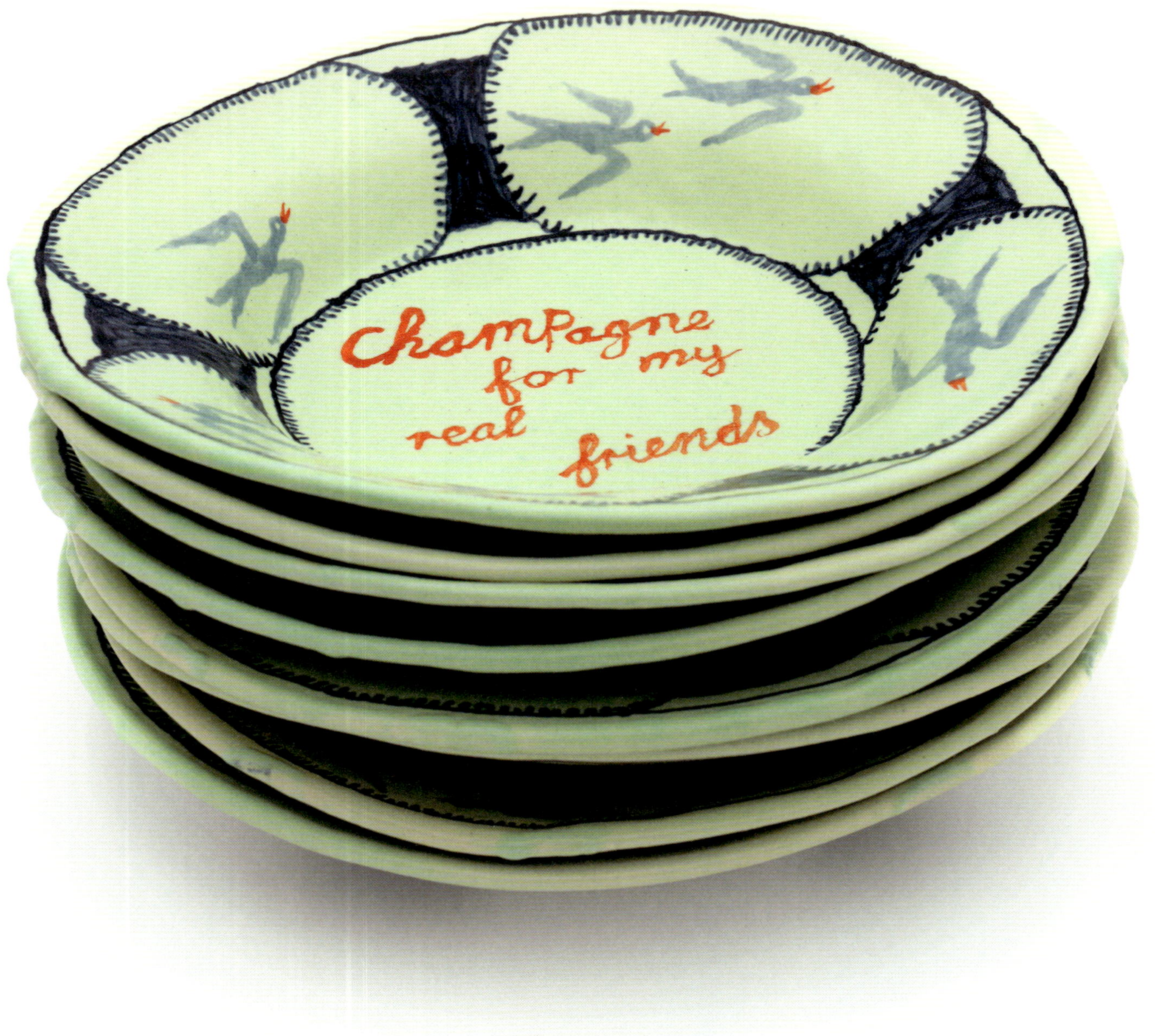

20 July 2024

Biographies

HYLTON NEL was born in 1941 in N'kana, Zambia, and grew up in the Northern Cape, South Africa. He studied fine art at Rhodes University and specialised in ceramics at the Royal Academy of Fine Arts, Antwerp. In the 1970s and 80s he lectured in Port Elizabeth (now Gqeberha); at the Michaelis School of Fine Art, University of Cape Town; and Stellenbosch University. In 1991 he moved to the small town of Bethulie, in the Free State, and in 2002 to Calitzdorp in the Klein Karoo, where he continues to live and work.

Nel, who describes himself as an 'artist-potter', has been exhibiting his work since the late 1960s. A first 'retrospective exhibition' toured South Africa in 2001/2, accompanied by a catalogue published by the Nelson Mandela Metropolitan Art Museum (then King George VI Art Gallery, Port Elizabeth). Recent surveys include *Hylton Nel at 80* at the Fine Art Society, London (2021); *This plate is what I have to say* at Charleston, East Sussex (2023); and *Things Made Over Time* at Stevenson, Cape Town (2024). He first exhibited with the Fine Art Society, London, in 1996, and joined Michael Stevenson Contemporary (now Stevenson), Cape Town, when the gallery opened in 2003.

Nel's ceramics have been included in curated exhibitions such as *On the Surface: Contemporary Ceramics* at the Rhode Island School of Design Museum (2021); *Unorthodox* at the Jewish Museum, New York (2015), *The Magic of Clay* at Gl. Holtegaard, Denmark (2011); *The Discerning Eye*, Mall Galleries, London (2007); *To Hold*, Farmleigh Gallery, Dublin (2006); *Table Manners: Contemporary International Ceramics* at the Crafts Council Gallery, London (2006); and *Seduced by Colour: The New Maiolica*, Gardiner Museum of Ceramic Art, Toronto; and in publications including *Contemporary Ceramics*, edited

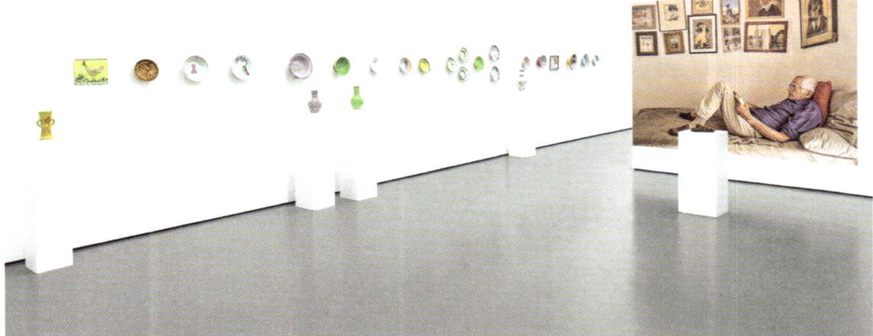

An installation view of Hylton's solo exhibition *Things Made Over Time*, 2024, Stevenson, Cape Town

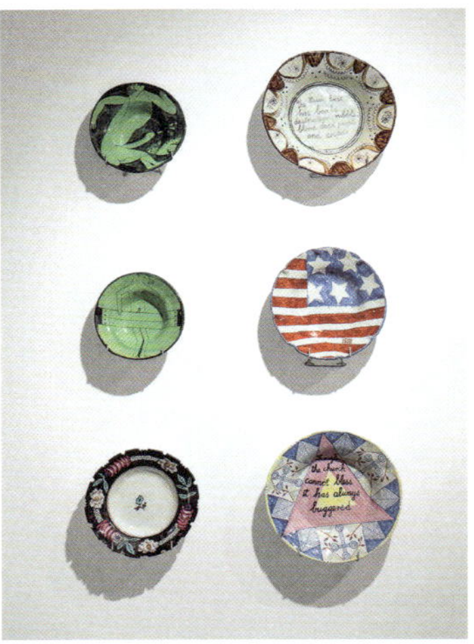

A detail from Hylton's 2023 exhibition *This plate is what I have to say* at Charleston, East Sussex / Photo: Courtesy of Charleston

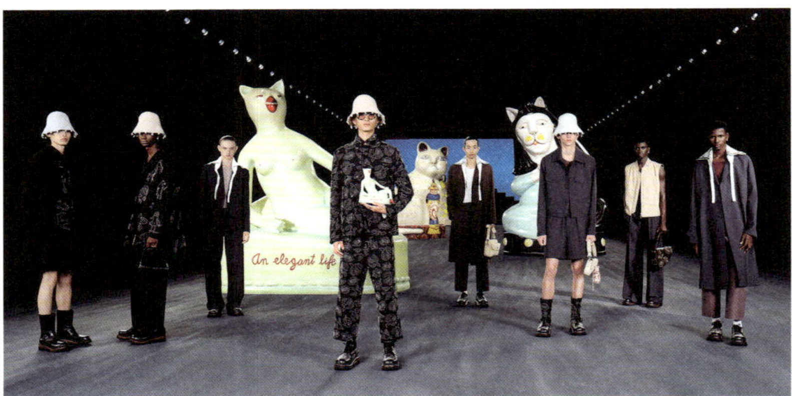

The runway of Dior Men's Summer 2025 collection, with Hylton's cats blown up large / Photo: Brett Lloyd, courtesy of Dior

by Emmanuel Cooper (Thames & Hudson, 2009), and *The Pot Book*, edited by Edmund de Waal (Phaidon, 2011).

Previous monographs on his work include *Hylton Nel*, jointly published by Michael Stevenson and The Fine Art Society in 2003, and *Hylton Nel: A Curious World*, edited by Michael Stevenson and published by Jacana (2010). This book is a third volume in this series.

Nel's words in this book are drawn from statements over the years as well as recent conversations with Marc Barben.

KIM JONES OBE is an English fashion designer. He studied graphics and photography at Camberwell School of Art before graduating with an MA in Fashion from Central Saint Martins in 2002. He became creative director of Dior Homme in 2018, also collaborating with Fendi from 2020 to 2024. He has contributed to magazines including *Dazed & Confused*, *Arena Homme+*, *Another Magazine*, *i-D* and the *New York Times T Style* magazine as stylist and art director. His Summer 2025 collection for Dior Homme was inspired by the life and work of Hylton Nel.

TAMAR GARB is Durning Lawrence Professor in the Department of History of Art at University College London. She has published widely on questions of gender and sexuality in modern and contemporary art as well as on photography from Africa, the work of women artists and feminist aesthetics. She first wrote on Hylton Nel in 1996, for the catalogue of his exhibition *A Prayer for Good Governance* at the Fine Art Society, London. Her essay in this book is a reworked version of a piece written for *Hylton Nel at Eighty*, also at the Fine Art Society, in 2021.

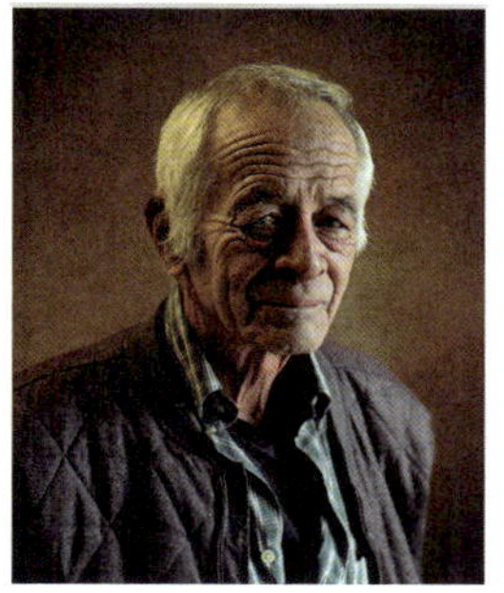

Pieter Hugo's *Hylton, Calitzdorp, 2016*, from the series *What the Light Falls On*

PIETER HUGO is a photographic artist living in Cape Town. Major solo exhibitions of his work have taken place at the Rencontres d'Arles; Museu Coleção Berardo in Lisbon; Kunstmuseum Wolfsburg; the Hague Museum of Photography; Musée de l'Elysée in Lausanne; Ludwig Museum in Budapest; Fotografiska in Stockholm; MAXXI in Rome; and the Institute of Modern Art Brisbane. He has photographed Hylton Nel on a number of occasions, including a commission for Dior. A portrait of Hylton taken on a trip to Calitzdorp with Kim Jones is included in his latest photographic series, *What the Light Falls On*.

The artist and the editors wish to thank all those who have contributed to this book, especially Kim Jones, Tamar Garb, Pieter Hugo, Michael Stevenson, Gabrielle Guy, Mario Todeschini, Francis Atterbury, and everyone at Stevenson and Hurtwood Press. Thanks also to all those who have supported Hylton's work over the decades through exhibiting his ceramics, writing about them, collecting and otherwise engaging with them, all of which has contributed to his extraordinarily rich life and career.

First published by Hurtwood Press
and Stevenson in 2025

Hurtwood Press Limited
SB113 China Works, 100 Black Prince Road,
London, SE1 7SJ

www.hurtwood.co.uk
hello@hurtwood.co.uk

Stevenson
Cape Town: Buchanan Building, 160 Sir Lowry Road, 7925 / Johannesburg: 46 7th Avenue, Parktown North, 2193 / Amsterdam: Prinsengracht 371B, 1016HK

www.stevenson.info
info@stevenson.info

Photographs of works by Hylton Nel:
Mario Todeschini
Cover and pages 15-24: Pieter Hugo
Inside covers and pages 41, 56, 72, 100, 156:
Gabrielle Guy

ISBN 978-0-903696-94-4

Editors: Marc Barben, Sophie Perryer
Design and layout: Gabrielle Guy
Artworking and lithography: Gabrielle Guy, Francis Atterbury, Roger Jones

Typefaces: Aperçu Mono Pro, PS Fournier Std
Paper: Symbol Tatami White, Arena White Smooth & Arena Natural Rough supplied by Fedrigoni

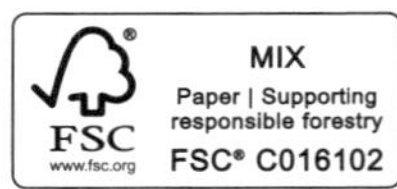

Printed in the UK by Hampton Printing, Bristol